Cocksh
&
Petton Remembered

The Social Development of Cockshutt and Petton From the Ice Age

'We dedicate this book to Dee Taylor
A lovely lady, greatly missed, who inspired us
to finish the work she began'

Researched and written by: Linda Baumgartle, Heather Bayne, Dean Bywater, Barbara Cooksey, Wendy Jones and Helen Willmoth.

Committee members also included Sue and Rick Johnson, Eddie Jones and Ann Ware.

A catalogue record for this book is available from the British Library.

This first edition, published in 2007

ISBN: 0-9545251-3-2
Further copies of this book can be obtained by contacting
Cockshutt Parish History Group, Chapel House Farm, Cockshutt Ellesmere SY12 0JJ

Typeset and designed by Naughty Mutt Limited
www.naughtymutt.com 01743 340 500
in Bembo 11.5pt on 13pt
Printing by Leiston Press, Leiston, Suffolk 01728 833 003

We would like to thank LHI for the Grant that made this book possible

FOREWORD

Bob Dommett

It is a privilege to write the foreword to this Cockshutt and Petton Compendium. It is a work you may carefully study or browse through at leisure. Either way, something will surely surprise you or bring back a memory of an incident or character from the past. There are a number of authors providing a variety of style. They are all to be congratulated.

Cockshutt is not a chocolate-box village but its people have always given a friendly welcome to all who come here. Whatever changes the future brings, I am certain this warm neighbourliness will continue.

Cockshutt, the village in which I was born
When the fields of corn by the scythe was
shorn,
When horses drew the plough, and milking
by hand
was the way of the cow.
Cockshutt, in which I was reared, when the
school
bells rang out load and clear
When on the stile I sat and by the gate I
stood,
thinking "By gum" the world is good.
Cockshutt, the village in which I was
married,
when water and coal had to be carried
Money was scarce, possessions were few,
you will probably say that's all they knew.
But we had Cockshutt, the place of my birth
The dearest place to me, on earth.
My old home was knocked down and I was
shattered,
But to the people who did it, it never
mattered.
A bit of old Cockshutt lay in the dust,
But the people who did it, they said it was a
'must.'
But old Cockshutt is valuable, to those who
care
For the people who cared, used to live there.
A home, with plenty of oak, and people who
once
drank there, will be glad that I spoke.
Cockshutt, the village in which I grew old,
With plenty of memories, ribboned in gold.
Of good times and bad, many of which I shall
always be glad,
Friends I've had, and friends I have lost,
Which to us all, is a heavy cosh.
Cockshutt, the village, in which I hope to die
and in our churchyard be put, forever to lie.
I thank my Good Lord and the people I knew
that kept dear old Cockshutt, one of the few.
I'll lie in God's garden
forever in peace,
till the blue in the heavens decides
to cease.   Anonymous

CHAPTERS

INTRODUCTION

Wendy Jones

It all started in 1994 when Dee Taylor of 'Low Grove', Hightown, Cockshutt thought it would be a good idea to capture the recollections of the senior members of the village before it was too late. Dee asked me if I was interested in joining her in the project to produce some tape recordings and a leaflet to go out with the tape. I agreed. Our first visit was to Cressage Village Hall for instructions on how to interview using a tape recorder, with Richard Walker of BBC Radio Shropshire. The most important point we learnt was to always have control of the microphone when interviewing. Our first interviewee was Mr Bob Dommett, 'Tyneholm.' Dee began the interview by asking the question, "What was the difference between where he had been teaching in an urban area in the south of England and coming to a rural school in Cockshutt?" Mr Dommett took the microphone from Dee and talked for thirty minutes non stop. So we had fallen at the first hurdle of how to interview! This did not concern us as the tape has been very useful and, as you can imagine, full of interesting facts and stories. In 1994 I joined many villagers in the Red Lion for the visit of Radio Shropshire to record 'Monday's Place' with Jonathan King and Michael Howells. I told everyone that I would be round to interview them for their memories as we were going to produce a tape and leaflets about Cockshutt. Unfortunately Dee, who was a writer and journalist, became ill and died in 1998 so the project was put on the back burner.

It was in the winter of 2002, when I produced a short history of the Church for one of the Family Services, that Helen Willmoth said she was interested in the old houses in and around the village. We got together and decided to resurrect the project and to try and finish it. We were told by Terry Goodall that Dean Bywater was researching the old pubs of the village so he agreed to join us along with Heather Bayne from Kenwick and more recently Barbara Cooksey and Linda Baumgartle who are writing about Petton. So what started in a small way has just grown like 'Topsy'. We realised we could not produce a book without funding, so we applied to the Local Heritage Initiative for a grant. After much form filling, forming a committee and opening a bank account we were successful and were awarded £21.313. This grant was to cover equipment, materials and printing of the book. We plan to produce a good quality book, a CD of all the recordings we have made and also a DVD of recordings and photographs that have not been included in the book. We would like to thank everyone for all the wonderful photographs loaned to us and the stories you have told us. We have been able to let everyone see what we have collected when we had our two exhibitions in the Village Hall both of which were really well supported. During the many hours of writing the book I longed to be able to have the ability to write like Dee Taylor. I am a retired P.E. teacher with no IT or writing background. It has not been easy for any of us, so I hope you will spare a thought for the effort we have made and remember all the 'comers in' who have tried their best to record the history of the village close to their hearts. All that has been written down has either been read or someone has told us and we have done our best to verify the stories but this has not always been possible in each case. Many of the stories have come from memories already written down by John Moore, Peggy Husbands, M D Joyce, Miss Rogers, Esme Rawlinson, E V Bayne, David Evans, Mrs Emma Florence Cunliffe and Philip Morris. The aim of the book is to bring together the recollections and memories that have been in print, albeit in a very small way, into a comprehensive history of Cockshutt and Petton. If events have been missed out it is because we have not been told, but we have tried hard to include everything.

I would like to thank all the writers and the committee for their commitment, also Local Heritage Initiative for their financial support. It has been a mammoth task which has been very interesting and enjoyable even though it has taken us so long. I do hope you feel the effort has been worth it.

WHAT'S IN A NAME?

Cockesete 1270; from the Old English 'cocc-scyte' a woodland glade where nets were stretched to catch woodcock. From the *Dictionary of English Place Names* by A D Mills

Cockshutt; 'cockshoot', Old English Cocc-sciet, 'cockshoot' (from cocc, 'woodcock'+ sciete, 'shoot')

A 'cockshoot' is a woodland glade where nets are stretched to catch any woodcock that might 'shoot' (dart) through it. 1270 La Cockesete. *The Penguin Dictionary of British Place Names* by Adrian Room

A strip of land can be Shot, Shoot, Shutt or Shute - all variant forms of the same word, usually denoting land on a boundary. This word also means 'corner land' and occurs in Cockshutt + Cockshoot.

An original sense - a shooting/darting of woodcocks

English Place Names by Kenneth Cameron

Petton (hamlet Shropshire); Pectone 1086 – Domesday Book

'Farmstead on or by a pointed hill'

OE; pêac + tûn

From the *Dictionary of English Place Names* by A D Mills

Tûn in OE = enclosure, farmstead, village, manor, estate.

Cocc in OE = heap, hillock, cock of wild bird – woodcock.

CHAPTER 1

THE BEGINNINGS

Meres and Mosses

How the land around Cockshutt was formed some 15,000 years ago

The very earliest find was in the Crosemere area where a Neolithic site was carbon dated – 14 to circa 3350 BC but there is no further information. This site can be found at OS grid reference SJ438295.

The ice sheet which covered the North Shropshire area some 15,000 years ago left natural depressions in the glacial drift when it melted. These hollows have filled with water and become known as meres and peat bog sites were left, known as mosses. The depth of the meres range from 1 metre to 27 metres in places. The meres are nutrient-rich and the area around is a botanist's paradise. The 'breaking' of the meres happens at irregular and unpredictable intervals, the interchange is almost overnight, and the usual colour and texture of the mere changes to that of a thick green soup. The fish take to the bottom and refuse the angler's bait. This state of the mere will last a few weeks in late summer and autumn.

Crosemere A Botanist's Paradise

The Crosemere Complex

A compound peat-lined basin of irregular shape with a low gravel ridge dividing Whattal Moss and Crosemere, the ridge dies away on the eastern side into Sweatmere and Lloyds Wood. At one time the whole area must have been a single mere two to three metres higher than the present level of Crosemere. Drainage work carried out in 1864 is believed to have lowered the level of Crosemere by at least two metres.

Rich waters of Crosemere and Sweatmere owe their high salt content to increased calcium and bicarbonate. Both meres are topped up by run-off from farm land and are drained naturally from the eastern end of the mere, which eventually joins the River Roden via ditches and pipes. At South Sweatmere by Crosemere the outflow has been planted with conifers.

Crosemere is about 38 acres in size, 800 metres long by 300 metres wide and at least 9 metres deep. The bottom of the mere is stone and coarse gravel through to sand, silt and dark organic mud which supports flowering aquatic plants and aquatic animals and fish. The mere has reed swamps in parts of the northern and western shores and the bottom falls steeply from about 1 metre.

Ellesmere Angling Club, founded in 1931, have the fishing rights on Crosemere. They fish for carp, tench, bream, perch and pike and little has changed over the past 73 years apart from the members!

Sweatmere is the smallest of the meres and very little water is visible today due to overgrown reed swamp and luxuriant alder trees. Wide areas of peat totally

Sweatmere 1999 (above), Sweatmere 1995 (below)

surround Sweatmere and its area of water has rapidly decreased in recent times.

The reed swamp is a floating raft of rhizomes not even attached to the bottom – this is unique to Shropshire. This raft is very strong and buoyant and can support a man's weight if he keeps moving. Surrounding this mere is the finest undisturbed tangle of alder trees in this country. It completely covers the whole land surrounding the pool varying from 5 metres to 50 metres wide. Underneath these alders the ground is fluid, treacherous humified peat or standing water. Alder has a complete dominance around the whole area along with some birch.

Close to Sweatmere on its western edge a stone causeway was found and among the stones half a limestone quern, a hand-mill for grinding corn, was discovered in 1949 and is now in Shrewsbury Museum.

Whattal Moss

This moss is a raised peat bog with a small area of quaking bog at the western corner, possibly over a kettle hole. Whattal Moss is largely under plantation but pine and birch dominate the quaking bog area.

Ancient Earth Works or Hill Fort

Saxon period – an iron rod and bronze fragment were found in the 1990s. Between Crosemere and Whattal Moss there is a natural causeway on higher ground of gravel which has at some time been entrenched and even stockaded. These earthworks and hill fort are =good examples of a medieval motte (earthwork castle) and overlook both the mere and Whattal Moss. This site was also thought to be an Iron Age settlement 800BC- 42AD. This low peninsular between Crosemere and Whattal Moss was known as Stockett. About

Antiquity No.	County	Parish
SJ 43 SW 9	SALOP	COCKSHUTT
SJ 431 3069 SJ 4356 3062	DMV of Stockett, site of chapel, 'U' Earthwork, Misc undated finds, quern stone	

(SJ 4311 3069) Earthwork (NR)

"A low peninsular (SJ 433 306) still called Stockett (little stockade?) approached by a natural causeway, which has evidently at some time, been entrenched and perhaps stockaded". In 1872 (1864 - T Salop A S 2nd Ser 4 1892 280 R Ll. Kenyon) cutting of a deep drain lowered the waters of Crossmere (Crose Mere on OS 6" 1954) by 6 - 10 ft (Crose Mere, Sweet Mere and Whattall Moss probably constitute the remains of one continuous barrier of water).

Excavation c 1894 of the ditch (at SJ 43093068) showed that the ditch had been steeper, filled with water and had connected Crosemere with Whittall (Whattall on OS 6" 1954) Moss. The mound west of the ditch had also been higher. Animal bones, a cylindrical piece of iron and a fragment of bronze (undateable, but thought to have been part of a sword sheath) were found.

Both ends (of the peninsular) are defended by banks and ditches. On the eastern defences [not evident on available APs (RAF 1946 & OS 1972)] a stone causeway has been found close to Sweat Mere. Among the stones half a limestone quern was found; now in Shrewsbury Museum.

DMV of Stocket "denoted only by the site of an old fort" at NG (SJ) 432307; formerly co-extensive with Whattall & Kenwick. [Not mentioned in Beresford. No indications of DMV on available APs (RAF 1946 & OS 1972)].

contd.

Antiquity No.	County	Parish
SJ 43 SW 9	SALOP	COCKSHUTT

Traditionally a chapel stood on the banks of Crosemere.

Stone quern (?)found 1949 (SJ 4356 3062) by Donald Moore (in Shrewsbury Museum).

An earthwork has been constructed at a point where the ridge of higher ground separating Crose Mere from Whattall Moss is at its narrowest. It comprises a level platform of irregular plan and on its west side, separated by a wide ditch, a regularly shaped bank with an almost level top projecting S from the main ridge. The platform is now split by a probably later track.

No defensive banks and ditches can now be seen at the eastern end of the ridge. Two much-spread banks at SJ 435 305 are probably the result of the digging of a wide drainage ditch between them. The footpath shown on the 25" from SJ 4357 3071 to SJ 4351 3043 is probably the causeway referred to by Miss Chitty.

No indications of a DMV or of a chapel were seen on the peninsular, which is now pasture.

Published Survey (25") revised.

About 1190-1194 David Fitz Owen, Prince of North Wales gave Stocgete, with its appurtenances, to Haughmond Abbey. Stockett, a group of houses, is shown on OS 1st Ed 1" 1835 at approximately SJ 431306 with access gained by a road leading from the A 528 Ellesmere to Cockshutt road at SJ 4250 3073.

1190–1194 a small hamlet was built by the roadside almost opposite where the road to Kenwick Springs joins the Ellesmere road but a little nearer to Ellesmere. There was a tollgate or stock gate across the Ellesmere road.

Another important find in the Crosemere area hangs in Rowley's House Museum, Shrewsbury. A dugout canoe was discovered in 1891, 6ft down in the peat and entangled in the roots of a large birch tree which had grown through both its ends. The canoe was quite soft down in the peat but very soon became hard on exposure to the air. A trough-like or punt type boat with squared sides and a flat bottom - size 10ft 9in long by 2ft wide, 1ft 2in high in the centre. The sides are 7ft 6in in length and they curve gently to the square ends at prow and stern. The floor is flat inside and out. It is documented that the boat was made not later than the Roman-British period.

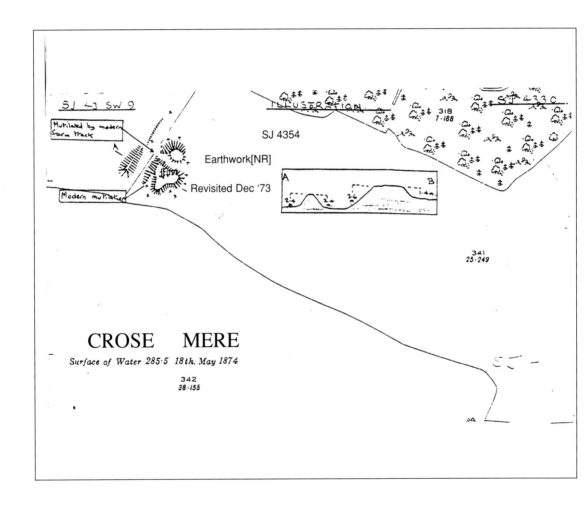

A bowl in the same wood as the boat has also been found in Whattle Moss, Croesmere. Finds in Petton, Bagley, Tetchill, Loppington and Ellesmere all point to the area being inhabited in the Late Bronze Age. It was a very difficult task to unravel the roots and great care had to be taken to bring the boat out. It was guarded at night and protected from the sun using green foliage from the trees and became a focus for people to visit. A Mrs Mary Haycocks described her visit to the boat in the press in 1891. A copy of this letter is preserved with the boat which was taken to Ellesmere Museum and put in a glass case after it was rescued by Mr Brownlow Tower from the Cremorne Gardens where it had been taken before it was put in Rowley's Museum, Shrewsbury.

About a mile from where the dugout canoe was found, lake dwellings have been identified at Pikesend, not far from Frankton Grange, on a promontory of peaty land which at one time had been surrounded by a lake or mere. The remains of 23 circular mounds, 12ft in diameter and 1ft or more in height, about 10 yds apart with some regularity in general arrangement were inspected by the Ellesmere Field Club in 1892. The tenant farmer was trying to level this land but stopped immediately when he was informed that it was the site of an ancient lake dwelling.

These artificial constructions at both Stockett and Pikesend were used as defensive dwellings by people post Roman and Medieval times. The whole area was a vastly wooded region so plenty of tree trunks were available for piles on which to build their dwellings and make their canoes.

Farming methods from earliest times to the present day have obviously had an effect on the meres and mosses of Cockshutt and the farmers around the meres are being encouraged to look after the area.

A farm Biodiversity Action Plan and a strategy for conservation of the meres and mosses has been put together by Farming and Wildlife Advisory Group Ltd. and English Nature who are looking after the Crosemere area for the owners. The farmers become stewards of this very environmentally sensitive area within the Cockshutt Parish. One comment from a farmer was that the water level at Sweatmere is increasing as the drainage ditches, which once drained the mere, are over time getting blocked.

Drawing by Derek Western of the Ellesmere Punt found near Whattal Moss.

-

CHAPTER 2
SITES AND MONUMENTS RECORDS AND ARCHAEOLOGICAL FINDS

D uring our research we visited Community and Environment Services in Shire Hall, Shrewsbury. Listed below are the Sites and Monuments around Cockshutt. Our thanks to the Economy and Environment Sustainability Group for allowing us to reproduce their records as they stood in December 2003.

Site Name *Parish, District, County*	NGR	Monument Types, Periods and Dates, and Form	
19559			
No 7 SHREWSBURY ROAD *Cockshutt, North Shropshire, Shropshire* Listed Building (II) - 1585-0/12/64 Listed Building - Shrewsbury Road	SJ43392927		
19634			
Churchyard wall and gate, Petton Church *Petton, North Shropshire, Shropshire* Listed Building (II) - 1585-0/12/187	SJ44022627		
19635			
Ice house apx 60m SE of Petton Church *Petton, North Shropshire, Shropshire* Listed Building (II) - 1585-0/12/188	SJ44082622		

Shropshire County Council: Environmental Record (SMR) *(Listing with status)*
18/11/03

Site Name *Parish, District, County*	NGR	Monument Types, Periods and Dates, and Form		
00841				
Petton gravel pit finds *Petton, North Shropshire, Shropshire*	SJ43002600	FINDSPOT	Prehistoric - 500000 BC to 42 AD	FIND
00843				
Whinnett Hill *Cockshutt, North Shropshire, Shropshire*	SJ40752865	EARTHWORK? QUARRY?	- to - to	CONJECTURAL EVIDENCE CONJECTURAL EVIDENCE
00844				
BA spearhead from Petton Moat *Petton, North Shropshire, Shropshire*	SJ44272648	FINDSPOT	Bronze Age - 2350 BC to 701 BC	FIND
00886				
Gesenok Well *Cockshutt, North Shropshire, Shropshire*	SJ41483044	WELL	- to	STRUCTURE
00887				
Stockett Gate *Cockshutt, North Shropshire, Shropshire*	SJ42503081	TOLL GATE	Post Medieval - 1500 AD to 1913 AD	DOCUMENTARY EVIDENCE
00888				
Dug out from Whattall Moss *Cockshutt, North Shropshire, Shropshire*	SJ43063110	FINDSPOT	- to	FIND

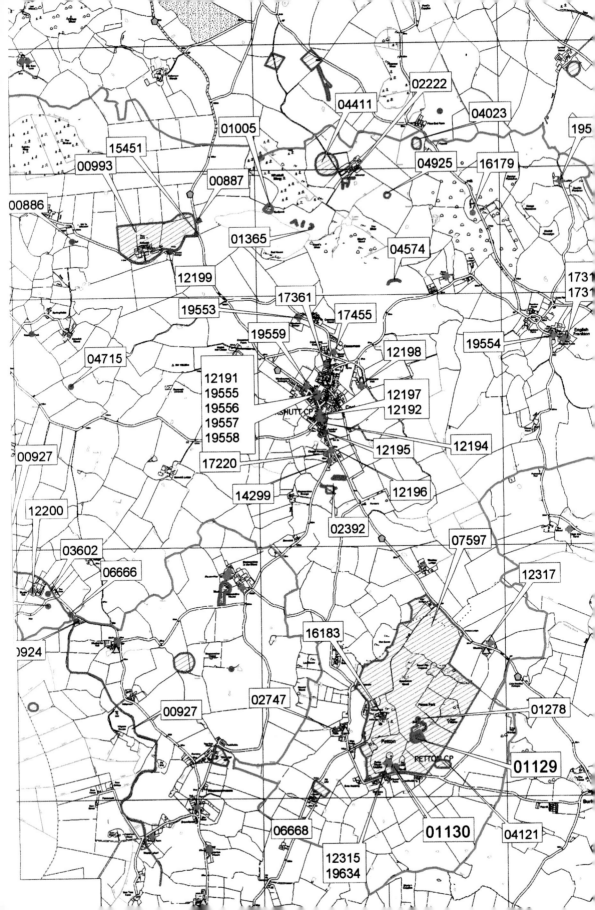

Site Name Parish, District, County	NGR	Monument Types, Periods and Dates, and Form		
00927				
Montgomery Canal Cockshutt, North Shropshire, Shropshire Ellesmere Rural, North Shropshire, Shropshire Llanymynech and Pant, Oswestry, Shropshire Oswestry Rural, Oswestry, Shropshire West Felton, Oswestry, Shropshire Whittington, Oswestry, Shropshire Baschurch, North Shropshire, Shropshire	SJ26262081	CANAL	Early 18th century to Early 20th century (pre WW1) - 1700 AD to 1913 AD	EARTHWORK, DOCUMENTARY EVIDENCE, STRUCTURE
00993				
Kenwick Cockshutt, North Shropshire, Shropshire	SJ41763054	DESERTED SETTLEMENT	Medieval - 1066 AD to 1499 AD	
		RIDGE AND FURROW	Medieval - 1066 AD to 1499 AD	
01005				
Motte Castle on the N Bank of Crose Mere Cockshutt, North Shropshire, Shropshire Scheduled Monument - 34915	SJ43103069	SETTLEMENT?	Iron Age - 800 BC? to 42 AD?	EARTHWORK
		DESERTED SETTLEMENT?	Medieval - 1066 AD to 1499 AD	EARTHWORK
		MOTTE	Medieval - 1066 AD to 1499 AD	EARTHWORK
01129				
Petton Park Moat Petton, North Shropshire, Shropshire Scheduled Monument - 32301	SJ44272648	MOAT	Medieval - 1066 AD to 1499 AD	EARTHWORK
		FISHPOND	Medieval - 1066 AD to 1499 AD	EARTHWORK
		(MOATED SITE)	Medieval - 1066 AD to 1499 AD	EARTHWORK

Site Name Parish, District, County	NGR	Monument Types, Periods and Dates, and Form		
01130				
Mound in Petton Park (Petton Motte) Petton, North Shropshire, Shropshire Scheduled Monument - 32299	SJ44092623	MOTTE?	Medieval - 1066 AD to 1499 AD	EARTHWORK
		MOUND	- to	EARTHWORK
01278				
Postulated DMV at Petton Petton, North Shropshire, Shropshire	SJ44202666	DESERTED SETTLEMENT	Medieval - 1066 AD to 1499 AD	EARTHWORK, CONJECTURAL EVIDENCE
01365				
Cockshutt, North Shropshire, Shropshire	SJ43393056	ENCLOSURE?	- to	CROPMARK
02392				
Cockshutt, North Shropshire, Shropshire	SJ43622849	RECTANGULAR ENCLOSURE	Early Iron Age to Roman - 800 BC? to 409 AD?	CROPMARK
02648				
Socketed knife from Grange Farm Cockshutt, North Shropshire, Shropshire	SJ39952995	FINDSPOT	Bronze Age - 2350 BC to 701 BC	FIND
02747				
Petton Farm Petton, North Shropshire, Shropshire	SJ43652655	FINDSPOT	Neolithic - 4000 BC to 2351 BC	FIND
03601				
Shade Oak Cockshutt, North Shropshire, Shropshire	SJ41252755	FINDSPOT	Bronze Age - 2350 BC to 701 BC	FIND

Site Name *Parish, District, County*	NGR	Monument Types, Periods and Dates, and Form		
03602				
Shade Oak *Cockshutt, North Shropshire, Shropshire*	SJ41252765	**FINDSPOT**	Prehistoric - 500000 BC to 42 AD	FIND
04023				
Pikes End *Cockshutt, North Shropshire, Shropshire*	SJ44343118	**RECTANGULAR ENCLOSURE**	Early Iron Age to Roman - 800 BC? to 409 AD?	CROPMARK
04121				
Petton, North Shropshire, Shropshire	SJ44472626	**BURNT MOUND**	Prehistoric - 500000 BC? to 42 AD?	EARTHWORK
04411				
Whattal W *Cockshutt, North Shropshire, Shropshire*	SJ43593102	**ENCLOSURE?** **NON ANTIQUITY?**	- to - to	CROPMARK CROPMARK
04574				
NAME field at Crosmere *Cockshutt, North Shropshire, Shropshire*	SJ44103010	**PIT ALIGNMENT**	- to	CROPMARK
04715				
Cockshutt, North Shropshire, Shropshire	SJ41462930	**POTTERY KILN**	Medieval - 1066 AD to 1499 AD	FIND
04925				
Enclosure c300m SE of Whattall *Cockshutt, North Shropshire, Shropshire*	SJ44053082	**CURVILINEAR ENCLOSURE**	Prehistoric - 500000 BC to 42 AD	CROPMARK

Site Name *Parish, District, County*	NGR	Monument Types, Periods and Dates, and Form		
06666				
Lime kiln battery *Cockshutt, North Shropshire, Shropshire*	SJ41432748	**LIME KILN**	Early 19th century to Early 20th century (pre WW1) - 1800 AD to 1913 AD	DOCUMENTARY EVIDENCE
06668				
Brick and Tile Works *Petton, North Shropshire, Shropshire*	SJ43452608	**BRICKWORKS**	Early 19th century to Early 20th century (pre WW1) - 1800 AD to 1913 AD	DOCUMENTARY EVIDENCE
		TILE WORKS	Early 19th century to Early 20th century (pre WW1) - 1800 AD to 1913 AD	DOCUMENTARY EVIDENCE
07588				
Kenwick Park *Cockshutt, North Shropshire, Shropshire*	SJ41002900	**PARK**	Post Medieval - 1500 AD to 1913 AD	
07597				
Petton Hall *Petton, North Shropshire, Shropshire*	SJ44002600	**PARK**	Early 19th century to Early 20th century (pre WW1) - 1800 AD to 1913 AD	
12191				
Church of St Simon and St Jude SHREWSBURY ROAD *Cockshutt, North Shropshire, Shropshire* Listed Building (II) - 1585-0/12/59 Listed Building - Shrewsbury Road	SJ43482921	**PARISH CHURCH**	Post Medieval - 1500 AD to 1913 AD	

zSCCMonList

Site Name	NGR	Monument Types, Periods and Dates, and Form	
Parish, District, County			
12192			
The Red Lion, SHREWSBURY ROAD	SJ43502907	**FARMHOUSE**	Post Medieval - 1500 AD to 1913 AD
Cockshutt, North Shropshire, Shropshire			
Listed Building (II) - 1585-0/12/65			
Listed Building - Shrewsbury Road			
12193			
Crown Hotel, SHREWSBURY ROAD	SJ43492903		
Cockshutt, North Shropshire, Shropshire			
Listed Building (II) - 1585-0/12/66			
Listed Building - Shrewsbury Road			
12194			
No 32 SHREWSBURY ROAD	SJ43512900	**FARMHOUSE**	Post Medieval - 1500 AD to 1913 AD
Cockshutt, North Shropshire, Shropshire			
Listed Building (II) - 1585-0/12/67			
Listed Building - Shrewsbury Road			
12195			
Cockshutt House, Cockshutt	SJ43552891	**HOUSE**	Early 18th century to Mid 18th century - 1700 AD to 1750 AD
Cockshutt, North Shropshire, Shropshire			
12196			
No 36 SHREWSBURY ROAD	SJ43592876		
Cockshutt, North Shropshire, Shropshire			
Listed Building (II) - 1585-0/12/68			
Listed Building - Shrewsbury Road			

Site Name	NGR	Monument Types, Periods and Dates, and Form	
Parish, District, County			
12197			
29, 31 & 33 Cockshutt	SJ43532903	**ROW**	Early 18th century to Early 19th century - 1700 AD to 1800 AD
Cockshutt, North Shropshire, Shropshire			
12198			
Crosemere Hall and attached garden wall, Crosemere	SJ43852928	**FARMHOUSE**	Post Medieval - 1500 AD to 1913 AD
Cockshutt, North Shropshire, Shropshire			
Listed Building (II) - 1585-0/12/52			
12199			
1 & 2 Kenwick Cottages	SJ42283031	**HOUSE**	Post Medieval - 1500 AD to 1913 AD
Cockshutt, North Shropshire, Shropshire			
12200			
Shade Oak Farmhouse	SJ41122767	**FARMHOUSE**	Post Medieval - 1500 AD to 1913 AD
Cockshutt, North Shropshire, Shropshire			
Listed Building (II) - 1585-0/12/50			
12315			
Fletton Church (dedication unknown), Petton	SJ44042627	**PARISH CHURCH**	Post Medieval - 1500 AD to 1913 AD
Petton, North Shropshire, Shropshire			
Listed Building (II*) - 1585-0/12/186			
12317			
Wackley Farmhouse, Petton	SJ44872722	**FARMHOUSE**	Post Medieval - 1500 AD to 1913 AD
Petton, North Shropshire, Shropshire			
Listed Building (II) - 1585-0/12/189			

Site Name	NGR	Monument Types, Periods and Dates, and Form		
Parish, District,County				
17293				
Span Cottage	SJ44563014			
Cockshutt, North Shropshire, Shropshire				
Listed Building (II) - 1585-0/9/51				
17312				
Lower Farmhouse, ENGLISH FRANKTON	SJ45542964	**FARMHOUSE**	Post Medieval - 1500 AD to 1913 AD	
Cockshutt, North Shropshire, Shropshire				
Listed Building (II) - 1585-0/13/57				
17313				
Barn apx 20m SW of Lower Farmhouse ENGLISH FRANKTON	SJ45512963	**FARMHOUSE**	Post Medieval - 1500 AD to 1913 AD	
Cockshutt, North Shropshire, Shropshire				
Listed Building (II) - 1585-0/13/58				
17455				
Rosemary Cottage, CROSEMERE	SJ43622954			
Cockshutt, North Shropshire, Shropshire				
Listed Building (II) - 1585-0/12/54				
19552				
Lshaped barn apx 10m NE of The Quaikin	SJ45503088	**BARN**	Post Medieval - 1500 AD to 1913 AD	
Cockshutt, North Shropshire, Shropshire				
Listed Building (II) - 1585-0/10/49				
19553				
Mere Farmhouse CROSEMERE	SJ43342983	**FARMHOUSE**	Post Medieval - 1500 AD to 1913 AD	
Cockshutt, North Shropshire, Shropshire				
Listed Building (II) - 1585-0/12/55				

zSCCMonList — Page 8 of 10

Cockshutt and Petton: Historic Buildings recorded on the SMR but not yet computerised

SMR No	Name	Period	Type	Evidence	NGR
14299	Methodist Chapel, Cockshutt	Post Medieval	Non Conformist Chapel	Building	SJ 435 287
15451	Toll House at Kenwick (may be duplicate of SMR Record 887)	Post Medieval	Toll House	Documentary Evidence	SJ 4254 3052
16179	Frankton Grange	Post Medieval	Country House	Documentary Evidence	SJ 4477 3063
17220	Shippon at Chapel House Farm	Post Medieval	Agricultural Building	Building	SJ 4354 2873
17284	Hay Barn at Burlton	Post Medieval	Agricultural Building	Documentary Evidence	SJ 458 259
17361	Brook House, Crosemere	Post Medieval	Farmhouse	Building	SJ 4356 2945

We also paid a visit to the Community Archaeologist in our research for the book. He told us a little more about the pottery kiln and pottery shards that had been found in a field in Kenwick Park.

The red dot in the field in Kenwick Park (see Archaeologist's Map opposite) is the place where they believe the pottery kilns are to be found.

Although buried in the field they are sure that there are pottery kilns waiting to be

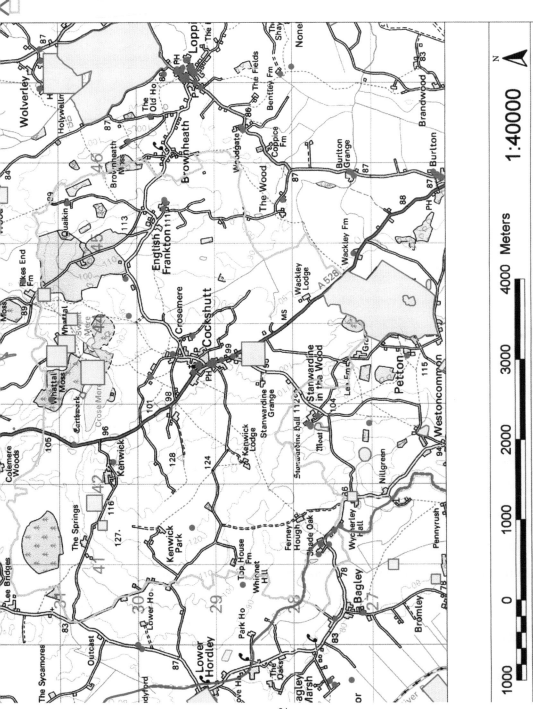

Archaeologist's Map

uncovered. In order to organise a 'dig' the archaeologist has to apply for funding, and of course this is not always available. The shards of pottery found are identical to shards found near Shrewsbury Abbey and Haughmond Abbey, another connection with Haughmond Abbey and Kenwick Park - is revealed in the book.

A former owner of The Red Lion in Cockshutt, Bob Greenaway, with the farmers permission, has been seen over the years, with his metal detector, in the fields around the village. Bob has found three silver denarius coins from the Roman period. A Roman soldier's pay at the time would have been about five denarii a week.

The earliest coins Bob has found were engraved with the head of the Roman Emperor Domitian. He was Emperor from AD18 to AD93. Also coins with the heads of Emperor Trajan AD98 to AD117 and Emperor Lucius Verus AD161 to AD169. The largest Bronze coin was from the time of Emperor Comodus AD180 to AD192. This is evidence that the Romans must have been in Cockshutt or certainly passed through the village possibly on their way to Chester. Bob has also unearthed many other coins including some from Saxon times, 20 hammered silver coins from Henry III onwards, coins from Edward I, II and III and Elizabeth I. The most prolific finds have been from the Georgian period, and fewer from the Victorian era.

Both other finds in Cockshutt were dug up in gardens in Crosemere Crescent. A large key verified to be 13th/14th century for a medieval door or chest, and a pottery shard of a Staffordshire slipware plate dated around 1680 to 1720 was found in August 2000. So next time you are digging the garden and find 'something' don't just throw it away, get it dated!

As you can see from the evidence found underground, the area of Cockshutt has been inhabited from the earliest times.

Domesday Book

Petton is mentioned in the Domesday Book but not Cockshutt. However, English Frankton does get a mention, as follows:

> 'Holding of Reginald the Sheriff under Earl Roger in Baschurch Hundred (English) Frankton. Robert holds from him. Aldith held it before 1066, 2 hides.
>
> In Lordship 1 plough; 2 ploughmen; 3 villagers with 1 plough. Value before 1066 10s; now 15s.
>
> Richard de Frankton holds 2 hides in Frankton of the fee of John Fitzalan.
>
> English Frankton – now in the Cockshutt Parish.'

CHAPTER 3
COCKSHUTT CHURCH

The very first chapel is thought to have been in the Crosemere area between Whattall Moss and Crosemere on the raised gravel ridge, but nothing more is known about it. A medieval 'barn like' structure with only one window was built under the auspices of the Knights of St John of Jerusalem who had a house in Ellesmere and manorial rights in Crosemere. The chapel of ease was established on the site of the present church because it was too far for people to walk to the parish church in Ellesmere for regular services. This chapel of ease was built in the reign of King Edward IV (1461-1483) and dedicated to St Helena. It is reputed that Helena was of humble parentage, the daughter of an innkeeper from Drepanum (now Helenopolis) in Asia Minor. Nevertheless, she became the lawful wife of Constantius Chlorus. Her only son, Constantine, became the Roman Emperor in AD308 on his father's death. It was her son's influence that caused her to embrace Christianity after his victory over Maxentius. From her time of conversion Helena led an earnestly Christian life and by her influence and liberality favoured the wider spread of Christianity. She erected churches on hallowed places in Palestine. Helena assisted not only individuals but also entire communities. She had two churches erected for the worship of God, one in Bethlehem near the Grotto of the Nativity, the other on the Mount of Ascension near Jerusalem. Her visit to Jerusalem particularly associated her with the discovery, near the possible site of Calvary, of a wooden cross on which Jesus was crucified. St Helena with the cross is depicted in the right hand stained glass window above the altar, in Cockshutt Church. Constantine was with his mother when she died in AD330. She was laid to rest in Constantinople in the imperial vault of the Church of Apostles. Helena was revered as a saint and the veneration spread early in the 9th century, even to Western countries. It is presumed that her remains were transferred in AD849 to the Abbey of Hautvillers in the French Archdiocese of Rheims, as recorded by the monk Altman in his 'Translatio'. St Helena's Feast Day falls on 18th August.

Prayer of St Helena *(Traditional language)*

Almighty God, who didst call thy servant Helena to an earthly throne that she might advance thy heavenly kingdom, and didst endue her with zeal for thy Church and charity towards people; grant unto us thy people that we may be fruitful in good works, and steadfast in our faith in thee, and finally by thy mercy may attain everlasting life; through Jesus Christ our Lord, who liveth and reigneth with thee and the Holy Ghost, one God, now and ever. Another theory about Helena and her birth is that she was the daughter of King Coel of Colchester, immortalised in the Mother Goose rhyme, 'Old King Cole was a Merry Old Soul'. This means that Emperor Constantine was the grandson of a Mother Goose hero. Since there was a Christian church in Colchester in AD250 about the time Helena was born, it is possible that she became a Christian as a young person, which would explain Constantine's interest in the faith. I leave you to draw your own conclusion.

Before the chapel was built in the reign of Henry IV (1443) mention is made of a 'bond' involving Richard Boesley of 'Cockshutte Greve' and Crowlesmere and in 1492-3 Baron Le Strange granted lands in Crosemere to the Shrewsbury Drapers' Guild who were known as 'The Fraternity of the Holy Trinity of the Men of the Master Drapers' in the town of Salop.

A 'Chapel of Saynt Elyns in the paryshe of Elsomer" is mentioned in several of Henry VIII's ecclesiastical commission enquiries. In 1558 Roger Gough, an ancestor of the famous Myddle historian, who lived in Tilley near Wem, left in his will to the Chapel of Cockshotte.

In 1646 the chapel was the scene of the farewell sermon of the Reverend Thomas More, rector of Myddle and vicar of Ellesmere. Thomas More was a strong Royalist, a Yorkshireman and the first rector who was presented by the Earl of Bridgewater. He lived in Ellesmere and was known as an excellent preacher and travelled to Myddle once a month. He would ride to the church stile, go straight into church and, after the service and sermon ended, get on his horse by the stile and ride back to Ellesmere. He did not look after the parsonage house and buildings very well and his money was spent by his children. Being a Royalist and a loyal subject of Charles I he went to London to escape the Parliament forces but in 1646 he returned to the area and was entertained by Robert Corbett Esq of Stanwardine Hall. During his stay at Stanwardine Hall he preached every Lord's Day in Cockshutt Chapel because he could not be admitted to either of his parish churches. Eventually he was run out of the district, returned to London and never came back.

This period of Civil War between the Royalists and Cromwell's Parliamentary Forces must have had some impact in the Cockshutt area as Cromwell's men were encamped in Wem but the rest of the region seems to have been loyal to the King. During the next few years the chapel of ease in Cockshutt fell into disrepair. It was 1657-58 when the churchwardens of Ellesmere restored the chapel. The chapel was further damaged by fire in 1664. The Tong parish church register collected a sum of 2s 6d for 'ye fire at Cockshutt in ye county of Salop'. Money was also collected in many areas of the county for its restoration.

A very important Cockshutt family started their clock-making business in 1716 , they lived at The Lodge, Kenwick Park. The sundial in the churchyard is dated 1724 and on it is 'Will Joyce 1724, Thos. Basnett, Salop fecit. The Joyce family will be dealt with in another part of the book.

Petton Church was built in 1727 and some of St Helena's chapel fittings were moved to Petton over the years. Abraham Rudhall made the smaller of the two bells, at present in the church tower, and it is thought that this small bell could have been in the chapel in 1740 before the new church was built and then transferred to the tower.

The Townships of Cockshutt, Crosemere, Kenwick, English Frankton, Brown Heath, Whettal and Kenwick Park were all part of the huge Parish of Ellesmere. In 1772, Baptisms were allowed. Fifty years after Petton church was built a new church was started in 1776 in Cockshutt and opened in 1777 dedicated to St Simon and St Jude. Burials were allowed in 1776.

Voluntary contributions of neighbouring gentlemen and inhabitants of the area financed the building of the church, the principal promoters being the Lloyd family of Crosemere Hall. In 1767 Cockshutt chapel of case in the parish of Ellesmere received £200 by lot from Queen Anne's Bounty, also augmented with another £200 again in 1768.

The plain red brick church is a mixture of Gothic and Classical forms of architectural styles quite common in the 1770s – the so called 'churchwarden' period, probably trying to get away from the very ornate Roman Catholic Church architecture. The bricks were made locally inside the parish at Brick Kiln or Brick Hill lane. There are two possibilities where the bricks were made, one in Kenwick Park and the other is out towards Stockett Gate from the village. Two farm tracks, one from Crosemere and the other up to Kenwick and Browis Castle meet the main road and this is the site of Brickhill Pit where youngsters used to fish for rudd. In the field on the opposite side of the lane to Browis Castle were remains of what appeared to have been kilns. Also a field that has a depression, adjoining the main road and near the entrance to the lane, is called 'Claypitts' so presumably clay was taken from this field for brick making. The other possibility is near Brick Kiln Farm, Kenwick Park.

The bricks are $8^1/_2$ inches by $2^1/_2$ inches and the church has a slate roof and tower. The tower has three unequal stages, the top-shaped belfry is slightly recessed with corner pilasters terminating in stone pyramids to a plain brick parapet. There is no entrance from tower to church directly. The belfry has round-headed louvre windows on all sides and a round-headed window to the second stage on the west side. There is a blind roundel to the bottom stage on the west and a round headed plank door to the south. The slate roof has coped verges on carved kneelers. The side windows are broad lancets. The interior of the church has a crown post roof in five bays to the nave. This was boarded up in the late 19th century but is now open again.

St Simon and St Jude were chosen Apostles to go and preach the Gospel. Their feast day is 28th October which is two days away from the Divine Service when the church was opened, so that could explain the choice of saints. On Sunday 26th October 1777 St Simon and St Jude's Church, Cockshutt was opened and the first minister was Thomas Roberts. The day after the opening of the church there was great merriment and a procession, led by a musical band, marching through the village and onto the market place where great quantities of ale were given to the villagers. The market place was a square where four roads met by the Crown and Red Lion. The road from Loppington ran past Crosemere Hall and came out facing Kenwick Park road and the Ellesmere-Shrewsbury road formed a crossroads by The Crown. The evening concluded with a supper and ball at Crosemere Hall.

The Lloyd family were very generous benefactors of Cockshutt church and they gave a silver chalice which bears the date 1776 and a platen which are still in use today.

Francis Lloyd of Crosemere Hall died in 1788 and was buried in the family vault at Ellesmere. A mural tablet was erected in his memory in Cockshutt church. Unfortunately it is now hidden from general view since the installation of the new piped organ in 1948. The family was asked about moving the tablet but they were advised that trying to move it would cause damage to the marble so they agreed to leave it.

The Reverend Thomas Roberts, rector of Petton, took the majority of services at Cockshutt, and when he died he was buried with his wife in the churchyard.

The silver chalice and plate with the receipt (above) and relating documents (below)

31 Jan'ry 1789

Mr Rich'd Joy's Receipt
for the Plate & Cloth
belonging to Cockshutt Chapel.

Crosmere & Cockshutt

103/6/5

I acknowledge to have received this Day of Francis
Lloyd Esq one of the Executors of Francis Lloyd late of
Crosmere Esq dec'd, one silver Flaggon, one silver
Chalice and one Silver Stand and one Table Cloth
being the Gift of the said Francis Lloyd dec'd to
Cockshutt Chapel and now belonging thereto and
which said Articles are now delivered to me for safe
Custody by the Directions of the Inhabitants of the
said Chapelry As Witness my Hand the 31st Day of
Jan'ry in the Year of our Lord 1789.

Rich'd Joy

Witness
Lewis Jones.

The churchwarden's account book which was opened in 1794 records that Ralph Downs was the minister, John Burlton churchwarden and Samuel Green clerk. At this time parochial funds were raised by a 'levy' known as a 'leurn' but by 1795 it was found to be insufficient and a new assessment was made. The amount varied from one farthing to three half pence in the pound. Ralph Downes only lasted a year in the job and in 1795 J A Cotton became minister.

When the church was built there was no clock in the tower, this was a later addition, but the date 1777 was put on the clock face. In the early 1960s when the church clock was repaired the clock repairers changed the date on the clock face to 1789 which is the date on the brass plate on the mechanism inside.

It was always thought that the clock was made by the Joyce family but the brass plate on the clock mechanism tells a different story. The clock was a gift from Mr Roger Jones of London in his will. It is thought that two clock makers in Ellesmere, who had been apprentices with the Joyce's in Cockshutt, but had chosen not to follow the Joyce's to Whitchurch, made the clock. Richard Bullock and Edward Davies manufactured the Cockshutt clock as a unique collaboration and maybe in memory of John Joyce.

The large bell

At about the same time as the clock was put on the tower two bells were put in the belfry. The smaller bell probably came from the original medieval Chapel of St Helena. This bell when rung was reputed to say "Tom Townsend" as a tribute to the licensee of the first Golden Lion and then he moved to The Red Lion when the Golden Lion became the vicarage in 1860. The other larger bell was made by John Rudhall in 1776 and the striker on the clock hits this bell on the hour.

The small bell which has no inscription and the larger bell are used for Sunday services today.

During the time of Reverend Cotton the font and pillar were added to the church and the minister gave a marble basin and in 1818 a new pediment was erected.

The old chapelries of Cockshutt, Dudleston and Penley had no houses of residence for the clergy so they clustered in Ellesmere, where on a Sunday morning various incumbents were seen setting off to their chapels like postmen. The curate of Ellesmere and later vicar of Cockshutt, Reverend Burrows, used to travel on horseback to both Petton and Cockshutt after assisting at Ellesmere first, one sermon sufficing for all three parishes. Very similar today but the vicar travels by car not horse!

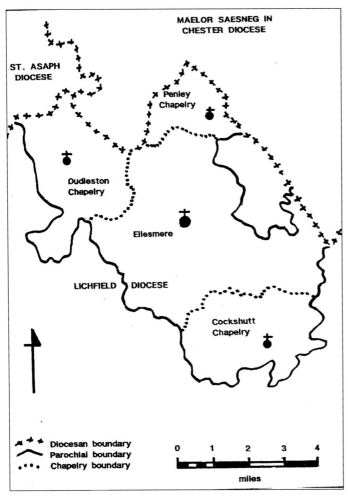

ST. ASAPH
DIOCESE

MAELOR SAESNEG IN
CHESTER DIOCESE

Penley
Chapelry

Dudleston
Chapelry

Ellesmere

LICHFIELD DIOCESE

Cockshutt
Chapelry

✚✚✚ Diocesan boundary
〰 Parochial boundary
•••• Chapelry boundary

0   1   2   3   4

miles

Penley became part of the St Asaph Diocese in 1920

Cockshutt church was licensed for marriages in 1860 and not until then did the minister permanently reside in Cockshutt. The Golden Lion was converted into the vicarage. Richard Spoonley was the first vicar to live in the new vicarage but he only stayed four years, when Reverend Edward Furmiston took over the reins and looked after both Cockshutt and Petton. The Reverend Furmiston was considered a somewhat eccentric person but he was liked by many of his parishioners. On Sunday he acted as organist as well as preacher playing a harmonium which he had introduced. Before the harmonium was brought into the church an orchestra composed of instruments referred to as bass-viol or violoncello, clarinet, oboe and bassoon played for services. The churchwarden's account book tells us that this orchestra cost the chapel warden 'a pretty penny' in strings, reeds and other sundry things. The interior of the church had a gallery for the musicians.

In 1868 Cockshutt became a separate ecclesiastical parish when the Reverend Furmiston became Cockshutt's first true vicar. His family had lived in the village for several generations. The church's fabric was consequently restored and the seats rearranged into their modern form to make the chapel's transformation into a parish church complete. Repairs were also carried out on the roof and the chancel arch was reinforced. Also at this time a small steeple on the summit of the tower was removed. The account book also reports that scarcely a year went by without some charge for cleaning or repairing the clock.

The book is not without its atmosphere when the minister and villagers had many 'tiffs.' One Annual Legal Vestry meeting declared that 'no person shall turn any horse or cow or anything else into this chapel yard without leave from the minister and chapel warden'. This has been crossed out and a note inserted that the 'vestry meeting had no power to make this order as the chapel yard belongs solely to the ministers and no one else has any right to it.' signed by the minister.

Throughout the church's early history the Lloyd family supported the poor of the village and in 1801, in his will, Francis Lloyd left an annuity of 6 shillings per annum to be given in bread to the poor of the chapelry forever. The church has always had families in the village who gave generously to the improvement of the church and its appearance. In 1841 Mr B Phillips of Wackley presented a handsome bier cloth and one pound per annum to the chapel clerk for taking care of the chapel and cleaning and sweeping the chapel once each month. 1847 saw the institution of a fire engine and a year later it was resolved that one pound per annum be allowed to Richard Haycocks for taking care of the fire engine which he undertakes, subject to the orders of the chapel warden and to exercise a sufficient number of times a year.

In 1868 a special meeting was called to consider the fabric of the church which was dangerous and in a state of decay. When the steeple was removed so were the church pillars. Earl Brownlow gave £100 towards the cost of seating arrangements for the congregation especially for the poor, the new seats to be free and open to all. £50 was also raised by voluntary subscription in the parish. Now as Reverend Furmiston was the vicar of St Simon and St Jude and the chapel of ease had become a parish church, a vicar's warden was elected and vestry meetings were held in the schoolroom.

Another continual expense was the churchyard gates as it was considered expedient to close the public thoroughfare through the church yard and the gates were kept locked except on occasions of Divine Service.

In 1870 the roof was re-slated and something had to be done about the inadequate burial ground. Lord Brownlow gave a quarter of an acre adjoining the north wall for extending the churchyard.

Another important year in this church's history was the arrival of the Robinson family in 1876 at Frankton Grange. The name Robinson has meant a great deal to Cockshutt until the death of the last family member at Frankton in 1965. Nicholas Robinson was nominated vicar's warden in 1882 and he financed the re-gilding of the clock. The church yard was re-planted with oaks, limes, poplar, weeping birch and copper beech presented by members of the Robinson family and the vicar and his wife.

The new vicar was Reverend Henry Jenkyn Wilcox who is the longest serving

REV. HENRY JENKYNS WILCOX
1881 – 1907

Henry Jenkyn Wilcox

vicar to date. Henry Jenkyn Wilcox brought his delicate and very neurotic wife and his colony of bees to Cockshutt in 1881.

' Honest' John Peel continued as the gardener at the vicarage and looked after the pony and low basket carriage for a while. The vicar had not been here very long before he found fault with the schoolmistress, a Miss Craty, who was asked to leave. Another long serving member of the community was appointed headmaster to replace Miss Craty, it was John 'Gaffer' Moore. One of his conditions when appointed was that he was able to play the organ for Sunday services. However Mrs Wilcox carried on her duty as organist for about ten years before her health failed and it was then that John Moore took over the duties of organist and choirmaster.

Cockshutt Church must have been a thriving place with three very influential men involved in the day to day running of the church and school, John 'Gaffer' Moore, Reverend Henry Jenkyn Wilcox and Nicholas Robinson. John Moore soon had an excellent choir of men and boys and they were proud to show what they could do during festive occasions such as Easter and Harvest. The vicar was not an eloquent preacher but he seemed to suit the congregation at Cockshutt. He was rather pompous in his manner and liked to show his authority when the occasion arose.

The main attendees at Sunday morning services were the Robinson family of Charles Backhouse Robinson, one of three principal landowners in Cockshutt, and his wife. Nicholas Robinson, who became a Justice of the Peace, his stately wife and their children, Nicholas, Charles, Frank, Harry and Euphemia.

Another family well represented at church were the Nunnerleys of Kenwick. There was a morning and evening service and Sunday school in the afternoon. Tommy Dickin always sat at the back and had a snooze during the sermon. One Easter morning service the vicar gave out the notices of coming events, always before the sermon, but this day he forgot to mention the Annual Vestry meeting and the old sexton Tom Tomkins, quite a character, bawled out at the top of his voice "Heigh! Yo didna gid out 'bout vestry meeting for Monday night". The parson was somewhat flabbergasted but appeared to take no notice. The congregation wondered what would happen next, and with all the fuss old Tommy had not had time to settle down to snooze. Tom Tomkins' concern about the meeting was very serious because that was when he received his salary for the year. No doubt the sexton would have been reprimanded by the pompous Reverend Wilcox, but nothing more was heard about it. The sexton was a typical Salopian rustic of bygone days. He used to spend many days in the old churchyard just tidying up but never overdoing it. He was one of the workmen on the Bridgewater Estate who were noted for taking things easy. You could not blame them, for their wages were very low, but they were provided with good cottages and gardens at a very low rent. Old Tomkins worked around the village for the Estate and one day was cleaning out the brook between Tatton's field and Alf Burrough's which was crossed by a wooden bridge. On this particular hot summer's day old Tomkins sat fast asleep, his feet dangling in the water below. He was one of the characters of the village, now asleep in the old churchyard where he had dug graves to lay to rest the many who had gone before him. During his time as sexton Tom Tomkins used to wind the clock every Saturday night and this custom was followed by his successor,' honest' John Peel. For many years it has kept time for the villagers, arousing the rustic workmen for their daily tasks.

Honest John Peel was gardener and sexton to 5 vicars during his 50 years in the village. He also helped to plant the trees in the churchyard which in 1981 had grown to magnificent proportions.

A few improvements were carried out in the old church during Reverend H J Wilcox's incumbency. In 1887 a new vestry was built at the east end of the church at the expense of Lord Brownlow. This was a necessary addition to the church as the old vestry, at the bottom of the church tower, had been the scene of a serious accident when the vicar's surplice caught fire during vestry prayers on Easter morning.

In 1888 a carved pulpit was installed with the inscription, 'BE YE DOERS OF THE WORD NOT HEARERS ONLY'. The nave windows were changed from plain glass to coloured glass and dedicated in 1897. In 1904 the alabaster step was put in up to the altar. Beautifying the church became very important to the members. Again it was the Robinson family who financed a large part of the new furnishings in the church.

John Peel

The beautiful three apse windows (below) were made by the very distinguished and foremost glazier of the 19th century C E Kempe. He was largely responsible for the revival of glass making along medieval lines. The windows depict St Simon and St Jude, the Crucifixion of our Lord and St Helena and St Chad. They are all memorials to Charles Backhouse Robinson who had died in 1894.

A new hymn board bearing figures of our patron saints Simon and Jude was designed and financed by Lord Brownlow. Ventilating windows were installed in the nave of the building. The chancel wall was covered with alabaster and was largely financed by a garden fete held at Frankton Grange by the Robinsons. The lectern, which is a copy of one in Lincoln Cathedral, was presented in memory of Euphemia, Nicholas junior and Margaret Hope Robinson. All the brass altar furniture and altar cushions, cross and candlesticks were added.

The porch was also built over the main door and the door handle is a copy of the door handles in Westminster Abbey and was made by John Peel (sexton). The old communion rails that now sit at the back of the church are 17th or early 18th century with slender turned balusters hinged in three sections - they are probably the oldest piece still remaining in church. It was during the beautification that a new altar rail was put in.

During his life Charles Backhouse Robinson of Frankton Grange exerted a great influence upon life in Cockshutt. His home was a regular meeting place for the village clubs and festivities. The church today bears ample evidence of their generosity and their prominent role within the church.

The death in 1907 of Reverend H J Wilcox brought the end of an era for the village community. He was a local historian, involved with archaeological digs at Crosemere and Pikesend, a gardener and keen bee-keeper; he was greatly respected by his parishioners. He is buried in the churchyard and a brass mural plate was erected over the vestry but is now over the main entrance.

Mural Plate

It shows a thanksgiving for the 26 years of his ministry. Mrs Wilcox presented a christening jug in memory of her husband in 1907, and it is still used today.

Reverend J Rowley Donald, a native of the Orkney Islands was the next vicar to come to Cockshutt, after the death of Reverend H. J. Wilcox. He was a very active vicar whose hobbies included boxing, diving and digging for historic relics in the vicarage orchard. Reverend Rowley Donald was a curate in Salford and stood in for his own vicar at Harvest Festival in Colemere Church. The vicar of Colemere told Reverend Donald about the vacancy at Cockshutt and he applied for the job after being shown round the church and vicarage by Mr Brownlow Tower, manager of the Bridgewater Estate for Lord Brownlow. Mr Brownlow Tower lived at Ellesmere House and was responsible for looking after the property and land in the Cockshutt area. During the 1st World War Reverend Donald volunteered as a private in the Army Service Corps and he left the parish completely in 1920 to resume his mission work in the Far East.

During the time that Reverend Donald was in the vicarage many alterations were made. The inside sanitation was out of date, there was no bath and no inside lavatory, so a well had to be dug in the stable yard and a pipe laid from the tank to fill it with water. The tank was on the opposite side of the road and was used by the village for their water supply. It was not quite clear whether the water was piped across or under the road to the well, before being pumped to the storage tank in the roof of the vicarage. The gardener, 'honest' John Peel, was required to pump the water from the stable yard well to the tank in the roof. Sometimes this pump did not operate and an investigation had to take place. Although the tank in the roof was full, Reverend Donald had to go and inspect that the pipe was not blocked. Having spent his youth in the Orkneys he was used to diving and swimming so he put on an old vest and old pair of flannels, got a short ladder and like a diver he descended to the bottom of the tank groping about until he found the outlet pipe. He came out of the tank like a drowned rat, chucked off his vest and bolted. The vest lay there for a week afterwards. John Peel was correct, the outlet pipe was not blocked because it was 1ft from the bottom of the tank.

The Reverend Donald was responsible for entertainment during winter months in the schoolroom. A boxing club was formed and run by him. He had come from Salford, Manchester and had supervised boys' clubs which included boxing. The Reverend Donald was no mean artist in the "Art of Bruising" as he called it and used to display his skill on some of the village youths. In one contest he challenged two youths, one after the other, Lathom of Myddle, who had received lessons beforehand, and Ted Husbands, a lusty youth from Crosemere. The fight was short and fierce with the vicar coming off worse. He was unable to appear in the pulpit for Sunday Service and on the following Friday night's match he had a considerably bruised face. Though the club continued for some time after this it is noted that the vicar did not don his gloves again!

The Bishop gave the Reverend Donald leave to enlist but he did not wish to be a forces padre. He joined as a fighting man but was subsequently accepted as a dispatch rider using a motorcycle. His wife and daughter moved from the vicarage to Llandudno. On seven days' leave from France he arrived at the vicarage only to find it unoccupied. Tom Evans and John Peel had been left in charge, and they told him of his wife's whereabouts so he borrowed a car from Alf Hulme, thinking that because he could ride a motorcycle he could claim licence to drive a car. Apart from the bump into the churchyard wall when starting off, all went well until he got to Llandudno Junction. Here he collided with another car. The policeman demanded to see his licence, which was not forthcoming, so he was summoned to appear before Llandudno Junction magistrates the following week. He brought his wife and daughter back to Cockshutt in a borrowed car! He set off a few days later to bike to Wrexham and to take the train to Llandudno. He was fined. When cycling home from Wrexham that night he lost a pedal and had to walk from Overton Bridge, about ten miles. When the war ended Reverend J. R. Donald returned to his parish for a short time. He then received an offer of a mastership of a school in Rangoon, so after storing much of their furniture at Mrs Burroughs of Crosemere, the family made arrangements for their voyage. They settled down in Rangoon and stayed for about two years and then came back to Cannock Chase where he became curate. A couple of years later he moved again to some outlandish place in the Peak District. Next he moved to Herefordshire, where he died in 1945. He was known as an eccentric and rather quarrelsome person who was difficult to understand. He had a quarrel with Mrs Tatton who was leader of the girls' choir and also with John Moore, who objected to boys who could not sing being allowed into the choir. Reverend Donald took over choir-master duties helped by Jack Sawbridge at the harmonium; John Moore was only needed for Sunday duty.

1921 was an important time for the churches in Cockshutt and Petton when they became a united benefice. Reverend John William Isherwood was now the vicar, another well travelled and educated man having also been a forces chaplain. During his few years in Cockshutt the church roof was repaired. Reverend Isherwood went up to have a look at what the men were doing and, so the story goes, he put his foot through the ceiling. It had been designed that way to conserve heat, so then he decided that it all should come down so ever since we have been heating that huge roof space. He also had another idea to make the chancel bigger and pushed back the wrought iron screen and choir pews, so that the pulpit stuck out. The exposed floor was a mess, because it was part tiled and part wood. Another change was to the outside when the ivy which had clothed the church to the eves was stripped off. There is some doubt about this date as the ivy on a wedding photograph about 1930 shows ivy on the church wall. Maybe it had re-grown! Reverend Isherwood left in 1924.

The new vicar in 1924 has been described as a 'vicar with too much money'.

The Reverend Walter Peppercorn (right) was another well-travelled vicar. He built a house on the Stanwardine Road just past Chapel Cottages and called it Bhim Cottage (Low Grove today), after a village in India where he had been. The house was built for families of low income at an affordable rent, a very generous addition to the village. In 1930 the wrought iron screens that had already been moved once by a previous incumbent were removed and replaced by high oak screens. These were paid for partly by the parish but mainly by the vicar or, as people suspected, Mrs Peppercorn, a peculiar looking woman who dressed beautifully.

(Left) As well as the new chancel screen a shield high above the chancel was hung on the archway over the chancel and it represented Mrs Peppercorn's depiction of the Book of Revelations, The Tree of Life and The River of Life.

(Above) Reverend Peppercorn presented to the church a silver box for communion wafers and it is still used for this job today.

Taken about the 1920s the church with ivy growing up the front wall.

In 1930 the extension of Cockshutt's churchyard, the cost of land and legal expenses came to £14.00. Old school drains, that ran through this part of the churchyard, had to be taken up, a new drain laid and two viewing chambers built and the wall had to removed and built on a new site. A fee of £3.8s 0d for consecration of the ground had to be paid to the Diocesan Register. The whole job cost £100.5s 9d. The congregation was asked to take home collection boxes to help clear the debt.

The memorial tablet on the wall near the lectern, to a Frank Harold Elwin son of James and Isabel Elwin of Cachar, India, was erected by Reverend Peppercorn in memory of a friend killed in action in the First World War.

In 1925 the old altar table was replaced by a new altar table of carved Australian Oak. The faculty permission to have a new altar states that the old altar must not be removed from the church without leave of the court. Is the table at the back of the church the old altar? The faculty was also for new altar rails, credence to footspace in green alabaster. The altar table in Australian Oak is beautifully carved and it's a shame to cover it with cloths. As well as the new chancel screen a shield high above the chancel was hung on the archway over the chancel and it represented Mrs Peppercorn's depiction of the Book of Revelations, The Tree of Life and The River of Life.

The tablet in memory of Reverend J H Wilcox was now hidden by the screen and it was moved to go above the main entrance.

The stone flagging in the chancel area was done and the pulpit had a 'face lift', the top and bottom taken off and the panelling made good with some old panelling from the vicarage.

In 1936 electric light was installed in church and two years later Reverend and Mrs Peppercorn moved to Gnosall in Staffordshire.

In 1938 Reverend Percy Gray Hardy became vicar of the parish. This was not an easy time as the threat of war was everywhere. A Nine Lesson Carol Service began in 1939 and carried on through Reverend Hardy's time in Cockshutt.

The first war victim to be buried in the church yard was RAF Sergeant Rear Gunner Eric Parker of English Frankton, who died of his wounds on active service. The village was divided about the type of memorial for the victims of the Second World War. The village had been working towards building a hall for the community since 1927 but the money collected was used to build an organ in the church, instead of the hall, as a memorial. The installation of the organ covered the tablet to Francis Lloyd. The names of the Second World War victims are on a brass plaque on the side of the organ. The conclusion made is that Commander Robinson didn't really want a hall because it would mean that organisations using the school, this provided a useful income, would go to the village hall. The dedication of the organ was in April 1948 by the Lord Bishop of Shrewsbury to the fallen of Cockshutt and Petton. At the dedication service the organ was played by Dr Gabb the deputy organist from St Paul's Cathedral, London. Reverend Hardy and Dr Gabb had met during the war. As a result of this meeting the church choir went to St Paul's Cathedral for a visit.

In October of the same year there was another milestone in the history of Cockshutt, a new Headmaster was appointed at the school and he also became the church organist and is still at the age of 90 years old playing every Sunday and for weddings and funerals plus any special events, Mr Robert Dommett arrived. Before the new organ there was an American organ, a little gem that went up to Petton. Miss Margaret Hulme was the organist from Crosemere Hall and she wanted to give up playing as she was getting married, so Mr Dommett took over at evensong on 3rd October 1948. Another occasional organist was Connie Parker of English Frankton but she was also glad to finish.

During the war Reverend Hardy was away from the village as a padre in the army. Various curates cared for the parish and some lived in the vicarage. Reverend Hardy was a grammar schoolmaster before he was ordained, and one of his former pupils was James Callaghan MP and a former Prime Minister. Free Will Offerings have always been an important and confidential financial support to the church and usually the minister dealt with FWO. When Reverend Hardy left Mr Dommett took over this important role and didn't manage to lose the job until 1980! Mrs Hardy also took an active part in the life of the church and village, being a keen Mothers' Union and Women's Institute member. There were no children.

When Reverend and Mrs Hardy moved away from Cockshutt the Reverend J A Mercer arrived for his last appointment before his retirement, but he really enjoyed himself, mostly because of the music. He loved singing and had a good tenor voice. The choir sang in four-part harmony and performed anthems and at least one cantata for Good Friday. Friday night's choir practice was a highlight for him and the choir, the four Ashley children, the two Dommetts, two Birch brothers, who could read music and sing solos, Jill Husbands, Margaret Stokes, Graham Humphreys and Trevor and Colin Gregory were all members of the choir, which also included Mr and Mrs Dommett.

Mrs Mercer was a 'professional' vicar's wife, a little older than her husband and she became very frail. She made it quite clear that anything to do with church flowers was the responsibility of the vicar's wife, even to throwing away the dead ones. They had three daughters, two were married and lived away. On one occasion, a visiting four year old grandson, stood up in the sermon and told his grandpa that he had said enough! After an evening at the Red Lion, it was not unusual for one or two to ask Reverend Mercer for a lift home. They were always lucky as his old Austin, with a hole in the floor, managed to take them home. Reverend Mercer spent many hours sitting beside Mr Dommett when he was learning to drive, after school was finished. The vicarage garden was very large and the vicar was grateful when Mr Dommett took over about half an acre. Reverend Mercer was a scholarly man, a graduate of Durham and a mine of information on saints, love and tradition.

Reverend J A Mercer retired in 1957 and Reverend Pedr Pollard took charge - quite a contrast. Reverend Pollard had had three careers. First as an army officer, finishing at the end of the war. He then joined the bank and at one time was a bank manager in Shropshire. He finally decided to go into the church. He was very interested in finance and was treasurer of the Diocese for the Mothers' Union and on many committees in Lichfield. Cockshutt had their parish share set high to show a good example. Mrs Pollard always sat at the front of the church and would signal to him with her hanky when she thought he had preached long enough. The Pollards had a very musical son, Peter, who was friendly with the Dommett and Ashley children and they still keep in touch.

Choir. Back Row left: Madelaine Dommett, Brian Ashley, Mr Dommett, Peter Pollard, Mrs Dommett, Middle Row left: Derek Ashley, Beryl Ashley, Barbara Smith, Graham Dommett, Rosemary Henshaw, Gill Husbands. Joan Henshaw, Reverand Pollard. Front: Graham Humphreys.

There were three Sunday services but the living was still just Petton and Cockshutt. Reverend Pollard and his family moved to Eccleshall when he retired as his mother-in-law was in hospital in Stafford.

The church was still being heated by the coke fire at the back of the church. It was lit Saturday lunch time to have the church warm for Sunday morning. The choir robed at the back of the church near the fire, the vicar froze in the vestry. There used to be a fire there but it was bricked up many years ago. The electric lights in church once had globes which clipped on to the top. Tom Gregory, the sexton and church cleaner and Mr Dommett changed the bulbs when needed. It meant carrying the tall steps from school and a very long handled brush so that the lights could be drawn towards the steps and whoever was on the steps could reach out, take the globe and change the bulb. After an unfortunate accident with one globe the two of them decided to remove the rest of the globes hoping no one would notice. The congregation did notice because the church was so much lighter and they wondered why they hadn't thought of it before. Dommett and Gregory were very relieved!

Reverend Lansdale arrived in 1961 and one of the first jobs he and Edmund Parker did was to get the parish share reduced to its true level. Reverend R J Lansdale was a very gentle man and suffered with serious heart problems. Quite often Sundays wore him out and he would have to stay in, much of the time in bed, until the next Sunday. He was a very musical man and played the organ and often commented on the voluntary, especially if by Bach.

Captain Robinson was church treasurer and Mr Dommett was auditor and one time when accounts needed to be ready he threw the books at Mr Dommett "I can't get these … things right. I know I haven't pinched the money. Sort them out!" In true naval fashion Mr Dommett answered "Aye Aye sir." What he had been doing was paying telephone bills and one or two other things from the church accounts. He was grateful to Mr Dommett, but from now on Dommett was treasurer and he would do the auditing. Captain Robinson always attended funerals in a top hat and tails. Although conditions in his house were very primitive his tall, slim, upright figure was always smartly dressed for church.

Reverend Lansdale died in Petton vestry, one Sunday afternoon when the congregation was waiting for him to come out for the service. Mr Dommett had noticed that he wasn't well when they walked together from the morning service in Cockshutt. As soon as Mr Dommett heard of the tragedy he organised the Reverend Stanley who lived in Crosemere Road to take the evening service. Reverend Stanley was a retired Anglican missionary from Canada. He called his bungalow 'Que Appelle' which was the name of his diocese in Canada. He was always happy to fill in whenever he was needed. The Lansdale's had two boys, almost too well behaved; probably they had to restrain themselves quite a lot because of their father's health. Both boys were bright lads and a real asset to the school. Mr Lansdale had a sister who was a nun and she and other nuns made the Mothers' Union Banner for church.

Although the village hall had been built the vicarage annex was used by many organisations as a meeting room and the PCC met there as well. In 1968 Mr Dommett was secretary. It was this year that part of the vicarage garden was sold at auction. Miss Rogers re-covered the kneelers in church. Repairs to the church roof were carried out after the January storm and it was agreed that the insurance should be increased to cover storm damage. The clock was again repaired and an annual fee was paid to provide an annual check and maintenance. It was in May 1969 that Miss Rogers agreed to become magazine secretary and write the monthly letter during the absence of a vicar after the death of Reverend Lansdale. New curtains for the church door were put in place, these were a gift from an anonymous donor.

The new vicar, Reverend Cyril Elsey, was inducted in November 1969.

Rev and Mrs Cyril Elsey admire some of the paintings entered in a Church Competion, (right)

When contacted in 2003 and asked about his time in Cockshutt he wrote in a beautiful hand, still living in Budleigh Salterton and in his 95th Year. He remembers one or two important events. The loss of the flagpole and cockerel from on top of the tower on a very stormy night, and he has one regret that he never saw it replaced. Also the removal of the chancel screen to the back of the church. The opening up of the sanctuary enabled a clearer view of the beautiful Kempe windows in the apse. In July 1972 permission was given to remove some memorials in the old churchyard. The interior of the church was decorated.

The vicarage was basically unsuitable for the vicar and his family so a new rectory was to be built on the tennis court and other land to be sold along with the vicarage. Reverend and Mrs Elsey did not move to the new rectory but decided to retire a year early and move to Budleigh Salterton in Devon in 1975. In Cockshutt church at this time the church service was very formal with sung psalms and canticles. Reverend Elsey had other regrets about his time in Cockshutt, there was no Sunday school and no choir.

The Reverend John Tye was the first occupant of the new rectory when he was licensed in April 1976 to become priest in charge at Cockshutt.

The new Rectory and Rev Tye

The church in 1976

1977 was a very important year for Cockshutt church as it celebrated its 200th anniversary. At the same time Petton was celebrating its 250th anniversary so they joined forces for the big event. A very informative booklet about the history of Petton and Cockshutt was produced by Miss Rogers and David Evans. The event ran for a weekend, Saturday, Sunday and Monday 4th, 5th, 6th June, with local history in the village hall and flower festivals in both churches and refreshments on sale. The school also joined in with 'Country Store' home produce, plants and handicrafts for sale, country clothes and dance over 200 years were demonstrated by the children.

The Sunday Holy Communion services were held at both churches with the Bishop of Shrewsbury officiating at the evening service in Cockshutt. On Monday there was a tug of war competition on the village hall field and a country and western dance in the evening. At this time the Petton and Cockshutt parishes were linked with Weston Lullingfields and Hordley. This arrangement seemed to work well as there were already close links through whist drives and bingo. No sooner had everyone got used to this when it was all change again and in 1980 just Petton and Cockshutt formed the parish.

The tower roof caused great concern during the late 1970s and a fund was set up to mend the tower. The altar table was moved forwards and a platform provided to put it on. There was also a scheme to plant a rose in the churchyard in memory of a loved one. The PCC decided to charge for the parish magazine. Den Birch had taken over winding the clock. Finally the tower was repaired and made waterproof in February 1982.

1982 brought Reverend John Durnell to Cockshutt, an ex-railway man and policeman before being ordained. He will always be remembered as a keen cyclist, preferring his bike to his car.

Miss Rogers and Mr Evans, with some of the old exhibits at the Cockshutt display.

Cockshutt..good for next 200

1977

Two people at opposite ends of the age scale are the co-authors of an interesting and readable history of the churches and parishes of Petton and Cockshutt in north Shropshire.

Nineteen-year-old student David Evans, of 1 Crosemere Crescent, Cockshutt, has written about the churches and retired teacher Miss E. M. W. Rogers, of Penrhos, Crosemere Road, Cockshutt, has written of the general history of the parishes.

Their booklet, selling at 30p, had been published to coincide with the churches' bi-centenary, Potton Church being 250-years-old and Cockshutt Church — dedicated to SS Simon and Jude — being just 200-years-old.

Evening classes

The seed for the history was set a few years ago when Miss Rogers, head of Myddle School for 16 years until retirement 10 years ago, attended evening classes in local history.

But it was only last December that she and David joined forces for research in earnest into the parishes, making good use particularly of the local studies library in Shrewsbury and of the County Records Office at the Shirehall.

The result is an interesting look at Petton and Cockshutt and brought right up-to-date with references to the villages' 20th century life.

Research findings have obviously had to be condensed to put them into

booklet form and Miss Rogers said: "It is fairly superficial, but we have tried to bring in every interesting point."

For David, a former pupil of Cockshutt School and Shrewsbury Priory Boys' School, research was made easier by having a temporary three-months' job in the records' office of the County Archivist.

He said: "I found it more interesting than anything I did at school, but I was born in Cockshutt and my relatives have lived here for generations.

He goes to study history at St Catherine's College, Cambridge, in the autumn — after a working holiday in a hotel in Norway.

Their research has shown Miss Rogers and David something of the resilience of Cockshutt. Said Miss Rogers: "Cockshutt today is still thriving and keeping up well and developing again. I think it must be good for at least another 200 years..."

The history booklet has not been the only contribution of Miss Rogers and David to the churches' bi-centenary. They also mounted a local history exhibition as part of a three-day festival on Countrywork and Countryways.

David said that with the co-operation of villagers, they had collected enough photographs and other items to easily fill the Village Hall.

Rev John Durnell

This is when it was all change again and Cockshutt and Petton became linked with Lyneal and Colemere and Welshampton. The altar table was moved back but on its platform. Mrs Durnell will be remembered for her distinctive hats. The church again was in need of re -organisation and decoration. The chancel screen which was high was moved to the back of the church and the large shield painted by Mrs Peppercorn was also taken down before redecoration. Churchyard maintenance has always been cause for concern when no sexton was in the post. The cleaning of the inside of the church has varied over the years from paid cleaner to volunteers.

In 1985 the Bishop of Shrewsbury officiated at the Thanksgiving Service for the redecoration of the church. Church fundraising became an important part of church life as the parish share continued to increase and the fabric and grounds of the church needed maintaining. Brenda Carr and her committee were the inspiration behind many events and worked hard for the church. The Fundraising Committee as they were called was separate from the PCC and meetings were held regularly.

The Plaque on the Organ noting refurbishment

In February 1990 the church clock was repainted and small repairs and restoration work were carried out free of charge, as part of Joyce's 300th anniversary celebrations. The ladies of the church took over the cleaning to save money and Mary Lindop and helpers made new altar cloths during winter of 1993 again to help save money. The British Legion, Women's Section, donated money for organ repairs as the organ is a memorial to Second World War victims.

Repairs to church and tower roofs were needed urgently and it was going to be expensive so the ladies organised many events. One important change was that Harvest became a Sunday lunch affair instead of Friday evening supper. Edmund Parker resigned as churchwarden, a position he had held for thirty years. Reverend John Durnell retired in March 1997 and it was September 1997 when Reverend Trevor Thorold was licensed at Cockshutt. Trevor got off to a 'sound' start when he went to ring the bell as part of the service and broke the bell rope, or as he says "it came down in my hand".

The first Alpha course was held in 1998 in the village hall and was well attended. Another break from tradition was the appointment of chalice assistants from the church members to help with communion. Another important fundraiser were the covenant gifts by members also known as Free Will Offerings or now Gift Aid, when tax can be reclaimed from the Government; and we must thank Bob Dommett, Edmund Parker and now Chris James for their diligent work to help boost church funds. Clare Jenkins is now in charge of Gift Aid in 2006.

Rev Trevor Thorold at Harvest

In October 1998 Bob Dommett celebrated 50 years as church organist. In 2006 Bob is still playing the organ for every service.

In June 1998 Paul Boyd took over the grass cutting in the churchyard and the Parish Council pay a donation each year towards the cost. Evidently Paul enjoys grass cutting so we are very lucky. In 2006 Paul resigned from the job of churchyard grasscutter and Jamie Cureton has taken over.

The large Cypress tree in the churchyard was causing concern and the PCC agreed to have it cut down.

Before and after removal of large Cypress tree in churchyard

In 1998 the church began to think about a Millennium Project and it was decided to install a kitchen, store room and disabled toilet. A hearing loop was also suggested and disabled access, but first the church had to be re-wired as a priority. Grants for the Millennium Project were applied for.

Above left:Fund Raising at Bellavista, Knolton to for Millennium Project. From the left : Martin Griffiths, Abb Griffiths, Carole Nicholas, Dave Jones, Daisy Smith Alf Smith, Pauline Povall, And Garden owner Les Jennison. Above right: Church Garden Fete at Stanwardine House. L – R Jean James, Wendy Jones, Margaret Dickin.

Another important improvement for the village and churchyard is the Garden of Remembrance which was started in memory of Den Birch who so lovingly looked after the church clock for many years.

The Garden of Remembrance

In 2000 Trevor and family enjoyed an exchange visit to Canada and Sandy and his wife came to the rectory to look after our four churches. Sandy will be remembered as the guitar-playing vicar who regularly entertained at the Terra Nova (Leaking Tap). During 2000 other refurbishment was carried out, the altar kneelers were re-covered and new door curtains put up and a new carpet was laid down in memory of Cyril Hambly to replace the previous carpet which had been laid in 1973 in memory of Edith Parker and Kathleen Thelwell. The Reverend Trevor Thorold or 'Trev the Rev' as he introduced himself to us in Cockshutt, has also instigated lay involvement in the church services. All the readings are read by church members and the 'Worship for Today Services' are very informal and lay led, using the modern worship songs. Trevor has been a tower of strength to many families in the village; his visits are to anyone who is sick, bereaved or just housebound, even if they have never attended church. His concern has been all-embracing and has brought the community together. He will always be remembered for his pastoral commitment, caring and understanding nature. He took the church into the community but did not expect anything in return. Trevor left the parish in 2005 and the Reverend David Ash became the new Priest in Charge for the Benifice in 2006. We welcome David, his wife Sarah and son Blake to our village and Benifice.

Sunday School

In the 1870s there was Morning and Evening Service and Sunday school during the afternoon at Cockshutt Church. The Sunday school has flourished at times and folded through lack of support at other periods throughout the history of Cockshutt Church.

The Girls' Friendly Society, which was a Church Organisation, was held in the Vicarage Annex in the early 1920s.

In the late 1940s a Youth Group met in the annex with Mrs Hardy, the vicar's wife. The group mainly consisted of girls enjoying craft activities. Margaret Husbands and Dossie Birch remember the country dancing to a wind-up gramophone, playing tennis on the vicarage tennis court and learning to make cakes. The girls also recall their time in the choir.

After the Second World War ended and the village was getting back to normality, Nellie Smith started a Sunday school, again in the annex. Christmas parties were also held in the annex and in those days were a very important event in the year for the children.

It was during the 1950s that annual outings to the seaside became popular. Tom Hyde's buses from Ellesmere were used, a great improvement from 'Lily of the Lake'. This was prior to the existence of Lakeside Coaches.

Myra Nicholas carried on the tradition of Sunday School followed by Jean Jones (Brick Kiln Farm, Kenwick Park). As a little girl Jean had attended Sunday school, which was held in the morning in church. She travelled into the village in a pony and trap driven by her grand-mother. The pony was tied up in the Crown Yard while they were in church. It was not unknown for the Jones family, three sisters, brother Tom and grandma to walk to Cockshutt from Brick Kiln Farm on a Sunday morning to attend church. Jean got married in 1958 and left the village. At this time Beryl Ashley helped by Carole Nicholas, became leaders of Sunday School.

It was in 1969 that Miss Rogers collected a group of young people together at 2.30 pm on Sundays in Church. Miss Rogers, the retired Head Teacher of Myddle School, was always interested in the children and had plenty of interest-ing tales to tell, but she was very stern when crossed. The group performed a play each year in both Cockshutt and Petton. One story that Miss Rogers related to the children was about Mary Jones getting the Bible translated.

Sunday School perform the Story of Ruth. from left Janet Whitfield, Kevin Holliday, David Evans (with the corn), Keith Whitfield, Jane Holliday, Pauline Gregory, Karen Whitfield and Dawn Smith sitting in front of the well.

When Reverend Elsey arrived in Cockshutt in November 1969 he felt young people should be encouraged to get involved in church activities and he organised a Church Youth Club in the vicarage annex. With the help of David Evans, a group of teenagers, mainly boys, met on a Saturday night supported by Reverend Elsey. He hoped to get more young people to attend church but it only happened occasionally. A table tennis marathon was organised and went on all through the night. It lasted twenty-four hours. When Cyril Elsey left Cockshutt in 1975 the group continued to meet in the village hall as the new vicar Reverend Tye now lived in the newly built rectory so the annex was not available as the vicarage had been sold as a private dwelling

A ten-hour sponsored football match on the village hall field again raised more money.

Left to right back - John Dickin Steven Hodnet, Philip Carr, Tim Vernon, David Dickin, Front - Alan Davies, David Carr, Kevin Holliday, Keith Whitfield, Roger Griffiths. Rev Tye at the back

David Evans, who had helped with the Church Youth Club for many years, went off to university in 1977 and the Reverend Tye continued with the group a little longer. Sunday school had folded during the time of Cyril Elsey.

It was in 1985 when Pauline Povall, Jo Norton and Louise Dean restarted Sunday School in church. They had children of that age and wanted a Sunday School for them to attend – so there was only one thing to do – start your own! They had between eight and twenty children during the time they were involved. For their first trip they went to see a pantomime. Picnics to Colemere and a visit to explore the church tower in Ellesmere were also enjoyed by the children. Jim Clough used to get involved and would play his violin for the children to sing. It wasn't long before Sally (Jim's wife) became leader and Sunday School was flourishing once again.

In 1992 Joyce Feeney, who had been helping Sally, took over the reins. Many outings were organised and lots of people from the village supported these trips. Joyce had a good nucleus of children who attended on a regular basis and Sunday School was once again very active.

All dressed up for Noah's Ark to take part in the Cockshutt Fete in 1996

Sunday School make puppets to perform in church in 1999.

The children performed a Nativity play each Christmas.

Joyce Feeney in charge of rehersals Nativity 2002

They also had an annual prize giving when each child received a suitable book. Joyce is still involved with Sunday school but Ann Simkins is the main organizer at the moment. Unfortunately the children have grown out of Sunday School and there do not seem to be any younger children interested enough to take their place, or any parents prepared to take their children to Sunday School. A Saturday Craft Club has been started to try and get the children interested through craft work, to possibly start Sunday School again on a Sunday or maybe another day or evening. Joyce Feeney and Cathy Thorold are the new organisers.

Sunday School outings no longer seem popular as there is so much else to interest children today, not like years ago when the annual Sunday School Outing was the event of the year!

Mothers' Union

The Mothers' Union in Cockshutt has flourished for many years but I am limiting my extracts to the minutes of a book from 1956 and going on to the 1990s.

In 1956 there were listed 38 members and as the years progress one reads against the register 'moved away or died' alongside some of the names. Mothers and daughters are not infrequent in those early years so 'Senior or Granny' was the identifying term by a duplicate name.

Members came from Pikesend, Petton, English Frankton and Cockshutt village. The meetings in those years were held in the vicarage on every first Thursday in the month at 2.30 pm and presided over by the vicar who always signed the annual reports. Gradually some meetings began to be held in the vicarage annexe and by 1958 the majority of venues would be either the annexe or church. Out of twelve meetings, seven were in church but by 1963 only two services were in church. Several January and February meetings were cancelled because of the severity of the snowfalls; which illustrates as we know the change in our climatic conditions. They also had a crèche for young children.

Speakers were largely drawn from neighbouring parishes from the clergy and indeed the vicar would suggest people he could contact as speakers. A fortnightly working party was also proposed in 1964 to sew and knit items for sale for the fete. These meetings were in members' homes. At that same meeting it was proposed that three veils should be purchased out of funds. (It is not reported why, but at confirmation the girls usually wore a white dress and veil). By 1968 the annual tribute to the MU was to be raised to 3/6d per annum but the purchase of Home and Family would remain an additional 7d per quarter.

A discussion at this meeting recommended that the Redemptoristine Convent at Chudleigh should be asked to undertake the making of the MU Banner. The sister of Mrs Lansdale, the vicar's wife, was a nun in this convent and she helped to embroider the banner. This banner is held, on show, in the church.

The following year, 1969, the dedication of the banner took place on March 24th, Mothering Sunday. The poles had been ordered.

By 1981 the report records that a typical meeting was twelve members; three to four visitors and about six children in the crèche. Subscriptions register as £1 per member.

In 1980 a comment in the reports drew my attention to a heading: 'A matter of Social Concern'. Their concern was for a group referring to themselves as 'Moonies' and their growing numbers, as there are now three hostels of them in the Diocese. This group of young people were involved in taking barbiturates, drinking meths and sniffing glue. Sadly this proved to be a resistant problem in some areas of society.

The overseas fund-raising and talks are by now registering in much greater number on the programmes and talks given to members are increasingly given by people who have spent Hollidays in faraway places or by visiting overseas workers; they illustrate their own regions or travels by talks and slide-shows.

Mrs Sutton was presented with a plant on the occasion of her Diamond Wedding; not too many we know, are lucky enough to survive to celebrate this event but the changing pattern of marriage will mean this is an even more unlikely event in the future.

During the late 80s and early 90s, many meetings were at venues of private homes, Glendower (Mrs Rene Jones/garage), Stanwardine Grange (Mrs Dickin), and Tyneholm (Mrs Dommett). Mr Dommett often welcomed members with a glass of his home-made wine, always an excellent and popular addition. I have been fortunate to sample this and can give a first-hand recommendation!

Christmas Parties at this period were always at the rectory by invitation of Reverend John and Grace Durnell.

A Coffee Evening held at the Rectory

Top left photograph, Ivy Nicholas, Nellie Sutton

Top right photograph from left, Dorothy Norton, Grace Durnell, Amy Dommett.

Bottom left photograph Dossie Birch, Mary Lindop.

At a meeting in February 1992 there was a demonstration of spinning and some garments were displayed which had been knitted from hand-spun and dyed yarns made by Mrs Dee Taylor. Our book is dedicated to her memory; she was a very talented lady.

The range of places the MU visited for services and outings are a barometer of the changing times and circumstances. They began with local villages and the earliest far-flung outing they made was to Coventry. Then one reads that they attended Llangollen, Stoke-on-Trent and Lichfield etc. Summer outings involved trips to the sea or zoo, all indicating that access to travelling further afield no longer presented a problem. The speakers begin by being local clergy and then expand vastly in range of experiences and contributions mainly based on overseas workers.

The entertainment for Christmas was in the old vicarage - fetes, games and teas; it moved to the annexe and members contributed to the fare and then it flowed back again to being at the rectory. They were homely family parties and games. A change crept in again with local pubs or hotels being booked for the outing. Transport was required, indicating yet again more affluence.

The attendance figures also reflect the change going from thirty five in the early days down to twelve. The structure of daily life has altered vastly over those years because now women with young children are generally at work at some part of their day. The young children are in full term nurseries and so the need for a crèche for six or seven children is no longer required. Mothers' Union does not attract this age group as it once did.

Chapel

The Primitive Methodist Chapel used to be on Stanwardine Road in 'Hightown' on the south side of the village and is now a pair of sandstone and brick cottages (below). No.1 Chapel Cottage has had its roof raised and has been made into a dwelling. This was probably done when the new chapel was built. No.2 Chapel Cottage must have been built up at the back as the old chapel was made into two dwellings. There is a suggestion that perhaps No.2 was also one of the many pubs in Cockshutt, Petton Arms, but we have no confirmation of this.

The New Primitive Methodists' Chapel, Cockshutt

Opened in 1891 this new chapel was of red brick with a slate roof and tall spire and built on land at the back of Chapel Cottages, very close to the Shrewsbury Road. The impressive looking chapel was furnished with pine.

It had a centre pulpit with rails round and rows of pews about ten each side with solid backs. The wall above the altar was painted blue and pine folding doors led into the schoolroom.

Primitive Methodist Chapel, Cockshutt

There was no heating at first except for three Valor stoves, but eventually tubular heaters were put along the back of each pew. You had to be very careful not to burn your knees! The chapel also had a stage and Methodists from the area would come to Cockshutt to perform for the villagers. A paraffin lamp was positioned by the doorway to light the entrance. Two large buttresses were built outside to support the large crack that had appeared behind the pulpit. The toilet facilities were outside around the back. The chapel was well supported and had two anniversaries each summer, one for the grown ups and one for the children. There were two services each Sunday, afternoon and evening, when many children would sing by themselves, recite poems, perform duets and group singing all for children aged three to fifteen years. Mrs Tatton was the organist and she helped train the children with the help of Miss Bessie Owen and Miss Maggie Birch (Chapel Farm). The Birch family of Chapel Farm were devoted chapel goers, Mr Willie Birch was a preacher.

For Harvest Home there would be two services and the chapel was decorated by the women folk, and on the following Monday evening a sale of vegetables and produce, kindly given, was auctioned for chapel funds. Mrs Ann Gibson would always make some of her treacle toffee for this, along with Granny Smith's well known treacle toffee. Sunday school was well supported and had an annual outing from the chapel. A farm cart with sides pulled by two horses was decorated with ivy, laurel and other leaves. There were benches for the children to sit on. The cart would take them to Whitemere or Colemere for the day and there would be a picnic hamper with drinks and sandwiches for everyone. Sometimes the trip would not be so far, only to Stanwardine Hall or maybe to Chapel Farm Field. But when Mr Timms 'Lily of the Lake' charabanc, fitted with hard solid wheels became available, outings went as far as Grinshill and Nesscliffe Hill, quite a long way for the children. 'Lily of the Lake' did not go very fast but to the children it was really speeding. It was an open air contraption with seats going the width of the vehicle and a door at both ends of every seat for passenger access. It had a roll-along hood fitted to the back to pull over should it rain. If the rain wasn't too much umbrellas would go up.

In 1930 a wedding was held in the chapel – Mr Lancaster and Miss Birch were married and a luncheon was served in the schoolroom of the chapel for 50 guests. The schoolroom was used during the war for the whole village to collect their coupons. Before the Second World War the chapel flourished and the Birches of Chapel Farm, the Birches of The Dobbin along with the Smiths of Apple Cottage and all their families helped run many fund-raising events.

In 1957 Heather Roberts was christened in the chapel, the last christening I believe. The final service in the chapel was 9th November 1969 at 2.30 pm. The chapel was demolished in the early 1970s and the plot was bought by Mr Dommett as part of the Tyneholm garden. Later planning permission was granted for a dwelling on the plot but nothing has been built to date.

During and after the Second World War the Roberts family of Petton Farm became very involved in the chapel and Quarter Day teas were held up in Petton Farm when the children were allowed to run around and play games. There was also a tennis court on the front lawn. Circuit meetings and anniversary celebrations were also held at Petton Farm. To get to and from Petton to chapel they would use Lea Lane.

The last minister was Reverend Wilson, the minister from Ellesmere, and it was during his time that the decision to close the chapel and pull it down was made. It was in 1970 that the Bishop of Lichfield gave permission to Reverend Cyril Elsey to give communion to Methodists in the village as long as the Methodist church minister agreed.

CHAPTER 4
SCHOOL

The original school at Cockshutt began late 1840s and was in one of the two cottages opposite the church wicket gate. Mr John Green lived in one and the School was in the other. Mr Green was a native of the village and his father Samuel Green is buried in the old churchyard between the front wicket and the war memorial. He was married in 1850 or earlier to a sister of Thomas Townsend of the Golden Lion, later to become the vicarage. John Green and his wife moved into the cottage opposite the church and had a fairly large family, two sons and five daughters.

Old School and School House

A new school was built by Earl Brownlow in 1856 to accommodate as many as 120 children. I don't know where they put them, but all these places were needed because the families were much larger as so many labourers were working on the farms. The Earl was only a teenager and it was his mother who handled his financial affairs.

The school was a red brick Victorian structure with white leaded windows. When it was finished Mr Green proudly marched his flock across the road to take possession of this wonderful new building.

The only record of this event is by John Green writing the date 1856 AD on the bottom of the right hand drawer of the old teacher's desk. All the desks were made in the village and a little rickety and rough. It was some 76 years later when the teacher's desk was sold to Harry Pratt the blacksmith, by John Moore. Government grants had become available to buy more up-to-date desks, firmer with an iron frame and also collapsible.

John Green was very strict and had a peculiar dry cough or scraping of the throat and when the pupils heard that noise they knew someone was in for a telling off. He was a good athlete famous for high jump and long jump. As well as teaching and being choirmaster he managed a smallholding using the field of about three acres attached to the school with a good cow house and pigsty, and also rented about four acres down Meadow Lane. He planted a walnut tree and other fruit trees in the schoolhouse garden.

The school house, built at the same time as the school, had a large brick oven for baking bread and also a cheese press. In the kitchen were rods with bacon hooks providing a means of hanging home cured bacon. In later years a vaulted cellar was built in the back yard covered by a slate roof with a store for firewood and peat. The cellar was entered by about a dozen steps and covered by double folding doors. This cellar was used as a dairy by John Green and shelves were put up to accommodate the milk pans. It was an ideal place for keeping milk cool.

John Green's eldest son Sam became a teacher and taught at Lord Brownlow's school on his estate in Ashridge, Buckinghamshire, and married the headmaster's daughter. Sam Green eventually became headmaster of the school and was also organist at Lord Brownlow's private chapel.

Sam Green's eldest daughter, Dorothy, became a noted Shakespearean actress and after retiring she gave private elocution lessons in London. John Green's eldest daughter, Jane, married the vicar of Cockshutt, the Reverend Edward Furmiston and moved to the Lake District. The Reverend Furmiston is buried in Cockshutt and his son also became a vicar in the Lake District.

John Green's youngest daughter married Mr Kendall, the Land Agent for Mr Mainwaring at Oteley Estate, Ellesmere. John Green was one of the founding members of the Oddfellows in Cockshutt and was held in great respect by the village. He lived until he was about 90 years old and died in retirement at Mere House (now Mereside Farm), Ellesmere. There is some dispute as to where he is buried.

The Education Act of 1870 raised the status of teachers to 'Certificated' and compelled all children from five years upwards to attend school. Mr Green was in charge of Cockshutt for about fourteen years and he was replaced by Mr Edwards who held the post for three to four years; then a Miss Graty took over. This was not a happy time as the teachers and the Reverend Furmiston had many quarrels. The school logbook had pages torn out of it and it was in a very dilapidated state. It was never known what HM Inspectors had to say about the missing pages. The school logbook begins in 1878 and in January 1879 there were fifty children on the roll. In February of that year all children were examined in arithmetic and the standard was very backward. In March 1879 a boy was expelled for gross misconduct but it doesn't say what he did!

During that year's harvest time the school was closed so that the children could help on the farms. The logbook reports that the weather, illness and harvest were responsible for poor attendance as not all the harvesting was finished when school re-opened.

On March 26th 1880 the school was closed in the afternoon as it was full of smoke from the chimney, the only heating in the place. By April 1881 standards were reported as beginning to improve.

In 1881 Reverend Henry Jenkyn Wilcox became vicar and decided the school would be much better if a man was in charge. The post was advertised and on the 13th March 1882 John Moore took up his duties. There were sixty pupils, boys and girls mainly from a farming background. John Moore had a pupil teacher aged about 16 to assist him by taking the infants. Between them they managed to teach sixty pupils of all ages and standards.

Initially each scholar paid two pence a week for their schooling, but it became free some years later. Attendance at school was both irregular and not strictly enforced. Many boys were employed on farms at busy times; harvest, picking stones, singling turnips when ready to hoe and, very important, picking potatoes in the autumn. The whole school closed during potato harvest for many years.

When John Moore became head of the school he also became the village postmaster. There was a sign, POST OFFICE, over the front door of the schoolhouse. The room immediately inside was used for postal work, sale of stamps and postal orders and this room became known as the office. Today the Post Office is in the same place, but it has moved around the village over the years. When John Moore commenced his duties in March 1882 he wrote in the logbook that he found the scholars backward and discipline very lax.

By April he wrote, 'order was much improved and attendance good'. In November many boys were late for afternoon school because they had been following the Hunt; they were detained after school. Several boys were caught climbing on the school wall and they were also cautioned for throwing stones as one boy had been hit. J Tatton and G Williams were punished for fighting and two other boys got into trouble for assaulting a girl on the way home. H Evans and E Hanmer were also punished for truanting. Life in school hasn't changed much has it!

Every year the school had an HM Inspection and a Diocesan Inspection. The Shropshire Education Committee decided the elementary schools, as they were known, should teach cottage gardening. About twelve boys were instructed for about an hour a week. Many of the boys liked to get out into the fresh air away from the confines of the classroom. One boy in particular Richard (Dick) Downes had no interest in his schoolwork so John Moore gave him a

John Moores Class during the 1880s. John Moore (seated) and his assistant (standing)

job in the garden to find a three-inch wire nail that had been dropped in the garden about three years before. It was not long before he found an iron bar 4ft long and 2in thick. He exclaimed to the Head, "My lord, Gaffer, anner it growed?" John Moore replied how good the soil must be in the school garden with or without manure, it would grow anything! Dick Downes used to help at the schoolhouse, during dinnertime, getting in buckets of coal and sticks for lighting the fire, carrying clean water from the pump across the road etc. He was paid for this work with scraps from the table.

In June 1886 the attendance in school was small in the afternoon because the Primitive Methodists had their Sunday school party. During this year two boys were punished for

indecent behaviour to one of the girls.

A course of Practical Gardening lessons were arranged and the school garden was to be kept tidy and free of weeds

During 1893 the school was struck by a deadly outbreak of Diphtheria and seven children died from this dreaded disease. The Ministry of Health found that the cause of the outbreak was due to the primitive sanitary arrangements. Old earth closets were in use for both boys and girls and the schoolhouse family. These arrangements were condemned and Lord Brownlow had new privies built well away from the school. These were automatically flushed from underground water tanks in the schoolhouse yard; they were fed from one of the village water tanks on the side of the main road opposite Stone Villa. The effluent was piped underground to the meadows some distance away and the fall ensured clearance.

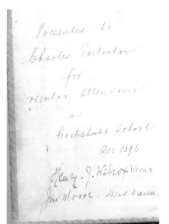

An extension was also built onto the infants' classroom and a new floor laid in the main schoolroom and up-to-date desks with collapsible tops were provided. The original desks were so badly worn and splintered that pupils continually had to have splinters extracted from various parts of their anatomy. These original desks had been made at Bridgewater Estate yard in Ellesmere.

A book presented to Charles Emberton for regular attendance at school 1896. It was signed by the vicar and the headmaster.

(Right) 1898 Miss Rider is presented with a China Tea Service for her forthcoming marriage.

COCKSHUTT SCHOOLS,

DECEMBER, 1903.

The Managers present to the Subscribers of 1901-2 the Reports of His Majesty's and of the Diocesan Inspector's of these Schools; and the annual balance sheet which it will be observed is this year divided into two portions—the first from November 1st, 1902, to March 31st, 1903, signed by the late Voluntary School Managers—the second from April 1st, 1903 (being the date when the Education Act of 1902 came into force in the County of Shropshire) to October 31st, 1903, and signed by the present School Managers.

They are glad to be able to point out that at the end of the Management as a Voluntary School on March 31st, 1903, there was a balance in hand of £93 18s. 4d., and there is also due to them the share of the next Grant from the Education Department for the five months commencing with the School year on November 1st, 1902 to March 31st, 1903, amounting to £53 16s. 8d., after which it is paid to the County Authority. The items also in the second balance sheet of books, hosiery, and carriage of goods amounting to £6 11s. 7d. were paid in error by the Treasurer, and it is to be hoped will be refunded by the County Authority.

From April 1st, 1903, the Managers are answerable for the School Buildings, yards and offices and Schoolmaster's house, and any alterations or repairs which may be necessary, and the only reliable income available for this purpose is the rent of the Schoolmaster's House, estimated at the assessment of £8 per year, what they receive for the occasional hire of the School buildings, and the above balance in hand on March 31st, 1903.

The Salaries of the Teachers, the cost of Books, apparatus, furniture, fuel, light, cleaning, fire insurance on furniture, stationery, postages, etc., are now all paid by the County Authority.

The Managers beg to express their gratitude to the Subscribers to whose support the present sound financial position of the Schools is largely due.

The School having now entered upon a new epoch they would like to call the attention of the Subscribers and others to the fact that the School was built by the late Earl Brownlow in the year 1855, and placed in the hands of the Vicar and Churchwardens in trust for the education of the children of the Chapelry (as it then was) of Cockshutt. The education was to be not only secular but religious, and in the principles of the Church of England. For the last 48 years the Trustees, the Managers and the Staff have endeavoured to fulfil their Trust, hundreds of Cockshutt children have been fitted for the struggle of life by receiving not only secular but religious teaching. During the whole of this period not a single child, as far as the Managers are aware, has been withdrawn from the religious instruction. Every year almost the standard of the teaching imparted has been raised, and the education now given to the children of the poor is in every respect not only equal, but in many respects superior to that obtained formerly by the middle classes in private schools. The old order has to a certain extent passed away, the Managers are only responsible for the upkeep of the buildings and the maintenance of religious instruction as a feature of the school curriculum. The Managers whose period of office ended on March 31st, 1903, hope sincerely that the future of the School may be even more successful than the past, and that the kindly feeling that has always existed between the Managers and the Staff on the one hand, and the scholars and parents on the other, will always be sustained whatever changes the future may bring forth.

The present managers under the Education Act of 1902, are:

Rev. H. J. WILCOX, Vicar and *ex-officio* Chairman under the above Act and the T...

Mr. W. NUNNERLEY, Churchwarden

Mr. BROWNLOW TOWER

Mr. NICHOLAS ROBINSON

Mr. CUNLIFFE, nominated by the Cou...

Mr. C. EMBERTON   „   „   Paris...

*(Left and below)
Management reports 1903*

Receipts. From Nov. 1st, 1902 to March 31st, 1903.	£	s.	d.	£	s.	d.	Expenditure. From Nov. 1st, 1902 to March 31st, 1903.		£	s.	d.	£	s.	d.
Aid Grant for 1902-3 paid Aug. 28th, 1902				50	0	0	Teachers' Salaries					70	0	0
Adverse balance Oct. 31st, 1902, as per last year's report				11	17	10	*Incidental Expenses—*							
							Books, etc.		2	10	3			
Balance in hand Nov. 1st, 1902				38	2	2	Fuel, Light, and Cleaning		7	6	4			
Government Grant	115	18	0				Repairs, etc.		14	10	6			
Fee	33	2	6	149	0	6	Insurance		0	16	9			
Other Sources—							Rates on Teacher's House		0	3	0			
Hire of Rooms				3	3	9	Superannuation		3	0	0			
Whixall Charity				1	15	0	Other Expenses		1	18	3			
Subscription from Capt. Cunliffe				2	2	0						30	5	1
							Balance in hand March 31st, 1903					93	18	4
				£194	3	5						£194	3	5

Signed by Managers to March 31st, 1903.
HENRY J. WILCOX. Chairman : NICHOLAS ROBINSON, Treasurer ; CHARLES EMBERTON.

Receipts. From April 1st, 1903 to Oct. 31st, 1903.	£	s.	d.	Expenditure. From April 1st, 1903 to Oct. 31st, 1903.		£	s.	d.
Balance in hand April 1st, 1903	93	18	4	Books, etc.		5	17	2
Hire of Rooms	1	0	0	Hosiery		0	9	5½
				Carriage of Goods		0	4	11½
				Sweeping Chimneys		0	1	0
				Receipt Book		0	1	0
				Rates on Teacher's House		0	5	3
				Diocesan Education Board		0	10	0
				Balance in hand October 31st, 1903		87	9	6
		£94	18	4			£94	18	4

Signed by Manager from April 1st, 1903.
HENRY J. WILCOX, Chairman ; NICHOLAS ROBINSON ; CHARLES EMBERTON.

John Moore and his class 1904

As well as being Headmaster and Postmaster John Moore also had a few acres and some animals to look after. Here he is with his daughter Dorothy and his chickens in about 1914.

A new lighting arrangement with suspended paraffin lamps was also put in while a new coke-burning stove replaced the open fire. School attendance was 140 pupils.

Boys and girls put on an annual concert every Christmas. Everyone enjoyed it, a very popular event. We're not sure who enjoyed it the most, scholars or parents and friends, but without doubt Joey Brookfield was a great favourite. The proceeds of the concert were used to buy prizes and certificates for good attendance and good work.

The following are some pupils who made good after spending their early years with John Moore at Cockshutt School.

R Downes known as Dick was quite a character he was the one sent to look for the wire nail in the school garden. He came from very humble parentage and lived in a very small house away up in the fields known by the significant title of 'Browis Castle'. He was one of a large family and used to do the odd job in the schoolhouse at dinnertime and be given the scraps from the table such as rice pudding, dumpling, tart, potatoes and onion sauce. Very often the onion sauce was mixed with the rice pudding but it was all the same to Dick who regarded them as dainty bits.

When he left school, like most boys he went to work on a farm as a waggoner's lad. His aim was to master dealing with the shire horses. When this was achieved he could move off to Liverpool or Birmingham to drive horses belonging to the railway and other firms. Dick went off to Liverpool and became driver of a team of horses. He did not stay long in this job and began to regret that he had wasted his time in school. He now began to attend night school in Liverpool, did extremely well and he was soon a member of the Liverpool Police Force.

When the war broke out in 1914 he joined up. John Moore had always kept in contact with Dick Downes and wrote to him at the front. He reminded Dick of the mixtures his daughter Sissie had given him from the dinner table. Dick had been wounded and the letter took a long time to reach him. Eventually John Moore received a reply from Edinburgh in which Dick did remember the mixture of rice pudding and onion sauce that Sissie used to give him but he assured him that he had had many worse mixtures since. Dick went on to confess that one day when he had been sent to the cellar to 'sprit' (take the long shoots off) the potatoes there was a little barrel of beer down there but no container to draw beer into, so he lay on the floor on his back and turned the tap on. "My goodness I did feel bad in school that afternoon so I got what I deserved"

After the 1914–1918 war Dick Downes returned to the Liverpool Police Force. He used to visit Cockshutt on his motorcycle for a day's rabbiting. After retiring from the Force in Liverpool on about £3 a week pension he worked for the Post Office in Ellesmere driving a van around the villages collecting and delivering mail. After his time with the Post Office he had a job as caretaker of the government depot in Elson Road, Ellesmere and at last he seemed to have settled down. John Moore received a 90th birthday card from Dick very neatly written and well worded which he would never have believed possible. It's a miracle and Dick was certainly a marvel. Dick became crippled with arthritis and died in 1954 after being bedridden from a stroke. He was a friend of the former Home Secretary Sir David Maxwell Fyfe and it is believed that he taught himself to speak Yiddish.

Denis Ashley's Overseas Club Certificate

*Peace Celebrations in Cockshutt Schoolyard (front) in 1919. Note the triangle on the window with a piece of wood –
this is where the postman used to hang his letter sack, each day, with the Cockshutt post inside*

Edward Hanmer also came from very humble parentage but made good. He was born in the
old tumbledown cottage in Crosemere. His father was a cowman for Richard Marsh and his
mother Jane was midwife for the parish and they had a large family.

Edward was a scholar at Cockshutt School in 1882. He left when he was about 12 years old
and like most boys went to work in a neighbouring farm. He soon left and moved to work
at Norley, Cheshire, a famous potato-growing district. In 1893 he married and emigrated to
Australia where he set up as a haulier in Footscray, a seaport, shipbuilding and manufacturing

town near Melbourne. At first he used horse drawn lorries and then changed to motor vehicles. He seems to have prospered well and soon owned a number of lorries. He was very interested in municipal matters and became a member of the Town Council. His name has been given to a sports ground and gardens. He also persuaded a nephew and two or three nieces to emigrate to Australia where they married and did very well for themselves.

In 1938 Edward Hanmer came to Cockshutt for a holiday and brought a photograph of himself as Mayor of Footscray and presented it to the school. Commander Robinson representing the school, as there was no vicar at the time, and John Moore was one of the party. Also on the photo are Samuel Hanmer (brother) and his wife, and Mr T J Marsh a school manager.

Edward Hanmer also came over to Cockshutt to celebrate his golden wedding. Although not a studious scholar, he became like Dick Downes, educated on the hard path of life.

Edward Hanmer presenting his photo to the school 1938

Another scholar who has done well in Australia is George Povall, son of Thomas Povall, a cow keeper of English Frankton. He set up as a farmer and milk seller in Yarra Junction which proved very successful. He sold out in 1944 and bought a smallholding but was still looking for a larger farm.

One of the first scholars to settle in Australia was Jack Tatton, son of Henry Tatton, Head Gardener at Petton and brother of George Tatton who was the local joiner and undertaker in Cockshutt in the 1940s. Jack Tatton had a varied career in Australia making a fortune in gold mining in Victoria and losing it. He settled in Cairns working as a clerk at the municipal gas works in the early 1940s.

Samuel Hanmer son of Jack Hanmer, and Arthur Roger of Whettal both became sheep farmers in West Australia. Besides these former scholars who emigrated to seek their fortune others have become prosperous farmers in and around the village, the Embertons, Parkers, Povalls and Marshes.

John Moore had strong nostalgic feelings for Cockshutt but they were all shattered when he visited the village in 1942, many years after leaving. The school house had lost its Wisteria and was occupied by someone other than the schoolmaster, but it had returned to a Post Office. The school garden tended with such care by John Green and John Moore had been cleared of fruit trees and converted into a grass patch with some pigs in an enclosure, and children used the area for playing. The church burial ground had encroached onto the school croft and very little of the original croft was left. The allotments were no longer of any interest to the villagers. The well-trodden footpaths had almost entirely disappeared. John Moore had no desire to visit Cockshutt again.

On his death at the age of 90 John Moore had left a legacy of his life's work which he had recorded in a notebook and which was made into the *Reflections of John Moore*, helped by his son. He had retained a vivid interest in all around him and his memory was good. He had a strong faith and devotion to our Lord which was the ruling principle of his life. He died in 1946 and is buried with his dear beloved wife in Cockshutt church-yard.

Samuel Jackson became head in May 1921 after the retirement of John (Gaffer) Moore. Unfortunately little information of the next six years is available. The only item that has been given to us is a book, *Just So Stories* by Rudyard Kipling, presented to Dorothy Birch (Auntie Dossie) who was the first scholar to pass the

Inscription in book

Minor Scholarship Examination from Cockshutt School in July 1924. The inscription in the book is signed by Samuel Jackson the headmaster. Auntie Dossie (Mrs Dorothy Norton) went on to become a District Midwife and told many tales about driving around Shropshire with no lights during the blackout in the war.

The only recorded events during the time Samuel Jackson was head were found in the punishment book which he started. This was the time when pupils were punished with strokes of the cane. It seems you were either caned on your hand or behind depending on the crime.

'Too lazy to use dictionary' was worth two strokes on the behind.

'Careless work and willfully dodging corrections' merited six strokes on the behind.

'Disobedience and swearing', 1 stroke on the hand.

'Laziness and refusal to do as told', one stroke on the hand.

March 14th 1922 one boy had a day off school 'To take a cow to Ellesmere' this resulted in strokes on the behind.

October 1926, 'Dishonourable conduct during research work in class': Three boys were given four strokes each, doesn't say where.

Games played were hopscotch, skipping, bowler, rounders, ball, and top and whip. Hopscotch was drawn on yards and the road as it was just dirt; string or old rope was used for skipping; bowler and spear was often an old hoop from a wooden tub; and the top and whip top was often the glass stopper out of a ginger ale bottle.

Writing was with pencils, pen and ink (inkwells were fitted in each desk); chalk, crayons and a slate with a slate pencil.

Hands were inspected for cleanliness and shoes or mainly boots had to be clean and polished, hair had to be tied back out of the eyes.

Heating was by open fire in the small room and a large closed- in stove in the Big Room. No one was allowed to leave their seats at any time without being told, they dare not speak to each other in lessons or look at other pupils' books or copy. If they did they were punished. The cane was used almost everyday on someone. There were two canes, one large and one small. If the large one came out it sent a shiver and frightened the class wondering who was going to get it.

July 1927 saw the appointment of Cecil Edward Hassall as headmaster.

Throughout the school logbook there are entries of staff being late for various reasons but it was all recorded. Many staff travelled from as far away as Whitchurch. Staff from the Ellesmere area came by bicycle and punctures were their reasons for being late. The weather was also a problem and sometimes staff had to walk from Ellesmere as the roads were impossible for cycling on. Trains and buses were often late and connections missed. It was nothing for staff to get a train from Whitchurch to Ellesmere and miss the bus to Cockshutt so they had to walk. Any absence by staff for whatever reason is all recorded in the logbook, most interesting reading!

Heating the large room was a big problem with the coal fire in the main room, now the hall. In 1929 the school received two Valor oil heaters to help with heating.

Ringworm and scarlet fever were recorded in 1929. In May 1929, the day before the General Election, the school held a mock election. The winning candidate was Kathleen Roberts (Liberal), John Beckett (Labour), Albert Gregory (Conservative) the other candidates. The children displayed great keenness and enthusiasm. The same year Kathleen Roberts received a certificate for the essay competition organized by the Royal National Lifeboat Institution.

9th September 1929 was the first mention of the Produce Show in the logbook. The boys obtained prizes for cauliflowers and beetroot grown in the school garden. Egg collection was also an annual event as part of Shropshire Hospitals appeal. In 1930 Cockshutt collected 267 which was 92 more than the previous year. By 1932 Cockshutt had sent 1,532 eggs since the appeal started in 1928.

In July 1930 the school was allowed to use a field owned by Mr T Dickin, Cockshutt House. The Cockshutt boys played home and away matches against Myddle for their first ever games of cricket, unfortunately they lost both.

In the September 1930 Produce Show the garden produced 1st for Lettuce, 1st for Beetroot and 2nd for Carrots. In 1930 John Nicholas was presented with a certificate for the Essay competition organized by the RNLI.

Miss Young's Class about 1930

October 1930 saw a new fire grate installed in the main classroom. Fire drill time was 1 minute 15 seconds to clear the school, by October 1936 it took only 30 seconds to evacuate the school.

In the 1931 Produce Show the school garden produced six prizes for vegetables so this bode well for the future of gardening in the village.

November 16th 1931, the school took part in 'Buy British Week' by doing a project on Britain and the British Empire and in January 1932 there were gardening and farming lessons to prepare the boys for the future.

Not only was the school inadequately heated the lighting was also poor. In February 1932 the logbook reports that owing to heavy darkness this afternoon it was practically impossible to do any written work even though all the lamps were lit.

During 1932 the senior pupils commenced a Land Utilization Survey and visited most villages around the area: Crosemere, Colemere Woods, Pikesend, English Frankton, Kenwick Park, Stanwardine, Weston Lullingfields, Bagley and Lee.

Permission to use the portable wireless, belonging to the vicar, had been obtained from the Local Education Authority so the seniors could listen to the schools programmes on geography and gardening.

In October 1932 members of the church choir were allowed out of school to attend the wedding of Olive Wilkinson of Mere Farm, who was the church organist.

The Robinson family from Frankton Grange were very important to both the school and church and in 1932 Captain Robinson was secretary of the School Management Committee.

One responsible job the school had was to look after the First World War Memorial in the churchyard. The Ex-Servicemen's Memorial Association expressed appreciation to the school children for their regular care of the memorial.

The logbook reports that during the dark afternoons and bad weather the children who lived some distance from school were allowed home early.

January 1933 the children held an exhibition of old photographs showing school, village and scholars of years ago.

In February the scholars were still listening to broadcasts on the wireless and wrote to Sir John Russell. These letters received from Cockshutt School were mentioned on the wireless and some of the information used in his programme.

A branch of the Council for the Preservation of Rural England was started in the school. Their main objective was to keep the countryside free from litter and encourage the children to take pride in tidiness (maybe we should start one again).

The end of February this year brought isolation to the village – 6ft-10ft drifts and traffic on all roads at a standstill.

During 1933 school trips began and became an annual event. Senior scholars, staff and some parents visited Port Sunlight and Liverpool. Measles in a neighbouring district meant several pupils were excluded because they had been in contact. In June of this year several were absent with pneumonia.

July 1933 the school bell was in need of repair so a whistle had to be used to assemble the children.

The Produce Show in September now included other classes than fruit, flowers and vegetables and the children took part in painting, essay writing, needlework, wild flowers and fruit as well as garden vegetables.

Another field in Cockshutt was to be used for football by kind permission of R J Marsh.

Cockshutt played Ellesmere on the racecourse field but lost 2-1.

1934 brought problems with the sanitary system, it had been tampered with by the builder of the new houses on Shrewsbury Road. The flushing system was working but only slowly.

January18th to 24th there was a serious measles outbreak and school was closed to stop the spread. The whole building had to be disinfected in accordance with Regulation 110 and pencils were destroyed and the pens had to be boiled.

In March of the same year a boarding pupil at Oswestry High School brought measles back to the village because she had been sent home.

Infant and junior teachers were given lessons in the use of the 'Beacon' method of teaching reading. This method of teaching children to read was used for many years.

In 1934 the school trip was to Messrs Cadbury at Bournville.

During the haymaking season in 1934 a mini whirlwind struck R J Marsh's field of hay. It

Mr Hassall's Class 1934/35. Front Row: Geoffrey Nicholas, Norman Birch, Bill Smith, Bill Allman, Robin Henshaw, Frank Dickin, John Sawbridge, George ('Dixie') Dean. Second Row: Tom Smith, Alf Smith, John Hanmer, George Hanmer, Roy Hanmer. Third Row: Mr Hassall (Headmaster), Alf Hanmer, Herbert Grice, Irene Roberts, Connie Jones, Millie Birch, Maud Hanmer, Nesta Dickin, Eileen Cook, Brenda Nicholas, Betty Hanmer, Back Row: Edgar Roberts, John Roberts, Len Birch, John Chidlow, Joe Grice, Stanley Austin, Tom Davies, Frank Mathews (Pitchford).

happened one dinnertime and it was a curious spectacle watching hay being lifted high into the sky.

School did not open on September 10th because the new heating system and decorating had not been finished. The children had an extra three weeks' holiday.

In October the outside of the school was painted.

1935 school trip went to Swindon. In July the school was closed once again because of a measles outbreak. At the re-opening of school ten days later only 43 children out of 80 were present, 26 children had measles and the others lived in outlying areas so no contact could be made because they didn't have local radio, newspapers, home telephones or mobiles.

In October the school flushing system was not working so the boys were flushing the lavatories twice daily by carrying buckets of water from the pump across the road to the syphonic flush.

On January 21st 1936 King George V died. The school closed on 28th January for his funeral.

The WI used the school as their meeting place but on March 19th one of the hopper windows was broken while they were there. In May this year the Infants and Standard 1 had organized games for the first time. The school trip went to London. School provided craft items to be displayed at the West Midlands Show.

Children were taken to the Head's house to listen to the broadcast of the departure of the Queen Mary and again two days later to listen to the schools broadcast from the Queen Mary.

During 1936 a long serving school caretaker, John Peel, died at the age of 81 having just retired the previous year.

June 22nd produced a severe thunder and lightning storm and torrential rain, the worst storm for many years.

The year finished with the shock news of the abdication of King Edward VIII.

Each year school finished with a Christmas party, it usually meant the school closed for the afternoon so the room could be made ready for the evening party.

1937 a very poor start to the year due to bad weather, heavy snow and blizzards with many children absent. There was also an epidemic of coughs and colds.

March 19th 1937 was a very important day for Cockshutt school, electric lighting was installed and a socket had been fixed for wireless and projector use. Now that they had an electric socket the school applied for the loan of a wireless set from Central Council Stores for school broadcasting.

There was an appeal for used postage stamps for the rebuilding of the Orthopaedic Hospital, Oswestry. 1,583 stamps were collected in school.

I have mentioned some of John Moore's ex-pupils; another was John Wellings. He left school in 1892 and visited Cockshutt in October 1937 bringing with him a football for the boys to use. Mr Wellings had worked in mining at Que Que, Southern Rhodesia in Southern Africa, since 1900.

It was in 1927 that the first meeting was held to raise funds for a parish hall. In 1937 Mr Hassall was very involved with the fundraising. He organized a 'Beano' celebration along with the Reverend Peppercorn and school was closed for the day so they could all take part.

October brought more severe weather, frozen snow and rain on top made conditions treacherous.

In 1938 the playground was causing a problem, it was in very poor condition and the Headmaster brought it to the attention of the School Managers.

The school received the sad news that Mr T Dickin, a very well known character in the village and school manager, had died. The choir attended his funeral and four boys represented the school.

In April 1938 Reverend and Mrs Peppercorn were leaving the village to go to Gnosall. Milly Birch presented Mrs Peppercorn with a handbag; and a map of Shropshire in 1599 was presented to Reverend Peppercorn. The presentation was on behalf of day school, Sunday school, choir and fellowship.

Football Team 1937/38. Back Row: Mr Hassall, Frank Pitchford (Matthews), Tom Davies, Edgar Roberts.
Middle Row: John Hanmer, Joe Grice, Len Birch, Front Row: John Roberts, Norman Birch, John Chidlow, Bill Smith, Alf Smith.

During the Easter Holidays the windows in the Infants' class were changed so all had plain glass instead of the diamond panes, this had improved the amount of light in the classroom and the hopper windows would improve ventilation.

The senior scholars visited London for the annual trip with parents, staff and friends, twenty-nine in all. They visited Madame Tussuads, walked through Hyde Park to Buckingham Palace and saw the inspection of the guards; walked along Bird Cage Walk past Westminster Abbey and the Houses of Parliament; they went underground to The Tower of London where they saw the Crown Jewels; Tower Bridge and the ships on the river. After tea they visited Trafalgar Square and into St Martins-in-the-Fields. They left Paddington station at 6.50pm and reached home about 11.40pm – a real day trip.

The Head reported to the Medical Officer and County Surveyor that there was an offensive smell emanating from the main drain outside school. This was attended to and a trap fitted to the grid opposite the school gate.

June 24th, chicken pox had broken out in school and some children had to be excluded because they came from the same houses. The epidemic lasted until October 21st.

John Sawbridge, our future shopkeeper, was awarded a special place at Wem Grammar School.

The Wisteria that had grown up the school house wall was chopped down and replaced with a Japonica which Mr Dommett remembers very well.

Another Beano was held for Parish Hall funds so school was closed for the day.

Many entries had been put into the Horticultural Show; paintings, needlework, essays, wildflowers and fruits. The school garden managed 3rd prize for cabbage in the Open Section.

On September 15th the Head attended a meeting in connection with The Air Observer Corps.

At the Armistice Service held in church, John Chidlow and Eileen Cooke laid wreaths on the War Memorial on behalf of the children of the village. The children were still looking after the Memorial and once again were thanked by the Ex-Servicemen's Association.

December was very cold and the children were given plenty of exercise to keep them warm.

January 11th 1939 was a very dark day and the lights had to be on, heavy snow fell and there were severe gales.

On the 26th January school received four handbooks dealing with Air Raid precautions and First Aid.

March: the school playground was measured for tarmac to be done this year!

This year's school trip was to Port Sunlight and Lever Brothers Soap works and then onto Liverpool where they visited CP Liner 'Duchess of Bedford', followed by tea and the amusements in New Brighton.

I have already mentioned that the school closed for Beano celebrations which had now become the Parish Hall Fete. Another annual event was the Oddfellows Club Day when the Oddfellows walked around the village with the huge banner. There was lots of entertainment in the Red Lion car park. This was held in June each year and the school was closed for the day, very important event in the life of the village and will be dealt with in more detail in another chapter.

September 3rd 1939, 11am, war was declared between Britain and Germany.

School did not open on the 6th for pupils but the teachers were in school to receive instructions. No evacuees in the village at the moment.

September 7th, school opened. The school playground was being tarmaced so it was very difficult all round but school carried on.

The blocked up entrance

September 11th, children received instructions on how to use a gas mask.

September 19th, seven evacuee children arrived in school, all privately billeted. The School Medical Officer was called to examine them.

Entrance to old Infants' was blocked up and a window put in, the entrance was now at the back. Tramps used to pinch sandwiches from the children's cloakroom before it was blocked up.

During the Christmas Holidays in 1940 the fires had to be kept going because of severe frosts.

The children were given plenty of exercise to keep them warm instead of ordinary lessons.

The snow followed at the end of January and attendance was low and the children were sent home early in the bad weather. This was one of the most severe winters in many years.

Very heavy snowfalls and the roads were practically impassable and only 34 children in school.

February continued much the same with very heavy snow, the worst winter since 1895 the newspapers reported, even heavy snow into March.

Cockshutt played football matches against St Gerard's, Liverpool, the evacuees at Loppington and at Cockshutt, and Cockshutt won them all.

The girls as well as the boys were caned but Mr Hassall was somewhat considerate at most times when he would ask if you were right handed or left handed and caned you on your non- writing hand.

The punishment book continued to record the type of behavior that warranted the cane.

Throwing away school property – 1 stroke on the hand.

Swearing – 3 strokes on the hand.

Playing truant from school – 4 strokes on the behind.

Bad language – 4 strokes on the behind.

Bullying a little boy and knocking his tooth out – 2 strokes on the hand.

Making rude remarks to a little girl on the way home from school – 8 strokes on the hand.

1940 Mr Hassall's and Miss Young's Classes, Mr Hassall, Percy Dulson, Alan Marsh, Ernest Dulson, Eric Williams, Frank Gwilliam, Miss Young, Middle Row: Dennis Birch, Stanley Hanmer, Dorothy Birch, Margaret Husbands, Gladys Hanmer, Pauline Hodnet, Myrtle Thomas, Betty Davies, Jean Husbands, Ethel Williams, Cyril Marsh. Front Row: Philip Emberton, Ron Roberts, Dennis Smith, Trevor Gregory, Raymond Nicholas, Frank Hanmer, Dennis Edwards, Brian Birch.

One day in May gas masks were all examined and re-fitted but not all the children had brought theirs to school. The ones who had their gas masks had to practice wearing them. Rehearsal of Air Raid Drill alarm lasted 10 minutes. Details of evacuation had been received from the Education Office and the vicar brought in gummed brown paper to stick on the plain windows if necessary in case of air raids. During the summer Holidays wire guards were fixed to the windows to minimize the danger of flying glass should the windows be shattered by a bomb explosion.

The Tobacco Fund, cigarettes were collected and sent to the forces. Cockshutt's collection went to sailors on the HMS Vivacious and cards were received thanking the school for their generosity.

During this year several evacuees attended school and there seems to have been two types of evacuee. Private ones, when families arranged their own accommodation with relatives in the village and the other evacuees who were sent to the area by the regions around Liverpool. In January 1941 twenty-seven evacuees arrived from Wallasey and the private evacuees came from Liverpool, Manchester and Birkenhead in smaller numbers.

By 1941 The Ministry of Information began their film shows in the school and continued for many years for the children during the day and for the adults in the evening.

When the gas masks were examined in the March, 100 out of 101 pupils had brought their gas masks to school and practised wearing them. As the school had many evacuees, a Mrs Paterson was sent to the school from Wallasey to help with them. Cockshutt School was chosen to participate in the scheme of the Ship Adoption Society. This meant sending letters to the sailors, along with cigarettes and cards. Letters of thanks were received from the crew of HMS Barcote.

A large piece of plaster had fallen from the ceiling in the Infants room and it was not safe to use so the infants and Standard 1 were taught in church.

By December 1941 there were 114 children on roll, 82 local and 32 evacuees.

The School House System was in use and the houses were - Darwin, Clive, Benbow and Hill. Each house had to take turns filling the inkwells, giving out the books ready for the next lesson during playtimes.

January 1942 brought a change of staff: Mrs Rogers (Miss Baker) moved to Ellesmere Boys School and as no teacher had been appointed and no supply teacher turned up, it was difficult for two days. A Miss Joan Millington then came as a temporary teacher. What a time she had getting from Whitchurch to Cockshutt each morning. She was late the first three mornings due to the train from Whitchurch being delayed. In her second week it was the bus that was late due to the bad state of the roads. On January 22nd Miss Millington arrived in school two hours late because she had had to walk from Ellesmere due to the heavy snow. More snow fell that day and how she got home is a mystery.

By the 10th of February Miss Millington had caught mumps which was in school and many children were absent. A replacement teacher, Mrs Spurgen, lasted only one day as she could not continue to teach in Cockshutt. No replacement was sent to cover Miss Millington's absence and it was March before she returned. The head had Standard 2 upwards but fortunately many pupils were still absent suffering with mumps.

A sad day for the village when the funeral of an ex-pupil John Chidlow, only 17 years old, was held in church. The school was represented.

May 1942: many of the gas masks were found to be faulty and they were sent to the Chief Warden for attention.

On September 25th the school closed for five weeks for potato picking, but it was the 14th December before school reopened due to boiler trouble.

The Ship Adoption Society ship attached to Cockshutt in 1943 was "Empire Cape" and the Merchant Navy Comfort Service supplied wool to the village, so the senior girls and their mothers began a huge knitting programme. Parcels of knitted items and books were sent to 'Empire Cape' many times during the next few years.

Letters were also sent to HMS Queen and HMS Wildgoose along with parcels of books. Christmas cards were also sent to all three ships.

Another effort during the war that the school and village supported was Salute the Soldiers Saving Campaign. The enormous amount of £10,028 was raised; the target for Cockshutt was £4,000. What an effort by everyone. Still noted for their generosity the village of Cockshutt continued with their support when the new Millennium Hall was to be built.

It was in 1944 when Miss Millington was sent home with a rash, 'it may be infectious' was the written entry in school log.

In March fuel ran very, very low and the emergency supply had to be used because there was no coal or coke available from Ellesmere.

The Ministry of Works wanted to remove the railings at the front of the school but the school managers refused to give consent because of the security of the children.

The senior pupils visited United Dairies, Ellesmere for a very interesting afternoon. Ex-pupils Corporal J H Birch (RAF) and LAC William Davies came back to give talks to the pupils on their travels in the Middle East, Mediterranean and India.

December 1944: Miss Young retired after 33 years as infant teacher; she was missed by all.

1945 started with very bad weather, heavy snow and both staff and pupils were down in numbers. The senior pupils helped the Head with the younger children.

The Master of 'Empire Cape', Captain Grieg, sent a letter and four photographs thanking everyone for their generosity over the last few years. PC Boardman (Shropshire Constabulary) gave a talk about road safety and inspected bicycles and gave advice.

Another ex-pupil, Sergeant Gordon Jones, gave a talk on Palestine where he had spent four years.

Mrs Bird who had taken over from Miss Young was given leave of absence to have a baby so back came Miss Young on supply.

July 1945 saw another big change in the school as Cecil Edward Hassall left to take up a position in Cambridge after eighteen happy years in Cockshutt.

Mr Herbert Evans became Head but school could not open on 3rd September as it should have and it was the 10th when the re-decoration of the school was finished. October brought the Horticultural Adviser bearing gifts, two spades, two forks, two lines and four handles. Unfortunately football was banned from the schoolyard due to two broken windows.

In November 1945 school received clothing coupons from the Education Office and these were issued to the families.

Dossie Birch received her Certificate for passing the Religious Examination in 1945

The village and school continued to support the Navy Comfort Fund by holding whist drives and dances.

A dance was also held in aid of the school party and an application was made to Ellesmere Rural District Council Food Office for a permit for rations for the party – this was granted.

January 1946, when school opened it was without Den and Dossie Birch who had reached the leaving age of fourteen. Two teachers were again late but Mrs Bird had been ill on the way and Mrs McFie had helped her to school. Mrs Bird had been affected by the severe cold morning and revived after a hot drink and a warm by the fire. They were both late the next day because they had to walk from Ellesmere as it was impossible to ride their bicycles.

The school curriculum was to be extended as the senior girls were to go to Baschurch Domestic Science Centre.

May 1946 was another landmark when school dinners were begun. The meals were transported from Wem and the washing up was done in the school house. 59 children wanted the meal so 62 knives, 62 forks, 62 spoons, 3 wooden spoons, 1 large knife, 11 dozen plates, 6 tea towels, 12 dish clothes, 3 oven clothes, 1 roller towel, 2 buckets, 1 mop, 3 servers, 3 ladles, 4 scrubs, 36 yards oiled baize, 1 kneeling mat, 6 flannels, salt and pepper pots and mustard pots were ordered and arrived. It was months before a crockery cupboard arrived to put all the pots in.

In July 1946 John Hodnet left school for Wem Grammar School and is now a School Governor, a Parish Councillor and a District Councillor and has been for many years.

A big event in the village calendar was the Horticultural Show always held on the first Saturday in September. Of course there was no village hall at this time so marquees were put up on the field next to Stone Villa, known as Harry Austin's field, and the fair used to come for a few days.

In 1946 Pearl Manders attended school from the Manders Fair. School meals were well established and discussions were held about a school kitchen but as they had no water supply no decision was made.

Transport was arranged for Petton children, which is still in operation today. School closed January 29th to February 13th because of severe weather.

The school was getting ready for physical activity as 63 pairs of pumps were ordered. The bad weather continued and blizzards made the school dinners late and there was no mail in Cockshutt. Fuel was short with no chance of delivery from Ellesmere.

Another milestone in school was when they had school milk delivered for the first time from Mr Higgins of Baschurch.

Mr Evans Class late 1940s. Tony Thomas, Tony Hanmer, Ken Hanmer, Trevor Gregory, Percy Dulson, Keith Sutton, John Husbands, Bernard Ashley, Keith Jefferies, Eric Pugh, Les Smith, Pam Millington, Joyce Williams, Olive Chidlow, Doris Taylor, Joan Carr, Mary Ashley, Edna Birch, Beryl Ashley, Keith Evans, Carl Smith, Sheila Davies, Ruth Tomley, Pam Smith, Myrtle Thomas, Betty Henshaw, Joyce Whitfield, Mary Hanmer, Derek Ashley and Teacher Mr Evans.

Gordon Whitfield started school April 1947, not a good time to start as there was an outbreak of sickness and the school lavatories were inspected. The refuse dump and pump for the water supply across the road were also examined. The Medical Officer called to see about the outbreak of sickness. The water supply was definitely dangerous! Wem Canteen instructed that no water from Cockshutt was to be used in school. A supply of water was sent from Wem daily. The washing up after dinner was to be taken back and done in Wem.

Fuel was low again in November and Reverend Hardy offered to loan some of his private stock.

Resurfacing the boys' yard caused many problems as it was done at the end of November but on 15th December it was unusable as it had not set. April the following year it was still causing concern because the surface became sticky in warm weather. The playground still was not satisfactory and a thick carpet of gravel was put on the yard in December.

The container of mince for school dinners had not been securely fastened and a large part of its contents ran over the pavement. Emergency rations came to the rescue when four tins of corned beef were used.

In December the fuel had run out again but as it was a warmer day school stayed open. The day after it was closed. Lots of children had colds.

School opened in January 1948 still having problems with the playground as the gravel had not solved the mess.

A crate of food from Bristol supplied by the Australian Food for Britain Appeal arrived and was distributed; each child received about one and a quarter pounds. In February school received dried milk chocolate powder from Canada.

In April, which was over twelve months after the job was done the playground was again sticky as the weather got warmer. Folk dancing began.

The Headmaster Mr Herbert Evans left and an acting Head was appointed. Mrs L G Lightwood would stay in charge until Mr R Dommett takes over in October 1948. When Mr Dommett came up from Ilford in the South of England for an interview and the job was offered to him he could not give an answer without consulting his wife. There was electricity in School House but no running water. Of course Amy, his wife, was not used to this. They had two children to consider as well and they had both hot and cold running water in their house in Ilford. The Chairman of Managers at the interview, Captain Robinson, could not understand his attitude; surely moving to a rural area you must expect these hardships. Frankton Grange did not even have electricity never mind running water! The school managers told Mr Dommett that they would have running water in the spring. Mrs Dommett did agree to come to Cockshutt and they both say it was a decision they have never regretted.

Mr and Mrs R E C Dommett arrived by train from Ilford having waved their furniture off in the morning on the day before. On Friday 1st October he was given the day off to see to the furniture when it arrived. They had stayed at the Red Lion overnight. There was a panic in the school so Mr Dommett had to go into school and Mrs Dommett was left to see to the furniture.

School dinner pots had always been washed up in the schoolhouse but that was stopped and Dossie and her mother managed in the school porch. The school then consisted of the Hall (two classes), the Infants' room and three porches, boys, girls and infants.

A general election was about to take place and Captain Robinson wanted to use the school house front room for the Conservatives' committee room as usual. That was another event that came to an end as Mr Dommett did not want to be involved in politics.

Soon after they arrived funds were needed for the school Christmas party so Amy and Bob decided to pay Captain Robinson a visit, they were quite unprepared as to what to expect. There was no water or electricity in Frankton Grange and it was a dark night as they walked up to English Frankton. Eventually they found a door and knocked, gradually a glimmering ray appeared and the door was opened to reveal Captain Robinson with a lighted candle. They followed him through corridors into a dark back room with uncomfortable chairs.

Mr Dommett had come from teaching music and maths in a boys secondary modern school to a school with an age range from 5 to 15, from cheeky East Enders to more subdued quieter children, not as sharp as the ones in Ilford, the class of 30 plus of mixed age, sex and ability was a challenge. Mr Dommett taught the seniors and Mrs Bird and Mrs McFie had the infants and juniors.

One of the first things Mr Dommett did was to ring the Education Office asking if he could take mixed PE. This had never been done at all as there were no facilities. The Education Office told him he could take boys and girls together for PE. The next day when this news got out one irate mother did not want her girl to have PE with the boys. They soon got over it. Facilities were very poor; a playground at the back was tarmaced but had a brick wall across the middle which separated the boys' lavatories from the girls' lavatories. The wall came down as soon as Mr Dommett could manage it.

It was very difficult teaching a mixed age and ability; the class and children had to learn to work on their own while another group was being taught. This situation only lasted a few years as a secondary school was built in Ellesmere and pupils 11 years of age and over were transferred there.

The school garden continued to be used and although the Headmaster was expected to provide the seed he could have the produce.

Life in the school house was difficult as there was no sign of running water being brought to the village. Mr Dommett bought a 20-gallon tank on wheels to fill at the trough opposite Stone Villa or the shop. The other pump was in the courtyard (where Kenwick Close is today) of four cottages but the water was not for the use of the rest of the village, though they did use it sometimes. The water was unfit to drink but I think they were the only ones who boiled it for drinking. Safe water was brought into school in containers with the school meals.

The school house had a flush toilet but mostly it was done with buckets. The stream which runs under the road and fields to the bottom of school house garden filled a huge tank which emptied and cleared the school house and school lavatories and took it away under the new part of the cemetery. There was a vertical cylinder under each seat but the trough must have been 12ft down and Amy Dommett was always worried a little child would vanish. This system was an improvement on the earth closets most houses had but it did go wrong from time to time.

Cows were milked in a shed at the bottom of school house garden and Mr and Mrs Dommett bought their milk there. They thought it was lovely, "much nicer taste than this bottled stuff."

There was no rubbish collection in those days or for a few years. There was a midden in the corner of the school house garden very full of school's rubbish as well as that of the school house. The School Managers had this cleared when Mr Dommett moved in.

Tom Gregory the school caretaker advised Mr Dommett to take his empty tins for a walk and push them down a rabbit hole with a walking stick. There never seemed to be a shortage of rabbit holes.

School coal was kept by the school house midden. School house coal had a brick outhouse but it meant the caretaker was often coming through the classrooms in winter.

The first Christmas Mr Dommett was in charge there was a nativity play performed. The Reverend Hardy was leaving for Newbury cum Newchurch and on January 25th 1949 he visited the school for the last time but it was May before a new vicar was appointed, Reverend J. A. Mercer.

Before the opening of Lakelands, as it is known now, Mr Dommett and the senior boys visited many local farms to learn about farming both crops and animals. The Education Committee bus was used to take 21 pupils and Mr Dommett to the West Midlands Show in 1950. The same year 16 pupils and Mr Dommett visit TES Thalamus in Camell Laird's dockyard, Birkenhead.

From left: Melvyn Smith, Edward Adams, Gladys Whitfield, Roy Burden, Bill Tomley, Winston Chetwood, Madeline Dommett, Gordon Whitfield, Mr Dommett standing behind the Naval Officers.

The Christmas celebrations were in church when carols, lessons (choral speech) and a nativity play in mime were performed in the evening.

January 1951 started very badly as the school had an outbreak of measles and it was April before everyone was back in school. In September there was another trip to Birkenhead to see the Festival of British Ships.

January 1952 changed the school forever when the senior children left to go to the new Secondary Modern school in Ellesmere. Mr and Mrs Dommett took charge of the new school in Cockshutt when Mr Dommett had 32 juniors and Mrs Dommett 17 infants. Mr Dommett continued his visits to local farms with the junior children.

The school trip this year was to Lichfield Cathedral and Wall Letocetum.

At last discussions took place June 1953 about a water scheme for the school and in July a piped water system was laid on during the Holiday. Mrs Dommett had waited almost five years to get running water in School House.

In 1953 the School House had a television in time for the coronation and they plucked up courage to ask Capt. Robinson if he would like to come down and watch the coronation on TV. He came and thoroughly enjoyed it and they all had a very relaxing time together.

Class of 1953. Included in the photograph: Gary Smith, John Griffiths (Petton), Malcolm Griffiths, Syliva Smith, Dorothy Whitfield, Cynthia Jones, Jean Vaughan, Gill Husbands, Beryl Ridgeway, Billy D ?, Barry Hawkins, Jeremy Howland, Hughie Baker, Michael Young, Keith Hanmer, ? Peel, Kathleen Adams, Susan Kemp, Rosemary Henshaw, Margaret Stokes, Joan Henshaw, Diane Worthington, Myra Gregory, Carole Nicholas, Susan Thomas, Adrian Nicholas, Derek Ashley, Norman Whitfield, Graham Dommett, Derek Jones.

Cockshutt School attends Ellesmere Music Festival. Back left: Dorothy Whitfield, Susan Kemp, Cynthia Jones, ?, Gill Husbands, Carole Nicholas, Middle Row: Pat Norton, Barbara Smith, Julie Griffiths, Rosemary Henshaw, Graham Dommett, Barry Hawkins, Barbara Whitfield, Derek Jones, Front Row: Jeans Jones, ?, Bob Dean, Barbara Whitfield, Pat Jones, Shirley Hawkins, Ann Wycherley, Pauline Bailey.

Mr and Mrs Dommett with the competitors on Sports Day in 1955. Carole Nicholas, Dorothy Whitfield, Barry Hawkins, Graham Dommett, Derek Jones, Cynthia Jones, Jack ?, Rosemary Henshaw, Barbara Whitfield, Jean Jones, Patricia Norton, Robert Dean, Gillian Husbands, Susan Kemp, Janet Kemp, Janet Smith, Barbara Smith, Julie Griffiths, ? Davies, Reg Hanmer, ? Scott, Barry Bailey, Alison Bennett, Maureen Smith, Isobelle Hulme, Valerie Hanmer, Kathleen Hanmer, John Griffiths, Kevin Holliday, Nancy Cori, Shirley Hawkins, Ann Wycherley, Jean Jones, Pauline Bailey, Jean Griffiths, Philip Ralphs, Don Hanmer, Priscilla Chedwood, Elaine Bennett.

Cockshutt attended the Ellesmere Schools Music Festival for the first time in 1954 but continued to take part in this music event for many years to come. The school received a new piano.

The school trip in 1955 was to Dudley Zoo.

After a long association with the British Ship Adoption Society Cockshutt no longer wished to remain a member and the Education Office were informed.

Carole Nicholas and Gillian Husbands were transferred to Priory Girls School, Shrewsbury and Graham Dommett to Priory Boys in 1956 and Barry Hawkins to Wem Grammar School. The school trip this year went to Chester and their first attendance at the Inter-School Sports at Ellesmere Primary School.

The Higgins family from Baschurch who delivered milk to school forgot the school on 5th March and the milk delivered on 3rd June was sour.

The school received an electric water heater for the kitchen.

The school trip for 1957 was to Hereford and Ludlow. This year the school desks were changed to tables and chairs.

School meals continued to be brought from Wem and Mr Dommett thought they were awful and began to take sandwiches, not a very good example but he could stand them no longer. One sweet which was served up each week was called Railway Pudding and the school adviser was asked why this roly poly type pudding was called this. She had to call it something. Eventually the meals were prepared in Ellesmere and there was a great improvement in taste and quality so the Dommetts went back to eating school dinners.

In June 1957 Reverend J A Mercer retired and in November Reverend P Pollard was appointed to the church. Friendship with Petton Hall School had always been close, both staff and pupils, and many sporting fixtures have been played at Petton because Cockshutt did not have a school field.

The Country Dance team in 1959 Roger Bailey, ? Hanmer, Robin Hulme, ?, Alan Davies, ? Davies, Jean Bailey, Isabelle Hulme, Kathleen Hanmer, ? Smith, Nancy Cori, Shirley Hawkins.

1960 saw a change to the playground wall bordering the road, it was rebuilt and the railings removed.

In March 1961 work started on the canteen extension. Also in 1961 there was another change of vicar and Reverend R J Lansdale took over from Reverend P Pollard.

Many road safety talks had been given over the years in school and in 1962 there was an inter-school quiz held in Cockshutt. The Challenge Shield was won by the Cockshutt team of Robert Hulme, N Crewe, C Hawkins and G Jones. Robert Hulme won the cup for the highest individual score.

The punishment book indicates that Mr Dommett did not cane on the behind but strokes on each hand were recorded. Impertinence warranted 3 strokes on each hand, also disobedience, inattention and cheating, but clouting a girl in the playground was 1 stroke on each hand, bullying was 2 strokes on each hand.

In June 1962 five boys from Cockshutt were awarded places at Wem Grammar School but Fred Bayliss, Brian Heap, Robert Hulme, Graham Humphreys and Richard Lansdale all wanted to go to Priory Boys in Shrewsbury. The Education Department met with the school and the parents and the boys got their wish.

During the Christmas Holidays a radiator burst so the boiler had to be put out, but the open fire was kept in day and night. It was 8th January before repairs had been done and school could open.

The school trip in 1963 was to Caernarfon Castle and there was also a visit to a performance by the British Dance Theatre Group in Baschurch.

October 1965 saw the funeral of Captain C G Robinson RN retired, who had been a school manager for many years.

There was trouble with the water meter, there had been a tremendous increase in already heavy water consumption. The inspector found that a washer had completely disintegrated and there was no control over the flow of water to the flushing tank.

Valle Crucis Abbey and Chester Zoo were the places visited in 1967.

At last the school was to get three new classrooms when work started in 1968. The former Infants' classroom was to be made into a kitchen, and the former main classroom a hall equipped with gymnastic apparatus.

In September 1968 there was a Headmaster and two full time staff.

The new classrooms

This year saw an outing to Jodrell Bank and Manchester Airport.

But it was 1969 when all the alterations were complete and the school kitchen opened and Miss Dossie Birch and Mrs Myrtle Holliday were ready to cook and serve dinners to the children. It was about this time that a telephone was installed in school, so Dossie did not have to go to the public phone box to ring for supplies.

Cockshutt Children Entertain W.I.

Cockshutt Children Entertain WI 1969. The children taking part under the direction of Mr Dommett were: Clive Pugh, Raymond Lawrence, John Dickin, Yvonne Harcourt, Katrina Roberts, Peter Sawbridge, Gary Owen, Nigel Jefferies, Kevin Holliday, Mark Smith, Gareth Phillips, Roger Griffiths, Keith Whitfield, Darren Griffiths, Josephine Bailey, Philip Simcock, David Dickin, Andrew Ratcliffe, Neil Crewe, David Carr, Steven Hodnet, Jane Schofield, Sian Phillips, Philip, Valerie and Carol Hanmer, David Dowdy, Susan Williams, David Evans, Pauline Gregory, Karen Whitfield, Michael Holliday, Sylvia Sawbridge, Shirley Pugh, Christine Nicholas, Lesley Peel, Susan Williams, Dawn Peel, Pat and Janet Simcock, David Dean and Richard Smith.

The school field was also used and they held their first ever school sports day on their own field. Sports day was arranged so that every child got a ribbon for something. In September the school bus collided with a Bibby's lorry at Stone Hill on the way home to Petton and Burlton. Despite considerable damage to the coach only two children were slightly injured, one had loosened teeth and the other a cut tongue.

Reverend Cyril Elsey arrived to become vicar after the death of Reverend Lansdale.

Miss Mona Morris began her long association with Cockshutt School in September 1970 in charge of Class 3.

It was January 1971 when swimming classes began in Ellesmere every Monday morning.

During the summer Holidays in 1972 Mo became Mrs Gordon Whitfield. By December of that year the number on roll had fallen and Mrs Whitfield had to leave. But over the years Mo has been back on the staff in different capacities and is still there for half a day a week working with children who need a little extra help.

In 1972 ex-pupil Carole Nicholas won a Winston Churchill Scholarship to America to study staff training and education for the under-fives. Carole was a teacher at Wilfred Owen Primary School in Shrewsbury and was presented with her medal by the grandson of the late Winston Churchill after a successful completion of the travelling fellowship.

The School in 1972

The annual school trips for next few years were Conway Castle and Llandudno, Welshpool Railway and Canal, Llechwedd Slate Caverns and Black Rock Sands and also a visit to a Farm Safety Trail at Walford Farm Institute.

Reverend Cyril Elsey left the parish in October 1975 and at the time of writing this (30th September 2004) Reverend Elsey is still living in Budleigh Salterton, Devon aged 96. He once described Mr Dommett, a dear friend, as 'indommetable.'

It was April 1976 before Reverend John Tye took up his position as vicar and in July of the same year Mr and Mrs Dommett (right) retired. That was certainly the end of an era.

Mr Corfield was appointed acting head but became Headmaster in October.

The playground was marked out for netball in March 1977. The football team continued to play matches with varying degrees of success. The 'new block' was re-roofed in May 1977.

The school began study days and visited

Blakemere, Llangollen, and the younger children looked at their own village of Cockshutt. The re-roofing was completed but the building was left in an unsatisfactory condition, but the builders did put things right after half term.

June 1977 was the date of great celebrations in both Cockshutt and Petton as the 200th anniversary of Cockshutt Church and 250th at Petton. There were displays of dancing and costume in school and a Flower Festival in church.

Celebrations 1977

Pony-trekking in Churchstoke was a new venture for the school. Sports Day, the Jubilee Shield was presented to the winning team.

During the summer Holidays Mr Corfield was married.

Football and now netball matches were played against other schools, some wins were recorded.

In January 1978 an after-school swimming group was set up with the help of parents.

June that year saw the first weekend away hostelling in Bishops Castle, 20 children and staff.

Comprehensive education came to the area in September 1977 but it was July 1978 before bus passes were issued to the pupils travelling to Ellesmere. The school said goodbye to Mr Corfield and welcomed Mr David I Davies (left) as Headmaster.

September 1978 Mr Davies came from acting head at Church Preen School near Church Stretton. He is a rugby coach for Wrexham RC and an amateur swimming coach.

The school won 2nd prize in the Ellesmere Round Table Competition 'Make a Guy.'

The Christmas treat this year was to see 'Toad of Toad Hall' at Theatr Clwyd, Mold.

January 1979 school closed because of a shortage of fuel but the staff had to report each day.

School opened on 22nd January despite a threat of pickets due to the NUPE strike. No incidents were reported in the logbook.

Garage donates football strip to primary school

Cockshutt Garage sponsored the school football team with a new kit. Back left: Adam Baker, Robert Benson, Craig Whitfield, Cockshutt Garage owner Terry Goodall, Headteacher Dai Davies, Nicolas Hulme, Jerad Gilbert. Front Row: Tom Boyd, Thomas Thorold, Michael Ashdown, William Stokes, Adam Vanner and Simon Postans.

The Duke of Westminster opens Kenwick Close 1987 with the help of Cockshut School.

One important contribution made by Dai Davies was his enthusiasm for music, acting and entertaining. During his time as headteacher the school performed many light entertainment events for the village and friends. One such event was his adaptation of the story about Pinocchio.

Pinocchio (Rhiannon Evans) is given a surprise by Jiminy Cricket (Sarah Hayward]

Characters from Pinocchio. Haley Whitfield, Clare Wrench, David Stokes and Amy Griffiths.

Clocks. Standing: Jack Price, Matthew Ashdown, Felicity Cooksey, Hannah Stokes. Kneeling: Adam Baker, Rebecca Raymond.

6000 D–Days 'The Academy' by David Davies (Dai)

There were many changes that occurred in the twenty-two years I taught at Cockshutt.

For example, the introduction of IT into the classrooms (which was more traumatic for the teachers, as they struggled in vain to keep one technological step ahead of their pupils!): bringing in SATs for seven and eleven-year-olds, which caused a great deal of concern among teachers and parents alike, and continues to do so today (except in Wales where they've already been scrapped): and also the introduction of the National Curriculum in the 1990s which split the teaching fraternity almost fifty-fifty for and against.

Despite these changes and increasing pressures on teachers, staff at Cockshutt felt that a balance within the curriculum had to be maintained. Of course, it was imperative that all children had the opportunity to succeed in the basic essentials of literacy and numeracy. However, we felt that other subjects such as art, music, drama and sport were equally as important for some of the less academic children, as these subjects also gave them a chance to excel.

Out-of-school visits were also much appreciated and it is sad to see that schools are now often reluctant to take children on outings because of litigation concerns if an accident were to happen. Our weekend expeditions to Criccieth and Harlech in particular were huge successes.

(Although I'm regularly reminded of the 'lost keys saga' at Criccieth when I meet certain ex-pupils, and I even temporarily lost one of my own daughters on a school day-trip to London – recovered safe and sound, I can assure you!). These memories, along with those of certain Christmas nativity plays and sports days, have certainly outlasted those of maths and history lessons, which have long since receded into the dim and distant past, it just goes to show that teaching is not necessarily all about the three 'R's.

Another significant factor that made the twenty-two years at Cockshutt such a great experi-ence was the excellence of the staff and the continuity that arose from their length of service, which allowed good working relationships to develop. Sandra Weetman (nee Couper), Dorothy Hambly, Andrea Howitt-Dring and Margaret Cummings, all spent many, many years teaching at Cockshutt – indeed some of them are still there to this day. And Dossie (remember that chocolate 'pavement' with pink sauce?), Den Birch and Mrs Daisy Smith between them had 100 years of service to their credit! I would also like to pay tribute to the school governors, in particular John Hodnet who was chairman of governors for most of the time I was at Cockshutt. They all played an important part of life of the school and contributed to the 'family feeling' I've already mentioned.

Dossie (right) retired as cook but continued as caretaker with Den. Dossie has served dinners to the children for more than 40 years – with over 20 years as the cook. She left school at 14, but was back in school within weeks, helping her mother serve the dinners.

As a tribute to Dossie and her life in the community, Dorothy Norton (Auntie Dossie), put pen to paper when Dossie was invited to the Palace in 1997.

The Lord Chamberlain is
commanded by Her Majesty to invite

....

.... Miss Dorothy Birch ....

to a Garden Party
at Buckingham Palace
on Thursday 17th July 1997 from 4 to 6 pm

This card does not admit

Finally, a school is of course synonymous with children, and I was fortunate to be in a place where it was a privilege to be involved with so many fabulous, talented children, all of whom were a pleasure to teach.

Ode To Dossie

Have you heard of Dossie the Cook?
Well if you've a minute just look in the book
She's worked in the school for 50 years
Not just with saucepans but cleaning gears

She's seen five headmasters come and go
Maybe there's something you'd like to know
But Dossie says she's keeping quiet
They all said they enjoyed the diet.

Scholars too she's fed by the score
They knew they could always ask for more
Her puddings too went to a great extent
Especially their favourite chocolate pavement

After plays and concerts she would excel
At tea and biscuits and cakes as well
The visitors would enjoy this fare
And look forward to a chocolate éclair

She loves to watch all kinds of sport
And what a team does she support
"Come on your reds" don't play it cool
Of course it's the famous "Liverpool"

After all these years with the Kremlin
If she picks up the phone she has them trembling
She likes to have a little fight
And if they're wrong she'll put them right

The County Council have been great
To show how much they appreciate
They brought her flowers, presents and things
And a County Badge, now that is something

To end it all they've gone one better
The other day she had a letter
To Buckingham Palace she's been invited
To the Queen's Garden Party – she's delighted!

Come - get your best bib and tucker out and don't forget your hat!

D Norton, 1997

Ken Williams and his reflections

I became Headmaster in 2000 after the retirement of Dai Davies who had built up a fine reputation for the school, which was recognized by school inspectors and the community. He was popular with parents and children, especially for his comic drama roles in the school productions, and an infectious laugh was his trademark.

The school's success was reflected in the increased number of pupils. He worked with the governors to add two classrooms to the building. The school yard was extended and resurfaced.

Once again in 2003, school inspectors recognized the school's friendly atmosphere, wide range of subject areas and good national tests results. The school takes pupils from the villages of Burlton, Petton, English Frankton, Hordley, Bagley, Tetchill and some from Welshampton and Ellesmere.

There are good links with the village playgroup and a parents' group 'The Friends of Cockshutt School' (formed in March 2001) who help to arrange fundraising functions for school equipment and travel costs for school trips.

Thanks go to the school caretaker – Mrs Rosie Jones – as the building is always sparkling clean for the staff and children. Visitors are greeted by the school secretary, Mrs Nikki Martin-Jones. Meals are cooked on site and served in the school hall by cook, Mrs Karon Farrell, ably assisted by Mrs Pam Hanmer and dinner supervisor Mrs Sue Smith.

Karon's kitchen saucery beats all-comers

Karon Farrell with pupils Jake Farrell, Jake Dean-Tucker, Alice Farrell, Nia Farrell, and Connor Humphreys after winning the local heat of School Chef of the Year 2003.

Strong links are maintained with the neighbouring church of St Simon and St Jude, and Lakelands Sports College in Ellesmere.

The school continues to offer a wide range of subjects and children are taught how to play brass, woodwind and string instruments.

2006 was a time to celebrate the 150 years anniversary of the school on its present site.

In 2006 Ken Williams and Mrs Cummings retired and Mrs Heather Dawson became the new Headteacher.

Above, School Pupils 2002/2003 and below, The School in more recent times

CHAPTER 5

KENWICK PARK

The origin of the name Kenwick is uncertain, but may well have been derived from the name Cena; Cenan wic meaning the dwelling of Cena. It may also have come from a longer name with Cen or Cyne as its first part. Cyne was common in Anglo Saxon name composition and wic was an Anglo Saxon word for village or dwelling.

Under Saxon rule, the Manor of Ellesmere, which was comprised of a number of smaller manors, including Cockshutt and Kenwick, belonged to the Earls of Mercia. After the Norman Conquest, strong Norman overlords were appointed to face the Welsh following the revolt of 1069, when much devastation was caused in the countryside. Roger de Montgomery was given Shropshire, becoming the Earl of Shrewsbury.

In 1102, Alan Fitz Flaald was made Sherriff. He was to receive grants that made his descendants, the Fitzallans, the greatest landlords in Shropshire, consolidating for themselves vast tracts of land facing the Welsh.

William Fitzallan founded Haughmond Abbey in 1110. As the Fitzallan family monastery, it was the first house of Augustinian Canons to be established in Shropshire and benefited from many gifts of land given by the Fitzallans and their vassals, the Le Stranges. It is recorded that the Abbot of Haughmond "held Stockeyeth, Newton and Kenewike; services to suit of court and to victual men at arms".

Henry II gave the Manor of Ellesmere to David ap Owain, Prince of Wales, in 1197. Later, it was seized back by the Crown before passing to Llewellyn, Prince of North Wales.

Between the years 1205 to 1210 Llewellyn 'conceded, gave and confirmed to Haughmond Abbey for the souls health of himself, his father and David ap Owain a whole moity (half) of Kenewike with its liberties and appurtenances, and also pannage for 60 swine wherever Llewellyn's own swine had pesson within the Hundred of Ellesmere', while in 1236 'Richard FitzWilliam, Forester of Kenewike, confirmed the pannage of Stockeit and gave assart there to the Abbot of Haughmond'.

Pannage was a term used to allow swine into woods to forage for food, particularly acorns and mast in the autumn. Pork formed an important part of the diet in those days, being far more popular than beef.

Assart was a term used for the clearing of woodland to bring it under cultivation. Field names such as lawn and park are evidence of ancient parkland while other field names such as riddings (rid of trees) stockings (land covered in stumps) and leasow (woodland pasture) bear witness that the land within Kenwick was subject to such clearance.

In order to improve the land, marl, a type of subsoil was dug from pits and put onto the cleared areas to improve the soil texture. The pits were dangerous to work in and frequently collapsed, drowning or maiming the diggers.

Tetchill Township

Parish of Hordley

1839

KENWICK WOOD TOWNSHIP
KENWICK PARK TOWNSHIP

The production of sheep was very important at this time, with ewe's milk being used to make cheese, while the wool was used for cloth. During the 13th and 14th centuries, Shropshire wool merchants were amongst the most important in the country, exporting high quality wool to European cloth manufacturers.

By 1276, the Manor of Ellesmere was given to Sir Roger Le Strange for life. He died in 1311 and it once more reverted to the Crown, but in 1330 it returned to the Le Stranges, when Edward III gave it to Eubolo Le Strange and his wife Alice.

During this period Haughmond Abbey continued to increase the amount of land it owned, with gifts from the Le Stranges and others. In 1333 'Roger, son of Thomas de Gesenok gave to Nicholas, Abbot of Haughmond a parcel of land in Kenewike called Takewike and later in the same year also released to the same Abbot all his right in a parcel of land called New Totewike in the field of Kenewike'.

Haughmond Abbey initially made up a proportion of its income from the rents of temporalities, but demesne farming was also carried out on a significant scale. The houses with lay brethren had an expanding grange economy but as the recruitment of lay brethren declined they were faced with problems. They relied on paid labour on their demesnes when they started to cultivate them directly. However, in the latter half of the 14th century they changed to rents, leasing out land in small portions and for short periods. This made up a high proportion of their income and they were in a better position to meet the rising prices and competition of the period.

It is uncertain when Kenwick was established as an enclosed park. They were usually created by Lords of the Manor for hunting deer by enclosing woodland and pasture with a high wooden paling, frequently constructed to include deer leaps at intervals. This allowed deer, often roebuck, to enter but prevented them from getting out, thereby ensuring that there was plenty of hunting within the park. It is thought that Kenwick Park was constructed towards the end of the 15th century and beginning of the 16th century. It belonged to Haughmond Abbey. However, there is evidence to suggest that a large area of land within the park may well have belonged to the Le Strange family and later the Stanleys (Earls of Derby) who owned the estates for one hundred years until the final decade of the 16th century when they sold all their land in Shropshire.

During this period there were many changes; Henry VIII ordered the Dissolution of the Monasteries and in 1539 Haughmond Abbey was suppressed with all the land being seized by the Crown. The land was sold off during the following two years.

Saxton's map of 1577 shows a park of considerable size. There are indications that it included an area from Wackley Lodge, through Stanwardine in the Wood to Lower Hordley, together with land bordering the north and east of what was to become known as the Bridgewater Estate. However by the early 1600s the palings surrounding the park had rotted and fallen into disrepair and the whole was effectively disparked.

In the early 1600s the Manor of Ellesmere and the Lordship of Myddle was purchased from the Stanley family by Thomas Egerton. His third wife was Alice, Countess Dowager of Derby (whose husband, Ferdinando – Lord Strange, 5th Earl of Derby had died in 1595). Thomas

Egerton became the Keeper of the Great Seal and was given the title of Baron of Ellesmere. The land in the Ellesmere area amounted to nearly 9000 acres and included a large area of approximately 1000 acres within Kenwick Park. A sketch map of 1602 clearly shows the area fenced in, with four gates giving access, viz The Cockshutt gate (halfway between Kenwick Lodge and Cockshutt); the Horderley gate (at the end of the lane which joins the Ellesmere to Hordley road); the Lee gate (close to the Marl pit on the Hordley to Ellesmere road) and Stockgate (where the Kenwick Springs road joins the Cockshutt to Ellesmere road).

Shortly after 1602 approximately half of the Bridgewater land in Kenewicke Park was let to James Croft who sub let parcels of the land to some 23 under-tenants with the intention of profiting from the sale of the timber as fuel for the glassworks which was situated on land close to where Lower House now stands, whilst at the same time clearing the land and enclosing fields. The Lodge retained all its land and was not sub let in any way.

By 1637, the Bridgewater rent roll had been substantially increased, partly due to the new enclosures of Kenwick Park and Tetchill Moor, though Tetchill Moor was described as 'a great waste of mosse and moorish ground overflowed with water and overgrown with alders and other underwood of no great value'. It first required draining before it could be let. Nevertheless, those tenants who held enclosures on Tetchill Moor and Kenwick Park had to improve their rents, Tetchill Moor by 1/- per acre and 4d per acre on Kenwick Park.

The 1640s were difficult years and tenants on the Bridgewater Estate in Kenwick Park were amongst many to suffer during the Civil War.

Oliver Harrison 'was undone by plunder and fire' while William Mullinex was described as a 'cavalier plundered divers times is poor'. Thomas Houlston, John Illitch and Mullinex were said to have "lost more than all the park beside".

The Bailiff for the Bridgewater Estate wrote that 'Note yet about the 23rd March 1643, I was driven from ye Lodge Ffarme, plundered by ye kings forces and lost corne, cattell and household stuffe, and God knows whether ev're I shall set foot in it again'.

During the years of the Civil War there was a temporary abandonment of rent collection from the tenants of Kenewicke Parke because so many had suffered hardship. It was not until 1647 that rent collection resumed and tenants were able to continue with clearing and improving the land.

In 1634 Richard Hatchett bought Lee Hall and also purchased land within Kenewicke Wood. This land passed down through the family until it was sold in the middle 1800s.

The Shropshire Hearth Tax Roll was compiled in 1672. This was a revenue tax which survived until the introduction of the Window Tax in 1690. For every hearth a tax of 2/- per annum was payable with exceptions granted for the very poor. The following details give a good insight into the size of the dwellings on both Kenewicke Park and Kenewicke Wood at that time.

Kenewicke Parke – Hearth Tax 1672

	No of Hearths		No of Hearths
John Joyce (Lodge)	4	Emanuel Davies	1
Rees Davies	1	Antony Shorey	1
John Whattall	1	Thomas Jacks	2
Ann Clark	1	Richard Bate	1
Roger Clark	1	Ursular Probert	1
George Mullington	1	Mr Hodson	2
William Suker	1	Richard Philips	1
Matt Sutton	1	Ed Davies	1
Edward Nunnerley	1	Th Harrison	1
Francis Meyrick	1		

Kenewicke Wood – Hearth Tax 1672

	No of Hearths		No of Hearths
Mr Finch (Shade Oak)	6	Lloyd & Joyce	2
Joseph Lester	1	Fran Lloyd	1
Randle Manning	1	Mr Vaughan	2
Wm Witcherly	2	Thomas Newnes	1
Frank Oateley	1	John Smallman	1
Wm Birch	1		

Throughout the 18th century land continued to be cleared and improved. There was a big drainage project on Tetchill Moor and it is recorded that tenants had to dig the ditches and build the road across the moor to Kenewicke Parke . Further drainage of Kenewicke Parke linked up with the Tetchill Moor system carrying the water to the River Perry. Undoubtedly this would have been the time when many ponds were dug in the fields, fed by the drains and ditches to provide water for livestock.

The opening of the canal to Weston in 1796 was of great benefit to the surrounding area. Limestone was brought from Llanymynech to be burnt in limekilns at Hordley and Weston, with coal brought from collieries in the Chirk area. The lime produced was used for spreading on the land to improve the quality of the soil. Slate was another important product brought into the area to be used instead of thatch for roofs. The canal was also used to transport quantities of timber to other places showing that there was still much timber felling and wood clearing being carried out during the 18th and 19th century.

The early half of the 19th century was a time of considerable growth. The 1841 census gives an accurate account of the number of people living within Kenwick Park and Kenwick Wood and Bagshaws Gazetteer records the following:

Kenwicks Park is a small village and township, 3? miles south of Ellesmere having 1054 acres of land which is the property of the late Earl of Bridgewater. At the 1841 census there were 22 houses and 120 inhabitants. The resident farmers are:

Edward Colemere	Thomas Hamson Kenwick Park
William Gough, The Lodge	John Hassall
Ann Harrison, Top House	John Reynolds
Jane Harrison, Old Cast	Thomas Jacks
Lazarus Harrison, Lower House	James Williams

Kenwicks Wood is a township situated 4 miles south from Ellesmere embracing 865 acres of land. In 1841 there were 23 houses and 137 inhabitants. The principal landowners are William Sparling Esq, Sir Roger Kynaston Bart., Thomas Bulkley Owen Esq, Mrs Sutton and Mr Joseph Hignett.

The resident farmers are:

Stephen Burrows	Edward Hayward
Sarah Nickson	John Shingler
Edward Stokes	

The tithe maps of that period show that Kenwicks Park township comprised solely of the land held by the Bridgewater Estate, while Kenwicks Wood township bordered Kenwicks Park from Wackley through to Lower Hordley and on the west side included a stretch of land on the Tetchill Moor side of the Hordley to Ellesmere road, together with some land on the north east side of Kenwick Park.

Field details at that time show that a high proportion of the land was under arable cultivation with only a small amount recorded as pasture.

The period between 1874 and 1914 was the time of the Great Depression in farming when cereal prices collapsed, mainly as a result of cheap imports, from such places as America and Australia. Farmers in the area moved away from cereal production to mixed farming, with greater emphasis being placed on milk production, pigs, sheep and horse breeding. The majority of the farms produced milk which was made into butter and cheese for sale at local markets or at the large cheese fairs which were held in Ellesmere, Whitchurch and Wem.

The end of the 19th century and the beginning of the 20th century saw a number of the farmhouses and farm buildings on Kenwick Park either rebuilt or adapted to cater for the requirement of such production. At the same time, many of the cottages and small holdings ceased to exist. Only the presence of old damson trees in the hedgerows gives an indication of where a dwelling once stood.

Towards the end of the First World War farmers were encouraged to give up cheese making on farms and sell their milk in churns to the local dairy in Ellesmere. It was then dispatched by train to London. At that time, city dairymen who kept cows on the premises were unable to obtain the necessary cattle feed as a result of German submarines sinking ships full of grain destined for Britain. A few farms continued to make cheese for a number of years, but eventually they too sold the milk to the local dairy. The introduction of the Milk Marketing Board in 1933 brought about a structured system of buying and selling milk throughout the country.

During the Second World War the War Agricultural Committee appointed a local farmer in each area to inspect and designate land that was suitable for growing potatoes and other vegetables, in order to feed the nation. There was also greater emphasis put on the growing of fodder crops such as kale and mangels for livestock.

The Bridgewater Estate, which had passed into the Cust Family (Earls Brownlow) during the mid 19th century, was sold off following the death of the 3rd Earl Brownlow in 1921. The majority of the land was purchased by the Wimbourne Estate, though a small portion was sold off privately.

In more recent times, the land changed hands several times, passing from the Wimbourne Estate to the Mercantile Marine Insurance Company in the 1970s before being sold to the Land Development Company. During this time, some of the farms were sold to sitting tenants. The remainder of the land is now in the ownership of the Ellesmere Estate.

Brickiln Farm

As the name suggests, this farm was originally the site of a brickyard in earlier times but ceased to produce bricks probably around the early 1800s. A marl pit just down the road may well have been the site from which marl clay was extracted and incorporated with sand dug from nearby land, to make the bricks.

Part of the house is very old and, following a fire in 1982, renovation work revealed the remains of a bread oven and some wattle and daub work in one of the walls.

Mr and Mrs Tom Jones live here.

Mr Jones has lived here all his life as have two gener-

Tom Jones as a small boy with Geoff Powell driver of the United Dairies milk collection wagon.

ations of his family before him. His grandmother used to recall how one night close to Christmas, a thatched cottage on The Grange farm had gone on fire and how the family had been given shelter at The Grange and at Brickiln Farm until accommodation was found for them elsewhere. For many years afterwards, the Jones family used the plot to grow vegetables and it was always referred to as Chidlows garden.

In the severe winter of 1947 the snow reached the top of the hedges and the marl pit bank had to be dug out by hand. The only way out of the park was across the fields to the Springs lane.

Hay harvest time was always marked by the delivery of a barrel of cider, used to quench the thirst of those working in the fields. Much of the work was done by hand with neighbour helping neighbour to turn the hay and pile it into haycocks, before it was loaded onto the hay wagons using a pitchfork.

Most farms kept pigs and one pig would be slaughtered each year. This would be carried out on the farm by Stan Richards who worked for Haywards, the pork butcher in Ellesmere. Farmer's wives would make black puddings and sausages, while the flitches of bacon and hams would be cured and wrapped in cloth before being hung from the large hooks which adorned the beams in most farmhouse kitchens and pantries in those days.

Every house had damson trees and these provided a vital source of income. In good years, the money received would pay for the rent and rates of the property, so not one damson would be left on the tree.

Rabbits were always in plentiful supply and provided many a tasty meal for farmer and worker alike. Prior to the myxamatosis disease there was a thriving rabbit warren close to the wood which borders Springfields.

Sometime in the late 1940s, Mr Jones remembers how a large dredger trundled from field to field across Kenwick Park, dredging out all the ponds in the area, to ensure that there was adequate water for the livestock. Water was always a scarce commodity. It had to be pumped, often by hand, to provide water for both the house and for use on the farm. Later, some of the farms did acquire mechanical means of pumping the water from the wells. It was not until the mid 1960s that the mains water was finally installed to the homes and farms on Kenwick Park. This, coupled with the installation of mains electricity some three years earlier, meant that Kenwick Park had finally 'arrived' in the 20th century!

The Nook

For many years, this house was known as Rose Cottage before it reverted to its former name The Nook. It was originally a two up, two down brick and timber cottage and possibly dates from the late 17th century.

During the first half of the 20th century Harry Fardoe and his wife, Polly (Mary Emma), lived here. Harry was the son of a Cockshutt cobbler and was a farm worker at Kenwick for some years. He farmed the smallholding at Rose Cottage with a few cows, pigs and hens.

In the summertime he would cut the roadside verges with a scythe nearly all the way to Cockshutt and, with the aid of his wife, they would make countless trips piling the hay onto a two-wheeled hand cart to bring it home and store for winter feed.

Rose cottage (above and left)

Harry Fardoe and Family (above)

After the Fardoes died in the 1950s, Mrs Stacey lived there for a while and the cottage was painted black and white. When she left, the cottage lay empty for some considerable time until Mr and Mrs Stanley purchased it. They renovated and extended it and lived there for many years until it was sold to Mr and Mrs D Batho, who added a further wing to the rear of the property. Right, The Nook Today, the present owners are Mr and Mrs Checketts

Reynolds Cottage

This house and smallholding dates back to the early 1800s and was occupied by John Reynolds. Around 1872 Sam Evans moved here and divided his time between his smallholding and working as roadman in the locality. He was a very popular person and a keen boxer, who achieved a reputation for his boxing bouts with Cockshutt's sporting vicar, the Reverend Donald. Sam (right) had four children and after his first wife died, he married again some years later and had three more children.

He died in 1926 and his daughter Nell married Geoff Howard and continued to live there all her life. In recent years the house has been renovated and extended by Mr and Mrs C Lea.

Kenwick Grange

The present house and buildings were built at the beginning of the 20th century replacing previous buildings on the site. A number of cottages existed close to this farm at one time, their former presence indicated by the odd damson tree.

Like other farms on Kenwick Park, this was a dairy farm, initially producing cheese, prior to selling milk to the local dairy. For many years it was farmed by Mr and Mrs Rogers and their family, before it was taken over by Mr and Mrs C James in 1954. They continued to produce milk there until 1961 when they changed to arable farming.

Lower House

The large square house was built around the 1830s with the farm buildings built in 1913.

When studying field maps of the area it is easy to see how and where various "industries" have developed and given rise to the naming of that particular field. Glass in its early days was not available on a large scale and only the wealthy would have access to it. The glassmakers were semi-itinerant, building their furnaces in wooded areas. They moved their 'cribs' from time to time from estate to estate for the timber. The crude production methods produced glass that would be very rough by today's standards. By the late middle ages, soda was no longer available and northern glassmakers turned to wood-ash from their own wood-fired furnaces as a flux, for a potash glass. Because the glasshouses were situated in forests that provided fuel and ash the glass made was called 'forest-glass' or Wald glass.

Kenwick Park is known to have been used by glassmakers, the field names give a clue, Glasshouse Field for example. A map in the Bridgewater Collection in the Shrewsbury Records Office dated 1650 showed a field in the tenure of Richard Phillips as 'glass house field'. Lower House Farm and Lower Farm, all part of Kenwick Park, have field names to suggest there were possibly three glasswork sites. But by the mid 1650s the Countess of Derby gave instructions to her agent that the number of charcoal-burners in the woods should be restricted. The land rent increased until it became unprofitable for glassmaking to continue. Today, a field is still known as the Glass Field.

Mr and Mrs L Hayward farmed here for many years. Mr Walter Downes started work here as a waggoner in 1938 before joining the army in 1939. He served for the duration of the war and returned to Lower House Farm in 1946. At that time there were about six workers on the farm together with two Italian prisoners of war, Salvatori and Samuel, who were delivered each day from the camp at St Martins and collected again in the evening. After the war, they 'lived in' on the farm for a few years.

On his return from the war Mr Downes became cowman and for about three years after the end of the war some of the land continued to be ploughed to grow corn and fodder crops. Part of a field would have potatoes, with a row for each of the workers. Soon the land was returned to grass and the sheep numbers increased.

There were between 4 to 6 working horses used on the farm, but often there would be between 12 to 15 other horses bought in from the horse sales at Shrewsbury or Wrexham and they would be broken in, first by halter and then harnessed to chain harrows . In common with all farms at that time, hedge cutting was done by hand and Mr Downes recalls that he did a lot of the hedge cutting by piecework in the lighter evenings.

Eventually, a tractor was purchased and Mr Downes was promoted to tractor driver. Gradually, as more mechanisation was introduced, the number of farm workers lessened.

Mr Hayward died in 1970 and for a while the farm continued to be run by his daughter and son-in-law until the lease was given up and the farm was merged with Kenwick Grange. Mr and Mrs James later purchased the property.

Today the house and buildings are owned by Mr and Mrs Trowbridge who have adapted what was once the cow sheds into stables for their horses, while the farm land has been merged with Kenwick Grange to become one large farm.

Kenwick Park Council Houses

The four houses were built to provide homes for farm workers who worked on farms in the locality. Initially the building of them began just before the war, but the worked stopped because the builder apparently ran into financial difficulties. It was not until 1940 that they were finally completed.

Among those who lived there in the early days were Mr and Mrs Price and their family. Mr Price worked at Top House Farm and Mrs Price used to rear the orphan lambs. Often they would be placed in cages along the grass verges (which were considerably wider than today!) and they would be fed from a bottle with milk brought from the farm.

Mr Walter Downes still lives in one house while another is occupied by Mr Percy Lunt, now in his 90th year. For many years, he worked on the farm at Winston, in Tetchill, until it was sold.

Springfields

Originally known as The Haycocks and within the boundaries of Kenwick Wood, which bordered Kenwick Park, this farm was known to have been in the ownership of the Bulkley Hatchett family throughout the 18th century until the mid 19th century, when it was sold to Edward Hayward.

It was purchased by Dr John Withington Roe in 1898. Dr Roe practised medicine in Ellesmere for many years, and after his death it remained in the Roe family. During that time it was farmed first by Mr Thomas Gilbert and then Mr Jack Philips, before Mr and Mrs E Bayne moved here in 1947, purchasing the property in 1960. It has remained in the Bayne family since that time.

Part of the house and the farm buildings date back to the early 1700s. The oldest part of the house would suggest that it was a relatively small dwelling but extensions have been added over the years. Here too, cheese making took place for a number of years.

The farm buildings were once a barn and malt kiln, together with pigsties and hen loft above, which were typical of that period. Alterations were made to the buildings in the early 1900s when it was adapted to accommodate milking cows. Marks in some of the old beams suggest that they may well have had a previous use many years before.

It is thought that at one time there had been a monastic dwelling here, but the only evidence found was when a field close to the house was ploughed in the 1950s and a considerable expanse of what was thought to have been a cobbled courtyard unearthed.

A carved stone stands in the garden as a memorial to Rob, who became known as Britain's first parachute dog during the Second World War. He was awarded the animal VC for his work with the 2nd SAS in North Africa and Italy when he made a number of parachute drops with men behind the enemy lines. Rob was owned by Mr and Mrs Bayne.

Kenwick Wood

This farm is the only property to have retained the name of Kenwick Wood. It also bordered the Bridgewater Estate of Kenwick Park. Some of the fields have unusual names, such as Hacksey and Heasel Husk, the latter suggesting that the land may have been raised up at some time. Close by, there is a small wood enclosing several ponds, which are said to be very deep. These may well have been marl pits at one time.

Another field is known as the Flax Yard. Flax was often grown in small plots. It was cultivated for its fibres and harvested by pulling up, rather than by cutting. It was usually made into bundles and immersed in ponds for retting. This process could take up to ten days, after which it had to be stooked to dry.

In the late 1700s the farm was known to have belonged to a Mr Boodle for a period. It was sold to Mr John Hayward in the mid 1800s, before being purchased by Mr R Roe. He built the farmhouse there in 1898 and it was farmed by Mr and Mrs Woolley for a number of years. During that time the ownership passed to Mr John Roe.

In 1927 it was purchased by Mr T Lea who built a large addition to the front of the house. In 1930, he also added more land to the farm when he purchased two fields from the Bridgewater Estate. For several years it was farmed by his daughter and son-in-law, Mr and Mrs Faulkner, before being leased to Mr T Brayne who farmed it until 1963, when it was taken over by Mr M Faulkner who lived there until he retired. It is now farmed by his daughter and son-in-law, Mr and Mrs G Lammie.

Within living memory, three houses have been demolished:

Browis Castle

This was a two up, two down red brick cottage which stood isolated across the fields from Kenwick Wood. It acquired the name of Browis Castle from Dr Roe, who lived nearby at Springfields. Whenever he visited the cottage the children appeared to have a staple diet of a kind of gruel made from bread and dripping, soaked in boiling water and seasoned with salt and pepper – a variation of the Welsh dish called brewis.

The farm to which it belonged had long since disappeared and the cottage itself, once the home of the Downes family and then the Parkers, was demolished in 1963.

Ferney Hough Cottages

On the back lane from Kenwick Park to Ferney Hough were two semi detached farm workers' houses. They too were demolished in the 1960s.

CHAPTER 6

COCKSHUTT REMEMBERED

We have begun with the physical and general attributes of the area to assess why people were drawn to settle in the region from the earliest times. The actual area spanned by Cockshutt runs to Colemere then across to Hordley, Brown Heath and Loppington – an area of 35 sq miles. It is a village straddling the A528 Ellesmere to Shrewsbury Road.

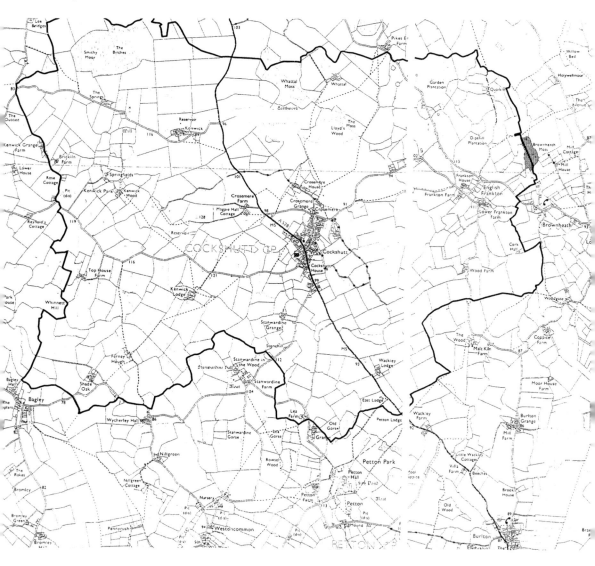

Boundary Map of Cockshutt Parish

Cockshutt has one shop, a post office, church and school. It used to be a totally agricultural village with the occupants being mainly farm workers. Farming methods have become mechanised and there are not now the number of farm labourers required. Added to this there has been a major change in the productive side of farming and this has affected the prosperity of the area. As we go over the type of changes we have researched you will realise just how big a change has taken place. There has also been a spate of building new homes and an influx of new people to the area.

We will now travel back to a period of time where a lot of people have memories recounted to them because their grandparents have left a verbal record generation to generation which we can endeavour to capture. In the process of research we have interviewed people and in a lot of cases traced some information from the Shropshire Records Office. This will always reveal omissions by accident if not design; information may be inaccurate because of the complexities of tenure. For example, the multiple repeats of a family name which despite the compilations of census reports shows the 'said' family have moved several times within the confines of the village. This may be because a more desirable property becomes vacant, so they up sticks and go. Thus accuracy becomes a figure of chance!

To believe also that the accuracy on the census is infallible is to be naïve. There will always have been those who for instance 'lodged' their children temporarily each night, to sleep next door at auntie's or granddad's when large families in too small houses made space a prime need. Some people may not have declared a 'tenant'. Others may equally have been econom-ical with the truth of occupancy to officialdom thus furthering the distinct possibility of names versus houses being inaccurate. Age is also not always going to correlate with birth certificates, which may be by design or ignorance of facts.

One unhelpful factor is that change has brought about destruction of properties; many of those no longer existing would today have had a conservation order on them. The site is cleared, redesigned for new modern housing with a very different structural layout then the new roads are renamed, renumbered; further to which comes a change of occupants and the alteration is complete.

 This would apply for example where the present Church Green and Kenwick Close houses stand. The 'all change' situation over the generations- four houses being reduced to two etc, makes the research just that little bit harder to correlate.

When I was first asked to join forces in this venture of recording facts about the village, my interest had already been aroused by observing small details that suggested a possibility of a dwelling although there were no longer any signs of the bricks and mortar.

Walking the dog along the Shrewsbury Road towards the Dobbin, not a stretch to linger and ponder with the heavy traffic passing, I had noticed a very pretty whitish-pink rose, perhaps an old fashioned climbing rose, but definitely not a wild rose, entwining itself in the hawthorn hedge. I was told there had been two cottages on this road and also allotments. Another sign of a disappeared dwelling was just past Rosemary Cottage. Two different types of rambler climb through the nettles and hedging trying to survive. One is a floribunda rose of tiny pink flowers. I have succeeded in taking a cutting of this so at least somebody's rose from long ago still survives if this wilderness is ever cleared for future building. There was evidence of a gate in the brambles and way back in the flourishing weeds and overgrowth perhaps a gnarled fruit tree. Who dwelt there?

Again I learnt that along this road that leads to Crosemere, there had been in total three cottages; of the other two I could find no trace. The area known as The Pinfold, a place for stray animals to be held, would be unrecognisable to any stranger. Beyond this stretch again and opposite the last smallholding was a really beautifully constructed pig sty. The brick is a glazed red brick with a rounded coping brick surmounting the wall top. If such effort had gone to building the pig sty, one can only but assume the cottage that it belonged to, must have been of a similar standard of work. The only evidence of its existence is a neglected orchard and some barns.

This same lane is, I am told, called Draw Well Lane and apart from the farms that remain, had several residents living there. At the end of the lane which would appear now to be a dead end with the right to cross a field to CroseMere its only purpose, does in fact make a left turn which is sometimes blocked off by a farm gate. This lane was a route to connect up with the main A528 to Ellesmere. I have tried to walk it on occasion but generally the nettles make it impassable. I suppose by virtue of neglect eventually this road or lane will have the hedges removed and the fields will envelop and absorb the lane and a bit more history will be lost.

The lane known as Meadow Lane can take some navigating in high nettle season or when the ruts and potholes become waterlogged and impassable to all but a tractor. I am never sure of my legal rights to tread these lanes: are they private or are they public? They honeycomb the district and are a delight to tread. The sounds of traffic fade, a hum of bees hovering over an abundance of wild flowers scattered in the hedgerows, birds undisturbed in the hedge and occasionally the surprise of a small wild animal moving in its natural terrain is a never-ending pleasure. One can find a peace and tranquillity so often denied nowadays.

Moving from a city where there are actually quite large tracts of land that have been deemed for public use whether by historic rights or by a gift, one soon learns that the vast green area of the country is really out of bounds. One would be trespassing to enter it.

The map shows a maze of footpaths criss-crossing the fields and research has shown that these tracks were not pleasure-orientated but were a very necessary short cut for labourers who walked considerable distances to work.

Ramblers are the only ones anxious to keep these routes open and are often in dispute with a farmer for their efforts. This surely would be a case for the previously mentioned disused lanes being kept usable – not for transport but for walkers. They would not then be a threat to either crops or livestock and in turn would supply that need to escape the car.

With my mini-surveying began an on-off interest in Cockshutt as it had been. Fortunately there are still many born and bred residents very willing to tell you of this 'lost' past. Very often they would say, 'I was born there or my grandparents lived there' so the delight in this information was really propounded when the photographs began to appear. Of all the 'lost' houses there is only one property we haven't been able to capture, which is sad. The house belonged to the Chesters and stood opposite what is The Briars today.

To the present generation wielding a camera from an early age, the cost of recording anything and everything is not a novelty. The photographs of the past are usually few and faded and highly treasured. The major benefit to be had from their emergence now is that with today's technology they can be reproduced and preserved for future generations.

A natural progression from being shown these photographs were to hear stories related to the dwellings and the way of life. We then began recording the anecdotes which was a privilege to be party to, but as they are in many cases quite lengthy, only snippets can be printed in text because of a lack of space. Fortunately, again with the aid of modern technology we can transfer both the tapes and excess photographs onto CD and thus the work will be permanently recorded and kept for future use. One can refer to data from libraries, study census figures or electoral roles but the dry notation does not put the flesh on the bones – only personal anecdotes can do that.

The village has changed with the disappearance of the old properties, with the addition of new properties and the alteration of many rural activities for employment. This would be seen as natural progression. Many new occupants today are incomers, some using the rural address as a dormitory as they work elsewhere. Other incomers retire to the village and may partake in local activities. Growth of an area brings about these changes and most people contribute with a variance of skills and interests which is healthy and is an addition to the rural skills already existing.

A major factor for any incomer to realise is that a village has been a very self-sufficient entity in its own right for generations. Needs and requirements to benefit the community are planned, financed and achieved by hard work and organisation. There is never voiced a thought that all they need to do is 'demand' and the government will provide, which would doubtless be the case in a town. Something carefully planned and saved for is equally appreciated and cared for.

Opening a window on the past of the village reveals a very lively community with a host of shops and pubs which far exceeds the present day. The village pub now is popular and well supported but how about having eight?

The village shop is an asset which sadly many villages have lost but how about several? The slow communication of the past meant that local demand required the trades to cover their immediate needs. We read of the following in Kelly's Directories: wheelwrights, a saddler, a carpenter, a tailor, a butcher, a shoe maker, a barber's, a sweet shop, a cake shop, and a chip shop. One cannot interpret these suppliers on the scale of today's shops. Animal feed and coal were also supplied from certain bases. The pubs would probably be a home brew and benefited from the passing trade of goods vehicles plying the main route from Ironbridge or Shrewsbury and on to Ellesmere Port and Liverpool. This latter point will be covered in a section on transport. Fresh milk, vegetables and eggs would be in no short supply, sweets and cakes homemade.

The community spirit of self-help was very much alive and kicking. Whilst the area had pockets of affluence, it also had many who survived on low wages without state benefits but who still created this activity and enjoyment. It did not require satellite television, broadband, cars and foreign travel to survive.

That would appear to be a cry for the 'good old days'. No one needs to be as gullible as that. Perhaps the homes for which we might express nostalgic regret for their destruction provided picturesque misery in reality. This may not have been realised at the time: rising damp, no indoor water or electricity are not comfortable. Warm dry housing and sanitation would not be given up readily by those who have experienced the alternative. Equally a right to health care without concern for the cost would not be exchanged for some of granny's cure-all recipes. I experienced many of these salves from my own grandmother who would apply them despite there being no complaint or condition giving rise to the need. 'Your blood needs cooling, your age requires it,' was sufficient. Have you ever suffered goose grease rubbed on your chest – it smells appalling and there were many other remedies. Our own GP conceded that, whilst they did no lasting harm, generally had a purgative value and were not infrequently unpleasant to taste, they did no good and served no purpose! So nostalgia is on the back burner but interest yesteryear, the fun and some of the hardships all help us to appreciate our present and respect the past. We read of garden trails for the purpose of entertainment and fundraising today. Now in the comfort of your armchair and within the confines of your own home, let us do a house trail beginning with High Town. That will be a surprise to many incomers for a start , we begin from the end of the village where Catch-em-All cottage stands.

Approaching Cockshutt from Shrewsbury the first pair of semi-detached houses on the right hand side was once upon a time four houses or cottages, numbers 35, 37, 39 and 41 Shrewsbury Road, all without electricity and all with earth closets and no water. Rainwater was caught in rain butts to supplement household requirements but the remainder had to be collected at a pump which is further down the road on the opposite side.

The pump can still be seen in the garden of what was the garage house – Glendower. It began as a wooden pump and was replaced with an iron one.

 This was quite a way to carry water when requiring it for the family wash or for bath night. Not surprising that the bathtub water was shared by several family members with just a top-up as it cooled. Lucky first, poor last!

A policeman working on a rota system lodged at no. 41 so there was a sign outside hung over the hedge saying 'Shropshire Constabulary'. Remembered names of the constables were: Dodd, Thomas, and Tart. Nellie Sutton who lived at no. 37 had fond memories of one constable when she was a child. When he came in for his meal at about 2.30 pm – 3.00 pm. he would trim off any fat on his meat and save it for her when she came in from school. She regarded this as a treat – a treat she enjoys to the present day which defies all the present day health rules; perhaps it even contributes to her longevity as she is a nonagenarian. These cottages had sufficient land on either side of them on which to grow produce to add to the pot!

Opposite these four houses is a house called Tyneholm, the first on the left as you approach Cockshutt from Shrewsbury. The field next to it was always referred to as Townsend Field by the Dickin family because Frank's mother's maiden name was Townsend and presumably she owned that land.

Tyneholm was built on land bought from Lord Brownlow, by a man called Edward Wilkinson about 1939-40. He was the district surveyor for the Urban District Council and the Rural District Council; they shared in harmony the services of this joint appointment for both councils. He covered such sectors as roads, buildings and sanitary inspection. The wood used within the house was of high quality being oak panelling, for example from Hardwick Hall and oak beams brought from the workhouse in Ellesmere when it was demolished. He was helped on the building of the house by Robert Henshaw who lived in the council houses on Shrewsbury Road. Water was supplied to Cockshutt in 1954 but Mr Wilkinson said he didn't require it because he had his own well; he had a hand pump in the kitchen over the sink to supply his needs.

Mr and Mrs Dommett retired from their posts as head and deputy of Cockshutt School and bought Tyneholm from Mr Wilkinson. They were advised that the water supply would be insufficient for the requirements and usage of a family of four, so had to pay for the water supply on the opposite side of the road to be ducted to their house. The Water Board refused to countenance the continued use of the well in case it polluted their water so the supply from the well was stopped, the well itself is still there. The chapel next door was in full use at this time and, in the days of Mr Wilkinson, had been able to use his quite extensive driveway to park their cars for Sunday services. This did not suit Mr and Mrs Dommett and may well have been one of the contributing factors to its closure. Increase by then in the volume of cars used does create a problem as to where people can park. This particular stretch of road can offer no suitable answer and pedestrians en masse would be at some risk of accident. It has to be said that 'en masse' might be a slight exaggeration as there was some decline in the attendance figures, which would also make keeping the chapel open an unrealistic proposition.

Cockshutt Chapel Ellesmere cicuit

The Primitive Methodist Chapel mentioned was a quite splendid brick-built structure, the foundations having been laid in 1889. It was very popular and well attended. Mr Dommett played the organ on one occasion for a soloist who was singing at a Harvest Festival. We have a newspaper article recounting a wedding service there. A Mr Cressit from Stanwardine was thought to be one of the founders of the church.

It does seem strange to have invested so much money and effort and then to knock it down. When the building was demolished Mr Dommett bought the site and extended his garden to include it. and used it as his vegetable garden .When asked if there were any conditions or ties to the land because it had been a church site he said, "No, but on the deeds of Tyneholm it did include a clause forbidding the sale of alcohol".

Prior to this large construction the Methodists had attended a little chapel on the

Stanwardine Road just around the corner. This chapel was altered after the modern chapel had been completed. It is thought the roof level had been raised to give an upper floor – evidence of this is visible on the gable end. The chapel then became two cottages.

Catch-em-all cottage (right) is a very picturesque thatched house and one of three in the village. It stands on the fork of two roads, one being the A528 and the other being the road to Stanwardine. The cottage has of latter years been extended. The name is unusual and how long it has rejoiced in this name remains a mystery. One suggestion has been that the former occupants were in an advantageous position to catch all those passing and have a chat! It has been occupied by a Mr and Mrs

J Husbands, a family name for several generations in Cockshutt. They were followed by a Mr Bill Smith and his wife Polly. Villagers do dub people with nicknames and maybe fortunately we are usually unaware of them. These two rejoiced in being referred to as Windy Bill and Polly Longfrock and as they are long since dead and gone this cannot cause offence. The Smiths were followed by Mrs Edith Jones.

Turning into the off-shoot road that leads to Stanwardine and Petton called Stanwardine Road a house side on to the road and backing on to the Thatched house is Chapel House. Over the years this house has changed its role; it was a shop when run by Mr and Mrs Edward Birch and their daughter Maggie. Some land went with the shop but in no way was it a farm. When that changed hands it was run for many years by a Mr and Mrs Latham until Jack and May Kynaston bought it in 1951 to run as a farm. They rented and added fields to the property as they became vacant. The outbuildings and barns were on the other side of the road to the house and, with the land not being compact and contained around the farmhouse, the cows had to be driven as far away as Meadow Lane. May recalls she did this on her own and apart from there not being much in the way of traffic, she did hope that everyone had their gates closed. It wasn't unknown for a cow to head off onto someone's garden and lumber around; they would have been quite likely to have entered a house if the door was open. Pavements at this time were an unknown entity. In 1984 May and Jack were doing some alterations to a room in the house and discovered a rather crumpled and sooty newspaper which turned out to be a section of the Shrewsbury Journal – that is the newspaper that preceded the Shrewsbury Chronicle.

They reckoned that the paper was about 134 years old; it spoke of the Crimean War and Florence Nightingale. Advertisements for clothing were showing furs, capes and spats. Sadly May no longer has possession of the paper.

There are eight properties beyond Chapel House, two being the sandstone cottages called Chapel Cottages, one the Chapel Farm barn which is now converted to a very attractive barn-conversion. There is a modern house and then Bhim Cottage.

On the site of this house there used to be a croft owned by Polly Ashley and on it she kept her one cow. She lived down Crosemere and her son George used to have the job of walking this cow down to be milked and back again; he watered it at the pump (left) on the way past.

George grew up to own a fleet of lorries which he kept on the site where modern bungalows stand near Brook House.

Bhim Cottage was built by Reverend Peppercorn about 1931 and named after a place in India he and his wife had visited. It was rented to Mr and Mrs George Birch. Mr Birch was a churchwarden and he lived there for a number of years. The Birches were followed by Jane and Tim Cox and finally it was purchased by Wallace and Dee Taylor and, as we said at the beginning we have dedicated our efforts of writing to Dee's memory.

Stanwardine Grange (left), or as I am told 'The Cottage' by some Cockshutt inhabitants, is a pleasing farmhouse set well back from the roadway, built about 1700. It has only ever had the Dickin family in it and prior to that the Dickin family came from Stanwardine House. As this is a working farm we will make further reference to it in the chapter on farming.

At about this point the road begins a slight gradient and atop this is a house called Stone Hill. This smallholding was once owned by Mr Tom Kynaston and although it cannot be verified I understand there was a plaque on the wall of the Primitive Methodist Chapel acknowledging his contribution towards the funds for building the chapel. His home was shared by his housekeeper, a Miss Stone.

They were followed by Mr and Mrs Geo. Birch, the gentleman working for many years at Petton Hall. After them came May Kynaston's uncle, a Mr Harry Thomas.

The owners today are David Mills and Margaret Pugh. They run a donkey home. I have deliberately not called it a sanctuary as by their own description they house the donkeys and in my abbreviation – teach them the 3RS! They relocate, retrain and rehabilitate them – so not a sanctuary! At any local events their donkeys prove a great attraction. On Palm Sundays a donkey always leads the procession from the village hall to the church in Welshampton. When they are loosed to graze in fields adjoining nearby lanes one can be fairly certain that local youngsters will have fed them carrots and stroked these donkeys.

Harriet feeding the donkeys (above). Below, Cockshutt garage, Cockshutt lorry, Garage with van

Further up this rise one arrives at High Fields the eighth property along this road. This house was built by Bill France; he ran a garage on the main A528 where until recently Jones Garage stood. This was a galvanised metal building where he repaired cars and sold petrol. He was helped by Eric Sutton. Bill lived at Clive but when some land became available at High Fields he bought it and built a house, approximately post–war.

When his wife died the property was too large for one person and he moved down to the bungalow 'Greenway' which is now occupied by the Dommetts. A family called Dent bought High Fields and they were followed by Ken and Annette Kynaston.

Stanwardine House and Hall are beyond here but that again will be described under the farming chapter. So we will about turn and make our way towards the heart of the village, back to the A528.

As we turn the corner we can just see over the hedge the iron water pump, this would have been open for public access and is in fact a listed artefact. It stands in the garden of a house called Glendower. This is a name to conjure with; Owen Glyndwr having played such a part in border country disputes. He was a great Welsh patriot and visionary and a thorn in the side of Henry V who despite the English government offering a large reward for his followers to betray him, never succeeded. The name became a legend in Welsh History. Maybe the legendary power of the name attracted the owners to name their house by it; who knows?

This house used to be owned by Bill and Rene Jones who ran the brick built garage alongside the house; they came in 1955. Their garage replaced a galvanised garage owned and run by Bill France. There hadn't been a garage in Cockshutt before 1926-27. The Jones' built up a fleet of heavy goods vehicles which, when not in use stood to the side and rear of the garage; speaking on a personal note, these Lorries were a regular sight at the Liverpool Docks.

Sadly the garage was demolished (above) in 2003 thus ending the repairs and petrol service for Cockshutt motorists.

Two new houses have been built on the site and newcomers to the village would never imagine what a hive of activity there used to be in this particular area. Passing two fairly modern properties, with donkeys grazing in the fields opposite, we come to Cockshutt House farm (right). When I first came to live here the barn was being used for a trial run as a Farm Shop. Two farmers' wives, Mrs Ashley from Cockshutt House Farm and Bim Johnson from Top House

farm had combined as a business proposition to sell meat, vegetables, pickles, jams and pies. They had worked very industriously to stock the freezers and shelves with fresh baking and produce. This enterprise was perhaps very demanding and in the end, enterprising and successful as it was, it closed and the barns were sold for home-conversions.

The farm used to be called Cockshutt Hall and then changed to be known as Cockshutt House. The Dickins occupied this farm for several generations. Thomas Dickin is forever captured for posterity in an oil painting of himself seated on horseback. 'Tummy' Dickin gets a further mention when we refer to sporting events in Cockshutt. There was a series of other owners by name of Phillips, Totty, Lee and Davies before the present owners Mr and Mrs Ashley.

Our next area of interest is No.32 Shrewsbury Road or Hazel Cottage. This property is recorded in the reference library as being late 17th century, refronted 18th century. The house has indeed had a varied career and changes which are ongoing to the present day. The property was once a farm, and then it was occupied by Tom Sutton, a carpenter. At the rear of the property where a modern bungalow stands was a yard where a large traction engine powered a drive belt.

Timbers were cut and all the usual carpenting work demanded in an area where farm carts would also be a requirement of maintenance. They were wheelwrights, coffin makers and general repairmen for all things wooden. Tom's son worked at Bill France's garage up the road. Bill Humphreys, who began as an apprentice to Tom Sutton, rose to being owner of the business and Hazel Cottage. He told me he'd

covered all beams in the house and filled in the cellar. Later occupiers have worked tirelessly to strip out all this covering but so far no-one has emptied out the cellar! The small building adjoining the house was the Office. In the fullness of time

Above, Hazel Cottage, The yard of Hazel Cottage, Looking towards Hazel Cottage today and yesteryear

Bill sold the main house but retained the office; he sold the yard as a plot for a bungalow to be built on and then built himself a bungalow on an adjoining piece of land. His proud boast to me was that he had buried the traction engine under a rockery in the garden of his bungalow. That could have been a leg-pull so it wouldn't be worth excavating unless a metal detector had made some pretty resounding noises! He was a very interesting character and an exceptionally talented carpenter. It was disconcerting when he said how many people he'd measured up for coffins and I'm sure there's no worry about their coffins not being good for a few centuries underground! When he asked how you were though, one wondered if a 6' by 3' was being weighed in the balance when one replied, "Fine!"

The coming of mechanised transport took its toll on businesses like this and indeed the standing stock of spare cart wheels were actually burnt! Eventually Bill sold the bungalow and renovated the 'office' turning it into a delightful pensioners' bungalow. One could say within a small area he'd come full circle.

Running at the side of the property is a lane called Park Lane known only to residents, no street signs show this. It runs from the A528 up to Hordley. If one walks up the lane a matter of yards past the bungalows, there is an area on the left always referred to as The Cherry Orchards.

A rather murky pond parallels the road and then as one begins the ascent of the rise, on the left is an ROC shelter built for use during the Second World War. To the passer-by this would appear to be no more than a concrete trap-door affair that has had the fastening welded to prevent it being entered. Should one be able to lift the door one would see a metal-runged ladder going down the side of a steep shaft. At the bottom it opens into two rooms where observation and recording of enemy aircraft took place when an air attack was likely and of the defence measures being carried out for our protection. These shelters were country-wide and fairly unknown to most members of the general public. It is a small reference point to our political and historic changes in recent years. Their role changed in the 1950s when the Cold War became a major threat to our defence system.

Continuing up the lane and coming to a slight bend one again would see a small pond on the left but now, no longer evident, was a cottage on the right. The greengage tree in part of what used to be the garden would be the only clue to what used to be the garden and is perhaps the only clue to its existence. A young lady by the name of Jenny Young used to live here and had to walk down to the tanks opposite the shop and fetch her water and then toil all the way back again. This would be done in all weathers and was no respecter of feeling poorly. She taught at the school for many years. The water from the pond opposite the cottage was used for the chores such as floor washing or for use on the garden and who knows what else! Running water from a tap is taken too much for granted.

Another lady who I was acquainted with lived there for a while; her name was Olive Ashley. The army were billeted in tents up Park Lane so they had no facilities to do laundry. Olive was a very hard working lady and to supplement her income she did washing or laundry for the army. No running water and every drop to haul up the hill from the village would make this a daunting task.

The Dommetts were good friends of this family and recalled parties when the children were younger when they could really let off steam with no concern for disturbing the neighbours. Again, a family who coped with no amenities and toilets which were just earth closets.

To go higher up this lane we come to farms which will be recounted in the chapter on Farms. We'll about turn and go down the lane: no clanking empty buckets impeding our walk!

At the bottom of the lane is a building called The Crown. This was originally a farmhouse built by Jed Salter in1689. It stands on the left of a courtyard, with the next pub known then as the Red Lion at the other end of the yard, the two virtually connected by two tithe barns.A modern row of three terraced houses flank the yard also. The barns are in a sad state of repair, if one ignores the modern housing, the yard itself has not changed much in three

Note the roof and sign change of The Crown

hundred years. The Crown was used as a farm, a public house and a Court House. It was subject itself to a number of imposed fines for unruly behaviour in its day.

One part of this yard used to be a slaughterhouse-cum-butcher's shop owned by the Dickins. From 1913 to 1950 Mr Walter Tomlinson was the village butcher and slaughter man. While referring to the slaughterhouse at this point draws to mind that Nancy and Ern Roberts used to organise and run bingo here, to raise money towards building the old village hall, but this was after its days of being a slaughterhouse. Worms used to come out of the wood where they sat! You'd certainly shout something, if not House!

The Red Lion nb. roof change and cows approaching along the road

The Red Lion minus plaster-rendering and the Smithy-pre-porch

The Crown and the Red Lion both had provision for stabling horses. In the case of the Red Lion they could actually stable six horses. The Crown no longer operates as a public house but only a few years ago it was still an attractive venue for a meal and a drink.

The activities I witnessed living opposite to its car park, surrounded as it was then by fields were the arrival of: a mobile Mother and Baby Unit for babies of Cockshutt having a weigh-in and health check. Another day a Blacksmith would set up with his van and shoe horses that were either ridden in or came in horse boxes. The Walking Hunt for hare coursing would arrive in a flurry of muddy workaday 4 x 4s with lots of jollity, shoes swopped for wellies, dogs barking and then in what seemed an instant they'd depart on foot up the lane. Hare coursing with beagles used to be done a lot but with the proliferation of rabbits, hares do not survive. Rabbits kill the leverets. Mr Hulme of Crosemere Hall said he always enjoyed jugged hare served with redcurrant jelly. Each public house appeared to honour a share-out of activities held in the village but the preferences for one must have gradually contributed to the closure of the other.

Workaday life within the pubs merits a chapter on its own but before moving on it is worth mentioning that the external appearance of the Red Lion or Leaking Tap as it is now known once had a very different roof structure.

I have read that the original shape and windows are still existent within the new roof formation.

Next door to the pub yard is another yard and house owned by John Wainwright, our village plumber. His house has a quite imposing appearance because it has an additional feature of a protruding porch with a room over it in the front of the house. The house originally would have qualified as a good size. It used to be the home of Harry Pratt the village blacksmith. He dabbled in running a smallholding, more as a hobby as he had land and outbuildings at the back of the property. He still shoed horses and 'shrank' the iron rims onto wooden cartwheels. Harry started his working life in 1901 at these premises and carried on his trade until he was seventy-two when he and his wife decided to 'settle down a bit'. After all he is quoted as saying, "Rose and I have been married for

The 'Smithy' today complete with porch

nearly sixty-two years". Harry used to drink with Walter Tomlinson and Walter Worthington, the latter living at an old pub called The Cross Keys further up the road. All three could remember an old mail-coach coming through the village on its journey from Chester to Shrewsbury and back. As they passed through the village en-route, the passengers threw pennies out of the window for the children. The last coach passed along this route in 1914, much later than any other route in the country.

Next along the road after the Smithy are a row of three cottages of some considerable age. The first one, no. 24 was where the Coronation Tank was placed a large sandstone trough or tank into which water from the fields above was fed. Richard Humphreys lived here, and his son Ellis was killed in the First World War.

In the tiny centre cottage lived Pryce and Sarah Roberts; in no. 3 lived Mr Bill Smith and his large family, and much later it was occupied by Sally and Jim Clough from Liverpool.

The row of terraced cottages

At no. 20 was Jim 'Tither' Austin, his brother Bill, the dog Gert and a wife. Tither is referred to as a 'character' – that can however be a euphemism lending charm, which depends on your point of view.

On land adjoining these cottages used to be a pair of cottages, one of which used to be the Old School. Mr John Green taught there and occupied the other cottage as his home. The construction of the new school in 1856 was the point at which the children/teacher crossed the road to take up their school activities. In later years the ex-school cottages became home to John Stone; Ned Davies and the children Melrose, Eva and Archie. Next door was Polly Smith and grandchildren Will and Tom. Tom became the husband of Beryl now living at English Frankton. Eventually when these families moved out, George Ashley bought them and let them become totally derelict with pigs apparently able to roam through their broken remains.

The school held an allotment opposite its gates, the produce of which was intended for the use of the schoolmaster. There was a walnut tree in the school grounds and in later years six. Smith recalls the walnuts being sold at fourteen for a penny. Someone else remembers rare grafted fruit trees that had been set there, perhaps in the school allotments.

The children were encouraged to dig and maintain the plot within school time. John Moore writes that a boy whom he described as a thorough dunce enjoyed this occupation of digging in preference to bookwork.

Modern dwellings on Church Green and Kenwick Close totally obscure today any concept of a sandstone building that was called The Cross Keys (right, with a typical sign below).

The fairly large pub was run for many years before it succumbed to a change of usage, and became home to the following: Mr John Brookfield at no. 14 and his son Joe, as a Saddlers Shop. Joe must have had learning difficulties because various recorded incidents whilst amusing, highlighted the problem.

It was not unusual to see Joe clipping weeds in the road with a pair of scissors or putting his head to the ground to see if he could hear any traffic. Fortunately in a small community a protection of kind deals with these incidents and he was referred to as a 'special person to us all' by another biographer.

The Cross Keys looking towards Ellesmere

In no. 12 was Lisa Husbands, grandmother to Nellie and Peggy Husbands. The story associated with this house was that in the 1800s a young lad who had quarrelled with the family decided to run away and go to sea.

As he trudged along the road, he realised that he had the key of the house in his pocket. Loath to retrace his steps; afraid of the consequences if he did, he pushed the key into a hole in the trunk of a nearby ash tree. The tree grew, the key remained visible for many years until eventually it disappeared from view. Many years later the tree was felled; no key was reclaimed. A later descendant of this same family lived at the cottage and was known never to have had a key for the back door. There was a large keyhole but the door was always bolted from the inside and padlocked outside. Fact or fiction: we'll never know and nor do we hear what became of the run-away!

Left, from the back; Elsie Birch holding Dot Birch (Mrs Norton)Nellie Birch Amy Birch and Tom Birch.

Right, Elsie Birch with Dossie as an Infant

Left, Dossie and her Grandmother Mary Ellen Birch at the side of the CrossKeys cottages; in the background can be seen Rose Cottage and Rag Row.

At no 8 lived Ellen Birch, Dossie's grandmother with her daughter Mrs Wilding, and Dossie and Den, the twins. Mrs Wilding walked with the post in all weathers all the way to Whettal to the Edwards': she was post-lady for quite some time. The Williams' lived in another cottage in the group and at no. 12 was Walter Worthington (friend of Harry Pratt) he had the well. It was available for the Cross Keys cottagers and others who asked. Mr Sawbridge from the shop said that his family preferred the water from this well as opposed to the one that was opposite their shop.

Demolition of The Cross Keys Cottages]

There is some reference to an iron pump being 'up the shut' which no longer exists. The said pump served houses 8, 10, 12 and 14 and was for their consumption. All that remains is the base stone at no. 17, the new bungalow. This does not seem in accord with mention of a tank.

The water provided by these various sources of tanks and pumps was condemned by the Health Authority as being unfit to drink.

For the Dommetts living in the school house, the Doctor advised they boil any water before drinking it or using it for personal washing, teeth cleaning etc.

The Water Authority then brought in water for the children's use in school hours. They, of course returned to using the condemned water on arrival home. The strain of bacteria contained in water which has drained through fields on which cattle graze does create a health risk; perhaps they had developed a natural immunity.

Travelling on from the Cross Keys towards The Dobbin there have again been changes and places that are no longer evident. Just after the last houses on the left going towards Ellesmere were allotments. Further on was a pair of black and white semi-cottages and a thatched cottage. The latter was so near the road a previous writer on Cockshutt suggests that this one might well have been a toll-house.

Nobby Austin lived in one of the pair of cottages near The Dobbin. Nobby's culinary skills or his hygiene seems to have suited him but left some wariness in Bill Smith observing him cooking. He was frying eggs in the frying-pan over the stove, behind him the cat was on the table with a mouse under the newspaper!

Dobbin Cottage. Jack Griffiths and son Robin

Mrs Ann Austin, his mother, owned a carrier cart and a horse that rejoiced in the name of Rosie. She used the cart on a daily basis charging only a few pence and was unofficially dubbed the 'Cockshutt mail'. The necessity and popularity of the service she offered cannot be underestimated. She took over this work from her grandmother, Mrs Nellie Bagnall, who operated the same thing only with a donkey and cart. Market days for Ellesmere were on Tuesdays and therefore small goods to be sold such as eggs, butter, apples, live chickens, holly wreaths at Christmas, were all stacked around the occupants' feet. Those travelling on Tuesday, booked in advance and then Ann placed two planks across the cart for them to sit on. When the cart approached a bank or 'The Tunnel', Ann would exhort the passengers by shouting 'Sit back wenches or sit forard wenches' as they acted by weight like a brake. These must in themselves have been rather precarious seating arrangements. Some passengers might also have a child on their knee, so the weight must have been to the maximum. Old Rose plodded at a slow and rhythmic pace. Only once on this route did they have a mishap; Ann engrossed in conversation slackened her hold on the reins and Rosie veered into a rut on the road. She plunged wildly for a moment, throwing the ladies over the hedge and into a field. All were merely shaken by the episode bar Mrs Austin whose arm was broken, resulting in no lifts for some time.

Mondays, Wednesdays and Fridays were kept for carrying articles that were large; for example a bicycle that had been for repair; a couple of sacks of coal; new items from Clay's Foundry, generally larger bulkier goods. Saturdays were usually kept to transport passengers. In wet weather there was a huge carrier umbrella that covered everyone in the cart and partially the rear end of Rosie. On cold days Ann protected herself against the elements with a large plaid shawl. One rainy day did create a minor calamity because she was returning from Ellesmere carrying some medicines.

The rain peeled two of the bottle labels off but, studying the shape and colour of the said labels and the size of area it might have been adhered to, she reglued them on. There were no reports of unexpected effects to the patients from the mix-up, so perhaps her guess was correct!

The last cottages before turning into Porter Lane are the ones referred to as 'at The Dobbin'. The name itself seems strange but as Dobbin is generally associated with horses and as this road formed part of the circuit of the steeplechase which first took place in 1837, perhaps that is a case of name by association.

We will turn back towards Cockshutt centre now passing two fields that only vary nowadays by what is either grazing or growing on them.

The field nearest the brook was owned by Harry Austin and was one place that annually drew the crowds as it used to have Manders' fairground and other events held on it. For now we'll leave that to be covered by the very hectic entertainments programme that the village held.

The sandstone house called Stone Villa was once a carpenter's shop run by a Mr Holland. We have a picture of Minnie Vernon in the pathway of the house dated 1896 when she was five years old. The actual age of the house must be about 1800. Her father was a carpenter and apprenticed William Matthews at this time; he lived further along the road in Primrose Terrace. Minnie seems to have been a very lively character and very keen on politics despite suffering for more than fifty years with arthritis. This necessitated many trips to doctors and specialists to try to alleviate the pain. Her stoic attitude to her condition meant that for as long as it was possible, she used to go to London and sit in the Strangers Gallery in Parliament

Stone Villa captured from a glass negative taken in 1896; Minnie Vernon aged 5yrs. sitting on the wall and above right, in more modern times

and listen to the House debate for hours at a time. Her local MP was so impressed with her enthusiasm, he arranged a treat one year for her to sit alone in the Sergeant at Arms Gallery. She really appreciated this honour, even when housebound because of her frailty the radio and newspapers meant she could keep abreast of her political interests.

Mrs Vernon's home was also the base for the local GP, Dr Rogers to hold a surgery. She was quite strict with the patients, who not infrequently started their queuing outside. Once inside however, privacy was not possible when it came to complaints and cures being discussed and overheard. George Tatton the wheelwright was the next occupant.

William Matthews, apprentice in 1896

Alongside Stone Villa is a pretty thatched cottage called Rose Cottage. The records describe this cottage as a 15th century cottage with later additions and alterations being originally a part cruck construction with a painted brick infill.

Very early occupants from this cottage would have seen soldiers and movement of the Civil War troops. Prince Rupert for the Royalist cause is reported to have stayed in the vicinity and, with Wem being a centre of military aggression, what might these people have heard, seen or who knows, have been involved in!

In more recent years Len Birch, an octogenarian from Weston Lullingfields was born here and photographed as a child by the gateway with his mother. The roof was no longer thatched but had a corrugated metal covering.

Rose Cottage, Len Birch and his Mother

Within a couple more years he was to move to the previously mentioned Bhim cottage at the High Town end of the village.

This cottage was also referred to as the Nurses' House. The District Nurses seem to have been lodged at various houses in the region. A Nurse Logan lodged at Cockshutt Hall/House for some time. At Stone Hill a Nurse Davies lodged and Nurse Norton, Dossie's aunt was District Midwife from Rose Cottage. Nurse Roberts was also remembered, as she, poor soul, was on call from Myddle Wood at all hours of the day or night. Unlike today, the new mother was expected to remain bed-bound for up to ten days during which time they required visiting.

A little cul-de-sac separates us from the next row of modern bungalows. Pause for a moment before crossing here and think that the privies for the next six houses were at the far end of this road.

Primrose Terrace, otherwise known as Rag Row. Right to left; Mrs Kirkham Mary Ashley (child) Violet Ashley (Mother)
Mrs Williams Margaret Husbands (child) Olive Chidlow(tot) Doris Mrs Husbands

Todays modern replacement of Primrose Terrace or Rag Rouv

No matter what the weather or whether it was pitch black outside, there was a long trek to the toilet for the next original cottages. They were not flush toilets but earth closets with no light switch to make it less scary at night and certainly no heating! Recounting one resident's memories of the problems there, he said if the toilet buckets were full up, you had to go and dig a hole to empty it.

The modern bungalows have replaced the sandstone cottages in what was then known as Primrose Terrace. The row at the present day sports an unofficial sign with the name Rag Row, although postally I am sure it is just Shrewsbury Road. I am not sure how it gets that name but it may just be a matter of humorous irony!

Primrose Terrace was a row of sandstone terrace cottages, originally with one room up and one down. The large landing upstairs meant the space was used as a sleeping area to make it appear to be two bedrooms. The ground floor was red quarry-tiled; one front gate between two cottages separated the front gardens and at the back they had an enormous garden each. That didn't compensate for the long trek to the loo!

The first cottage, no. 19 after Rose Cottage was occupied by Adelaide Sawbridge (right) ; she also ran this as a shop selling home-made sweets. As her family grew up and prospered they moved further down the road to where the present village shop is. Her house then became in turn a Tailor's shop run by Mr Phillips, then a furniture repair shop with a Mr Ted Birch and later still by Mr William Matthews the previously mentioned apprentice-carpenter employed at Stone Villa.

Listing other occupants along this row going towards the school were; the Chidlows and John and Patty Allman. Jack was a roadman or, as they were sometimes known, a lengthman. Each man would have a length of road to keep clean and tidy. This applied to by-roads as well but not the lanes. Great pride was taken in keeping the village smart and tidy. Patty his wife had a reputation for always being kind and helpful to the sick and dying.

William Husbands, Ashleys and Matthews complete the list. A Mr Billigge 'The German', also lived for some time on this row. During Adelaide's time I believe that someone on this terrace also acted as a barber. There were far more people serving the community then than we can list today. The present Post Office was the School House where John Moore (Junior) was born in 1888.

We begin the last terrace of houses after the church; the first was the Post Office for some time run by Mr and Mrs Jack Brookfield, later by a Mrs Aubrey. The Post Office has been a moveable feast in its time going to no. 23 to Gladys Stokes then back to the School House where Mrs Dorice Peel was postmistress. The mailbags hung outside school totally unattend-ed when awaiting delivery or collection. One of the school windows was left open for items going in via the window. This location was followed by a move down to no.3 Crosemere Crescent where Mary Gregory officiated as postmistress.

Long before the council houses were built on this lane, there used to be a brick built hut in the field near to a shelter and stable which housed the shop's horse and corn store. In this hut the postman, having cycled from Ellesmere, stayed each weekday evening sorting out the mail. He would deliver the evening post at 5.00 pm, wait until 6.00 pm to empty the letterbox, then he would cycle on to English Frankton and Brown Heath and then on to Colemere, via Pikesend, to empty their letter boxes and cycle back to Ellesmere.

*Clockwise from left, Early transport for the shop, Edwardian children waiting near the shop,
Chris Sawbridge delivering with his cart, This picture shows a wall outside the shop*

The shop, as recounted earlier, began in a very small way in Primrose Terrace and then moved to the last house on the next larger terrace of houses. Adelaide's son Chris in 1898 took up the trade and by the turn of the century was specializing as a baker and confectioner. To expand the trade he sold paraffin and foodstuffs and animal foods, storing the latter in a covered hut next to the postman's hut down the lane.

He collected this food from Weston Wharf at Weston Lullingfields, a very busy terminal of the canal. He also brought back coal. They needed a cart for bulk transport and purchased a delivery trap for the bakery goods. Delivery of goods covered a fairly wide area of Colemere, English Frankton and Loppington. The picture of the trap also shows how the front of the shop appeared, with a garden and path leading to the door. On busy days there could be a queue outside!

Chris was married to Lizzie and she and Mary Brookfield from just up the road had both been in service as maids in Frankton Grange. The driver of the trap was Jack Sawbridge, Chris's son. He was organist in church but suffered with epilepsy and died in his twenties. Jack's brother Laurie who had trained as a draughtsman returned from London in 1921 and gradually took over the business; the old man continued to bake until he died.

Laurie acquired a motor cycle-combination and delivered the goods in that. Life was obviously speeding up a bit at that time!

Inflation however meant the baking of bread on a small scale was no longer economical and baking had ceased by 1948.

The family still recall when talking about transport that, should they require a lift to or from Baschurch Station, Laurie would use the cart; the fact that it had recently been used to transport coal was of no consequence! Laurie faced coping with food rationing during the war when people had to register with their ration books. In 1946-47 there was a very severe winter when Cockshutt was cut off. He always had to ensure that there was enough flour in for these occasions. Saturday nights were late-night opening when accounts were reckoned up as a lot of weekly trade had been done on credit; this was the night for the cash to be collected in and this was a time of some of those queues previously mentioned!

Laurie did run an unofficial taxi service often taking the vicar from parish to parish. John his son had trained and served in the RAF but on marrying Rose (she was his third cousin), he took over the shop from Laurie who retired in 1965. The shop joined the Mace group of independent grocers when it was first formed in 1960.

In 1968 the small room which had formed the shop and served the community for the past seventy years, was completely demolished and a new self-service store was built on the same site. In 1970 Sawbridges took over the news agency. The generations of Sawbridges running the shop, starting with Adelaide's tiny shop, the bakery with Chris, delivery of goods by both Chris and Laurie and finally the supermarket run by Rose and John were a story of a family business success.

The sons had each begun their working lives training in other work but when retirement was claimed they each took up the cudgel and continued and expanded the grocery business. John's son like his great grandfather trained as a baker and confectioner, this time in London and the better prospects, naturally enough ended the line of Sawbridges in Cockshutt. In 1992 they sold out.

Across the lane is a building occupying the corner and referred to as the Annexe (left). On this wall there used to be a metal circular sign; the background colour was an orangey yellow with black writing. It was an Automobile Association, AA, sign (right).

This sign has been removed and restored by the present owners of the Old Vicarage.

The Old Vicarage – formerly The Golden Lion. Below, the roadside entrance

This used to be the coach house of the Golden Lion pub, but is now a private residence. The Golden Lion was run by Thomas Townsend who was actually born there in 1810. They moved across the road to the Red Lion, owned by Lord Brownlow. There is a 'Sales Catalogue' dated 8.12.1815 when the Townsend officially took over ownership of the pub 'messuage and farm'. The Golden Lion then became the Vicarage for many years.

The Vicarage Annexe in later years is recalled quite frequently in Cockshutt memories as it served home for a variety of functions.

Nellie Sutton recalled a Whist Drive held upstairs on a Monday which she attended once a fortnight; money raised on this night was given to The British Legion. On the alternate Mondays a Mrs Gregory ran events to support the church. On Nellie's Whist Drive nights she would call into the Annexe earlier and light the fire before going on to deliver her father his evening meal which she had done daily for the past seventeen years. The WI used to meet in the Annexe and there were dances also held there.

On a much more serious note there was a thatched cottage down Crosemere Lane, just after Yew Tree cottage. Two modern bungalows occupy the site now. This cottage was black and white in appearance and built very close to the edge of the road with steps leading up to it. It was the home of Mrs Williams and her daughter, now called Nancy Roberts.

The thatch caught fire and gutted their home (right) so they sought temporary accommodation at the Annexe. In later married life Nancy and Ern Roberts used the slaughter house-cum-butchers at the Red Lion for the Bingo night and then later they moved across and used the Annexe.

This was in the run-up to fundraising money for a village hall.

The vicarage gardens encompassed the present day vicarage and down Crosemere Lane to the Alley Walk. The bungalows on the right going down the lane did not exist although the pair of cottages belonging to Tom Ward and Harry Lunt just after Skittle Alley was there.

The vicarage garden was described as a lovely sight in spring with the orchard all in blossom. The gardens being so extensive were used for social functions. Bill and Blodwyn Smith got married from the vicarage and had their reception on the vicarage lawns.

Blodwyn had been in service there for sixteen years. In the early nineteen-thirties Reverend Peppercorn, described so often by so many people as the vicar with more money than he knew what to do with, or wealthy and eccentric, but more importantly a very good man. He is well remembered for what he overall called a 'Beano'. Under the umbrella of this title he had (a) a museum; (b) a garden fete; (c) an exhibition.

It was a *Grand Affair* for Cockshutt! In the church magazine he wrote a puzzling sentence, 'Let there be no mistake about it. The clue was in a sentence and all would be revealed in the next issue. 'Beano'. The inspiration for this money raising activity was a closely shared one with the school head, Mr Hassell.

The two men worked tirelessly organising the various activities. The title 'Beano' was subsequently to be used over a period of years when staging other mammoth money raising events.

The village had to partake in costume and items of rural historic interest were procured by the Vicar to be props of the period. John Sawbridge in period costume was photographed on one of these props, a velocipe, (top left). The date of this event was 1935.

Laurence and Terry (Theresa) Sawbridge were also photographed in costumes that had been procured, (middle left). Villagers would line-up in costume to watch the parade (bottom left).

Other activities hosted by Reverend Peppercorn were dances on the vicarage lawn after the parade of The Oddfellows Club.

Reverend Peppercorn also launched a model hot air balloon. Part of the fete activities was to release ordinary balloons and his secret ambition was that they be released on a south westerly wind and actually reach Scandinavia. John Sawbridge's reached somewhere in Yorkshire but Scarborough was the furthest recorded. A target measure was placed on the vicarage wall for all to see both the aimed for and the achieved figures.

The following year Reverend Peppercorn and Mr Hassell organised similar events for the fund and plans were drawn up for the village hall's construction, but 1939 saw world events that put the whole programme on hold.

The money raised was saved but after the War there was a lot of controversy about founding a suitable memorial. Laurie Sawbridge was a trustee of the money and he felt that as the money had been raised for a new village hall it should therefore be known as the Memorial Hall.

Reverend Peppercorn who had played such a part in organising the fund had retired and moved away. A new vicar had replaced him called Reverend Hardy; the vicar wanted a new organ for the church and the casting vote saw its replacement and a very small plaque is on the side of it commemorating the lives that were lost.

There was some discontent about this by those who had contributed time and effort into the fundraising and were not church members; they saw nothing for their efforts. One can only add from the aspect of the present day that the reason for the existence of the organ is very easily overlooked.

One of the vicar's resident at the vicarage at a much later date had an 'interest' which involved him digging holes all over the place in his search for historical artefacts. Each to his own!

Leaving the vicarage we have one more house to visit. The pair of houses just after the new vicarage appears to be two semi-detached houses today, but was in fact, four cottages originally. The occupants of these houses were; Thomas (Moody) Jones; Granny Chidlow where there was an iron water pump; Williams', and Joe Gregory.

Somewhere at this juncture and exactly where I cannot trace, Cockshutt appears to have had an area forming a square or market place.

Important events of the village took place on this square; meets of the local hunt, village 'wakes' and merrymaking and an annual agricultural fair that was held until May 1850. The alteration in layout that created this market place was formed by the road from Loppington going past Crosemere Hall and coming out opposite the road to Kenwick Park thus forming a square or market place.

Bear Baiting took place in the square, usually in the autumn when the bear was brought from Loppington on a regular circuit of this attraction. Charlotte S Burne in Shropshire Folklore says that a Mr Robinson of Hanmer owned a bear which could account for the popularity of the sport in Salop. Another local man, name of Peate, also had a bear which used to be taken to the various 'wakes' and kept at an inn.

 At Cockshutt there were three inns in the centre of the village and each procured a bear as an attraction. The landlord paid the bear-keeper ten shillings for the three-day stay; and the latter also received 2d or 3d for three runs at the bear from the owner of every dog. He had a sort of weapon called a paddle, with which he prised open the dog's mouth when fastened too tightly on the bear. Each poor bear was baited three or four times each day at intervals and the keeper made a collection from the company each time, so he must have made a considerable profit altogether. (Any hotel carrying the sign The Bear Hotel bears witness to the old sport of bear-baiting). As a small boy Mr Townsend used to hide stores of apples and nuts etc in cracks in the stable walls for his own use. The bear found them all and ate them! The last bear baiting in Salop was at Loppington in 1825 on the occasion of the vicar's daughter's wedding. It became illegal in 1835. For entertainment value only, Peggy Husbands wrote that a dancing bear was brought through the village by a man who also brought a Hurdy-Gurdy machine or barrel organ. In this respect there was no suggestion of harm or suffering coming to the bear.

Crosemere Lane has changed drastically from being a dusty lane bordered by the vicarage garden down to Skittle Alley, two cottages and then fields on the right and on the left only the shop back garden and two cottages to beyond The Briars. It takes imagination to envisage it as it was. Cows were herded up and down the lane; there was no street lighting and no pavements. The photograph (next page) of fields in the present crescent before the council houses were built show haymaking with Jack Brookfield and Laurie Sawbridge and John Sawbridge as a little boy. (He is in his mid-seventies now).

Anyone who remembers pictures like this will feel nostalgia for a slower pace of life but I am sure the speedy methods of a combine harvester remind one that we have more people to feed and there is no room for nostalgia! This land they are reaping was rented from the Bridgewater Estate.

The large tree (left) where Rose Sawbridge and her sister are perched was opposite Yew Tree cottage. There were fruit trees on this field where, according to John in later years, many children used to go scrumping.

The council houses in Crosemere Crescent were built in 1952. Mains sewerage came in the 1960s. The building followed the curve around forming the Crescent to Meadow Lane. The Council obtained and purchased the land from the Bridgewater Estate.

On the left going down the lane, Yew Tree cottage (facing page) has had a series of tenants and owners. Thomas and Annie Ashley's son Fred; the Fardoes listed in Kelly's Directory as a shoemaker, moved up to Kenwick Park; Olive Ashley for a spell and for a while it was also remembered as a cake shop and card shop.

The thatched cottage, The Steps, next to Yew Tree was home to Mrs Husbands, a lady getting on in years but still working as a 'milker'. She had quiet cows, we were told. The later account of the fire destroying this thatched cottage we have already read.

The next cottage going down the lane was opposite The Briars. Where The Briars are built was known as The Cornfields and was host to cricket matches every year.

Opposite, however, was a quite sub-stantial black and white thatched cottage, complete with cellar, known as The Corns. It was owned by Samuel Chester and his wife Jane. In the 1871 Directory it refers to a William Corns living there and in 1911 it is listed as Corns Old house. When Sam died, his wife moved away and it was bought by George Ashley who knocked it down.

Again the landscape at this point is much altered and unrecognisable to today's phases of construction. The next farm after the Chesters' small-holding was Cunningham owned until recently by Randal Carr, and is now a new housing development. This farm used to be called Crosemere Farm, more of which we will read later.

Above, Yew Tree cottage and below, The Steps has been replaced by a modern bungalow

Crosemere Farm and an aerial view

Brook house; white section is the dance hall, below Brook House today

George Ashley's haulage vehicles parked where the bungalows now stand

FARMS AND COTTAGES

Brook House

Brook House is on the left and has a garage fronting the lane and with a timbered porch to the house front; this at first glance gives it a black and white cottage effect. This is an attractive addition to a house externally that couldn't be more different from its original design which is shown in the photograph.

In 1804 it was listed as a Malt Kiln and again in 1834 it is still recorded as a 'Malt Kiln and land'. Many further occupants in its history since then are named but accounts of it in recent memory are rather difficult to envisage. Kelly's Directory 1891 says a Lewis Rodenhurst ran a shop and also sold cattle feed. It acted as a warehouse for Wem Mill storing cattle feed. The Rodenhursts then moved to Loppington.

They were followed by Mr and Mrs Gwillams. This couple appear to have been very enterprising as they ran a shop and a chip shop and, biggest surprise, a dance hall.

This all appears to have taken place in what we see now as the area occupied by the garage. Then, it was a two-storey building. The dances had 'live bands' and were held upstairs and the shop activities were downstairs. They sold out to a Mr and Mrs Speake and their daughter Gertie and they continued it as a shop only; when they decided to move on they went to the pub The Cross Keys in Burlton.

Granny Ashley was the next occupant and later George Ashley ran a haulage business/garage, keeping his cattle wagons where the new bungalows are now. When the upper floor of the old dance hall was demolished the large oak timbers were used to build kitchen units and a kitchen table in Brook House.

Apple Cottage

Just after Brook House is Apple Cottage. Again, in the present day it is a single dwelling but it used to be two cottages. It stands on the corner of Porter Lane and Crosemere Lane. When built in the mid-seventeenth century it had originally a black and white exterior; it was later clothed in a brick layer. The thatched roof was replaced by slate after the height of it had been raised by removing the oak ceiling timbers. The interior otherwise still retains the heavy black oak beams and inglenook fire. As farm labourers' cottages they did not have a staircase to upstairs, just a ladder; this was not unusual to sleep in the loft area, under the thatch.

Granny Smith lived in one cottage and one can presume that her name gave rise to the cottage. Bill and Blodwyn Smith had left Cockshutt after their marriage but when visiting Granny Smith (his mother) it was decided to return and temporarily they moved in next door. He took up work at Crosemere Hall. The varying farmsteads occupied by the various branches of the Marsh family will be related in a section on farms.

Rosemary Cottage

The lane we now enter going towards

Apple Cottage, a recent view and a much earlier photo. The cottage began life as 2 black and white farm cottages

Below, Rosemary Cottage

the Crosemere Mere is called Draw Well Lane. The oldest property we see is called Rosemary Cottage. This attractive thatched cottage is a late seventeenth century cottage, timber framed with a red brick infill and straw thatch roof.

There have been a series of alterations and additions to the property. A Tom Hanmer on the census is called a cow keeper and lived there; he had a son also called Tom and it was he who gained the nickname 'Sticky Tom'. This was because he rode a bicycle to work at Stanwardine House and en route home he always collected any sticks he found for his fire, bound them in a bundle and tied them on his bike. In 1941 Sticky Tom worked as a farm labourer at Stanwardine House and whilst there, received a bullet in his backside after a passing Spitfire shot down a stray Barrage Balloon. He was unfortunate enough to be in line of fire from the stray ammunition.

After Tom, a lady by the name of Miss Anderson lived there.

The house needed modernising and this wasn't financially viable, so, advised by a Mrs Studholme she made application for money to upgrade the cottage and it was granted. Her means for gaining this capital was to set the money required against the asset of the property. In those days that would have been quite an innovative thing to have undertaken. There was no immediate family and the loan could be repaid on her death. The cottage, just like Apple cottage had no staircase, so with the money now available she installed not one, but two staircases - one at each end of the cottage. Being flippant, it springs to mind the song in "Fiddler on the Roof" one long staircase going up and the other coming down and one more going nowhere just for show!

She refrained from the third and must have felt vastly improved to have stairs and not a ladder. Beyond Rosemary Cottage, another black and white cottage, no.13 that has disappeared was the home of Mr and Mrs William Peel; he was fondly known as 'Nippy' but I haven't learnt why. In later years she was remembered by Mrs Hulme of The Hall as a 'sweet little old lady'. She was always absolutely immaculate and wore a rough (sack) apron. Her husband suffered with very bad asthma. The cottage was a timber/plaster construction and growing alongside it was a very large sycamore tree. In a high wind it was said that as the tree shook, the cottage also trembled.

Cottages 13 and 14

Opposite them, in yet another black and white cottage no.14 (right) that has disappeared was Granny and Granddad Ashley – Bill/Polly, parents and in-laws to George and Ivy Ashley. The grandmother kept a cow up on the croft where Bhim Cottage was built. They all had to carry their drinking water from the pump at Crosemere House. Neither of these cottages remains.

Crosemere House

Crosemere House (right and centre right) was the next property which in the 1911 census lists William Henry Owen (surveyor) as occupant. This very substantial looking house used to be part of Lord Brownlow's Estate and was the home of the land agent of the estate. It was later purchased by George and Ivy Ashley. It was a small farm of about thirty acres and did not form the mainstay of George's working life as his occupation was as a haulier, owning a fleet of vehicles.

Further along by the 'Mere' gate or footpath that leads to the mere, stood another cottage now no longer existing.

All that remains is a very well constructed pigsty which has acquired a preservation order on it! One wonders what the house itself was like. This was the home of Mr and Mrs Jack Hanmer. He was known as 'Little Jack' and Marie his wife always wore a man's cap.

She was a great friend of Mrs Austin along with Mary Ellen Birch and Sarah Jane Hanmer. They'd all been lifelong friends and it was these three who were to suffer the accident being thrown off Mrs Austin's carrier cart when Rosie the horse sensing the slackened rein, fell asleep and then misjudged her footing throwing them all off!

Now one looks at a bare patch of ground, a pigsty, a discarded boiler and a few gnarled fruit trees: that is all that remains of what was someone's home. There must have been a rare old commotion when the tale of their shopping trip and accident was brought home.

Mere Farm

Opposite their cottage is Mere Farm (right), a smallholding that was home to the Wilkinsons; Laurie Sawbridge from the shop was often up there visiting with young John. The Wilkinsons' daughter, Olive, was organist at church for many years. Later this place was occupied by the Rodenhursts. We'll retrace our steps past The Grange and Rosemary Cottage and into Porter Lane. Walking towards Loppington we have the very attractive new properties on the right, and with the usual trick of time it is almost impossible to envisage it as it was.

We come to a weedy watery piece of ground on the left known as The Flash. Crossing the lane and going towards the potato storage sheds, one comes to a plot of ground known as Charlie Green. On the south side of this stood a house photographed by David Evans in 1977 which had been referred to as The White House. It had once been a pub called the Green Gate. It then became divided into two cottages; in one lived Dora Hanmer and her son Tom. She was grandmother to Raymond Richards and great grandmother to Jackie. She used to take surplus eggs from her hens to be sold at the shop. Next door lived a Mr and Mrs Cooke and their three daughters, Kitty, her sister Eileen and Adelaide who died. Kitty was the last resident of these cottages and in later years moved to live in a house in the row just before the Millennium Hall.

Halls and Farms

The houses and cottages described so far around Cockshutt are built fairly compactly around the village and outlying it are several large Halls and Farms.

Stanwardine in the Wood

A very large and imposing looking Hall. In the earliest recording Stanwardine relates to a moated circular mound which was the site of the original mansion. This moat/mound is a

Stanwardine in the Wood and opposite right

listed site. The name of the hamlet – Stanwardine in the Wood, along with its moat, indicates that this was a medieval farm planted in a clearing in virgin forest.

The present day Hall is an antique mansion built in 1581 by Robert Corbet. It is irregular in shape and was not all built at the same time; additions have been made at different periods. The house is built with red sandstone brick from Grinshill, with stone facings and mullioned windows. The bricks are of the small Elizabethan type and have mellowed beautifully with age.

Robert Corbet, brother of Sir Andrew Corbet of Moreton Say, constructed the house and his son enlarged some of it after his death. It was to be extended again at a later period.

There are three gables to the front, and atop the centre is a stone, carved with the Corbet crest, The Elephant and Castle, whilst lower down, but above the porch is a shield with the coat of arms and crest of the same family. Above the right hand gable is a weathercock with the Corbet badge the 'Raven'. In times of conflict between the Royalists and Cromwell in the 1650s, the Corbet family knew some difference of loyalties. Robert Corbet and other branches of the family stood for Parliament; the head of the Corbet family, Sir Vincent was a royalist.

The last member of the Corbet family to own Stanwardine in 1700 allegedly gambled the ownership and deeds playing either at cards or in a snail race and lost to Sir John Wynne of Watsay.

Since then Stanwardine has always been a very large and imposing farm house. The Hall has many outlying farm buildings

The Hall was sold to a William Sparling of Petton in 1818 when it became part of the Petton

Estate; the deeds were transferred to him in 1839. A Mrs Cunliffe of Petton sold the estate again in1920.

In 1923 there was a fire at the Hall, started in the outbuildings. It burnt many cattle which were tied up by their chains which in turn became red hot. A number of calves were destroyed by the roof falling in when a workman opened a door to let them out. The bull broke away and ran amok to the village of Weston. Butchers were there dressing what was fit to salvage for food. Two of the domestic staff was awarded certificates for bravery, namely, Miss Lizzie Reeves and a boy called Harold Gregory.

Mr George Townsend was awarded a medal for succeeding in unfastening the red hot chains off some of the animals' necks.

Many years later in 1977 the family were to again experience a fire, this time within the house on Christmas Day. A chimney fire on Christmas morning damaged the mezzanine floor bathroom on the eastern side of the house.

In 1940 the Hall was used by the 51st Regiment Royal Artillery (Midland) as a regrouping place after Dunkirk – 1940-July 1941 with troops billeted there. A field at the back of the Hall is referred to as the 'Gun Park'. One of the rooms is referred to as 'The Guard Room'. In 1941 a Spitfire shot down a stray barrage balloon. Part of the balloon is still used to cover the billiards-table.

The Hall was bought in 1957 by the present owners, Mr David Bridge, his wife Margaret and their three children. The son Peter Bridge and his wife Fiona live there now with their children.

Land that had belonged to Stanwardine House (now in private ownership) was purchased and added to the Hall Estate; there are other apartments within the Hall for other family members.

Crosemere Hall

A red brick house of generous proportions.It has five bedrooms, drawing room, dining room, a very large hall and an equally large kitchen. There are numerous smaller rooms and bathrooms. Special features of interest were, for instance two areas showing the original structure of the walls of the older part of the house. Each panel is now covered with plate glass to preserve it; one section showed a heavily compacted daub and plaster covering - the second showed a trellis-type structure with the wattle/daub filling. In the main hall there is an exposed area of Elizabethan hand-made bricks, the bricks being both smaller than average and of an irregular size.

One half of the house is much older than the other, the older side having wide planked doors secured by heavy metal latches. Floors are uneven and the beams quite heavily notched. The inglenook fireplace in the drawing room (once two rooms) is enormous and is complete with inset areas to either side, one being the old bread oven. It was thought that one half of this very large room used to be the original kitchen. The kitchen used by the present owners is very large and has several hooks in the ceiling beams from which the flitches of ham would hang.

Crosemere Hall above.
Below, One of the first cars in the village at Crosemere Hall

The fireplace in the oak-panelled dining room and also the one in the bedroom above were of very impressive size and grandeur in two shades of marble. This fireplace and the panelling were thought to be the legacy of the Lloyds.

In the outbuildings of red brick one can define the shapes of doorways designed for coaches. The house was owned at one time by the Lloyd family; they were Shropshire Gentry.

When they owned it, the thought is that it was a much larger structure as would befit their rank and stature. An Edward Lloyd is known to have lived here around 1535 having bought it from the Parcy family recorded as early as 1451. One notable family member was a Francis Lloyd whose initials can still be seen on the staircase. He was disciplined by his father in 1676 and deprived of certain property benefits for his general bad behaviour!

The actual recording of this is as follows; - He had undutifully and disobediently demeaned himself to his father and extravagantly, prodigally and profusely spent and wasted much of his estate.

Fortune smiled on him again when in 1688 his marriage settlement included 'the mansion house, orchard gardens, buildings, barns, and stables and dove house'.

Within the gardens today there is still a dovecote.

The house was rented when the Lloyds moved away; the Lees family rented it and it was rented by the present owner's father, Mr Hulme in 1918; then he bought it.

The massive loft of the house has a closed-off section which must amount to one third of the loft area.

It has two doors to its approach, one up a small flight of steps and the second leading to a platform area. Within this third of the loft it was known and used for cock fighting, a sport that was illegal in the 1800s.

'Nanna' or Gubshill Sunshine 9th

At one time the Hulmes had one hundred cows, made cheese and kept pigs. Granny Ashley used to sometimes come over to babysit and her husband would milk the cows for the 10.00 pm milking. The special cow that was of international acclaim was called 'Gubshill Sunshine 9th' but known by the children of the family as 'Nanna'. She was fondly remembered with great affection for having a very sweet nature. The acclaim

The milkers. Standing; Jack Richards, Andrew Vaughan, Jack Williams, Tom Hanmer, Bill Cooke. Seated; Edwin Humpage, Miss Lewis, Mary Husbands, Fanny Husbands, Patty Allman, Beattie Sutton, Tom Sutton.

previously mentioned was because she gave 22,400 gallons of milk or 100 tons of milk in four years. A certificate was issued 1st December 1955 from the British Friesian Society, as owned by J S Hulme.

The sheep rearing has been the mainstay of the farm for the past fifty years, Pankymoor Prelude being the one which made history in 1998 as the best known in the country for having sired more than a million pounds of progeny. They still hold some of his semen for reproduction now.

Bill Smith worked for the Hulmes and was involved with the clipping for all

Stanley and Robin Hulme with Pankey Moor Prelude

the shows. "Everywhere we went we got first prize".

To get this standard for showing, every night after we'd finished milking we'd work with three wild lambs on halters. By one or certainly two weeks they'd come and put their feet on your chest – and try to nibble your tie; they'd become so friendly but this was all part of the handling for showing'. Bill is recorded as saying; "We've taken prizes wherever we went – Chester even".

On a less serious note he described there being a pit by the side of the Hall where they scalded pigs (dead!) and scraped the hair off.

There was a handle at each end of this 'boat' which if you jerked it, took the other person by surprise and over they'd go!

Bill further testified a lot lived in the Hall as staff; four shared one bedroom. They were: the two Richards brothers; a Tom Sutton who was the son of the wheelwright and his sister who also lived in.

Old Mrs Hulme, the grandmother, would come to the back stairs and call up, "its six o'clock, time you were up". In recounting this, Bill failed to acknowledge that they were young men whereas she a grandmother had obviously been up even earlier in order to give them a call. Tom Hanmer who lived at Charlie Green was the chief drainage worker. Three girls lived in, Bill's sister who made the cheese, a Miss Schofield and another sewing-machine worker.

Crosemere Hall, according to Bill was THE cheese-making farm in the area; he used to carry the milk buckets on a yoke across his shoulders, tipping it down into vats. There is a large photograph of all the milkers when dairy farming was in its heyday.

A further task of Bill's around the farm was to take out all the carpets when required and give them a good beating with a carpet beater.

At harvest time a hot meal was delivered to the men in the field. A photograph of the harvesters shows a man holding a cider-flagon; it was actually an old Rennet bottle being reused. Rennet was bought from the factory at Ellesmere and used in the production of cheese. The Rennet factory used to throw 'waste' over a piece of ground nearby and this attracted lots and lots of seagulls. You can still see the name of the Rennet factory above Dykes in Ellesmere.

For the benefit of the uninitiated such as myself, I took the pains to look up in the Oxford Dictionary what the definition of Rennet actually says;

1. Curdled milk found in the stomach of an unweaned calf containing rennin and used in curdling milk for cheese, junket etc.

2. A preparation containing rennin made from the stomach membrane of a calf or from certain fungi for the same purpose.

3. Rennin is an enzyme secreted into the stomach of an unweaned mammal causing the clotting of milk.

Well, that puts me on track and anyone else who may have been unaware!

I have veered off course with all this high tech. discourse so I'll return to activities within the Hall.

At Christmas time the house overflowed with family and a tradition they followed many years ago was to hang the top of an inverted Holly tree from the rafters and decorate it.

Mrs Hulme always remembers her mother-in-law as a most generous hostess who loved entertaining and always seemed to have a full house, bridge parties etc. She was an excellent cook and her own recipe book has been preserved and handed down in the family.

Shade Oak

The name of the Hall or manor 'Shade Oak' is derived from the magnificent oak tree within whose shade it once stood. The tree was felled in 1922 when it was no longer considered safe. No tree was ever planted as a replacement.

The buildings and barns of this black and white house were originally surrounded by a deep moat as were its neighbouring manors of Wycherley, Petton and Stanwardine-in-the-Wood. The two latter manors were said to be marked as 'forts' on an old map. The moat has largely been filled in, but in the 1950s work on the site revealed large slabs of stone indicating the position of the drawbridge. Earlier that year a cannon ball was found at a depth of about three feet between the house and barn and the site of the drawbridge.

About seven hundred yards to the North West of the manor and rising above the surrounding flat countryside is Whinnet Hill. This was described as a long oval grass-covered mound which was possibly an earthwork mound of the Neolithic period and later used by the Saxons.

Legend has it a battle was fought within this region but no proof exists of this.

Shade Oak built in Tudor Style may occupy the site of an earlier manor house but if so no traces of the original exist. The earliest recorded date is within the house carved in the oak panelling – 1659. The previous recorded description of the house, to which I now refer, was written about 1958. The farming then was 'dairy farming'. A massive oak, iron studded door to the dairy is referred to; the size and grandeur suggested it would once perhaps have been a door from elsewhere in the house – perhaps a main entrance.

A Roger Finch owned Shade Oak in 1724; a Richard Williamson in 1776 and a century on, Pembrey Hollands was proprietor. This man had twelve sons who all boarded at a school in

Chester travelling to do so using packhorses. It is probable that William Powell was the next occupant. A small gravestone at Weston Lullingfields' graveyard testifies to 'death by drowning' said to be in the moat, of his eighteen-month-old daughter. He in turn was followed by Richard Hinton as a tenant farmer of Shade Oak as it was part of the Oteley Estate. In 1921 Samuel Hockenhull of nearby Wycherley Hall bought Shade Oak for his son –William Henry.

He died in 1946, leaving Shade Oak to his wife and younger son. The house is still in the possession of the Hockenhull family.

Shade Oak was established in 1973 as a home of National Hunt Racing and Breeding by David Hockenhull and his wife Ann. It is now run by David and Ann, their son Peter and his wife Emma.

Shade Oak as a house has reflected the changing faces of architecture. Timber-framed houses with brick-infilling during the Tudor period fell out of fashion from Queen Anne's time up to mid-Victorian times. Anybody blessed with such a house did all they could to disguise the 'old fashioned' timber built house.

 Plaster was the cheapest and quickest means of a cover-up or alternatively bricking over external features from ground to eaves where the effect was very obviously on show. When the tide of fashion turned again and the antiquity of the original features was to be prized, then patient restoration to reveal all, where possible, was applied. Coats of paint hiding lovely oak panelling took hours to remove.

During some time of the restoration work an underground passageway was discovered. By lifting two sloping boards a four feet drop into a cellar was revealed only six feet from the entrance to an underground passage.

It is believed the passage originally led either to the moat, even under it or to the drawbridge. The bricked up entrance is still intact though the passage no longer exists. Was it a priest hole for concealing a visiting priest? Drawbridges and moats being for defence purposes, an underground escape route would not have been created unless troubled times suggested the need. Retrieval of a cannonball also indicates a hostile attack, very different from the peaceful surroundings today.

Frankton Grange

This house was comparable in size to perhaps Stanwardine or Petton Hall. A very large residence with a staff in its heyday of twenty to twenty-eight servants, male and female such as kitchen staff, cook, pantry-boy, maids, grooms and gardeners, butler, coachman and sewing maid.

At least three generations of the Robinson family lived there. They carried rank and were; Captain, Major and lastly Commander Robinson. He being the last, died in 1965. Listed in the 1881 census, reading the names of occupants of the Grange made interesting reading when comparing it with today's attitudes and views.

Charles Robinson aged seventy-four, occupation, gentleman. Wife; Euphemia.

Two views of Frankton Grange

The name 'Euphemia' is not one that trips easily off the tongue nor is it easily forgotten.

Nellie Sutton's grandparents worked at the Grange so no doubt Nellie was visiting them when she recalled meeting Euphemia.

The child had collected flowers and been given a vase to put them in; as fast as she placed them in it, Euphemia removed them. This naturally frustrated the young Nellie to such a degree she began to 'cuss' quoted Nellie. The whole object of the exercise on Euphemia's part had been to provoke her and be amused by her 'cussing'.

An incident that created a minor stir of excitement and speculation was to involve the Robinsons. An aeroplane was seen to land in a field belonging to the Marsh's. Some said the aeroplane had run out of fuel but this was not correct. The aeroplane belonged to a Mr Crossley from Burleydam and he was paying court to Miss E Robinson. This obviously was

Frankton Grange and staff

unusual for everyone concerned or otherwise, but it has to be said his attentions were not successful. To return to the census; the son and daughter-in-law of Charles Robinson lived at the Grange with their one year old son.

The listed servants living-in (many had cottages on the estate and did not live-in) was also of interest.

Harry Dinn	servant-footman,	b. London
Ann Gough	servant-housemaid	b. local
Alice Todd	servant-lady's maid	b. Bedhampton, Hampshire.
Ann Davies	servant-nurse aged 48yrs.	b. South Shropshire
Esther Appleby	nurse (midwife) aged 46yrs.	b. London, Middlesex

The position in the house does not confine itself to their 'employ' but precedes it by 'Servant'.

The distance selected servants come from is of note and the ages of the two employed for childcare could be ones that have been retained having reared the previous generation.

Euphemia was referred to as a leading light in the WI with a Mrs Higginson, the WI being held in either the Annexe or the School.

A cottage called Gardener's Cottage that still carries that name today is now a considerably extended private home. It used to be the home of the head gardener of the estate. There was also a lodge or gatehouse, home of Philip Williams, and another lodge occupied by the butler. Various other staff also had tied cottages. There is a large photograph of the Grange with the staff ranged in front of it on the gravel drive, all in their respective uniforms. Another smaller photograph of the house taken in the garden is of two ladies which depicts a very gracious age.

The Robinsons as a family played quite a part in certain aspects of Cockshutt life.

The church benefited handsomely from their generosity, so subsequently the name of Robinson meant a lot to Cockshutt. Nicholas Robinson played an important part in the church affairs.

In 1882 he was nominated Vicar's Warden, a year in which the clock was regilded.

Contributions to the church in memory of family members reflect their high standing in Cockshutt.

The care and maintenance and updating of the Grange was obviously non–existent and the property was in decline. It seems very sad that no consideration was given to salvaging and preserving it for future generations. Properties on this scale are few and far between depicting a very different aspect of our social history.

Wackley History

Wackley Lodge Farm belonged to the Brownlow Estates of the Earl Brownlow. The brick construction of the farmhouse is described as a 'Georgian brick and slate building' and in the 1998 Sales Catalogue it is described as having some twentieth century extensions. It would be hard to fix a date on the house construction because the present owners have found several internal walls to be timber and plaster. The levels of both downstairs and upstairs floors vary thereby creating steps up and down into some of the rooms.

The cheese rooms are for example well below the natural floor level. It would appear the Georgian construction has enveloped an original smaller wood/plaster house.

There is a large sandstone cellar under the main house which is the footprint of the property. A gutter/drainpipe to the rear of the house has the date 1898. The main house has five bedrooms and in total thirteen rooms. The rear wing of the house, no longer accessible from inside, is the part of the property which used to house living–in farm hands and domestic staff; it has seven bedrooms.

The water for the property is not supplied by Severn Trent; the house has two wells and a further well for rainwater.

A unique feature amongst the main outbuildings is a block called a 'Higgory' (right). This basically was a row of well built pigsties over which is an upper level which housed hens.

Reading through the deeds of the property, in 1898 the Earl Brownlow was engaged in raising by mortgage the sum of £25,000 putting Wackley as surety.

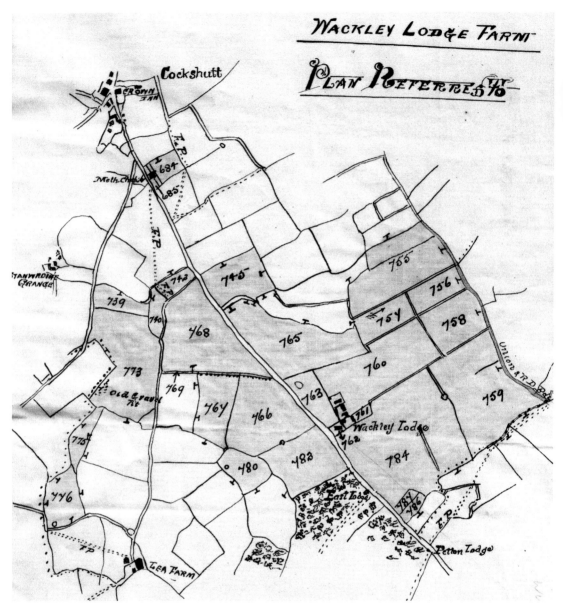

WACKLEY LODGE FARM

PLAN REFERRED TO

Repeatedly throughout any transfer of the property, a clause is always included that all beds, veins and seams of coal, brick-clay, sand and other minerals at a greater depth than 100ft from the surface are not transferred with the property.

By 1903, the interest on the loaned money was paid, so a further £6,000 was sought and paid by the Trustees.

The Earl died in 1927 with the sum of £29,000 outstanding.

This was paid by Richard Christopher Tower. Wackley was then sold out of the Brownlow Estates in July 1930, the new purchasers being jointly Margaret Elizabeth Emberton, Charles

Clockwise from Top left, Wackley yard in neglected state, Wackley yard restored, Frontage to the road overgrown, House and frontage restored.

Edward Emberton and Badon Blake. From this date the ownership of Wackley remained in the hands of the Emberton family, passing from father to son.

The exchange of ownership in 1998 saw the usage of Wackley having been a productive arable and stock farm, change to be a Reclamation Business of countrywide renown. Some acreage is rented out but parcels of land had already been sold prior to 1998 to other local farmers. The new owners, Mr and Mrs Powell took over a property in great need of restoration work as years of neglect had seen the buildings and yards neglected and totally overgrown with weeds. The presentation now is one of immaculate organisation with manicured grounds that are a credit to the owners.

Wackley under the Embertons
(an account by Charlie Emberton)

Charlie Emberton said his father worked in 1904 at the age of sixteen as a tenant farmer at Wackley Farm which belonged to Mrs Cunliffe of Petton Hall.

His brother farmed at Wackley Lodge Farm which belonged to the Bridgewater Estate. A letter survives from Colonel Ferral absolving him from military service as at sixteen he was farming on his own. Extra rations were allowed and applied for when threshing was taking place on the farm, the policy being, there were more men working on the farm, therefore extra mouths to feed. The men used to move from farm to farm as a team and the farmer's wife had to feed them; this would not have been possible without the extra rations.

Mrs Cunliffe used to write to Charlie's father and he said she had dreadful handwriting and always wrote on black edged paper.

She had a lot of 'military members' in the family so therefore there seemed always to be someone for whom they were 'in mourning'. True or not, this was their interpretation!

Mrs Cunliffe died in 1926; she was the last surviving member of the family. When Charlie's grandfather died, his father bought Wackley Farm. Grandfather had always attended Petton Church but was buried under the shade of a tree at Cockshutt Church.

Letters from Lord Brownlow's Estate to his father tried to persuade him to buy Petton Hall for £3,000; this was beyond his financial means. A Burlton man bought it and thought he could run it from his office – he couldn't. It brought a 1,000 people to the sale. There were twelve cottages belonging to the Petton Estate with Wackley. "Father buying the farm could not afford the cottages so the agent suggested they meet at the 'Raven' in Shrewsbury. After a few whiskies, the agent - Towler, said they would 'toss for it'- if father won he got the cottages. Father won!" There are actual documents which show this transaction.

Charlie's father served on the District Council for fifty years to March 1962.

Charlie's early memories (he is now 77/78) were of attending Cockshutt School. He walked to school as a young child from Wackley but in later years he cycled.

He recalled a Miss Young and a Miss Collins as teachers. He retained his confirmation book and another school book that his father was given for regular attendance in 1896 signed by Mr Henry Wilcox. The Head teacher was Mr John Moore.

All the naming in their family in the male line is a C. Emberton or Charles Edward Emberton in full.

When it came to eating his school dinner, he ate his sandwiches in the Red Lion. He went to Ellesmere College in 1937 at ten years of age. His aunt died in the influenza epidemic of 1918; she was only twenty-six years old.

Wackley Lodge Farm *(seen though the eyes of an employee)*

Percy Lunt left school at fourteen and worked at The Grange (Dickin's) where he did milking and odd jobs i.e. farm work. In 1935, at the age of eighteen he took employment at Wackley which was farmed by Mr Joe Emberton. Wackley was a large mixed farm with approximately 100 acres of arable crops. The remainder was grass. There were between sixty and seventy milking cows which were all hand milked and there were also sheep and pigs.

There were six full time men working the farm, with extra casual labour taken on at the busy times, particularly at harvest.

Percy Lunt worked with the horses along with Moses Hanmer and they started work at 6.30 am and finished at 5.30 pm.

He lived in, along with two other men and one or two girls. He was paid one guinea a week and his keep. He would get all his meals but sometimes if they were ploughing etc. a fair distance from the farm, they would have sandwiches and would not get back to have their dinner until 3.00 pm, after which they would have to clean down the horses and feed them.

Those 'living-in' would eat separately from the family and their meals would be taken in the kitchen.

Wackley had six working horses and for ploughing they normally used two horses, but if the land was heavy going they would sometimes use three.

Wackley also took colts from other farms and they had to be broken-in and then reined alongside the other horses until they were returned to their owners as good working horses.

He recalls one horse that was brought to them by Mr Pickering who had bought it from a sale at Lee. The horse was prone to kicking out with her back legs and so they had to be very careful and ever watchful of her actions. Gradually they trained her to farm work and she was returned to Mr Pickering. He sold her to a man who ran a Timber business in Shrewsbury and one day she kicked out and killed the man!

He remembers how they used to have a pony and cart which he used for taking sheep and pigs to market at either Shrewsbury or Oswestry (usually about twenty sheep or a litter of pigs – approximately ten or twelve).

The milk produced on the farm was made into cheese which would be sold at market (probably Ellesmere) and cheese fairs.

Whey from the cheese-making process was separated and whey cream used for making whey butter (which was softer in consistency than butter made from cream) The remaining whey would be fed to the pigs.

Joe Emberton had a brother Tom who farmed at Ferney Hough.

Tom and his wife moved into Wackley and Tom sometimes used to do some milking etc. and his wife helped in the house. They had a Morris car, but up until then transport for the family had been a pony and trap.

Percy worked at Wackley for three years.

The Crosemere Farms

The bottom of Crosemere Lane forks into two, one road to the right going to English Frankton, Loppington and eventually to Wem. The other lane continues straight ahead to the junction of Porter Lane crossing this road and going on into Draw Well Lane leading to the Mere. At the point where the lane divides, there was a farm to the right called Crosemere Farm. The division of the roads created a triangle on which stood Crosemere Manor Farm and crossing Porter Road on the left stood Crosemere Grange Farm. For present day

reference none exist as farms today within the village. Crosemere Farmhouse itself is now divided into two separate houses. The stockyard was brick by brick removed and an estate of modern houses has replaced the once busy yard. The actual farm stock and running of Crosemere Farm was transferred to a new purpose-built farm (top left) that continues to flourish on the other side of the A528, just before Magpie Hall.

The Manor House was not being farmed in latter years and was a private dwelling; it has since been demolished and now two very beautiful modern houses stand in well-tended gardens with sufficient land on the site to complete a probable two or three more houses. The original Manor Farm is shown centre left.

The site has little to remind one of what once stood there; a brook with ornamental bridges over it would be the nearest landmark but then, nature allowed it to ripple and patter over the stones, bedecked

with water weeds and wild flowers in no way achieving today's ornamental effect. Todays replacement Manor is shown at the bottom of the previous page.

The Grange was recently sold, the property has been renovated and updated as a private dwelling house and is no longer a working farm.

The complexity of naming these farms with such little variance for the names of each was made even more confusing by the occupants all sharing the same family name of 'Marsh'. It was interesting and complex to sort out and we were greatly helped by an old lady in Ruyton-XI-Towns who had been born and raised at Crosemere Farm along with six siblings.

Betty (Elizabeth) Moseley nee Marsh, aged ninety-five years was a wonderful character to talk to, albeit via her daughter Margaret. She was wheelchair bound, very frail and profoundly deaf. She'd suffered a stroke, had had cataracts removed from her eyes and had osteoporosis. Conversation with her was conducted by her daughter Margaret; visual aids such as photographs and some written work made the breakthrough possible. Despite all these difficulties we found a very mentally alert old lady who managed to convey a very wicked sense of humour and was a source of information on anything presented to her. Her failing strength and age meant that despite her willingness to help, we had to stop the pressure of questions because it was too physically tiring for her.

Had all this been possible a couple of years earlier, we knew she would have so enjoyed expounding on her recollections. We left feeling great respect for a very remarkable old lady; we equally felt great regard for Margaret who took time out to be so helpful, in a daily life that was obviously very busy.

One of the first observations made by Betty was to reprimand us and today's powers that be, for changing the spelling of Crosemere. It was always spelt Croesmere and pronounced

'Cro-es-mere!'

We left with a very complicated family tree which showed the links between the three farms and also showed the link to Crosemere Hall and the Hulme family.

We can see on the family tree, where the Hulmes joined the Marsh family. Accordingly we were told the Hulmes came from Fennymere and before that from Cheshire. We also knew that the Dickin family linked into this tree by marriage and the family tree showed where.

The details of the family members will not be of interest to readers but selected items might be.

Betty was born in 1908, one of seven children. She had a brother William Stanley whose name is on the commemorative plaque in church; he was killed in 1917 aged 21 years. We have photocopied a couple of embroidered postcards he had sent to his mother. His brother, Richard James, known as Jim volunteered for the army; he was the eldest boy and he was refused. He had fallen out of a damson tree and broken his arm and was therefore not accepted by them.

He married a cousin from the Manor; his father bought the Grange for him to farm but when he (the father) died the mother made Jim a joint tenant with her so he couldn't be put out.

The shared tenancy was a double-edged sword because she also made him sign the pledge at twenty years of age! Jim was Cyril Marsh's father.

One sister, Frances had been regarded as a 'blue stocking' because she was clever and went to Oswestry Girls' High School and then went on to London to complete her education by 1919. That would be unusual for the period for a girl.

Betty is shown in a delightful picture (left) as a very sweet faced little girl, standing by her pet lamb.

Her grandfather farmed at both the Manor and Crosemere farm. We have a photograph of William and Fanny Marsh taken in 1901 with their eleven children. They were the next generation to farm there after the grandfather. Two of Betty's sisters, Sarah and May, remained at home to care for their parents and then eventually retired to Ellesmere.

The next generation of Cyril's family, a sister, cared for Jim when he retired to Myddle. Betty herself is now being cared for by her daughter Margaret. It is not very often in our modern day that the elderly are still cared for by family. Our circumstances and homes do not always make this possible.

The next generation known by many today, were Jim's children at Crosemere Grange (left). Cyril Marsh married Joan and had two children, Roy and Sylvia.

Cyril was one of six children – the youngest child Stanley died at twenty-two months with meningitis. This is a complaint to strike fear in a home today although we know there are drugs to ward off its severity. In 1930 there would be no such hope. Cyril retired to Oswestry and the farm was sold.

Betty did recount also that her mother – Emma (nee Hulme) had a brother who had farmed at Kenwick Lodge and had nine children. One child, George, had served in the 1st World War; he survived it but spent some time in Shelton suffering with shell-shock. It was a very cruel war.

Kenwick Lodge Farm

Stanley Hulme retired from farming at Kenwick Lodge Farm (left) in 1985 having farmed there since he was twenty. The sale of farm stock was held on the 15th March 1985 when the final curtain was drawn on a very long agricultural career.

He moved there as a child with his father, James Hulme; he was one of nine children, three girls and six boys.

The farm was part of the Earl of Bridgewater's Estate so they were always tenant farmers.

When asked to give some description of Kenwick Lodge as a house externally or internally he said the house was almost a replica of Birch Hall in Ellesmere. When he actually went around the Hall, he felt it was quite weird to go from room to room but not be seeing his own personal effects there.

As a boy, Stanley attended Cockshutt School, the Head being

Mr Hassall; he described him as a very cruel man and told the story of two children, the 'Price boys' that qualified such a comment. The father was an agricultural worker who had to be up and out early leaving the boys to fend for themselves for both dressing and getting their breakfast. Their mother was dead. If the children, who were walking a considerable distance to school, were late, he caned them. Nothing can be added to that, no justification, just pity looking back over the years to a very sad situation. Stanley was at Cockshutt School from five to eleven years of age; he then went as a 'termly' boarder to Tilly House, Wem. The other boys in the family had been allowed to cycle this distance and not had to board but because he was undersize for his age, it was decided it would be best if he boarded. He hated it and resented this isolation from the family but had to accept it, until the age of fourteen when he left school.

He was friends all his life with a series of well known figures in the area, one being his namesake Stanley Hulme from Crosemere Hall.

He said "there weren't too many Stanleys in the area, the parents of both had been friends, so why with the same surname did they proceed to Christen their respective children – Stanley, it didn't seem reasonable". His nickname of 'Stumpy' which again he disliked was one way he could be distinguished from the other Stanley.

His elder brothers moved away from home, four of them going into farming in other areas of Shropshire. As he grew up it was therefore expected that he would work alongside his father. His father remained in charge of the running of the farm but Stanley was the trainee to its management. They had one 'live-in farm hand'.

The farm had in total 278 acres and was classed as being mixed farming or arable. They had on average more than 100 British Friesian cows, kept hens for domestic purposes and had some sheep.

Feed supplies for the animals and lime for the land were delivered from Weston Wharf. A steam-powered lorry made the delivery.

Minerals were fed to the cows in their feed and water for their drinking was catered for by large ponds on the land in the days before they had mains water. Water for the household use was from two sources - one being soft water collected in butts off the house and used for washing, the second source being from a well. If the pump in the well failed, Stanley remembered being winched down on a rope; it was 22 yards or 66 feet which sounds even worse, before you reached the water. It was approximately 1953 before they had mains water and then the cows also benefited by the supply as a water feed could be supplied to various troughs placed between some fields.

The household had rigged up an electrically-powered pump as an approach to updating the water supply, in one of the open sheds.

Stanley remembered in those early days of hand milking, a Miss Parry walking up from the village twice a day for the milking; that would mean her being there to start work at 6.00 am regardless of the weather and for this seven days'a week task she was paid five shillings.

Finally Stanley tells of a cottage for an agricultural labourer working at Kenwick Lodge in the row of four houses just after the village hall as you leave Cockshutt for Ellesmere. Others in the row belonged to other farmers in the area.

Once the mains water was on supply, Stanley put iron bars over the well to cap it and then concreted the yard but warned later tenants that the well site could be a potentially weak spot if heavy plant was using the yard.

The domestic arrangements of the farm in those early days was not something Stanley had cause to remember too clearly but he did recall that wash-day before electricity and mains water was a very long task for those involved in the laundering of the clothes etc. The brick built copper had to have a fire lit beneath it and all water used to fill it was brought by hand from either the butt or the well. The dairy made an addition to the amount of washing to be done on top of that of the household.

Cheese produced on the farm was generally sold at Wem as his parents tended to prefer Wem to Ellesmere and that included the attendance of the Doctor when required.

For many years the daily collection of milk was by Joe Guest now aged 93 years. He lives in Ellesmere and still feels fit enough to cycle to his favourite pub, the Railway. He recently attended the funeral of Stanley Hulme of the Hall, but felt he had to arrange a lift as cycling to Cockshutt might prove to be a bit taxing!

He first of all began collecting the milk churns on a flat-topped wagon and later progressed to the milk tankers. Milk was taken to the United Dairies.

In about 1940 when Stanley was seriously employed and involved with the farm, the Army billeted men to the farm. They were soldiers with trades and were supposed to be out on night duty but invariably only one kept the night patrol. At the entrance gate they sometimes had a beacon lit, powered by a diesel generator. It would appear there for a variable space of time and then be removed by machine to some other area out of Shropshire, this movement and length of stay being variable in order to create land-marking confusion to enemy bombers. The Ministry of Food during this wartime period dictated exactly what had to be ploughed and grown, for example beet or potatoes, as war years were a great strain on the nation's food supply.

These war years also, saw an insurgence of troops in the area; Americans! They started something previously never heard of locally and that was black and white dance nights in Wem. It was hoped that people's colour prejudice would in some way inhibit any unruly behaviour between the girls and soldiers.

Describing his social life in the area he told how in his youth he played cricket sometimes on the area which is now the housing estate of The Briars or on the Townsend Field.

He went to the visiting funfair as a boy but a hobby that grew to be a lifelong skill and source of enjoyment was dancing. He attended Rosa Hubbard's ballroom dance school in Shrewsbury until the skill was mastered (not staying to take it on to medal level) and never looked back. He occasionally went to Gwilliams at Brook House but more frequently went to the dances held upstairs in the old Town Hall in Ellesmere. Downstairs there was a bar and also a cinema.

He attended the Farmers' Dance nights until only recently. Tennis was played on a court at the back of the school garden which was opposite the present day school.

There were also two cottages on this side of the road, one of which had been the original school and next door being the school house; Stanley remembers when it was voting day in the elections, the school no longer occupying these premises, one was used for the Conservative vote and the other for the Labour vote. No mention of the Liberals and certainly no worry about political correctness!

The Crown and the Red Lion were later to become a base for much revelry with his circle of friends and their choice of which inn to sponsor depended as much as anything on the current landlord.

At one time he recounted that the licensee of the Red Lion was called in to the Police Station in Ellesmere and asked if the pub ever closed and if not weren't they afraid of losing the Licence?

The reply that Gaffa (Jack) Dickin owned the pub, the slaughterhouse and butchers behind and a farm meant he supposed he wasn't overly concerned. The next night the Sergeant appeared at the bar and is supposed to have said if he couldn't beat them he might as well join them. This account may have grown with the telling!

Foot and Mouth broke out in the area in 1961 with only a few cases in the locality. A restriction order on movement of livestock and the necessary precautions to prevent the spread of the disease meant the outbreak was not too severe except to those it affected. There was a second outbreak in 1967 and more farms were affected but Kenwick Lodge was again fortunate to escape it. They took the usual precautions; milk to be collected and churns being returned were all left at the gate. Corn feed being delivered was again left at the gate. Although they didn't suffer the loss of cattle the restrictive process for animal movement meant they were experiencing and heading towards a financial crisis because they had fifty breeding sows and couldn't sell them.

Top House Farm

Top House Farm is a long rectangular building which faces south. The original dairy was on the north-west corner of the house with doors giving access to both the yard and the house; it was always a very cold room, hence its usage.

The kitchen had a large inglenook which had once been its source for cooking and heat but in more modern times housed the Rayburn. There were beams in the ceiling of this room. There was a well outside which still had the remains of the old generator beside the pump for the days when it had been used for extracting the water. Mains water came to the farm in 1953 and it was one of the last properties in the area to get power.

Margaret and Alf Johnson took over the farm in 1976 and were there until 1997. They took over from a Mr Thelwell and before him was a family called Harrison.

The Park Estate had been variously owned by the Earl of Bridgewater (Lord Brownlow), then by the Prudential and also by Mercantile and General.

Originally before various farms were sold off, the Estate covered between 7,000 and 8,000 acres. Top House farm was one of the last farms in the area to use horses. Mr Thelwell was a very good milk supplier, a fact one could ascertain by just looking at the enormous stand by the gate where the 10-gallon milk churns stood. The churns were on a raised stand so that when full the milk collector could just roll the churns across and onto his flat wagon. Mr Thelwell had what was called a 'flying herd'. He bought the cows, milked them and sold them on. He kept a very good milk parlour.

Alf gradually established changes in how he ran the farm. He built up a Pedigree herd that he bred himself, of British Friesian cows and had at one time one hundred cows. Cows once stood in the cowsheds in stalls, sometimes for nearly six months, tethered with a halter around the neck, unable to make any free movement. Alf built sleeping quarters for them known as cubicles. The cow had really an enlargement of the original stall by this method. It did not wear a halter, had a food manger and a straw bedding area where it could lie down.

He also had an open shed area where several cows could be kept, free to move or lie down in an area of bedding straw. They had water troughs and food supplies.

He had one part-time hand and one full-time hand. The milk was sent to the Ellesmere Dairy in 1985.

The Milk Marketing Board gave out quotas for the farm stipulating a limit on the milk supply. If one exceeded the quota for their farm they were to be penalised.

To combat this excess milk they needed an outlet; it is exceedingly hard to dispose of surplus milk - one can't just throw it away or the water table would suffer. Alf was very innovative and paid to install an ice-cream parlour and bought the necessary equipment and began making ice-cream. They were fortunate enough to have a very good Italian recipe, so the ice-cream produced was of excellent quality and taste. He and Margaret then had to work out a marketing strategy to sell it and did so very successfully, so much so that today years after their retirement, 'Top House Farm Ice-cream' is still a very popular brand.

The farm covered 249 acres and was mixed farming. The cereals grown; wheat and barley, were for their own use. The crops generated feed for the animals which was processed; it supplied bedding and hay for eating.

There were signs of two cottages having been occupied on one part of the land but only the footings and the signs of a stone road were the clues to their existence. In their own farmhouse some windows were boarded up without any logical reason why this should have happened.

The possibility being that the window tax introduced by William Pitt in the early 1800s saw many houses similarly block up windows in order to evade paying the tax.

In 1967 Foot & Mouth disease had cleared many of the livestock in this region, Mr Thelwell's included. Although he did gradually pick up from this, his days of farming were coming to a close, hence the sale in 1976.

East Lodge built 1892

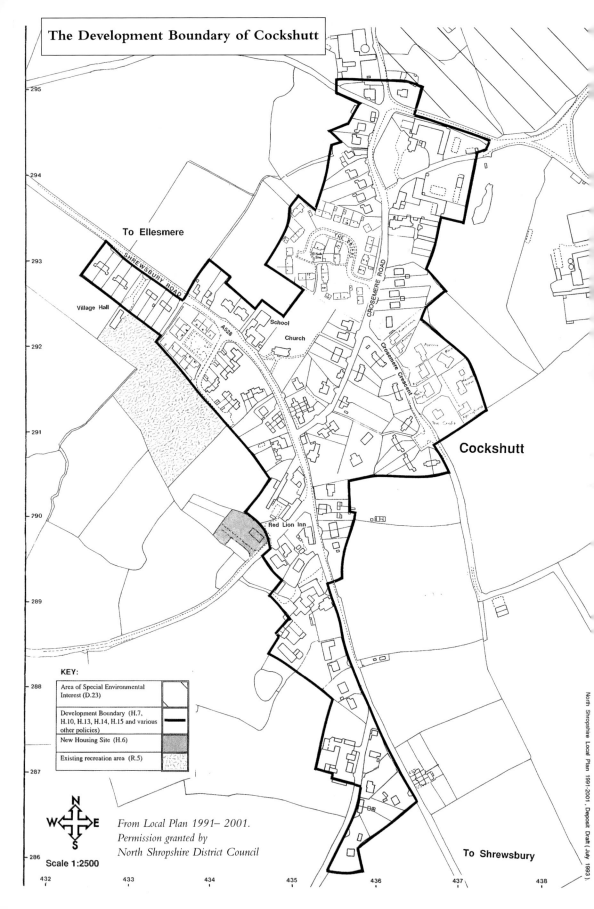

The Development Boundary of Cockshutt

To Ellesmere

Village Hall

School

Church

SHREWSBURY ROAD

A528

CROSEMERE ROAD

Crosemere Crescent

The Croft

Cockshutt

Red Lion Inn

KEY:

Area of Special Environmental Interest (D.23)	
Development Boundary (H.7, H.10, H.13, H.14, H.15 and various other policies)	
New Housing Site (H.6)	
Existing recreation area (R.5)	

From Local Plan 1991– 2001.
Permission granted by
North Shropshire District Council

To Shrewsbury

Scale 1:2500

North Shropshire Local Plan 1991-2001, Deposit Draft (July 1993).

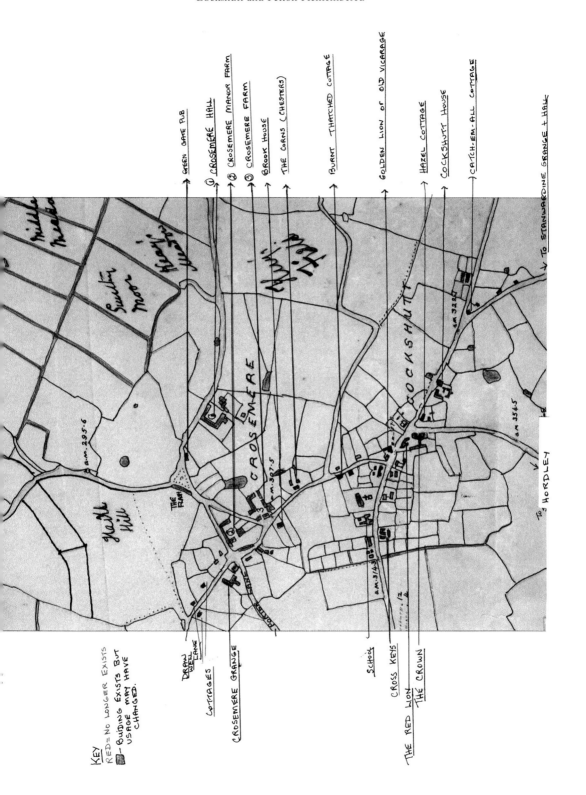

Labels (top, pointing down into map):
GREEN GAME PUB
① CROSEMERE HALL
② CROSEMERE MANOR FARM
③ CROSEMERE FARM
BROOK HOUSE
THE CORNS (CHESTERS)
BURNT THATCHED COTTAGE
GOLDEN LION OF OLD VICARAGE
HAZEL COTTAGE
COCKSHUTT HOUSE
CATCH-EM-ALL COTTAGE
→ TO STANWARDINE GRANGE + HALL

Map place names: Middle Meadow, Sandy Moor, Sharp Hill, CROSEMERE, COCKSHUTT, THE RAW, To HORDLEY

KEY
RED = NO LONGER EXISTS
■ = BUILDING EXISTS BUT USAGE MAY HAVE CHANGED.

Bottom labels:
DRAW WELL LANE
COTTAGES
CROSEMERE GRANGE
SCHOOL
CROSS KEYS
THE RED LION
THE CROWN

Champion Ploughman

We cannot refer to farms without mentioning the skill of ploughing which was often the subject of local competitions and, for some, even became legendary when the competitions entered into the realms of All England Championships.

A well-known character in the Ploughing Championships was Mr Tom Evans of East Lodge, Shrewsbury Road. He worked at Top House Farm for a short period of two years under Mr Thelwell and attended his horses but before and after that period he had worked on other farms, driven lorries and so forth. He excelled in the skill of ploughing and farmers where he worked would allow him to practise on their land but in his own time. His list of championships was most impressive; British Isles Champion; British National Champion; All England Champion and also he earned the same titles in Ireland and Wales.

There weren't large sums of money to be gained in these competitions - sums of £8 or £10 being the average in those days. In 1949-50 to enter into these championship events you had first of all to enter into the Cruckton Ploughing Event. Farmers would then back the winner which paid for the self-financing of travel and entrance fees. Some would be willing to lend horses to be used. If at that time you didn't win that event, you were not eligible for the higher competition levels.

Tom said he learnt his ploughing skills as a young boy; his father worked on a farm and horses were the means of labour then. He took his father's lunch to the field in his own school dinner time and he'd take the horses a length or two while he was there and then return to school.

He left school and worked on a farm at the age of fourteen. He worked a fifty hour week for 10/- pay. Locally in Shropshire (Tom was born over the border in Wales) he learnt a lot

Tom Evans Champion Ploughman

of his horse handling skills to the championship levels from 'Tom the Lion'. Tom had his own methods for achieving these very skilled results: he worked a pair of Shire horses but they walked on the level alongside of the furrow.

Many pairs of horses worked with one walking in the furrow and the other one on the level.

The Tottery or Swingle Trees as they were called were wooden rods which were attached to the traces and kept them in their place when horses were ploughing. They could be altered in their attachment to the plough. Tom had some Tottery made to his specifications from Bill Humphreys.

Chains made a further adjustment. (Swingle trees are Old English but 'tottery' seems to be local word to this area and could be derived from the Old Dutch meaning 'to swing' which I suppose is the sort of movement they made).

Today Tom says maybe only a couple of highly skilled Ploughmen will enter a competition; the Shire horses now cost thousands of pounds.

He expected to pay a top price of about eighty guineas; the horse standing 15 two-thirds hands on average. He usually ploughed $6^1/2$ inches deep and 7 inches wide. The ground to plough could be very variable from area to area. Sometimes he would go and have to take on a pair of horses he'd never seen or handled before.

The photographs taken at these events showed marquees, huge crowds and other events all happening within fairly close range. Even the other competitors who could number in those days up to twenty-two, would be working their furrow in close proximity. Their turning and calls could coincide with your horse needing to ignore the nearby instructions. 'Tom the Lion' gave sound advice on how to counteract this.

The perfect furrow

'Go with rags in your pocket and an ounce of tobacco twist. When interruption is threatened – put rags inside the horse's ears so he couldn't hear and put some twist around the bit and it would give the horse something else to think about!'

I can't vouch for whether this advice was followed but Tom the Lion lived and breathed ploughing according to Tom, so therefore the results Tom achieved may owe something to heeding this advice.

Some of his horses did not react well to blinkers or the bit and he wouldn't use them if the horse didn't respond to them.

The competitors entering these ploughing events came from Cornwall, Scotland, Somerset, Ireland. Tom would also travel to follow and enter events. In order to get to some of these distant places he recounted buying cars for sums such as £10 or even £16.

When working at Top House farm he worked alongside Bill Price and Alf Smith. He recalled Tom Thelwell buying a grey colt; they put it in the loose box and then put the mouth tackle on it and left it for a day.

Then they took it to Harry Pratt the blacksmith to have it shod. Tom then decided to ride it back to Top House Farm. It took off up Park Lane like a rocket, with sparks flying off its new shoes. Tom managed to turn it at the top of the lane but finished up at the same breakneck speed hurtling back to Cockshutt. The third time going back up the hill again it finally gave in and walked calmly into the yard.

They wasted no time then, by later in the day setting it to the plough. It was broken-in and caused no further problems. Ideally Tom said that any horse to be broken-in and set to the plough should first have been ridden.

Observing as we talked, the speed of cars traveling to and fro from Shrewsbury he observed that many of the fields on this route may not have field gates.

Going back to before the nineteen-fifties he said droving up to thirty animals to the Smithfield Market in Shrewsbury was not unusual. The gates of all the fields then were always secure or otherwise the cows would invade the crops in the fields.

Another country pursuit which Tom indulged in was airgun shooting; he belonged to the Montgomeryshire Air Gun League.

The target was a box shape within which was a white square. Central to the square was a tiny hole the size of a pencil end. The shot had to enter through this hole - not a near miss - and a bell would ring when you had achieved a Bull's Eye.

The arrival of the tractor and gradually more sophisticated equipment meant the demise of the use of the beautiful Shire horse. No championship could be achieved without a complete rapport between man and the horses. Tom has moved on with all the modern means available in mechanisation today but one only has to observe him look at a photograph of the gentle giants, describing their names, colour and special foibles to know they were extra special to him and we've lost a great deal with their disappearance from our lives. That sadly is progress but men like Tom represent this bygone age and we are most grateful to him for sharing these memories.

Health

The problems and worries that ill-health brings, lurk with every childish ailment and every accident that befalls a worker. With the benefit of age we look back and remember sunny summers, happy occasions, and sickness can't have been too bad as we are here now - we survived. The reality fades!

Paying for a Doctor's visit would not be something one rushed into: the resultant prescription would add even more to the pressure and be a further burden on limited resources. The advice accompanying a visit with regards to 'best treatment' for the patient could also be beyond practical ability of the family. It would for example be difficult to isolate a child when the house was already overcrowded. Adults faced an equally difficult hardship: 'Stay home and rest, recuperate and you'll be fit in no time.' Stay home and there will be no money to put food on the table and pay the rent.

It could finish in no other way than to struggle out and get on with the job. People who paid the monthly subscription to the Oddfellows Club had taken the precaution when they were fit, to put something aside for the days when they were not. The cost wasn't high but it guaranteed help towards the welfare of its members and pays the Doctor's fee.

The person suffering with the tonsillectomy mentioned later was covered by this insurance. It would not be enough to replace the missing wage packet, but at least the Doctor's visit and resulting prescription would be covered. Oddfellows is an organisation that still flourishes to the present day.

Large families mean frequent pregnancies. Where possible, most villagers would know a neighbour who had attended births and self-taught themselves the basic principles of midwifery.

By and large it would work. It would again be doubtful if the proper Midwife or Doctor would be the first to be sought for such an occasion if funds were low. The lack of equipment and medication has over centuries resulted in babies and mothers suffering and even dying as a result. The instructions that they remain confined to bed for the regulatory ten days would be impossible for most women. The man of the house earned the wage so perhaps a grandmother or neighbour or other near kin would step in to help but, with other children to cope with, the sheer luxury of rest would be impossible.

We know now that lying in bed, be it for postnatal care or post-operative care is not good for the patient; the opposite is true, they must be up and out of bed. Just for once the laws of health care being broken would be by fluke, the best thing for the postnatal mother.

The avoidance of prescribed medicines would also result in quack-products being administered. In many cases herbal treatments practised over years would solve basic problems. Other salves were not so desirable and yet would be regularly administered and suffered at the hands of some keen mother or grandmother. I mentioned earlier my own endurance tests. Favourites were brewed up every year ready for winter ills. Large sticks of the chemist's liquorice were purchased – (not the sweetie kind) and boiled up with some other ingredients and bottled. We had rows of cough mixture prepared. Taken with a dilution of hot water it took your breath away and you forgot to cough!

It may even be known to have worked. It had its own side effects as the present day medicines do – no one given a large spoonful of cough mixture would be constipated and yes; you didn't cough!

The lack of services in any populated area will have had its resultant knock-on effects for health. Water draining over surface land where cattle have had a right to graze, pollutes the water. The Education Authority condemned the drinking water for use in the school but every night the children returned to their homes and used this self-same water.

To illustrate how water pollution is a serious problem is proven in nearby Welshampton. The death of the African Prince, Jeremiah Libopuoa Moshueshue visiting there in 1863 caught a fever and died. His death was a result of sewage filtering into underground water systems.

Sewage is a major disposing problem and every earth closet presented this on a daily basis. Going somewhere and burying it means it drains into the water-table.

In the severe winter of 1891-2 there was an outbreak of an influenza epidemic. Hardly a household escaped and although there were no deaths directly attributed to it, great hardship was inflicted on the poor. In 1893 an outbreak of diphtheria occurred where some twenty houses were infected with about 56 cases of it resulting. The unsanitary conditions of the village attracted considerable attention in the local press.

Goods purchased today are overwrapped and zealously purchased by us all.

We require tips to dump the waste because much of the packaging of the products is not biodegradable.

The average cottage would by comparison have produced very little household waste that couldn't be disposed of either on the fire or on the compost heap.

The general lack of services at this point includes lack of pavements, no drainage systems and lack of street lighting.

The problem contributing to flooding in some areas today is the opposite side of the coin : too much paving and tarmac with no natural drainage to soak up excess rain. That is a minor addition I know to the overall global warming that we are told about.

The causes of flooding in some areas can be explained when a farmer with his years of experience in land management adds the following wisdom; the controversial building of houses on unsuitable land in Wem which later floods was very much a man-made problem.

Watercourses altered, blocking drains causes a back flow. The local river is not just confined to the zone they are building on – one looks further to its reaches nearer to Cockshutt. Sweatmere is becoming too 'wet' because drainage from it is not being maintained. The 'Estate' should drain the outlets to the River Roden. The badgers are blocking the drain-runs and so the water is backfilling into the woods. This overflow of water builds up with the alterations in Wem. It seems to make sense to me but there speaks a man very familiar with dealing with nature, understanding it and his main priority not being to build on Brownfield land.

Local Services nowadays would, under the community charges, cover the various aspects described. They would also include the benefit of a police force and fire service.

The former may have attended to gun licences, certainly held sway for the Licensing Act for Public Houses and will have had local criminals to put before the magistrates in the courts. 1847 saw the institution of a fire engine and a year later that 'one pound per annum be allowed for Richard Haycocks for taking care of the Cockshutt Fire Engine which he undertakes subject to the orders of the chapel warden for Cockshutt to exercise a sufficient number of times in a year'. I am sure the present-day churchwardens are happy not to have that on their rota of duties.

Work and Pay

In order to be able to survive, one has to have money to pay for food, clothing, a roof over your head and have some money over (if you are lucky) for pleasure, so one has to work.

We cannot go into detail of all the forms of employment but there were no rights for a wage structure, hours of work or the conditions within employment until fairly recent years.

The many hardships endured by people we have spoken to emphasize the fact that this is within living memory and the most notable factor being the early age they began to work.

For women, the majority were destined to be employed in service. Nancy Roberts was employed as a live-in member of staff for two shillings and six-pence a week.

She no doubt at that time thought that being given two days off a week was not too hard and the demand she was in for ten o'clock at night would be to serve both her interests for safety and also be for the convenience of her employers. The number of hours she would work was not recorded. Another lady – Blodwyn Smith – said her employers 'entertained a lot and gave dinners at night'.

That would mean domestics were washing dishes until the last guest left or perhaps stayed overnight, requiring drinks, fires in bedrooms lit etc. The late night would provide no respite on the following morning when the same early rise would be expected.

A girl leaving school at fourteen could expect to go into service, begin each day at 5.45 am and work endless hours.

Peggy Husbands described dark mornings when she began her work in candle light.

Scrubbing floors, yards, wooden furniture, endless use of cold water, chapped hands and wearing a rough apron of scratchy sacking. Water had to be pumped and carried. If she had the luxury of hot water the addition of washing soda caused her hands to bleed.

Living-in provided no comfortable bedroom to retire to at the end of her labour but rather an unheated attic room with an iron frame bed with a chaff filled mattress. The bare floor and nails in the wall on which to hang a change of clothes completed the picture. She was fourteen.

Nelly Sutton described living-in, in a very large newly built house; the floors were all bare wood which had to be polished both upstairs and down; again water for their every need, be it for the above stairs family or for her cleaning and domestic purposes had to be pumped and carried. For this service she received the princely sum of £2 per month.

In addition, because they must have discovered an aptitude in her, she was set to making endless ready-cut wool rugs the number of which she lost count. Interestingly she fell ill at this place with severe tonsillitis which necessitated being admitted into the Ear Nose & Throat hospital to have her tonsils removed. She was so ill she nearly died and when discharged was sent home in a wheel chair. Her employers saw no reason for her requiring a period of what we would call sick leave for recuperation but thought the problem has gone, and she should return to work.

Doubtless we have in this description the worst case scenario but these are memories of people living today. Not quite the 'good old days'.

There was also a description of a lady called Elizabeth Clawley born in 1861. If we feel fourteen was too young to be going to work as a live-in servant, this lady began work at twelve years of age in Babbinswood.

These children employed at such a young age, we know, were conditioned to know that that was their lot in life, but they must have yearned for their parents, a kind word, and a hug. This was sheer exploitation of children. She married at twenty years of age and lived at Pikesend in a tiny 400-year old cottage with obviously no facilities; here she bore nine children. Shopping in Ellesmere she had to walk laden with her baskets the nine mile round trip whatever the weather. She must have felt very blessed if she was given a lift in a pony and trap. To earn extra money she did stone picking in the fields, potato picking or helped manually with the harvest. Diseases of Rhinder pest, Foot & Mouth and Anthrax all struck severely in her lifetime.

One would think all these tribulations would have been enough to make her view life from her own perspective and yet shortly before Princess Elizabeth became Queen, she made and posted her an iron-holder in red white and blue.

She received a reply thanking her. It was, to say the least, a selfless act in her more than busy life. She and her husband were both employed at Frankton Grange, she being indoor staff and he working outside as a gardener.

The Outskirts of Cockshutt

The study of the homes and people living in the centre of the village leaves the offshoot lanes fringeing the village with some straggling of cottages. We have accounted for the end of the village called The Dobbin, bordering Porter Lane and the A528. If you continue on the main road towards Ellesmere, there is an off-shoot lane to the left; up there is a new farmstead which was built to replace the original Crosemere Farm which used to be in the centre of the village.

Beyond this new farmstead is a house called Magpie Hall (right), occupied in 1911 by a Mr and Mrs Jack

Hanmer and family. It is a strange name for a house and even more so to call it a Hall as by its proportions this would not merit such a grandiose title.

Outcast

The Radio Shropshire interview in the village, when people chipped in with memories and anecdotes of Cockshutt caused the reporter to refer to the Kelly's 1937 Directory and ask who lived at 'Outcast' As a stranger myself this name conjured up a series of imaginings, including pity for anyone who'd been apparently shunned and isolated. Needless to say this was another name that required explaining. A John Bellingham, cowkeeper was listed as living there as had several generations of his family. It was a 'beautiful little place, far from anywhere' recounted one of the radio listeners. It was a Smithy in its time so perhaps 'Cast' refers to the horses casting a shoe, who knows; definitely not a family 'outcast'. In 1871 a Richard Jacks farmer, is listed in the Cassey Directory as living at Old Outcast. Perhaps dialect and pronunciation has changed the title.

Stockett

This hamlet existed just after the turning for Kenwick Springs on the Shrewsbury Road and was also on the other side of the road where one sees fishermen park their vehicles to go down to the Crosemere. There are no houses whatsoever left of this hamlet.

The accepted translation for the name is generally taken from the Anglo-saxon; Stoc is a trunk of a tree, a fenced place and Geat or gate is self explanatory. Stocgeat has become Stockett meaning 'the gate of a fenced place'.

The natural causeway to the mere had at some time been entrenched and perhaps stockaded. In 1872 the cutting of a deep drain lowered the waters of Crosemere by six to ten feet.

It is thought that at one time Crosemere, Sweet Mere (sometimes written as Swet or Sweatmere) and Whatall Moss were once a continuous barrier of water. In this excavation of the ditch in the soil west of the ditch, animal bones, a cylindrical piece of iron and a fragment of bronze which may have been part of a sword sheath, were found.

In 1190-94 David Fitz Owen, Prince of Wales gave Stocgete (Stockett) with its appurtenances to Haughmond Abbey. In 1236 Richard Fitz William, forester of Kenewike, confirmed the pannage of Stockeit and gave assart there to the Abbot of Haughmond.

Two words in that excerpt mean the following;

Pannage is 'the feeding or right of feeding swine in a forest particularly on acorns and mast or, the payment for this'. (One could interpret here that a price was paid to the Abbot for the right to graze swine).

Secondly assart is a piece of land cleared of trees and bushes and fitted for cultivation. Old assarts of land were identified as enclosures of very irregular form with wavy boundaries; they form an irregular field pattern. This really speaks for itself; if trees in woodland have to be felled and cleared the boundaries will be variable. Kenwick was once a forested area of land.

A map of 1836 shows Stockett as a small group of houses and it is believed there may even have been a church or chapel on the site. The 1841 census for Kenwick, Stockett and Whattal numbers only nine houses and fifty five souls. Just how many of the houses can be placed at Stockett is unknown. Reverend Henry Wilcox copied out the Cockshutt Register of Christenings and Burials in the Chapel of Cockshute. Births for Stockett were as thus;

1795   – Thomas Richard

1811   – Charles Davies

1812   – Mary Wilkinson.

He made a further note in the abbreviations, in which he stated 'Stockett no longer exists' – 1879.

CHAPTER 7

FARMING

The opportunity to visit a farm and discuss farming changes that have arisen over the years does require conversation with a farmer! That is not always possible; the weather, the time and the nature of farm-work naturally dictates that the opportunity to 'chat' is going to be hard to arrange!

Individual farms have been visited during the writing of this book and the method of farming applicable to that particular farm has been recorded. It is the overall view of the changing landscape in the Cockshutt region that has not been accounted for.

The site of a farmstead has always been determined by water and the lie of the land; what is then grown relates to these factors. When water was not readily available, wells had to be dug. Ponds had to be created in the fields to provide a place for the animals to drink. The site of the wells and ponds in the fields can be seen in and around our local farms. Mostly the wells are closed, the ponds no longer essential, but left for the wildlife or duck flighting ponds. Piped water to the farms has been a major benefit to the general functioning of the farm.

The size of the actual farmhouse is the first indication of a major change that has transpired over the years. These houses, usually of generous proportions, included a whole range of service rooms for brewing, baking, cheese and butter making and washing. They were also designed to accommodate a large labour force. Many of the men employed slept in almost dormitory conditions. This labour force was not confined to men; women were also needed to fill the role of domestics, cleaning and laundering clothes, milking, cheese and butter making.

The primitive conditions of the time meant that water had to be drawn and carried to perform any of the tasks in and about the farm. There were endless fires to light and maintain indoors; machinery used for both indoor and outdoor tasks was very limited and very basic in the functions it performed.

Today farming is highly mechanised and therefore the labour force has been vastly reduced, those remaining having acquired new skills.

The farmhouse and arrangement of buildings around it reflect the connection between the working functions, such as storing of straw, cowsheds, pigsties, storage of root-feed, fertilisers, stabling of horses and, out of view and sunlight the wooden farm carts.

(The carts were kept out of direct sunlight where possible, as that actually shortened their life expectancy.)

A common factor of all these buildings was ease of access between the farmhouse and the principal buildings. A yard was crucial to the functioning of the whole.

These very buildings give us the second indication of change. Present-day farming has ceased to require the range of sheds that were built.

In many cases there are no animals at all and so the buildings are in themselves redundant, or no longer suitable to new enterprises. The trend to sell and use these buildings, converting them to dwellinghouses has been very rapid in today's construction industry. Converting to cash, buildings that were rapidly falling into disrepair has been a very visible 'change'.

The farming scene years ago required, as we have said, a large labour force. The system of mechanised farming was in its infancy, so most tasks required the use of horses. Ploughing and harvesting, transporting goods and livestock, collection of milk, marketing – all relied on the use of horses.

There was a support network of labour and skills, essential to the farm, which was provided by the blacksmith, wheelwrights, carpenters, saddlers and harness makers. These men were to be the last links in the era of the horse and cart.

Agriculture has always been linked with the unseen intervention of politics, which for its own purposes creates a need for change. In 1846 Peel's government repealed the Corn Laws which had given farmers security against the import of cheap foreign cereals. Britain adhered to the political consensus of free trade. It was believed that this encouraged enterprise to seek new markets abroad.

At this time major industrial changes were taking place. A density of population in towns put demands on the farmer by the government, to increase production cheaply in order to feed the masses.

For a while farmers were protected from cheaper imports because other major producers of grain had their own domestic problems. Russia had war in the Crimea and North America had its own civil war. That seems a far cry from Cockshutt and other rural areas in this country resulting in serious changes here, but it did!

The recovery from these wars meant an upsurge in imports of grain into Britain; other countries protected themselves by a tariff wall but Britain did not. Farmers struggled to cope with this influx of wheat; the economy of arable farming had reached an all time low and they were forced to change. The slogan 'Down corn, up horn' was applied. Our local farms changed in appearance with more livestock and fewer crops. The barley crop was still produced on home ground for the breweries and so long as the horse was the chief means of operating machines and being used for carting and transport, then oats as a crop was grown to feed them.

Milk producers of this time of agricultural depression fared better than most because the milk itself and by-products of butter and cheese increased in demand.

The production of milk, butter and cheese in Cockshutt, Wem and Ellesmere area was highly successful. The arrival of a rail-transport network and the Llangollen canal, plus rapid cooling systems for the milk meant the sale and despatching of the milk could be speedily sent on to the towns. (★hence Ellesmere Port)

It has been said that had our local cheese was so good that it had been given a recognised brand name such as *Ellesmere Cheese*, it could have stood competitively with other cheeses that have survived such as Cheshire Cheese, Lancashire Cheese or Wensleydale Cheese.

Pride in a beautiful farmhorse

Sadly it went into general sale and that successful product is just history except for Shropshire Blue!

The increase of cows and dairy production benefited pigs because their numbers increased to consume the whey from cheese making. Both breeds of animal created vast amounts of manure which had to be seen as a financial asset! The 'liquid gold' was therefore used prolifically as a fertiliser on the fields. This distribution of fertiliser over the fields in those early years relied on the labour force to spread it. The manure and straw was hand-forked and thrown over the fields – literally muck spreading. It was a heavy, unpleasant task so, hardly surprising, acquiring a mechanical muck-spreader was a very desirable asset on the farm.

The production of milk began originally with small dairies, milking being done by hand. The 'corn to horn' policy had increased the number of cows, so the milking process had to be increased in efficiency. Various experiments were conducted to produce milking machines and by the time of the Great War most of the technical difficulties encountered had been overcome. A milking bail for mechanised outdoor milking was developed in the 1920s and was used in an improved kind, on at least one local farm.

The increase of animals on farms demanded good pasture land and large-scale production of hay to feed them. Many of the operations at harvest continued to be done by hand throughout the nineteenth century, although a number of machines had been developed to increase the rate of working and save labour. Grass mowers for hay-making were available in the 1850s. The hay fork continued to be used for spreading and raking grass during the drying process. The hay when dry was forked and pitched onto horse-drawn carts and taken either back to the farm to be stacked or set up in a field as a hayrick. We have pictures of this taking place in Crosemere Lane!

The sheaf binders and threshers came into being to speed up this process but the combine harvester was not introduced into Britain until the mid 1920s, and was not widely used until

Taking a break in the field at harvest time

Grazing cattle, a typical rural scene

after the Second World War. Today these machines and their operators are often 'contracted' to farms at harvest time, because economically it makes sense to hire the machine for the period required as opposed to owning it and having it stand idle when not in use, though that runs the risk of failing to meet deadlines and timely operation. The hayricks and standing sheaves of corn are no longer to be seen.

The hive of industry in terms of man-power for the very labour-intensive tasks has been replaced by modern efficient machines. The changes came gradually but they do affect the overall view of our countryside. In years gone by, even children were employed for the harvest, the school being closed for two weeks: the potato-picking holiday continued into quite recent times. It has also been suggested that the traditional harvest spread or supper laid on at the farm as a reward to celebrate the work achieved, was usurped by the Church. The mechanisation process meant a decline in labour on the farm, and therefore no call for a harvest supper. The Church stepped in to celebrate with a Harvest Festival.

Silage stores today are an innovation in the process of feed. Green fodder can be cut after only two months growth and whilst green; it is not left to be spread on the fields until golden and dry as before. Clamps for storage are set up, the fodder compressed, covered and then weighted down with tyres. Less manpower to do it; therefore a very tiring task if later cut fodder is added to it though mostly moved and fed by hydraulic grabs and forks. Some things like tired muscles never change! The silo is another visible object of change.

Agriculture has, rather like a barometer reflected the unseen intervention of politics. The industrial revolution invented not just machinery in the factories, but machines to be used on the farm. This reduced the number of hands required on the farm so they, in many cases, migrated to the towns. Others would be absorbed in their migration, to allied industries associated with the farm. Local market towns to find larger livestock markets were being set up, providing separate markets for each different breed of livestock. Slaughterhouses were often built fairly near to them; the carcase trade increased a road network to facilitate this movement. Dairies were no longer small and on the farm themselves; the milk was now sent to major distribution centres such as the now derelict Dairy on the canal wharf in Ellesmere. New jobs arose at milking machine factories such as Fullwoods.

The Great War was responsible for the recruitment of many men, and sadly many died in this great conflict and this depleted the availability of labour. Land Army girls were first introduced to supplement this loss of labour; it was an operation to be repeated during the Second World War. Horses were replaced by machines which was both a practical and a visible change in all rural areas.

The Government in wartime faced the crisis of our food imports being destroyed; we were unable to sustain our food requirements. Farmers had to fill this breach and were told to grow potatoes and sugar beet. Some areas of land were forcibly acquired to camp soldiers (Hordley) or have ROC posts on them. Troops were at Stanwardine. Aircraft and tank bases required space. This form of change was vitally necessary for our survival as a nation, but not a natural development of the countryside. Cockshutt witnessed it all.

Harvest Time in the lane: Chris Sawbridge. Harry Pratt. George Peel. Geoffrey Nicholas.

Harvesting the modern way at Stanwardine

Potato Grading at Crosemere Hall; Pam Hanmer and Alf Smith

The control over farming during the war years did not stop when the war ended, but continued under MAFF and DEFRA. Farmers were often forced to plough up old pastures in order to replace cereals previously imported from Canada. They were given grants by MAFF to remove hedges to expand the field sizes and grow more. Only larger farms in this area could expand and specialise in this way; they did not carry it through to the extent done in the south, where fields achieved almost prairie-like proportions. Smaller local farms still mostly retained their hedges.

The war had concentrated all 'metal' production to be used for the planes, tanks, guns etc; tractors had been on 'hold' until this need ceased. An agricultural committee was formed to control the farm sale prices on machinery, to prevent a ludicrous escalation of prices. The post-war recovery, the mechanisation of tools and tractors became from then to the present day, big business, in which large sums of money were invested. This progress was to be the final nail in the coffin of intensive labour forces on the farm.

After the war there was an explosive growth in the use of agricultural chemicals, herbicides, insecticides, fungicides and fertilizers. This was accompanied by intensive farming of cattle, poultry, pigs and sheep. Farms began to specialise, a typical example being Mr Hulme's farm founding a flock of pedigree Suffolk sheep in 1952. They became famous in this country and abroad, achieving accolades over the years for the breed.

The problem in any area of specialisation can be the risk that if something serious goes wrong, a great deal of money and years of effort can disappear almost overnight. Serious diseases, have been brought to our attention by the media, are an example of this.

Rinderpest or cattle plague was noted earlier in the book; it last occurred in 1877. Anthrax, a very contagious disease to both animal and man, was mentioned in an incident at Marsh's farm. Foot & Mouth epidemics that ravage one farm can totally miss another. The devastation emotionally and financially cannot be under estimated. The epidemics were recounted for official enquiries in 1922, 1923-4 and 1953. A major epidemic affected Cockshutt farms in 1967-8. The year 2001 became the next major outbreak but none happened within the confines of Cockshutt. Dealing with the control of these epidemics essentially required speed of reporting the first outbreak, followed by major action controls. We have previously discussed how this tragedy affected various local farms because the forcible restraints of movement of healthy livestock meant near financial ruin to other farmers unable to sell on their animals.

The unseen influences that lay down rules and regulations affecting farming in the past were once again interfering in farm management in the following ways: - increased development and use of chemicals which benefited production, also resulted in over-production. There were, metaphorically speaking, lakes of wine and milk, mountains of butter, beef and wheat. Equally bizarrely there were people in the world starving to death!

The European Community introduced a quota system for milk production, coupled with price controls, thus reducing the levels of butter and milk production to manageable levels.

This drove many uneconomic producers out of business or they had to switch farming methods yet again. Top House farm, we have mentioned as a typical example of coping with this ruling when they developed the now renowned Top House Farm ice cream.

Another political influence in 1988 was a voluntary 'set-aside' scheme. The fields selected were very 'visible' in the area as weeds grew prolifically (and seeded).

Some concession was made to control the devastation of husbandry, by allowing the field to be mowed, but no financial benefit could be derived from the mowing. Subsidies were available for this compliance. The definition for the word subsidy is: 'a government payment or concession granted to an enterprise – e.g. farming, by which prices can be kept down or a particular market for a product can be stimulated, as it is perceived to be in the public interest'.

Tom Lindop and Randal Carr ploughing in a competition

The official controlling body for these dictats was first of all a body referred to as MAFF. This in full is; The Ministry of Agriculture, Fisheries & Food. The title today has been altered to DEFRA. This translates to Department for Environment, Food and Rural Affairs.

Many of the rules of farming can be read on the web-site of DEFRA and, reading as a totally non-agricultural person, I can see benefits for some of these rules and regulations being laid down and adhered to by all for whom farming is their livelihood.

Rules regulating slaughterhouses are essential for both animals and workers. Many years ago animals were slaughtered at the back of The Leaking Tap or Red Lion as it was then. The sheer numbers of today's stock, density of houses and people in the vicinity, means private slaughtering is just not a possibility. Similarly the information that villagers brought their own receptacles to collect their daily milk supply to the same area is not acceptable today. The same situation existed in the suburbs of the towns: a horse-drawn vehicle came around the houses carrying milk churns from which recipients had their milk bailed and poured into whatever container was proffered. Hygiene has become a primary motive in the improved health of people. Tubercular Testing of cows is necessary, as is the pasteurisation of milk and the containers used in the process etc. in the commercial dairies.

Burying animal carcases on the farmer's own land is no longer permissible, a record of why it died in the first place being necessary, especially considering the previously mentioned diseases.

As with all things in life that begin with common sense, it doesn't take long before rules and regulations overstep the mark and red tape abounds.

Hedge-cutting was mentioned recently which caused major problems for some sheep farmers. The rule says; 'the hedge must not be cut back more than two feet on the field side'. This does not give any thought to sheep being liable to pick up large thorn cuttings in their wool and worse still in their feet.

I have as an outsider learnt that if there were fifty ways to commit suicide, the sheep would know them all!   That was added just for light relief! – but, seriously this hedge-cutting rule is overriding common sense.

The final note to be included with reference to DEFRA is their description of the following advisory rules:

'A new agri-environment which provides funding for farmers or other land managers in England who deliver effective environmental management on their land: to conserve wildlife:

To maintain and enhance the landscape quality and character of their land: protect the historic environment and natural resources: promote public access and understanding of the countryside: natural resource protection.' All this is a minor part of a very lengthy document!

Recently a farmer, who was interviewed (not locally) on his reflection on farming today, had the following to say;

"Without the subsidies, no-one would farm. Farms that can't diversify will go under. There is cause for any farmer to feel that the Government doesn't seem to realise we should be able to supply a great deal more of our own food. The countryside is only a great place to walk in because the farmers look after it and the animals graze it. The animals are fast disappearing and under the 'New Environmental Stewardship schemes' farmers may just finish being park-rangers".

Let us hope his genuine feeling of despair will not become a reality.

Cockshutt and its surrounding farms have managed to change with demand and their workers have toiled in all weathers and conditions to keep bread on the table.

Supermarkets need to remember just where it all comes from!

Congratulations to the following for their services to agriculture: Long service medals have been received over the years by Len Birch, Les Birch, Frank Hanmer and Raymond Richards and in 2006 Don Hanmer. Frank Hanmer received his bar to the medal he had already received.

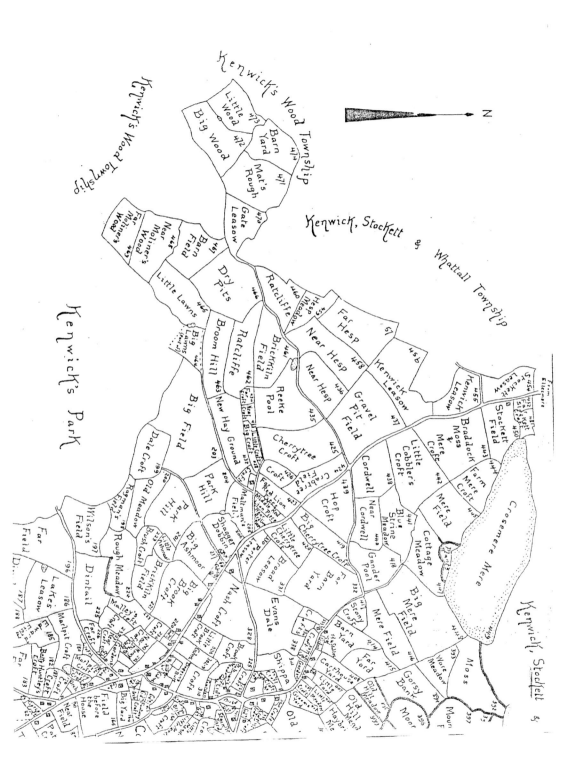

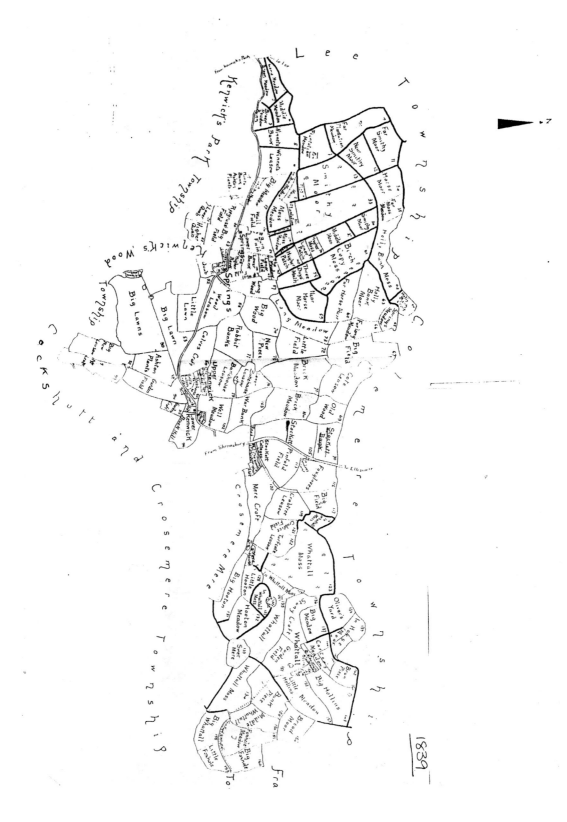

CHAPTER 8

TRANSPORT

Coaches

The reason for numerous public houses in Cockshutt was not primarily because the locals had a much greater capacity for drink than average but rather that they saw the opportunity to earn cash from the vigorous trade travelling from Ironbridge, Shrewsbury through the market town of Ellesmere and on to Liverpool or Chester. The coaches and passengers and Waggoners required refreshment and a change of horses and they supplied it.

The use of horses for coach transport did not as one might suppose, mean that the animal being the means of a livelihood was well-treated. They were often driven so brutally they had to be retired after three or four years. In 1821 twenty horses dropped dead on one mail coach route alone. The term stagecoach referred to the 'stage' being the distance between changes or halts, usually ten miles. Horses that had proven to be biters, jibbers, kickers or roamers were sold to coach proprietors where their vices did not matter. They cost between £27 to £37 each, the very best being £100. Hardly surprising, the cheaper ones were not regarded as anything more than a replaceable commodity. The life of a Waggoner would be no less hard; they were at the mercy of the weather, rutted roads, highway robbery and not permitted to mix with passengers when stopping at inns en route. They ate in the kitchens and often slept in the hay near the animals.

The class of coach varied; a lightweight Diligence with springs for instance, travelled fast with low fares and conveyed three passengers. The slower stage wagon carried a lot more passengers cheaply but in much closer proximity with a likelihood of some unpleasant characters as companions. In 1828-29 the Bang-up daily left Ellesmere at 2.00 pm; the High-flyer left Ellesmere at 2.30 pm. The Bang-up did not operate on Sundays.

The British custom of keeping to the left, made good sense when viewed from the coachman's seat. The whip hand had to be free to control the horses and to cut at the oncoming teams that threatened to block the way.

The coach journey from Shrewsbury to Chester was taken in a smart vehicle painted in brilliant yellow and black with four horses. The coach left Chester from the Grosvenor Hotel passed through Rosset, Gresford, Wrexham, Overton-on-Dee, Ellesmere, Cockshutt and Baschurch arriving at the Raven Hotel, Shrewsbury.

The journey after leaving Ellesmere behind took on an almost switchback route towards Cockshutt as it travelled at a speed of almost ten miles an hour. The wildlife, a glimpse of Oteley, Whitemere, Crosemere, and the Berwyn Range made for a most scenic route.

As the coach passed a turning to an unfrequented by-way, Porter Lane, it passed a pair of semi-detached cottages set well back from the road and a tiny timbered cottage at the road-side as if at one time it had been a tollgate keeper's cottage.

From this point the road was lined on one side with a row of evenly spaced horse chestnut trees, with the old racecourse on the other side known as the Dobbin.

There used to be a milestone that stood at this 'top of Dobbin' stretch of the road but it was removed just before the Second World War. (Any helpful signs of place-names and/or mileage disappeared so that if the enemy landed they were not aware of their whereabouts.)

The approach to the village at this point caused the coachman to stand up, take a post horn from a wicker case and give some rousing blasts to warn the villagers, particularly children that the coach was approaching. This would be at about four or five pm , after the children had escaped from school. They would rush to meet the coach and scramble for pennies thrown to them by the happy passengers.

From the pedestrian viewpoint, the sight of the smart four–in–hand coach and horses passing by was quite an event. The coach proceeded at a steady trot through the village to its next stopping place, the Boreatton Arms Hotel, Baschurch, before going on to Shrewsbury. The coach would then make the return journey to Chester. It did not run on Sundays.

This was not the mail coach. The Ellesmere and Cockshutt mail was carried by a horse-drawn cart from Shrewsbury, the driver being a well known character known as Ned Wycherley, a native of Burlton.

This same mail cart used to leave the mail bags and private despatch case for Frankton Grange hooked over the school railings, in all weathers, awaiting the attention required for sorting or sending them on to the Grange or other recipients. No-one ever tampered with them. One evening the mail cart came along, the horse slowed down as if it were going to stop by the school as usual, then instead of stopping it went trotting along. Someone noticed that the driver was not on the box and it subsequently transpired that the driver had either fallen off or was thrown off somewhere along the Ellesmere Road. A horse and trap requisitioned from the Red Lion was soon sent off in pursuit and the driverless Mail Cart was soon overtaken at Harmer Hill some six miles away. One other incident involving an accident with the Mail Cart occurred at what is called locally as 'Derby Bank' – just outside the village going to Shrewsbury. The cart overturned at this accident blackspot but fortunately cricketers playing on the nearby Townsend field were soon on the scene to render assistance to the hapless driver and his horse!

The Mail Coach had right of way on the road. The arrival of steam power threatened the livelihood of innkeepers, waggoners and coachmen; that was how the Times in 1839 saw the change of transport developing.

Before we close down on coach transport there were some interesting rules that applied to their usage.

1. 1734   Teams of horses had to be changed every day. The Red Lion and the Crown could both house horses making this change.

2. 1753   Outsides carried on the Shrewsbury stagecoach had the following etiquette; 'No ladies carried inside of stages unless wearing a hat'.

3. 1784   Mail coaches established

4. 1824   The first blow to the forthcoming upgrade of transport was when the Stockport-

Darlington Railway opened. In 1849 the Shrewsbury to Birmingham railway opened. The village would begin to feel the effects of this change to speedier transport as people chose to travel by rail.

5. 1850   Chester to Holyhead railway opened.

6. 1874   Last of the mail coaches.

By the 1880s the last of the coaches were running. Inns, horse sales, fodder, waggoners, would all take a downward toll financially as would the need for eight pubs in the village.

Canals

The development of rail transport was to affect the village but probably of much more local alteration to the landscape around Cockshutt was the canal system.

Canal mania in the 1790s swept the country almost to the equal of the railway network. Telford's experience of canal construction before taking on the Shrewsbury Canal had been restricted to one year working on an ambitious scheme to link the Severn, the Dee and the Mersey. Shropshire had the industrial heart of iron production at Ironbridge and this meant transport of goods to the towns. In 1792 William Jessop, a leading canal engineer came up with an ambitious route to extend the route surveyed by John Duncombe of Oswestry, from the Mersey at Netherpool across the Wirral to the Dee at Chester, southwards to Ellesmere to join the Severn in Shrewsbury. This system involved the crossing of two steep sided valleys of the Dee and the Ceirog at Pontcysyllte and Chirk. The new venture called itself the 'Ellesmere Canal Navigation', Ellesmere being the nearest to the centre of the proposed system.

The building of the canal was sectionalised and work begun pending funds being raised, especially for the masonry piers for the aqueducts.

Work was started on the section from Hordley Wharf to Weston Wharf which boasted four lime kilns, stables, a weighing machine, a clerk's house and a public house. The canal was carried on a further half a mile in anticipation of its link up to Shrewsbury.

The debate as to exactly how the link should be made to go to Shrewsbury involved all the major engineers of the canal building era. A proposal was made which, had it been developed, would have meant that as long as this form of transport existed, Cockshutt would have had a very different history. The proposal was to leave the Ellesmere-Whitchurch line at Colemere instead of Welsh Frankton.

According to this plan, instead of descending through Frankton locks, the canal would run on a level until it reached the outskirts of Shrewsbury where locks would be grouped. This line would pass via Cockshutt, Burlton, Myddle, until it followed the Parliamentary line at Leaton Heath.

At Myddle a secondary branch would communicate with Wem and the Grinshill Stone Quarry, also on the same level. The inclusion of Grinshill Stone Quarry would have meant they could undercut the price of Portland stone being used in London.

This whole idea was turned down and Cockshutt probably basked unaware of the near miss they'd have experienced of canal life on its doorstep. Canals for a start were largely dug at the hands of imported labour of Irish Navvies. They could create quite a problem being housed and fed alongside of their workings, leading, one has to say a very hard life.

The easy line therefore from Hordley to Weston Lullingfields was not begun until after 1796, a distance of four miles. The extension for its continuation for the further development to Shrewsbury never got beyond about half a mile outside of the village of Weston petering out in the middle of a field.

Today, if one tries to trace the line of the canal at Weston Lullingfields, one can, by looking carefully realise that a shallow hump in the road is actually a bridge which crossed the canal. To the left going from the village and aside of this bridge is a stone built building that was once part of the Wharf. Follow around the side of the building that is at the side of the road and the pulley windows are just discernible in the rear of the building where haulage of cargo was carried out. The base of the building now, houses tractors and farm equipment.

Ellesmere

Welsh Frankton *Colemere*

Hordley *· Cockshutt*

W

Bagley *Petton*

· Burlton

Weston Lulling- fields

· Myddle ·

Baschurch

Shrewsbury

SHREWSBURY CANAL

RIVER

SEVERN

I Montford Bridge

This route failed to be chosen.

Left, all that remains of Weston Lullingfield canal warehouse.

The widened area both here and beyond was obviously once a turn-around for barges. No water, high weeds, undergrowth and no canal equipment, make this a place that is unrecognisable to its erstwhile use.

Returning to the road and looking over the field

running on the other side of the bridge it is just possible to see the line or lay of a long hollow or the dry canal bed disappearing off on what would have been its route behind Wycherley and across to the rear of Shade Oak and on to Hordley. The banks of the canal have been bulldozed out of existence.

In 1951 the line in Shade Oak was demolished, a few years later Sycamore Bridge went and about 1960 Hordley Bridge vanished. A burst in the bank at Dandyfield in May 1917 was the excuse for limiting the navigation to Hordley Wharf. Another burst on the Llanymynech line near Welsh Frankton in February 1936 was not repaired. The basin adjacent to Hordley was filled in and the canal line abandoned.

This saga of the local canal history may seem to bear little relevance to life at Cockshutt but Weston Wharf played a big part in its source of supplying goods required. The original list of requirements for the start of building the Wharf had been for the construction of lime-kilns.

Lime was a vital commodity to Victorian farmers before the widespread use of modern fertilisers. Lumps of limestone quarried at Llanymynech were barged to be burnt in the kilns to be reduced to a fertiliser to spread on the fields.

A reconstruction of a Lime-kiln

Rail and Road Transport

In 1846 the Ellesmere Canal became part of the Shropshire Railways and Canal Co. They were general carriers to Chester, Liverpool, North and South Staffordshire and North Wales. Eventually the increase of railways meant that the LMS took over all carrying of goods previously transported on the canals.

The network of railways provided rapid transport and employment for many. The line at Ellesmere was the Cambrian Railway. Each line was owned by different companies linking one another depending on where their company built the line. Today, young people would be unaware of the liveries of these rail companies, the GWR/LNWR being but two of them. (These initials stood for the Great Western Railway and the London and North Western Railway).

Where stockyards were situated, as in Ellesmere, the hauliers could deliver or collect goods for local distribution. Sawbridges pony and cart was a forerunner replaced by George Ashley with his fleet of haulier wagons. This extended the delivery range and collection of goods by road with its links to the rail-road system. The expansion of a good road system then widened this periphery of delivery.

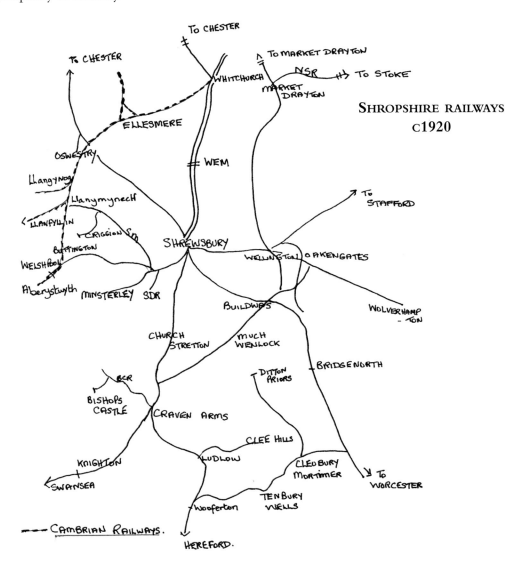

SHROPSHIRE RAILWAYS
c1920

OTHER LINES WERE SERVED BY: GREAT WESTERN: JOINT GWR/LNWR
LONDON + NORTH WESTERN RAILWAY + OTHERS

Passengers wishing to go from Cockshutt to London could make this journey from Ellesmere. A timetable from the first decade of the century showed nine trains a day to London via Whitchurch, and six back, the journey taking about four and a half hours. This length of time for a train journey seems excessive when we know the speeds a train can travel today; however there are other problems to encounter today when a journey from Shrewsbury to London can take seven hours because we have no direct connection to the Capital - we have taken a step backwards! The freight was not just confined to crated goods but actually took milk in tanks to London. Cattle were also moved by rail. The closure of the Ellesmere line came in 1962, a victim of Dr Beeching's rail closures.

The next upgrade of a road haulage transport based at Cockshutt, was Jones's Garage, Shrewsbury Road.

This proved that road transport was now one of the dominant means of conveyancing goods. They owned a large fleet of vehicles which until recently operated from the village, but in 1995 the garage itself was sold and the vehicles were moved to a different location.

In the 1930s the village outings used the 'Lily of the Lake' coach from Timms garage Ellesmere. This open-topped vehicle known as a charabanc is described as a long brake or car with transverse benches for excursionists.

In 2003 the Ellesmere Lakeland Coaches provide many a village outing with very comfortable transport. All a long way from Mrs Austin's cart with Rose the horse, described earlier.

Before leaving the subject of transport one has to note that even what we consider a familiar feature - the main A528 Shrewsbury Road, it is easy to forget that not long ago this was a much narrower and stony road subject to potholes and ruts. Lanes running from this road were mere dust-compressed tracks. When we have mentioned the possibility of turnpikes or tollgates on this road, the government had given permission to groups of people to make a road and therefore charge a toll to use it. Telford and Macadam were the first engineers to work out how to make good roads. The Macadam roads had no large foundation stones; smaller stones were put in layers and topped with broken stone and grit. When carts that we have mentioned, began to use these roads, they quickly wore away and pot-holed. To improve on this, the small grit was then topped with tar and thus became known as a Tarmacadam Road.

Peggy Husbands wrote in her anecdotes about the roadmen, the dictionary definition of this being; 'a man who keeps roads in repair'.

She says her Grandfather was a roadman in his day and she was born in 1910! In her own memory this job was still ongoing as she recalled a Mr Jack Allman carrying out this task. Each man was appointed a length of road to clean, repair and tidy. This applied to the by-roads also but not to the lanes. These men were referred to as 'length-men'. It is well to remember how short a time this change has come about. Coming from a city, I can remember any area of building or road works always had a little sentry-box by the 'hole' and a man referred to as a Cocky-watchman sat guard throughout the night; he had a metal brazier fire burning beside his hut and made his requisite 'billy-cans' of tea, had his frying pan at the ready and so kept himself sustained on his nightly vigil. Gradually roadworks were fenced or, as they termed it, 'roped and lamped'. The lamps required filling and lighting as they were not then up to solar or even battery power. One of the tasks for a workman who had worked in the daytime was to return at dusk and light the lamps. This was as recent as the late 1950s.

Roads are used for transport and are the arterial network of an area. They also attract 'characters' that take to the road; today we would call them vagrants – people who for one reason or another keep on the move. Peggy Husbands refers to certain 'characters' well known in and around Cockshutt.

They had wintered in the workhouses and walked the roads in summer, sleeping rough. Some names people may recall were; Moses Kirkham, Jack Cawley, Billie Done, Neddy and Tommy Kynaston and a Mrs 'no-nose'; all referred to as milestone inspectors. A very hard way of life.

Whilst commenting on this moving populace, the gypsies who pursue a nomadic life of a different type refer to the grass verge along any roadside as the 'long meadow' for very obvious reasons.

CHAPTER 9

SOCIAL LIFE

Most young people today would seem to feel there is 'nothing to do' despite having a wide range of electronic devices in their homes, and IT facilities in the village hall and library. They Holiday abroad and enjoy trips of a lesser nature throughout the year. "I'm bored," is not what one should expect to hear.

In very much earlier years a Cockshutt resident in a more outlying part of the village quoted her grandmother enjoying an annual event of dancing around a Maypole. I could not find any trace of this in Cockshutt. She then went on to recall another very popular country sport – Cockfighting. This was definitely something that Cockshutt took part in. The grandmother had then said her father kept his best cocks in the attic when the sport was banned in 1849. I would have to presume that for some while Cockshutt would be equally reluctant to give up this entertainment. There is quite a large cockfighting stage in the attic of Crosemere Hall which would facilitate a number of participants. The next one recorded is at Fernyhough in the attic rooms. There were receptacles for confining the cocks used in the fighting with apertures measuring fifteen inches by twenty-four. The sport of cockfighting was not unknown in the open but to take to attics would suggest a certain amount of secrecy. No doubt there were other venues for this activity which may not be either recognisable as such to the present day tenants or they are just not made known publicly.

Listening to older people describe their activities for entertainment they largely devised them for themselves. A bicycle was without doubt a necessary item in order to follow the invitations for fun and they were fortunate to know their lives were not at great risk when riding their bicycles to various venues, especially in the dark in wintertime. Today's children are not so lucky in that respect!

Paraffin lamps were the first lights or lamps that were vitally necessary to see where you were going when there was no such thing as street lighting. These were rather unpredictable in behaviour: they could go on fire or in a high wind they went out. To illustrate this I will recount Nellie Sutton's mishap with this as a means of lighting. Riding her bike to a dance at Myddle (a 6d. hop) the lamp went on fire on her handlebars. She threw it into the hedge but by then her hands became all black and she was wearing a white dress. On arriving at Myddle, she asked for water and soap to clean herself up and was given a bar of carbolic soap. All evening she was self-conscious about the powerful smell of the soap which blighted her enjoyment and she was convinced it would put anyone off asking her to dance! We can all feel her predicament all these years later!

The next progressive form of lighting was to have an acetylene lamp. This means of lighting one's way, was to my ears quite a dangerous distraction. I looked for a dictionary reference which was the following; 'a colourless hydrocarbon gas burning with a bright flame used in the past for lighting and in the present it is used in welding'. This lamp operated by a carbide and water system; a small screw top to the lamp turned the water on and if you miscalculated and released too much water you drowned the light.

The carbide when too wet wouldn't operate. All very dodgy and although there was no legal requirement to light up, the alternative wasn't really an option was it?

Dancing and cycling were not deterred by such problems of lighting. Nellie said that she attended many dances at Brook House and everybody of her generation also endorsed this as a very enjoyable dance hall. Nancy Roberts said 'live bands' there were really good. There were dances held at the Annex but space was a bit cramped. The Cockshutt Ball took place in the village school but that was an 'invitation only' affair. All catering was done by the ladies organising the ball. Mrs Hulme senior used to make the sweets. Sometimes the ball took place at Petton or Ellesmere.

The school hall also held more ordinary dances and again we can thank Peggy Husbands for giving details of the bands; they were obviously successful to be remembered in such detail. Harold Colemere's 'toe-tickling' band, the 'Savana' with Con Johnson, Norman Dawson and George Godwin on drums. The 'Midnight Serenaders' came from Welsh Frankton with Miss Doris Brayne as pianist and during the war years they had soldiers' bands.

The place to go was over the brook that runs out of Crosemere to Sweatmere – around this corner was the best 'beach' where there was a gradual slope into the deeper water. Mr Hulme remembered taking a pig-turnel to the mere and using it as a boat, almost as one would use a coracle. There was once a small stage or jetty for sailing and fishing at the edge of the mere. In wintertime, the mere used to freeze over, the winters being more severe than now. I have been told that Lawrie Sawbridge used to be a fine skater and was joined on the ice by many of the villagers including Ivy Ashley. To emphasize the severity of the cold, Mr Hulme recalled that Mainwarings had their coal delivered by a coal cart that drove over the Ellesmere mere to get to Oteley. In order to toboggan or sledge you first called at Tom Sutton's for an offcut of wood and narrow metal strips off an old mattress base as runners and you made your own. One time, so I'm told, the 'lads' collected lots of gorse and branches and made a bonfire in the middle of the frozen mere.

Garden Fetes held at Frankton Grange were an attraction to Connie Dakin and she also went to garden parties in the vicarage garden, as did many more. Reverend Peppercorn's and Mr Hassall's 'Beano' is to be found in another part of the book.

Peggy Husbands enjoyed Sunday school trips when they would be taken on a farm cart with the ripple sides on and decorated with twigs of ivy, laurels and other greenery. They would travel as far as Whitemere or Colemere taking picnics and drinks. If a distance such as that could not be managed they'd have to settle for Stanwardine Hall or just the Chapel field.

Progress in travel meant that in later years they used one of Mr Timms' charabancs called 'The Lily of the Lake' and go as far afield as Grinshill Hill or maybe Nesscliffe Hill. That was really travelling!

The tyres of the charabanc were hard and solid, the seats being the width of the vehicle with a door on each side to access them. There was a roll-along hood for use in really inclement weather, or, you carried an umbrella. It didn't travel fast as we understand speed today but the children found it all very exciting.

As the season progressed and harvest came around and Peggy recalls 'rabbit-running'. When a field had been newly cut the rabbits were exposed of coverage and would 'run' with the children in hot pursuit trying to catch them. Rabbit stew was quite a tasty dish, only losing favour from which it has never fully recovered following the outbreak of myxamatosis which decimated the animals so cruelly.

Children's games were for many years' traditional games that required little in the way of apparatus or equipment and often entailed chanting rhymes to go with the

In summertime there was swimming in Crosemere mere. It always seems to have been 'warmer' in the old days, many families would gather by the mere and take a picnic and take their swimming togs.

The Dickin Family trying to get their Landrover up towards Stonehill. Right, the Road from Cockshutt to English Frankton in Winter.

Lilly of the Lake, Seated in the front Richard and Gladys Roberts and standing towards the back is Dossie's mother.

game. The 'season' for the popularity of a game changed like an unwritten code that would dictate the new 'in' game. A study of these children's games discovered that the time for 'change' would not only happen in your own area, but would like a wind change, sweep the country!

Skipping that involved complicated rhymes and 'running-in' might just as suddenly change to become whip and top. The less money available for real tops and hoops reflects the ingenuity of the owner to adapt to the change and invent a substitute. Ideally a painted coloured top and whip would be desired in order to see the colours merge as the top spun. I was told by Peggy Husbands that she used a glass stopper out of a ginger-ale bottle as a top. A hoop with a stick could be improvised with the hoop off an old rain tub. Hopscotch was almost a code in its rules of play but required only stones, one to scratch out the lines and numbers on the floor and the other to toss to a square. Hand clapping rhymes were always a seasonal game requiring memory and dexterity. Chain games of people rhyming and looping down the line ducking under someone's linked arms; bouncing a ball against the wall with several members of an off-the-cuff team seemed to require no written rules but everyone could master it. We know that many of these rhymes are derived from historical events, the most common being Ring-a-Ring of Roses from symptoms of the plague or Black Death. I once stood and listened to a rhyme about the 'Fever van taking you away' and knew that the rhyme had no meaning whatsoever to the callers. I had had scarlet fever as a child and only by being an only child, did I escape being taken away in the Fever Van to an Isolation Hospital.

Adults pursued a variety of entertainments

Oddfellows

Cockshutt Oddfellows with their Banner ready for the Parade. Back Row – left ?, ?, Tom Worthington, Bill Hanmer, Den Ashley. Middle Row – Tom Hanmer, Bob Birch, Henry Birch, Jack Williams, Albert Gregory, Arthur Hanmer, Bill Husbands, William Smith, Ellis Hanmer, Bill Williams, Tom Harrison. Front Row – Bill Price, ?, Bill Wilkinson, George Tatton, John Husbands, Jack Birch.

The Club' as it was known in the village had the grand title of The Loyal Egerton Lodge No.4380 of the Independent Order of Oddfellows Manchester Unity Friendly Society. The Oddfellows Club offered medical insurance long before the NHS; in fact it was started in about 1730 with a branch in Ellesmere in 1840. The earliest minute book of the Cockshutt Loyal Egerton Lodge was 1905, available in the Oddfellows office in Wem. I believe the Loyal Egerton Lodge was founded by Mr J Green of Cockshutt and Mr Henry Townsend of Tetchill Moor in the late 1800s. I have not been able to research further back than the auditors report for 1904 which was adopted in September 1905 when Brother Thomas Husbands presided. In 1906 Brother George Tatton was in charge and in 1908 Brother John Austin. Before you could become a member of 'the club' you had to have a medical and take a certificate along with you to a meeting and if you were accepted you were initiated.

Everyone is very secretive about this but evidently they had a special handshake and password. The Egerton banner was very ornate and embroidered with the words, 'Help and Sympathy in Time of Sickness'. A Grand Master, Noble Grand Master, Vice Grand Master and Brothers were elected by the members and a warden appointed to visit the sick; there was also a management committee. Meetings were held on Saturday evenings at 8.00 pm. It wasn't until 1912 that they considered the

Juveniles on Parade

necessity of opening a female branch and steps were taken to do this. Names of absent members were entered in the Fines book and if no written apology was received the rules dictated that a fine had to be paid.

Each year in June 'the club' paraded around the village for the annual 'do'. In the early years it was held on the last Thursday but later it was held on the first Thursday in June and school was closed for the day. There was also a juvenile branch to the lodge and they had their own banner to parade around the village. The members of the club assembled at the Lodge house. This was at first the Crown Hotel and later the Red Lion. Members wore their regalia and held their banner aloft. What a sight it must have been as the parade, led by a brass band walked from the Red Lion down Crosemere and back up for a service in church. Any juvenile who was 16 years and under who had attended regularly and paraded had their dinner free, and they were each given 6d to spend. All members had dinner in a marquee in the Lion car park, the cost in 1921 was 4s 6d. each. The Lion yard was also the venue for a fun fair, hobby horses and swing boats and stalls down the driveway, and at times spilled out into Park Lane. In the early days Pat Collins provided the fun fair and later Greatorex and then Manders took over. The band played in the yard as part of the entertainment and they had to provide their own refreshments and transport. The bands changed over the years but most years it was Ifton Brass Band; Wem Town Band and Grinshill were also used. In fact tenders were asked for and it was the cheapest band with the most players that usually got the job.

The day was finished with a dance on the vicarage lawn but some effort had to be put into getting the area ready for dancing. Lucky spot dance prizes were 50 cigarettes for the gent and a box of chocolates for the lady. Ernest Harrison was called upon to MC the evening which if wet was held in the school. It was the band of the day that provided the music. In 1923 Bomere Heath Band was used and J Dickin was at the Lion now and the meal was 3s 6d to include a pint of beer, juveniles 3s.

In 1924 the Lodge entered the financial market and loaned a man in Wem £250 at 5% interest. They had invested some money in Swindon Corporation in 1920 and when it expired in 1925 they were asked if they would continue for a further five years at 4?% but Cockshutt members wanted 4? % and as Swindon were not willing to pay the extra, the £400 was repaid to the club. In 1926 they invested £300 in Mersey Docks and Harbour Board at 5?%, they decided to invest for ten years. By 1926 the cost of the meal for the annual 'do' was again reduced to 3s 3d and juveniles 2s 3d and it was decided to treat all members over 50. In 1927 there was a recruitment drive and 10s was offered to the member signing up the most juveniles. Edward Davies won the prize for introducing the most boys to join. It was in 1927 that Brother Wilkinson was elected to represent the Loyal Egerton Lodge on the committee to discuss a village hall for Cockshutt and he was instructed to vote in favour of a hall. The properties mortgaged in Whitchurch had been inspected in 1932 and some were found to be in a very bad state of repair. Notice was served on the mortgagee requiring him to execute the necessary repairs or in default repay the mortgage money. What happened between 1933-1960 I could not find out as the minute books are missing from the office in Wem.

During the break in records the war came and the National Health Service was introduced which must have affected the Oddfellows. By 1960 the parades had stopped and a day trip was organised instead. The meetings were now held in the Crown. The banner was still in Cockshutt as Brother Worthington inspected it. I have tried to find its whereabouts but have had no success. The day trips were in August to all the usual destinations - Rhyl, Southport, Blackpool and Llandudno. By 1973 the club had fewer than 50 members but they didn't wish to join up with another lodge if at all possible and a special effort was made to increase membership. During the 1970s Sister Thomas presided at the meetings and it must have been very unusual to have a woman in charge. The last date of the minute book is August 1976 and the Loyal Egerton Lodge, Cockshutt closed. The remaining members became part of the Wem Branch and this is still the same today.

Cockfighting

There were numerous outdoor recreations in the last hundred years which were popular sports at most village fairs. Bull-baiting, bear-baiting, badger tubbing, whipping the cat, bare knuckle fights and cockfighting to name but a few. The sport of cockfighting goes back many centuries being thought to have come via Persia into Greece. The famous 'Shropshire Reds' probably originated in Rhodes. The responsibility for introducing cockfighting into Britain must rest with the Romans.

In the twelfth century it was a recorded amusement of the English people and in particular to schoolboys. It would appear that schoolboy cocking was an annual event every Shrove Tuesday. The school was used as the cockfighting pit after the desks had been moved. The schoolmasters augmented their annual income by charging each pupil 'cockfighting dues' which paid for the purchase of fighting cocks. Money was also paid by breeders and owners to the schoolmaster as entry money and an extra sum for admission. Only really in the thirteenth century did grown men share an interest in cockfighting.

Royal patronage secured its popularity; Henry V111 had a cockpit attached to his Whitehall Palace. This patronage continued into the next century but was banned in the Cromwellian period. The restoration of the monarchy gave it new impetus. Experts wrote books both advising on what made for the best cockfighting bird and then rules of play had to be recognized and applied. A referee was present to deal with disputes over decisions. The cocks had combs and wattles cut or 'dubbed' thus giving the opponent bird nothing to grip. The tail was trimmed to give mobility and again make it less vulnerable to its opponent. The natural spurs of the cock were cut short and steel or silver spurs were then attached to the legs with blades or points from 1? to 3? inches in length. The cocks fought hungry as a rule so they needed guarding from an unscrupulous opponent giving them a meal, even poisoning a bird or maiming it.

The area chosen for the fight was referred to as 'the pit' and outdoors was an area approximately 16ft to 20ft in diameter, with six to eight corners. It was surrounded by banked up earth covered with sods and had a padded barrier of some two feet high surrounding it. In rural areas this would be less elaborate, the village green, a stable yard at an inn or privately at country mansions and manors. Reverend John Sparling had a cockpit at Petton Park; Shade Oak we have already mentioned and Crosemere Hall.

Until 1571 many competitions took place in graveyards as the clergy were quite ardent supporters of the sport. It was the commonest means of gambling which was its chief reason for popularity between 1750 and 1849. Stakes in some regions went from 10 guineas to 200 guineas; by the nineteenth century it was even known for sums of 1,200 guineas to exchange hands.

With gambling the measure of 'luck' encouraged superstitions to bring good luck. If the cockpit was sprinkled on the morning of the contest with earth from the nearest churchyard, then spells and charms would be broken and 'the best bird would win'. Place names or pub names can indicate its erstwhile history, e.g. the Fighting Cocks at Oswestry. Lee Bridges near Ellesmere was the scene of a special cocking on Easter Monday and Tuesday in 1799 between gentlemen of Cheshire and Shropshire, stakes being from 2 guineas a battle to 20 guineas in the main.

The cruelty of this sport degenerated further when the meaner sport of tying a cock to a stake and letting six to eight men each with a long-lashed whip take it in turns to whip the cock to death. A variation on this was to set the cock alone in the pit and spectators had shies at it throwing pieces of wood.

If the spectator could knock the bird over and catch it before it stood up, they could keep the bird. In 1835 an Act was passed making the practice of cockfighting a misdemeanor in certain circumstances. Cockfighting was prohibited by law in 1849 but it did not necessarily mean an end to cocking. Enthusiastic cockers were inclined to defy the law.

In the 1880s many cockers were convicted and fined. As with all things prohibited they tend to go underground, hence an outdoor activity took place within premises – lofts for example. The phrase is still used in normal premises to describe the roof space as the 'cockloft'. This would be when the 'cock fighting pit' in Crosemere Hall loft started to be used.

Cockshutt W.I

Cockshutt W.I. was founded in 1925; Mrs Betty Mosley (Marsh) and her sister Miss S Marsh were among the founder members. Euphemia Robinson and Mrs Higginson were very early members and 'leading-lights' at this time. The meetings were held in the Vicarage Annexe and we know from reading about the Whist Drives that a fire was lit in the room to provide heat: it seems quite cosy to read of that now! Our archive photographs of Cockshutt W.I show 'occasions' being celebrated in the school hall. Below, a fancy hats parade.

Looking at the numbers (over fifty people on one) the Annexe would not house so many tables being set-up.

The fiftieth Anniversary in 1975 was a very special occasion with a lovely cake made to mark the event; Miss S Marsh was the guest of honour. A cup for the Flower and Produce show was presented at this meeting and this show was then to be an annual event.

Back Row from left	Middle Row from left	Front Row from left:
Mrs W Worthingto	Mrs Aubrey(PO)	Mrs N Sutton
Mrs O Ashley	Mrs L Sawbridge	Mrs R Hulme (Lodge)
Mrs B Smith	Mrs Williams (Old PO)	Mrs Nicholas
Mrs Rodenhurst	Mrs Hulme (Crosemere)	Mrs Birch (Dobbin)
Mrs L Gregory	Mrs Hulme (Kenwick)	Mrs Pollie Smith
Mrs Williams	Mrs N Smith	Mrs Vaughan Jones
Mrs M Kynaston	Mrs B Hanmer	Mrs Parry (Pikesend) Standing.
Mrs I Nicholas	Mrs E Robinson (Frankton Grange)	

25th Anniversary - a meal in School Hall

Table on the left, left side: Beryl Carr, Hilda Carr, Mrs Cank, Mrs Carr, Mrs Evans, Mrs Gregory, Mrs Chidlow, Mrs Roberts, Mrs Sawbridge, Mrs Worthington, Mrs Allman, Mrs Williams. Right side of the table: Mrs Hanmer, Mrs Latham, Miss Latham, Miss Cooke, Mrs Ralphs, Mrs Williams, Mrs Gregory, Mrs Nicholas, ?, Miss Patterson, ?, Mrs Husbands, Mrs Smith. Table on the right, left side: Mrs Jarvis, Mrs Williams, Mrs Smith, Miss Smith, Mrs Wilding, Mrs Sutton, Mrs Chidlow, Mrs Sutton, ?, Miss Williams, ?. Right side of table: Mrs Parker, ?, ?, Mrs Kynaston, Mrs Hanmer, Mrs Williams, Mrs Birch. Top table (standing): Mrs Birch, ? Marsh, Mrs Hanmer, Sarah Marsh, Mrs Hardy, ? , Mrs Hassall, Mrs Hulme.

The ladies standing at the back left of the photograph, are the helpers including the Girl's Club. Mrs Ashley, Mrs Rodenhurst, Beryl Evans, Gladys Hanmer, Margaret Husbands, Heather Evans, Dossie Birch, Brenda Nicholas, Betty Hanmer.

WI Xmas Party

Back Row left to right – Mrs Griffiths, Mrs Husbands, Mrs Aubrey, Mrs Wilding, Mrs Worthington, Mrs Ashley, Mrs Smith, Mrs Rodenhurst, Mrs Gregory, Mrs Williams, Mrs Kynaston, Mrs Nicholas, Mrs Smith, Mrs Sutton, Mrs Carr, Mrs Ashley, Mrs Williams. Middle Row left to right – Mrs Sawbridge, Mrs Williams, Mrs A Hulme, Mrs J Hulme, Mrs Smith, Mrs Hanmer, Mrs Robinson, Mrs Ralphs, Mrs D Gregory, Mrs Parry, Miss M Latham, Mrs Dickin, Miss R Hulme. Front Row left to right – Mrs Vaughan Jones, Mrs Birch, Mrs Sutton, Mrs Worthington, Mrs T Nicholas, Mrs Birch, Mrs P Smith, Mrs Chidlow, Mrs R Gregory, Mrs Roberts, Mrs Mercer, Mrs Vernon.

In 1976 according to records from The Journal (forerunner to the Chronicle) the monthly June meeting was in the school hall with entertainment by the children. Mr and Mrs Dommett were retiring at the end of term and the W.I. made a presentation to them. At this meeting they discussed arrangements for the forthcoming Senior Citizens' outing. They were also supporting a 'Bring-a-bottle' stall at the Oswestry Orthopaedic Hospital.

1985 The Diamond Jubilee of Cockshutt W.I. was celebrated by a dinner and entertainment. The secretary (Joyce Hayward) was very busy coping with a widespread list of guest invitations, many of the replies of which have been retained. Cards of congratulations came from Erbistock W.I and Ellesmere W.I. Mrs Barbara Hampson who was County Chairman from 1983-5, attended and contributed a rendering of 'Little Brown Jug', which entertained members so much, their thanks for the overall event included mention of it. Some replies from retired members who had moved away to other areas of the country were delighted to have been remembered but with advancing years and infirmity had had to decline the invitation. The strength of friendship both near and far was certainly reinforced by the celebration. Below, The Diamond Jubilee Card and signatures of the members present

Right, Cockshutt Celebrates its 70th Anniversary.

1995 the County suggestion that the W.I. branches should make a map of their own areas to be interpreted as they saw fit, presented a challenge to members. The map for Cockshutt was begun during Mona Whitfield's presidency and a committee was formed to discuss the design. The project took two years to complete. Below, The village map and some of the people who contributed.

The presidency had changed over by then and the hanging and protection of the map and framing of it fell to Wendy Jones. Events had to be organised to raise the necessary cash to do this. The map itself was described as a quilt style map

COCKSHUTT

1925 – 1995

consisting of collaged/embroidered homes and pubs, church and school in the village. The school partook in the formation of the map (left) by sewing their names on 'leaves'. A tree is central to the quilt representing future growth, the leaves being the next generation.

The names of all those who had contributed to this map were beautifully listed as a key to the map on a framed manuscript made by a very talented man called John Husbands. His calligraphy was an item in its own right and hangs alongside the map in the Millennium Hall.

September 1997 was the next to last meeting in the Old Village Hall as the 13th December 1997 saw the grand opening of the new Millennium Hall by Dr Edwin Sawacha of the Millennium Commission.

1997 was quite a year in the calendar of events. Representing Cockshutt W.I., Wendy Jones, the president, and her husband Eddie were both invited to the Institution and Licensing of Reverend Trevor Neil Thorold as (1) Salop area Local Ministry Adviser and (2) Priest in charge of the Parishes. In 1998 Wendy was instrumental in organising and collating a collection of recipes for the Cockshutt Cookbook. A similar book had been made twenty years previously but the updating of it was decided to be a fundraiser for the Millennium Hall. At a book launch with refreshments provided by W.I. members, the sum of £330 was achieved and donated to the hall. The first meeting of the W.I. in the new hall took place on the second Wednesday in January.

1999 was a year that created a furore when an article appeared in the Shropshire Star in the July in which the National W.I. had reported the following: 'Our declining Villages'. They then proceeded to list nine points that contributed to this decline and listed four villages, Cockshutt being one of these! I will rewrite the headings we were judged on and their results;

1. Description; a long established agricultural working village, gently expanding.

2. Population; mainly established families with a relatively small proportion of newcomers.

3. School; yes. The Primary School used to be a Church School and is now a State School.

4. Shops; One village shop selling the basic necessities. Also a Post Office.

5. Pub; there were two until recently, but one has now been turned into a house. Historically, there were several pubs in the village.

6. Church; congregations are steady.

7. Community spirit; said to be 'pretty good' although there is a discernible split between

'locals and newcomers'. A new village hall is generally heavily booked.

8. Transport; the bus services have recently improved but doesn't seem much used. In practice, villagers are car dependent.

This article coming as it did from National W.I. Headquarters was strongly refuted by Wendy Jones and Helen Eatough. No recognition of Cockshutt being in crisis was felt to be applicable. The recent fundraising events for cash required for the hall all emphasized considerable enthusiasm from all village members both newcomers and old, for its continuing growth.

The survival of the shop, post office, school and pub were all evidence of a strong community.

Council Clerk, Helen Eatough underlined this fact by pointing out that Cockshutt was designated as a growth village under the North Shropshire District Councils 10-year plan.

To conclude on the subject of our W.I, we continue as a happy group of friends who meet monthly, raising funds, meeting other W.I groups from our surrounding villages, helping at any events in the village and generally caring for any in our midst which we feel applicable. We also enjoy a wide range of speakers coming to all our monthly meetings.

The W.I. as an organisation has a considerable say in subjects of national importance where our voice can be raised on a political level - in spite of its *faux pas* where criticism of our village was raised, and that was very rapidly refuted, in strong terms!

We are fortunate to have a fairly large collection of photographs from a

Above, guest of honour Mrs Betty Moseley (Marsh).
Below, Members and Friends Celebrate the 75th Anniversary

variety of functions held over the years which can be viewed with nostalgia. They record faces many of whom are no longer with us. This is not a moment to be sad but rather to rejoice in the happy memories of them and value the contribution they made. 2000 was another important 'milestone' for the WI in Cockshutt as a founder member of the branch, Mrs Betty Moseley(Marsh), was guest of honour at the 75th Anniversary Celebrations.

Cockshutt and District Royal British Legion Branch Women's Section

This Cockshutt Branch was founded in 1967 at a meeting in the Village Hall on 25th April. The following were elected at the meeting:

Chairman   Rene Jones

Secretary   Margaret Husbands

Treasurer   Myrtle Holliday

Committee: Peggy Husbands, Nancy Roberts, P Smith, S Hardaker, N Smith, Edna Evans and Dossie Birch (still a member today).

Personel have changed over the years for various reasons and numbers have declined but they still meet on the third Wednesday of each month in the Village Hall. The annual events are a June Outing and a Day Trip when other members of the village are welcome. A Garden Party, either July or August, at the home of one of the members is always lots of fun. Each month the meeting is addressed by invited speakers, many of whom entertain and enlighten the members on their particular subject. Refreshments are served by the members on a rota system, these are traditionally sandwiches and a cup of tea at British Legion.

Left: The Band leads the Parade. Right: Church Parades are attended when Men and Women's Sections from other Branches join in. Below: Members on Parade. Dennis Williams (Standard Bearer), John Hodnet, Rene Jones, 3 County Reps, Tim Wycherley..

Proud of their standard, Cockshutt Women's Branch, dedicated their standard in1984.

Members at a meeting about 2000. Back row-left Joyce Hanmer, Amy Davies, Bessie Austin, Pat Burns. Front row-left Jean James, Jackie Richards, Dot Ford, Milly Whycherley, Nellie Sutton, Amy Dommett.

Below: Rene Jones receives her Long Service Award Left to Right Rene Jones, Dorothy Norton (Auntie Doss), Nellie Sutton, Jean James, Mary Gregory.

The Cockshutt Women's Section Standard is carried by Lisa Williams throughout the area at other Church Parades as well as our own. For many years these Parades were headed by a band. Remembrance Sunday

is also a time for marching down the village and laying wreaths on the War Memorial in the Churchyard after the Church Service. The Cockshutt Women's Section are also responsible for flowers on the War Memorial each week from March to October, each member taking a turn twice a year.

New members are most welcome to join us if you believe in our motto – SERVICE NOT SELF. During the life of the organisation Rene Jones, Nellie Sutton, Ev Clark, Dossie Birch and Myrtle Holliday have all been presented with Long Service Awards.

Present Chairman, Jean James, lays the Women's Section wreath on the War Memorial on Rembrance Sunday 2003. (left)

Cockshutt and District Royal British Legion Men's Branch

After the initial forming of the British Legion in 1921, the Cockshutt Branch remained active until after World War Two. The Branch then folded and the Branch Standard was laid up in Church where it still remains.

On 10th September 1971 the British Legion was given the prefix of Royal . On 20th June 1983 with seventeen members present, Major Jim Pearce opened the inaugural meeting of the Cockshutt and District Branch of the Royal British Legion. The headquarters were to be the Red Lion Hotel, Cockshutt.

The committee elected at this meeting; –

President   Lt. Cmdr Jack Investor Lloyd

Chairman   Mr Wilfred Parry – Ex Army

Secretary   Mr Terry Goodall – Ex Royal Navy

Treasurer   Mr Alan Jones – Ex Army

County Delegate Mr Bill Davies – Ex Royal Air Force

The new R.B.L. Standard was dedicated in Church on 30th October 1983. (left)

Mr Dennis Williams (left) was appointed Standard Bearer and he has faithfully carried the flag at local and national level ever since.

In 1984 a Service Committee was formed:

Chairman Mr Terry Goodall

Secretary   Mr Qu. Griffith

Member   Mr A Griffith

The two Mr Griffith's still serve on the Service Committee today.

One of the highlights of the year was the Mystery Trip, arranged by Terry Goodall and Lakeside Coaches, Ellesmere. Strange, but we always used to end up in a Pub, the most remembered one being at a certain venue in Overton on Dee, a total disaster but great fun all the same. Over the years fund raising events have been many and various. The Branch has made thousands of pounds for the Poppy Appeal and Branch funds. Some of the events include Clay Pigeon shoots at Stanwardine Hall, the home of the President of the Baschurch Branch, and long serving Cockshutt member Mr David Bridge. Several Walks have been arranged, a Dog Show, Bingo Evenings, a Horse Racing Evening, and entertainment by Three Men In A Bow Tie. A Sponsored March from Shrewsbury to Cockshutt in full World War Kit by Mr Alan Biggs, a sponsored 9 hour guitar playing by Dennis Williams and Three Sods Operas, a Naval term for a Variety Night.

The residents of Cockshutt and District have always gone out of their way to help the Branch whatever the Fund Raising event may have been.

One of the most successful events was held on 7th to 9th September 1992 when Alan Biggs visited eight different RAF Stations around the country in 54.50 hours using as many different modes of transport as possible. Driving, walking and flying in several different aircraft types brought in over six-hundred pounds for the Poppy Appeal.

Over the years the RBL members have grown older and small branches like Cockshutt find the going more and more difficult. We are always ready to welcome any ex-service men and women, or any member of the general public who believe in our cause to join us. The motto of the Royal British Legion is – SERVICE NOT SELF.

Above: Dennis and Alan. Top right: Church Parade through the Village. Bottom right: Members of the Cockshutt Men's Section on Remembrance Sunday 2003

Indoor Short Mat Bowls Club

This club was started in January 1990 in the old Village Hall. Special carpet and equipment as well as bowls had to be bought before they could begin to play. The carpet arrived in strips and was sewn together to form the two lanes. The club has been very well supported over the years and continues to meet every Thursday evening in the new hall where more room is available. The Bowls Club always support the Village Hall Fete by running a stall and getting dressed up for the Fancy Dress Competition on a float when we were allowed to parade down the village.

Whist and Bingo

Whist has been a part of the village for over fifty years when the Vicarage Annexe was used as the venue. Both Whist and Bingo were used as fundraisers for the first Village Hall. Bingo and Whist were on alternate Saturday nights and are still fairly well supported after all this time.

Cockshutt and District Flying Club/Pigeon Club

In order to be a licensed flying club Bill Smith and Alan Jones went to the British Legion Club in Saltney, North Wales to meet the Union of Racing Pigeons Association, in 1979/ 1980, to get permission to become a flying club. This was the start of Cockshutt and District Flying Club (left) and their boundaries were determined by the Association. The Club was by invitation only. The Club have met over the years in both the Crown and the Red Lion Pubs.

Pigeon Show in outbuildings at the Red Lion. Left Andrew Lawley (Ellesmere), Bill Smith, John Edwards (Tetchill) Alf Smith, Ivor Williams (Baschurch) Micheal Sumner (Ellesmere).

The first race of the season is in April, with the old birds. The distance increases with each race until the birds are taken across the channel. There are about six cross-channel races each season, In the second half of the season the young birds of four to five months old are trained, again letting the birds make their way home from further afield each time. During the winter months when the birds have finished their moult and are in good condition there would be a show.

All prize money for the season's results comes from subscriptions, entry fees, raffles and donations from local people and businesses.

K C Knight (known as Danny) is shown right with his Trophies and Cups he won in 2003 along with £475.60p at the Presentation Evening of the Cockshutt Flying Club.

Keeping pigeons is not as easy as it used to be; new laws have allowed the increase in the birds of prey, which certainly makes life very difficult for the pigeons. Hawks particularly find a pigeon easy prey – they can be seen perched near the pigeon loft just waiting for the birds to be let out!

Cockshutt Girl Guide Company

Mona Whitfield began the Cockshutt Girl Company in 1971. They met at the Vicarage Annex on Friday evenings. Helpers included Barbara Hampson, Margaret Dickin, Joyce Whitfield and Marilyn Yates and all had their turn at running the Company.

In 1971 about fifteen girls were members. (right). In 1983 six Guiders attained the Queen's Guide Award. This was the last year of this award which became known as Baden Powell's Trefoil afterwards

The six girls – Karen Yates, Louise Dickin, Carole Evans, Vivienne Powell, Judith Webster and Lara Taylor (shown bottom right), were trained by Brenda Elwell–Sutton, who had come to live in the area from Scotland. Not only did Brenda help the girls with the Queen's Badge, she also trained Marilyn to become a qualified Guide Leader. The last camp the Cockshutt Guides took part in was the 'Big' Tudor Rose 75th Anniversary Camp held at the West Mid Showground.

The Cockshutt Guides folded due to lack of members in 1985 and Marilyn Yates moved to the Ellesmere Guides and is still involved today.

Cockshutt Scout Company

The 1st Cockshutt Group (left) was started in the early 1990s by Mark Smith helped by Tim Norton, Russell Lewis and Kim O'Brian. Caroline Griffiths was elected Chairperson, Gill Webb, Treasurer and Julie Gamble, Secretary; they all had boys in the group. The Group met one night a week and always had an interesting and different activity to do.- map reading, Five-a-side football tournaments, and paper picking to help keep the village tidy, to mention but a few. They also went camping, walking, to swimming galas, pot-holing, and fishing.

Church Parades were important on St George's Day (left) when Boreatton Band would lead the march.

Local area events were attended, and the Group once manned the telephones at BT Shrewsbury Exchange for Comic Relief Day 'phone in. Other Charity work was also well supported by Cockshutt Scouts. Unfortunately due to lack of support and Mark Smith not being able to spare the time the group folded around 2000.

Cockshutt Cubs and Beavers

The Cubs and Scouts join in activities in the Old Village Hall.

The Cubs started about the same time as the Scouts when Thelma and John Owen were the first leaders.

Cubs are shown left serving the starter course for the Ellesmere Ladies Circle 'Safari Supper' to gain their Community Badges.

Helen and Chris Ashdown began Beavers and Sandra Jones and Dave Vanner all ran the Beavers at different times, but again due to lack of support and time both groups folded around 2000.

Playgroup

The memories of Iona Blundred about starting a Playgroup in the village

As a young teacher of Reception class children I couldn't understand why Parents were worried or upset when they brought their children to school for the very first time. As a mother of twins approaching their third birthday, I realised they were fast coming up to school age and I then knew what the parents of the children I had taught went through So I decided to start a Playgroup in the village, and my children could make friends with lots of children, and would settle into school life when it was their turn to go.

After many 'phone calls, visiting councils, paperwork and going around the village collecting unwanted toys and games I finally opened in May 1972 with ten children. I started off opening two mornings a week which later became three mornings.

The children came from the village, Bagley, Hordley, Stanwardine, Burlton, Petton, Spun Hill, Weston Lullingfields and Brown Heath. There were many fundraising activities to provide paint, toys and equipment; a coffee evening, stalls at fetes, jumble sales, pottery party and later rides on a miniature steam train to raise money to buy a large piece of equipment – the slide.

I was given regular supplies of computer run-off paper for drawing and writing and I used to go to a newspaper firm in Oswestry, who gave me ends of rolls of paper that was used to print the newspapers. I relied on a Mothers' rota for help in the Playgroup.

In May 1973, I left for a brief period to have my youngest son and Marjorie Kettle and Marilyn Yates took over. They also took the children on a trip to the Fire Station. When my son was four months old I went back and my baby spent many happy hours watching the children and later even trying to join in some of the activities.

The Slide

Although we had to try to raise money in various ways to pay for equipment, I remember one fundraising event that stands out above all others. It was the year of the drought, 1976. We arranged a fete with Wem Town Band to open it. There were lots of stalls, pony rides and games. I thought this would be brilliant on the field in lovely weather. The day arrived and *It Rained* all day. We had to cram everything, except the pony rides, into the village hall!

During my time running the Playgroup we put on concerts, had sports days and had a Nativity play, and of course Christmas parties. Mr Dommett was Father Christmas in 1976.

From the Playgroup a Babysitting Service was started in the village using a token system which worked very well for many years.

It was at Christmas 1978 when I left to go back to teaching and the Playgroup was taken over by Marilyn Yates. Marilyn was helped by Jo Frater from Burlton. In 1981 Jane Barton joined Jo to run the group, with the help of a Mums rota. They tried to start a Mother and Toddler group but they had very little support. Lyn Bowley, Fiona Denning and Sue Hill kept everything going until 1987 when the numbers dropped. Sue Hill moved the Playgroup to her house 'The Old Vicarage'.

A new committee was formed by mothers in the village who wanted to return to the village hall with a Playgroup. Caroline Griffiths, helped by Joyce Feeney and Gill Webb, set up Playgroup again in the village hall in September 1988. The old village hall did not have much storage space and it was difficult to put everything away after each session, but it had to be done as the hall was used so much in the evenings.

The annual outing was usually to Farm World in Wrexham, always popular when animals are to be seen and touched.

In 1996 Jayne Gray became Playgroup Leader with the help of Caroline Griffiths, Maura Birch, Kay Hanmer, Mandy Middleton, Sally Vanner, Julie Bywater, Jayne Raymond and Angela Evans as volunteers and Sue Smith as assistant. The Playgroup began to spread its wings and many visits were organized including the Fire Station, Park Hall, Telford Town Park, Ellesmere to see the birds and play on the swings, and Shade Oak to see the foals. Visitors were invited to the group at the hall and the children met a policeman, a doctor, a health visitor, the Vicar, Dave and his donkeys, and exotic pets with snakes and spiders etc. There was always a Christmas Party with games, entertainment and Father Christmas.

They did go to Park Hall for a Christmas Party and Father Christmas a few times, it saved the mess in the village hall, and the children really did enjoy themselves. During Jayne's time as Leader the group had three OFSTED Inspections and had good reports each time. Assistants came and went but Sue Groombridge, Tina Jones, Jean Pugh and Sue Mellor all contributed to the smooth running of Playgroup. A Mums' rota was replaced by voluntary helpers who did the same hours each week so there was continuity. We were very lucky to have Cathy Thorold, Holly Hayward, Bunty Tweedle, Natalie Williams and Helen Philips. Cathy and Holly became assistants and Holly is still working in the Group.

When the Millennium Hall was built the Playgroup moved into a purpose built activity room with storage space. The tables and chairs and other equipment could now be left out most of the time and this was very much appreciated by the staff. The Playgroup began to grow and extended the hours to five days a week, 9 am. to 3 pm. Just like schools the numbers fluctuate but it continues to be successful.

During these years a very successful Mother and Toddler Group was set up and became very popular one morning a week, when they met in the lounge so that the toddlers had space to move around.

To celebrate the Queen's Golden Jubilee playgroup organised for the village to all have a go at doing as many stitches as they wished until the tapestry was finished. It took some time to finish but we did make it.

Playgroup has close links with Cockshutt School and its staff, getting the children ready for 'Big School'. Jayne resigned as Leader in December 2003.

A fair fundraiser

Cockshutt Playgroup held a spring fair in the Village Hall.
-Eleanor Thomas, Mrs Sandra Thomas.
-Mrs Julie Gamble, Mrs Cathy Benson, Mrs Debbie Hayward.

3—Mrs Joyce Feeney, Mrs Val Lewis.
4—Mrs Janet Chambers, Mrs Gill Williams, Mrs Caroline O'Brien.

Pictures: Bob Carter

From top left anti-clockwise: Visit to Farm World. The Play Bus pays a visit to Cockshutt Playgroup. More fund raising. Christmas Party at Park Hall. Jayne paints Harriet's face during her party at playgroup. The children enjoy Harriet's Birthday party lunch. The Golden Jubilee Tapestry

Football

When the village hall was built in 1967 Alf Smith ran a youth club in the village. John Griffiths and Graham Humphries organized a football team but they seemed to have to play against much older men and it was very soul-destroying for the lads. In 1970 another football team was being formed at Walford College known as 'Basil's Bruisers', after a member of the team. In those days 'Crossroads' the ITV soap was recorded at the college and sometimes the filming got in the way of friendly football matches. Believe it or not this was the beginning of the Cockshutt Football team. Derek Jones from Hordley brought the lads to play on the village field, which in those days was two fields and the pitch was the other way round, running north /south. Friendlies were organized every Sunday morning and by 1974–1975 the Wem and District Sunday League was formed, Cockshutt being one of the founder members. It was also in 1974 that Cockshutt FC had permission to use Chelsea FC old badge – a lion with CFC underneath. The team was relegated to the 2nd Division in 1975 but they had lots of support from the village. Nancy Roberts was in charge of refreshments and Rene Jones did all the laundry. Fundraising was very important as village hall and field fees were high. Strip had to be bought and new footballs were always needed. Players were asked to pay £1 each to insure themselves each week. 1976/1977 was the best season they had and won promotion to the 1st Division and they won the Consolation Cup – they were the first 2nd Division team to do so.

From left clockwise: Successful team 1976/77.

1980s Team: Ern Roberts, Phil Ralphs and Jack Northwood all helped the Cockshutt teams.

1991 Team: In 1991 Cockshutt were 2nd Division cup winners and enjoyed a better season. Derek Jones on the right, Jack Northwood Middle back and Reg Price in the hat behind the team.

The 1994 Team

During season 1978 the Market Hall, Ellesmere was used for training every Wednesday evening - it was now getting serious! The following years were not without problems both on and off the field, with not enough fundraising being done, and the form on the pitch needed improving. It is very difficult to get players to join a losing side.

In 1995 Cockshutt reached the 2nd Division Cup Final and also the League Cup Final! The League Cup Final was played against Gobowen Celtic at Wem. The programme contained the following pen pictures and information from the club.

DALE GRIFFITHS: We all think Dale, our goalkeeper, is a dead ringer for actor Tom Hanks, especially his character Forest Gump. If he wins a trophy this year don't ask him for a speech or he may burst into tears.

DARREN GRIFFITHS – Brother of Dale: Darren is built like the proverbial brick lavatory – and smells like one sometimes. At every match he ceremoniously smears himself with Vaseline – he says it's for chaps – or something like that! Anyway, I believe him.

DAVE WELLS: Dave is the only player in the team who hasn't scored a goal yet this season. Even our goalkeeper's got one! Maybe he's saving them up for the final. Mind you, Dave bagged some last season though – all in the wrong net unfortunately!

MIKE GRIFFITHS: Mike is priceless- 'cos he's an antique – almost! Cockshutts oldest player, he continues to amaze us every week by still being alive at the final whistle. Born and bred in Cockshutt and a founder member of the club, he claims he can still remember when all the fields around Cockshutt were still fields … and still are! Oh, and you could leave your front door open. Probably.

ALAN DAVIES: Alan has returned to Cockshutt this season to be our player manager after a successful period at Plant Utd. Although an excellent manager, his creative and imaginative fabrication (fibs) of how well he plays on the field is perhaps more fitting to fantasy football management!

SHAUN BIRCH: Shaun tells us he carefully prepares his state of mind the evening before a match by drinking some sort of 'secret tonic', probably 'milk of amnesia', as he can't seem to remember how many he's had by the morning. Well either that or he's been in the pub all night.

GARY ROBERTS: Gary kept the club alive last season, bravely taking over as player manager under difficult circumstances and steered us away from relegation. Definitely the 'biggest' character in the team, you may hear his dulcet tones carry from the dressing room at the end of each match – 'cos it's not over 'till Gary sings.

PAUL BIRCH: Nicknamed 'Gudgeon', for some strange reason, he always manages to get hurt while fiercely battling in midfield each week. As a result he continues to use more and more bandages for strapping as the season progresses. He should soon acquire the nickname of the 'midfield mummy'. Oh, and he's got a lovely smile as well.

JOHN EDWARDS: John reckons he's often mistaken for soccer stars Ian Rush and John Aldridge, (always by stunning blonds incidentally!) whenever he's in pubs etc. in Liverpool. It's funny that! Yosser Hughes never got a mention though?

JOHN STEVENS: Always the last man to arrive to get changed – often with seconds to spare till kick off! His excuses would fill a page… 'the alarms broke – the car broke down – my wife's hamster escaped!' etc.etc…

JASON PRICHARD: Imagine the results of a genetic cross-breeding experiment involving Michael Barrymore, Matt Le Tissier and Rodney from 'Only Fools and Horses' – well that's Jason. Our top goal scorer this season so far, we've all decided to stop passing the ball to him 'cos we're a bit jealous.

JOHN BARRY: John is a superb all-round player. A spectacular goal scorer, always in space and available for a pass – he has excellent vision, skill, balance and speed … makes you sick really doesn't it.

GARY JONES: Dependable, honest, romantic, good-looking, great sense of humour and an altogether smashing bloke … are just some of the things Gary has paid me to write when describing him today.

ELWYN LACOURSE: The clown of the club – loves to dress up – as Father Christmas for the old ladies who love him, also as his sister who all his workmates want to date.

DEREK JONES: Derek, now our secretary, was a player and founder member of Cockshutt Football Club way back in the early seventies. Strange to think that when Derek was dribbling down the field, most of the team was dribbling down their bibs!

MARTIN JENKS: Martin was present throughout the qualifying rounds but must unfortunately miss today's game as he's recovering from a cosmetic operation on a 'sticky out' collar bone, but it looks nice now though. He tells us he might have a nose job next season or maybe breast implants – he doesn't know yet. Decisions are such a bitch!

JACK: A loyal member of the' backroom staff ', Jack Northwood comes equipped with several rolls of tape which we all scrounge off him to hold our socks up. He contributes most generously towards the club and eases pre-match nerves with many wry comments.

REG: Special mention to Reg Price, who rain or shine comes to support us, and helps to put up the nets, flags and retrieves lost balls. Travelling to almost every away match he must surely be one of our most loyal supporters.

In season 1994/1995 Terry Williams began to play for Cockshutt. Terry had been living and working in the former East Germany in Kelbra, a semi-rural town at the foot of the Hertz Mountains, similar in size to Ellesmere but smaller. SV Kelbra, the town's football team was founded in 1920 and is the hub of the town. Terry became the first non-German player in the team and was often featured in the local press match reports. In 1995 Terry arranged for a handful of British Gas (who he worked for) and Cockshutt FC players to travel to Kelbra to play a friendly match. This was the start of friendly matches every other year in alternate countries. Kelbras's first visit to Cockshutt was in 1998. The home team was always victorious in the 'friendlies' but rivalry was forgotten at the final whistle and long-lasting friendships were made. In 1999 Terry Williams died while playing football in Manchester with his workmates. The Cockshutt trip in 1999 to Kelbra, along with some Ellesmere Rangers players, who Terry had also played with, had already been discussed and Terry's family decided that the arrangements should stand so in May 1999 the visit to Kelbra took place. The next exchange is scheduled for Easter 2004 when Kelbra visit Cockshutt. It has been a fitting memorial to Terry who loved football and wanted to bring together communities that he loved. They loved him in return.

It was in 1999 that Cockshutt Football Club folded due to lack of players.

In 2004 The Leaking Tap formed a new football team known as The Tap, and played in the Wem Sunday League. Unfortunately they only managed a season but were well turned out in a sponsored strip by 'On Course' of Wem. Again it was lack of players that caused the team to fold.

Cockshutt '84

In 1984 another team was formed in Cockshutt to play Saturday matches and known as Cockshutt '84. Some of the players played for both Cockshutt teams. It was Frank Morris who was one of the organisers of Cockshutt '84 but after a very successful first season the team folded two seasons later.

Choir

The formation of the Cockshutt Male Voice Choir was a result of a village concert produced by Terry Goodall and performed in the old village hall in 1995. It was a case of 'What do we do next'? A group was formed to sing and entertain with sketches written by Tom Jones. The group entertained at many local events and sketches were written for the organisation they were performing for, e.g. British Legion Ladies and The Women's Institute to mention a couple. Eventually the group concentrated more on the singing and enjoyed learning Welsh songs. 'Land of my Fathers' became their signature tune. Tom Jones was the conductor and Terry Goodall, Emlyn Evans, Don Dobson, Albert Griffiths, Alan Biggs, Tim Wycherley, Peter Allen, and Alan Jones practised once a week and Myra Evans accompanied them. In 2001 Tom Jones was unable to continue as conductor due to his wife's ill health. The group enjoyed their singing so much that most joined other choirs in North Shropshire and continue to sing.

Lunch Club

After the Millennium project was finished in church the fund-raising committee thought it would be a good idea to make use of the new facilities. It was decided to hold a lunch for anyone in the village who would like to come. For a nominal fee of £2.00 they would get a lunch; the menu included - soup and a sandwich, Hotpot and cheese and biscuits, Cottage Pie and a piece of cake. In summer salads and trifle etc. followed by tea or coffee. Three teams were set up and the lunch was to be on alternate Fridays. This was started in July 2002 and is still going strong. All expenses are taken out and the profit goes to church funds. We have celebrated Mr Dommett's 90th birthday and Mr and Mrs Dommett's 65th wedding anniversary. Christmas is always special when we have a party and the schoolchildren come in and entertain us. There is a real atmosphere of friendliness and enjoyment, a real village get-together!

Mr Dommetts 90th birthday party at Lunch Club with guests. Right, Helpers at Lunch Club

Golf Society

The Golf Society (below) was formed when Bob Greenaway was at the Red Lion - just for a social outing for local members and was well supported but numbers dropped and the outings stopped. The society had folded for about two years when Glyn Downes took over the organisation. About six events are played each year using different Golf Clubs in Shropshire. Each event is a competition for a trophy donated by local businesses. Sponsored events for local charities have also been arranged. Each event finishes with a meal at the Golf Club or back at the local. Plans are being made to venture further afield to look at other Clubs. About 12-20 players take part and although mainly local to the village, guests are invited.

Dice

This began during the time the Rawlinsons were at The Crown.

Every Monday the same crowd was in The Crown - there were about twelve of them. They would stand by the bar to play 7, 14, and 21. Each in turn threw three dice, the first to throw the sum of 7 named the drink, the dice went round again and the one to throw 14 paid for the drink. Round the dice went again and the one to throw 21 had to drink what had been chosen and paid for. If he or she hadn't drunk the drink before the next game started they had to buy a round for all the players.

They could only name a short drink in deference to the ladies who could not be expected to drink a pint. One night nearly ended in disaster when the Landlord Eric Rawlinson came round the bar and whisked up the dice and put them in his pocket. Everyone looked surprised, just then the door opened and in walked the Police. They felt sure the Police had heard the dice clatter on the bar but they found nothing. The game of Dice was illegal in pubs so they were lucky that Eric was so sharp otherwise he would have had a heavy fine.

Horse Racing

The first recorded Steeplechase to take place in Cockshutt was in 1837. The day was fine for 1st December, and about two thousand people were present. There were carriages and gigs, with horsemen, footmen and waggoners. The inns were full, also the houses, bakehouses, blacksmith's shop and the sheds accommodating both horses and people. Everyone was getting ready for all the fun of watching the chase. The start of the steeplechase, at one o'clock, was one hundred yards from Stanwardine Hall, owned at this time by Mr Stephen Denstone, one of the competitors.

The map of the course shows that it was well over four miles long. From Stanwardine, around the back of the village of Cockshutt, crossing the road at The Dobbin and then down Porter Lane and cutting across the Crosemere Meadows past the Hall to Wackley up to Old Gorse near Petton Lodge and back to Stanwardine. The ground was wet and heavy with some strong fences, sunken fences and big ditches for the horses to jump. The horses were very well turned out and the jockeys in their colourful silks must have been quite a sight. In this first Steeplechase, which was delayed by an hour and a half, there were 7 horses. 'Tarporley' – ridden by its owner Mr Denstone, in orange and white was the winner on the day; 'Bootjack' ridden by Mr Watson in black and white he came in second; 'Miracle' ridden by Mr T Clay in purple and crimson,; 'St David' ridden by W Sparling Esq and owned by Mr Kynaston, in green with a red cap; 'Pavilion' ridden by Mr K Bowens in orange; 'Rat Tail' ridden by Mr Burtonborough in yellow and purple; and 'Roy More' ridden by Mr Minors in blue and white. Each horse had to carry 13 stones. 'St David' was the last of the 3 finishers. The Officials for this first race were J R. Kynaston (Steward), A. W. Corbet,

W Sparling (Junior), Dryden R. Corbet, Clement Hill, P Charlton, and Captain Tudor Williams Junes Barker. These officials include many well known and important families from the surrounding area. It must certainly have been one of the highlights of the sporting calendar.

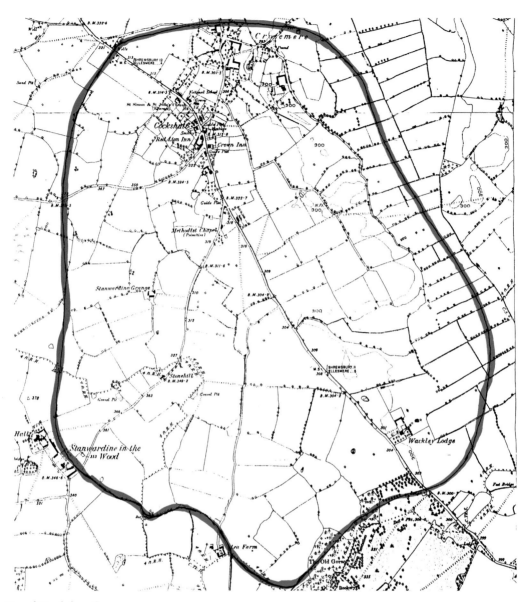

Map of Steeplechase Course

There were no serious accidents but a few falls and spills, most horses and riders having had at least one fall, and the winner 'Tarporley' was given enthusiastic applause by the people of Cockshutt. After paying the usual expenses, he would have been entitled to £20 for his owner rider. Mr Denstone's neighbours subscribed to the cost of having his portrait painted by one Jones R.A. and it was presented to him at a Grand Dinner at Stanwardine Hall.

Another account of horse racing in Cockshutt was on 1st November 1852. This was a three-day event which included dancing in the evening, and took place on fields around Cockshutt. I believe this was on the field by The Dobbin and still known as the Race Course Field today.

The account of these races in 1852 has been taken from the original poster, which has been framed, and is in the possession of the Lindop family formerly of Ferneyhough Farm.

Included on the race card was a Ladies Subscription Purse, which the Ladies of Cockshutt had contributed towards the Prize Money. The Owen Glyndwr Stakes and a Handicap Hurdle Race were also on the card. The horses or ponies were much smaller than the race-horses we have today, the races were for horses or ponies no more than fourteen hands high and the owners had to live within twelve miles of Cockshutt. There were so many competitors that heats had to be held and the Handicap Stewards were to be found at the Cross Keys Inn. The winners received their prizes at the Red Lion Inn and the Race Ball took place on the 2nd November at the Crown Inn . On the race day lots of amusements were organised including Bag and Foot races and the wind-up was held at the Golden Lion on 3rd November. One amusement that was forbidden by order of the Stewards, was Thimble Rigging. This is the trick game with three thimble-shaped cups and a pea, the bystander takes bets on which cup covers the pea?

Racecourse field in Cockshutt by The Dobbin was also used by the farmers to race their Shire horses which usually pulled the plough. The cart horses were ridden bareback, using just a set of reins, around the outside of the field. Alf Hulme had a good horse called 'Bob' - very nasty to deal with but a winner on the track.

Dog Racing

This was on Harry Austin's field now part of Crosemere Farm. Any dog would do. A stuffed rabbit on a winch was wound in as a lure. Someone would hold your dog at the start and you would shout it home over the winning line. Bill Ralphs was an organiser of the dog racing and would appear in a white coat and bowler hat for the event. Needless to say the bookies would be in attendance at both the horse and dog racing.

Beagles

The Cockshutt area is hunted by the Shropshire Beagles and they used to meet at The Crown (right). They did use Bagley when Jack Ivester-Lloyd, a very well known Beagler and author, lived there with his daughter after his retirement. Petton, Weston Lullingfields and Frankton Grange have also been venues over the

years. Burlton Inn has become the latest meeting place. The beagle is a smaller dog than a foxhound and the huntsman are all on foot and they hunt the hare. The Beagles are shown (left) as they set off up Park Lane.

Shooting

There are three shoots in Cockshutt area – Crosemere Hall, Petton and Frankton. All are private traditional old-established shoots that have been in existence for a very long time. Each shoot buys in pheasant poults at 6–8 weeks old and rears them ready for the season. Not only pheasant but duck, partridge and woodcock are part of the 'bag'. The Petton shoot is mainly on the old Petton Hall Estate where the Cunliffe family used to reside. Crosemere Hall shoot is on their land and includes the area around Sweatmere. Frankton Grange Estate is the area for the Frankton shoot and was used when the Robinson family lived at The Grange. The land is still used today. All three shoots have about 8–10 guns and each shoot uses a different day so there is only one shoot in operation at a time, and only once a week during the season. The gun dogs and the 'beaters' make up the gathering and the day is usually finished off with a meal at a local pub.

Left, Don Hanmer leads the way back from a Crosemere Shoot with some of the 'bag'.
Right, Frank and Don Hanmer sort out the 'bag' after a successful Crosemere Shoot.

Darts and Dominoes

Both The Lion and The Crown (right) had teams. Every Friday night was Darts and Dominoes night, one week at home and the next week away. Competition was very keen as all the pubs around were in the league. The nearest pub in our league to The Crown was five miles away and the furthest fourteen miles away. The rivalry between them was terrific but mostly friendly. The Crown had a very good Dominoes team. There were nine in a team and you could play both darts and dominoes if you were good enough.

Fishing – Angling Club

Ellesmere Angling Club was founded in 1931 and has fishing rights on seven local waters including Crosemere. The waters contain good stocks of carp, tench, bream, perch, and pike. They have a membership of approximately 330. There are 100 outside members and the remainder are classed as local. They must live within a radius of ten miles of Ellesmere, so anyone from Cockshutt can join and fish the Mere. Day tickets are not available for Crosemere – only Blakemere and the Canal offer these. Nothing much has changed over the last seventy years or so, except for rent or subscriptions increases.

Cockshutt Fly Fishers

With the enthusiasm of Brian Roberts (Sam) and the negotiating skills of Terry Goodall, for three short years Cockshutt had a Trout Fishing Club. In 2002 the Club agreed terms for fishing in Noneley reservoir. Seventeen members were needed to fish so the costs could be covered (only a few miles from Cockshutt). The three-acre rectangular pool stocked with rainbows and brownies provided a quiet retreat and sporty fishing. A rectangular reservoir might sound very dull, but in fact the dense growth of bullrushes and floating weeds provided rich feeding for the fish, and a dazzling array of dragonflies, with kestrels, buzzards and barn owls adding to the rich natural history. The water supply is piped from the nearby river which is used to irrigate crops grown in fields in the summer.

Horticultural Show

Over the years many silver cups had been awarded to the winners of the Show Classes and we had some difficulty trying to locate these when we were researching the Show. So much time had elapsed and for safe keeping the whereabouts were so secret that people had forgotten where they were last seen. On our first exhibition displaying all the information and photographs that had been generously donated by the village in September 2003 we were very pleased to have on show all the cups that were awarded last in 1976. Quite a find in the Parish Clerk's attic!

It was perhaps in about 1888 that Cockshutt held its first Flower Show on the vicarage lawn by the kind permission of Reverend Henry Wilcox. Rabbits, poultry, fruit and vegetables were on show, as well as flowers. The first, second and third prizes were one shilling, sixpence and threepence respectively, presented by a local celebrity. All was going well until a hulla-baloo emanating from William Marsh's farm practically cleared the grounds. Old Nanny Murray from Watergate Street, Ellesmere found that the crowd rushed right past her stall of cakes and sweets, which she had set up on the pavement outside the vicarage double doors, in its hurry to get to Manor Farm to see what all the noise was about. She wished she had stuck to her regular round of selling 'twenty fresh herrings for a shilling'. The news spread quickly. A cart horse had broken loose in the stables and had walked up a flight of steps onto the hayloft above. How to get the horse down without broken limbs brought forth much and varied advice from neighbouring farmers and their waggoners and of course from the crowd. Eventually the pitch-hole in the outer wall was knocked out until it was of a size to admit the passage of a large horse. A load of straw was spread thickly beneath, and with much coaxing and pulling on the halter the horse was eventually persuaded to jump through the much enlarged pitch-hole to the straw below, little the worse for his astounding adventure. Later he was sold to Mrs Marsh's brother, Edward Harrison of Top House Farm, Kenwick Park and until his death of old age, some fifteen years afterwards, he enjoyed some measure of fame for his exploit. So the first Flower Show commenced in a very humble but exciting way.

Some of the prize winners and officials at the Cockshutt Flower Show on September 3, 1960.

As years went by its popularity became so great that it became necessary to hold it in a tent set up in Harry Austin's field. It was well patronized and the exhibits of flowers, fruit and vegetables were highly creditable for a small parish. In the evening a dance was held in the tent. The show prospered well for several years, then the farmers, or at least some of them, introduced horse racing and this displeased the vicar (Reverend H J Wilcox) and he withdrew his patronage so that gradually the show declined and came to an end.

The show restarted after a break during the Second World War but lack of support forced its closure again.

From left clockwise:

May Kynaston admires one of the flower arrangements.

Joyce Whitfield receives the Rose Bowl

WI organise the Show

Margaret Griffiths, 1976 Show Secretary

The Women's Institute also took over the running of the show for a few years. After a break of four years the show was resurrected in 1976 and Mrs Dommett presented the prizes - it was the same year that she and Mr Dommett retired from school.

Although held in Cockshutt the event was known as Petton with Cockshutt Horticultural Show. It has changed throughout the years and now includes a children's section and arts and crafts but of course the flowers and vegetables, cooking and preservatives are still important. When the show was in the marquee by Stone Villa, Manders Fair was there as well and the event was a 'big day', in the life of the village.

The first Saturday in September has traditionally been Flower Show Day. George Tatton from Stone Villa used to help with the hobby horses and swings so that he could take Joe Brookfield with him and let him ride on them. The school entered vegetables grown in the school garden and won many prizes. I hope to encourage this event to begin again if I can get some interest. The Show did restart September 2004.

Keep Fit

Keep fit to music, and circuit training classes have been held in both the old and the new village hall. These have not been continuous, but well supported when organised.

Youth Club

Alf Smith started the first youth club in the new village hall in 1967. Graham Humphries and John Griffiths also began a youth club football team but matches were very difficult as they had to play against teams of men.

Youth Football Teams. About 1968: Back Row from the left – Bob Poole, John Griffiths, Phil Orme, Gareth Dean, Mike Griffiths, Charlie Brookes.

Front Row- William Williams, John James, Graham Humphries, Derek Jones, Keith Meddins, Graham Hughes.

About 1970 Back Row from the left – John Dovaston, Andy Barratt, John Griffiths, Harland Butler, Phil Orme, Mike Hesp, Tony McBride.

Front Row – Alan Smith, Mike Griffiths, Brenard Thomas, Martin Lysons, Brian Gough.

Ern and Nancy Roberts were always very involved with the village hall and continued to run the youth club after Alf finished his stint. Ern and Nancy organised both day trips and Holidays for the members. On the photograph (above) are shown, David Dickin, John Dickin, Keith Whitfield and Roger Griffiths among others in 1968.

A holiday to Anglesey under canvas; day trips included visits to Royal Albert Docks Liverpool followed by ten- pin bowling in Chester, the Houses of Parliament with an overnight stay in London, and the New Cathedral in Liverpool. Cockshutt village hall was the place to be for the best discos in North Shropshire - people came from Whitchurch and Shrewsbury to dance to a live band.

Below, Pat Morris and Derek Davies help to serve the 'goodies' to the 'old folks' at a party organised by the Youth Club. Ted Smith, Nellie Smith and Mrs Stacy enjoy themselves.

A Saturday Craft Club was also organised for the youngsters in the village and was very well supported. The youth club bought the football strip for the football team out of their funds for a cost of £200. Eventually the Cockshutt Football Club was formed – they were founder members of the Wem Sunday League. The newly formed team included some of the youth club players and became the team for Cockshutt. When Ern and Nancy decided they had done their bit for the youth of the village Syd Davies took charge in 1983 and kept it going for a few more years before it folded due to lack of support.

Fox Hunting

The hunt was recalled by Stanley Hulme as he had always been a hunt supporter from a young age. He belonged to both North Shropshire Hunt and Sir W.W. Wynne's Hunt (Wynnstay). One meet used to begin at Loppington and the other at the Frankton Grange. Stanley remembered that faggots were placed down foxholes to prevent the fox going to ground. There were about forty horses, plus foot followers on their bikes.

Cockshutt is on the boundary of two main foxhunting packs, Sir Watkin Williams Wynne and North Shropshire. Sir W.W. Wynne's hounds have been hunting since the early 1700s and started as a pack to hunt hares. The hounds have always been kept at Wynnstay near Ruabon and were privately owned by the Williams Wynne family until 1944 when they had to begin to have subscriptions. The North Shropshire Hunt was founded in 1834 when Sir Rowland Hill was the first master. The hounds have always been kept at Lee Bridges, Preston Brockhurst.

There are many stories out on the hunting field in and around Cockshutt and Petton, possibly the most famous being 'Owd Tummy Dickin' of Cockshutt House who rode to hounds for many years. When too old to follow the chase on horseback he hitched his hack to a trap and drove to various vantage points he knew well. There is also a story that he trapped a large dog fox in a culvert by his house and when the hunt came the same day he let it out for the huntsmen to have a great chase down the meadows to Burlton. However the wily fox was far too artful and he took sanctuary in Squire Vaughan's Spinney in Burlton, who was opposed to hunting.

Petton Hall used to be an important venue for Sir. W. W. Wynne's Hunt to meet. Mrs Emma Florence Cunliffe would greet the huntsmen in the park beneath the magnificent beeches and oaks which were a feature of the park. John Moore writes about 'a frosty morning in November when the beeches and oaks were still cloaked in their autumnal glory of russets and browns, while under the trees lay an ever thickening carpet of fallen leaves'. Horses and their riders and hounds had travelled for the meet; for in those days there were no motor vehicles to convey them to the rendezvous as there are today. Redcoated huntsmen mingled with horsemen more soberly attired but all superbly mounted. Ladies were present riding side saddle, for at that time it was quite unthinkable for a lady to ride astride. They were dressed in a habit most becoming for the occasion – a long black skirt draping their legs which were otherwise encased in riding breeches and top boots, a well tailored black jacket neatly waisted, a white cravat and a black bowler hat to which was attached a veil to protect the face completed their attire. And how charming they looked when well mounted. While the

Hunting from Stanwardine Hall

reception was taking place refreshments were served by the servants from the hall. There was a claret cup and biscuits for the ladies, while the gentlemen partook of spirits or beer with bread and cheese, which was brought round in large shallow wicker baskets. The same hospitality was extended to the foot followers. Second horsemen were there each having a spare horse on a leading rein ready for his master as soon as required. The Crown was used in the 1960s as a meeting place when glasses of sherry were handed around as the stirrup cup while the horses and hounds milled around the outside of the pub. In 2003 Sir. W. W. Wynne's and North Shropshire Hunt met in the area at Stanwardine Hall, Shade Oak, Burlton Inn, Loppington and help to keep the fox population under control.

Cricket

According to Esme Rawlinson, Landlady of The Crown, the main topic of conversation as soon as June arrived was cricket. Harry Pratt's field was used first of all and many comic matches took place when everyone would dress up, the women included, and great fun was had by all. Cricket balls have landed in The Red Lion barns and also straight over the pubs into the road.

The villagers dress up (right), to play cricket on Harry Pratts field. Joyce Whitfield, Karen and Keith Whitfield (just their heads), Kevin Holliday and John Husbands (far right).

The more serious matches took place on Randle Carr's'

Cornesfield where the Briars estate is now. As this was a grazing field for Crosemere Farm a lot of work had to be done to get the square ready for batting and the outfield suitable for fielding. Once the square had been cut, about six wickets in all, it was fenced off so the cows couldn't get on it. The field was used by Crosemere farm as an area to use while the cows were waiting to be milked. Of course this meant they left cow pats everywhere on the outfield so before each game the men had to go round with a shovel and bucket and sawdust was put over the spot from where the cowpat had been collected. The outfield was cut and a silage trailer used to take the grass away. Arrangements were made for a knockout competition each year and teams came from Wem, Ellesmere and Shrewsbury. Hanging behind the bar at The Crown were a number of pewter tankards all different shapes, sizes and patterns each belonging to a cricketer. Before each match the men would have their own tankard filled and take it down to the pitch. This came about because a glass got broken once and they thought this much safer. There were as many as thirty two teams that took part. The chief groundsmen were Bill Ralphs, Johnnie Husbands and Frank Holliday. After collecting the cow pats sawdust was put over the spot.

The umpires were Eric Rawlinson, Johnnie Husbands and Bill Ralphs. The last winner of the knockout cup played in the evenings was Telepost, Shrewsbury - they still have the cup displayed in a cabinet at the Sorting Office. There was an entrance fee collected at the gate and a raffle was held each match. The cricket equipment was borrowed from Petton Hall School.

CHAPTER 10

INNS AND BEER HOUSES, PUBLIC HOUSES OR 'PUBS'

In the 18th and 19th centuries Cockshutt was renowned for its fine cheese. The parish was originally an area of 1,533 acres, all owned by the Earl of Bridgewater. Another claim to fame was that in 1815 Cockshutt could boast of having eight public houses, not necessarily all in business at the same time – The Golden Lion Inn, The Red Lion Inn, The Crown Hotel, Petton Arms, Lloyd Arms, The Green Gate, Kenwick Hotel and The Cross Keys.

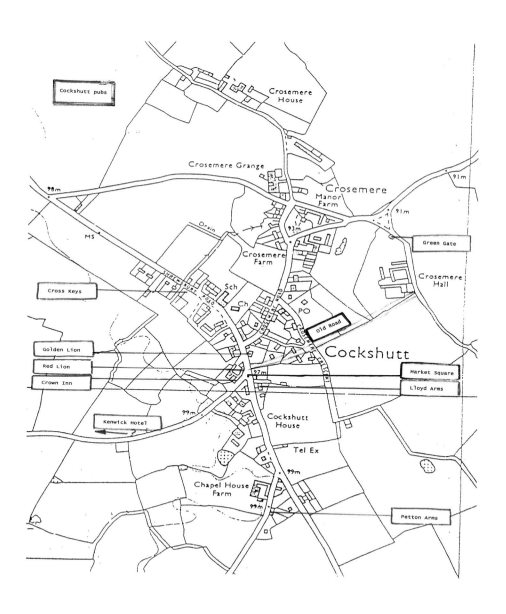

The Red Lion and The Crown were the largest and longest serving establishments and have both been supported by the village over the years. The villagers often changed their allegiance from one pub to the other and then go back as their fancy took them, or maybe a change of Landlord would make them move. Seven pubs have closed down over the years and at the moment the village is served by The Leaking Tap (formerly The Red Lion)

It has been very difficult to find any information about some of these pubs, but you must remember some of them would be just a single room within a house where ale was served and probably brewed on the premises. Sometimes these places would be beer houses and frequented by the many farm workers employed on the land. These beer houses were scattered about the village so no labourer would have far to go to get a drink. The largest public houses are situated on the main road through the village and were also coaching inns that could offer stabling, refreshment and a bed if needed. Working travellers both tradesmen and waggoners could obtain a hearty supper of beef, pickles and ale, a night's rest in the straw of the loft above the stabled horses , all for 9p.

The Crown Hotel

The Crown (below) dates back to about 1689 and was built as a farm by Jed Slater; it was a black and white half-timbered building. The Crown became a public house in the late 17th Century. People travelling to the village would tie their horse and cart to the rings fixed into the wall, which are still there today. During the 18th Century the house was remodelled and additions were made. It was rebuilt in painted brick on a rendered sandstone plinth to the front and right gable ends and a slate roof was fitted.

The Crown Inn, Cockshutt was sold at auction on Friday 2nd January 1829 by Mr Perry, of Pride Hill, Shrewsbury, at 3 o'clock.

'An old established and well frequented Inn or Public House, called the Crown Inn situated

in Cockshutt, aforesaid with commodious stabling for 14 horses, convenient cow-houses, piggeries, garden, large and capital brew-house and cellaring, suitable offices with excellent pump. Also two pieces of capital Meadow Land, nearly adjoining, held with the above premises, well supplied with excellent water and containing about 4 acres (more or less). The premises are in full business, and are situated on the Shrewsbury to Chester Road, where the Mail and two other Coaches pass daily. Mr Mathers, the tenant, will show the premises and further particulars may be known on application to Mr Perry.'

The Crown clearly could compete with the other public houses in Cockshutt, having the advantage of stabling for so many horses. This was a vital sales advantage in an age of horse drawn transport.

The innkeeper in 1841 was John Trevor and his family. After his death his wife became innkeeper until 1881 when Edward Jones was in charge until 1885.

Some reference has been made over time to the Crown having been used as a courthouse but there appears to be no evidence to support this. Indeed, the number of times the various licensees were fined for permitting drunkenness on the premises would almost certainly not suggest it was ever a courtroom. The dates for these said fines were: 1874, twice, 1876, 1878, 1881 and finally for keeping an open house after hours! This catalogue of fines must have threatened the inn with the Brewster Sessions being liable to withdraw their Licence from the Licence holder. For reasons unknown some leniency would appear to have been shown.

It was William Colemere who took over for a few years, but in 1891 John Fardoe was the licensee, and in 1901 a Joseph Walford was in charge until William Horatio Jones who advertised the inn as 'good accommodation for cyclists' took over in 1905. By 1909 Lambert Jones and his family took up residence in the Crown and stayed until 1961.

Tom Jones was licencee at the Crown when he married Barbara, and he promised he would only stay for 1 year, in fact they stayed about 8 years. In 1961 they moved to the Fox in Bagley and stayed for 27 years. The photograph (right) shows Barbara and Tom retiring from the Fox after being in the trade for 35 years.

About 1960 the Crown was fitted with a nuclear fallout warning system, which was positioned just above the telephone. There was a little box containing a device which emitted a high pitched warbling sound to warn the village of a nuclear attack. There

Cockshutt's role in war effort

Cockshutt villagers need never worry if the Russians decide to invade.

For tucked away in one of the most unlikely of places is a nuclear fall-out warning system.

Above the telephone at the Crown Inn, at Cockshutt, there's a little box containing a device which emits a high-pitched warbling sound warning of a pending attack.

When the warbler is heard, it is licensee's Mr David Oliver's job to wind up a siren kept in a shed to let the villagers know of imminent danger.

The attack warning system is part of a nationwide link-up set up to warn everyone about nuclear particles falling into the atmosphere.

Since its installation 10 years ago, the system has only been used once a year — for testing. Mr and Mrs Oliver, who recently took over the pub don't take much notice of the warbler — it's there if it's needed. But they hope it won't be . . .

David Oliver, licensee of The Crown at Cockshutt with the nuclear fallout device.

was a blue siren warning light that accompanied this apparatus. The cessation of the Cold War saw the removal of this system.

For the eighteen years from 1961 the Crown became the home of Eric and Esme Rawlinson and their two daughters . New to the pub trade but very keen and quick to learn and not afraid of hard work, having come from a farm, Eric and family settled down to their new life. Esme kept a notebook on the events of the Crown and its characters and did intend to write a novel about the hectic life of a Landlady and her family. Unfortunately she never did get around to getting it finished but I will share some of her memories with you.

On their first night in charge all the men in the village turned up to see the new landlord and have a free pint! The place was packed, smoky and the language left a lot to be desired! They had been in the pub for about a month and learnt what it was like to work a fourteen-hour day. When the Rawlisons came to the Crown the smoke room contained a jukebox, a large hole in the floor and smelt of stale beer and tobacco.

The decorating began in the small room behind the bar which was painted and papered, chintz curtains were hung at the windows and a carpet was laid together with tables and chairs for people to sit, it became known as 'the snug'. Very soon after this improvement the farmers began to bring their wives on a Tuesday night and it was very funny to see how different they were in front of their wives. They were very subdued and on their best behaviour. Very soon the snug became too small and the smoke room was next to get a makeover. The bar was built out into the room. This was hard work causing a lot of mess which had to be cleaned each evening before opening time. More beams were exposed and it took days to scrape them clean but it was worth the effort. Red velvet curtains were put up and leather seats around the room, a log fire was made in the grate, and an old piece of carpet was laid as they couldn't afford a new one. Doing the place up was certainly good for trade, as we found country people are notoriously nosy.

The customers played games that Eric and Esme had not seen before. One game was arm wrestling. It was strange to see two men going red in the face trying to put the other one's arm on the table, a common pastime these days. Another of these pub games was called 'bird', when each member of the game had to have in his hand one to three coins. Then in turn they would have to guess how many coins there were altogether in everyone's hands. The loser bought the round of drinks.

The sheepdog at the pub had a very sweet tooth and bets were taken to see if someone could hide something sweet that Prince could not find. They soon gave up as Prince beat them every time. Unfortunately Prince was knocked down in the pub car park and was replaced by a golden retriever which Eric had trained as a gundog ready for the shooting season.

The Petton shoot would start off in the bar at the Crown and it was amazing that anything was shot at all. The shooters would stumble out of the pub, many very unsteady on their feet. Maybe if they saw three pheasants there was always a chance if they aimed for the one in the middle! The shoot also finished back at the Crown with their dogs and whatever they had shot - pheasants, partridge, hare and other game. These were laid out and names put in a hat. When your name came out of the hat you could take your pick of the game. This weekly event during the season made a lot of extra work, as the feathers and mud from their boots had to be brushed up. After the clean-up the serious job of drinking and playing dominoes and darts would begin.

The pub began to serve meals and it was Annette, one of the daughters, who took over the job as cook.

There were two very important events in the village that affected the pub in various ways, cricket and the horticultural show.

As spring gave way to summer the talk in the pub was the coming cricket season. First the team had to be sorted out and work had to be done on the field. The evening Knockout Competition was arranged and teams from as far away as Shrewsbury had entered. The pub's pewter pots were used to take down to the field filled with drink and after the match it was back to the Crown for a few pints.

The show was one of the highlights of the village calendar. The Crown had an agreement with the show organisers that they would close on time. It was the only day when the bell was rung to call time, and this was so that everyone could go to the show dance. The day after the show was something special when most of the flowers that had been exhibited were brought to the pub so they could be displayed on the bar and around the rooms. The men were not too happy about having flowers on the bar! But this was one time when the landlady had her own way.

Always involved and used as an event head-quarters (right), the first 3 Ladies home from a Sponsored Walk from Shrewsbury to The Crown in aid of the Cobalt Unit at the Royal Shrewsbury Hospital. Left to Right - Jean Tudor, Delphine Hulme and Tracey Edwards.

The end of harvest was another busy time when the farmers would arrive at lunchtime and still be there at closing time. The front door had been locked but obviously not the back door, because suddenly the police walked in and wanted to know if it was late closing or early opening? There was a deathly hush in the room and the six farmers looked very crestfallen. The sergeant told them to get off home but "leave your drinks where they are, I will overlook it this time." After the police had gone, Eric and Esme put the kettle on to make a cup of tea. About half an hour later there was a knock on the back door and another farmer had arrived wanting to know where everyone was. They told him the story about the police and he thought that it was a waste of good drink, so he downed them one after the other. What a mixture – lager, beer and whisky! He then went happily on his way feeling much better.

That was the last time they had a visit from the law. A young fellow had taken over from the sergeant and would warn Eric if they were to have a visit, so they could close on time. On his nights off the young policemen would call at the Crown for a drink and everyone left on time because he was there, but not the policeman. He would talk and drink much longer. One night about midnight the back door opened and a voice shouted 'police'. It was Stanley Hulme (Stumpy), and coming into the smoke room the only person he saw was the policeman. A very embarrassed Stumpy, his face which was always red was even redder. He didn't know whether to come in or turn round and run out. Fortunately the policeman was a great sport and offered to buy Stumpy a drink. The two of them talked and drank happily for at least an hour.

Shortly after this incident tragedy struck the village in the form of Foot and Mouth disease. There had been a shoot that day and as usual they were still in the Crown when the telephone went. Before answering Eric always asked if there was anyone not here. The wives and girlfriends used to check on the menfolk, as they didn't know where they were. Some of them didn't approve of their men drinking and others hoping to hear they were in the pub and not out with another woman. The message was glum and Eric announced that Foot and Mouth was suspected at the cattle market. Many were pleased that it had been a shoot day or they would have been at the market. During the outbreak, which spread like wildfire, the Crown had four veterinary inspectors staying there, and they worked from seven in the morning to ten at night – they needed breakfast before they went and a meal on their return. The Crown quickly became known as the 'Foot and Mouth' pub – the vets, farmers and slaughtermen all drinking at the same bar, but strange as it may seem, there were more farmers that didn't catch Foot and Mouth than those that did. The floors and carpets were disinfected each night and the farmers washed their boots when they left the farm. Maybe this all helped to prevent the spread. This was a horrible time, the countryside was so quiet, the acrid smell of burning flesh of the dead animals filled the air but within six months of the all-clear the fields and farms were back to normal. Of course some farmers did not go back into milking but they were soon following their chosen way to farm.

The public bar had new dominoes tables and a new carpet and this worked wonders as the lads made sure their boots were clean when they came in. They also brought their wives and girlfriends. One nice thing about keeping a pub is that the customers confide in you and it made them feel more like friends. From very early days Esme got used to the bad language but on the whole the customers did not swear in front of her and when the women began to come into the pub there was a big improvement.

1967 The successful Crown's Dominoes Team from left - Back Row- Den Ridgeway, Eric Rawlinson, Frank Hanmer, Alf Smith, Tim Wycherley, Derek Griffiths. Front Row – Graham Woolley, Reggy Husbands, Ron Whitfield, Frank Holliday, Bert Hanmer.

Christmas has always been an important time of the year in the Crown and the first event was the Christmas Draw. It was Peter Brown that started it when he arrived with six turkeys and a duck he had bought cheap on the market. The turkeys were dead but the duck was waddling around at the back of the bar. If a stranger had walked in he would never have believed his eyes or else he would have thought they were mad, but then it was the Crown, a most unorthodox place.

From this first draw grew a gigantic affair. Each year the draw got bigger and people would come from miles around - the Crown was packed. No-one made a profit, all the money went into the prizes. Peter was in charge, everyone was so jolly and it was very good for trade. Sandwiches and mince pies were served and it was a lovely way to start Christmas. The day after the draw the pub was decorated, with a big tree in the corner of the lounge, streamers around with Christmas roses and holly. A crib was placed on the mantelpiece with cotton wool as decoration.

The customers really liked to see the pub ready for Christmas. On the nights before Christmas the carol singers used to come around. The Young Farmers were the first to come, then the Youth Club, followed by the Women's Institute. They each had their own night and never once in all the years did they clash. Christmas Eve was when the world and his wife came to the Crown; the place was packed with people singing carols and popular songs. At lunchtime on Christmas Day the customers were given a free drink, the only time of the year when that happened, except of course for birthdays. The pub always closed on time after lunch, as the women had stayed at home to cook Christmas Dinner and it was only fair to send the menfolk home.

After Boxing Day there was a lull until New Year's Eve. One New Year's Eve when everyone was in a merry mood and the ladies in their long dresses and paper hats, Dorman Smith, one of the staunch bar-lads, put his hand up the chimney and covered it with soot, he then went around kissing everyone and wishing them a Happy New Year whilst blackening their faces at the same time! Fortunately everyone took it in good part and started a Conga around the place and everyone laughing and singing, out of the front door and in at the back. After New Year the pub was much quieter and it gave Eric and Esme time to relax and talk to their customers warmed by drink and a cosy fire.

Stumpy spent many hours in the Crown at all times of day and night. If the pub was closed when he wanted a drink he would knock on the back door beaming all over his face and he would say "Any chance of a quick one?" Of course there always was.

When Eric and Esme left the Crown after 17 years in 1978 , David Oliver became landlord for a short time.

Abby Bywater took charge in 1980. Every Saturday was horseracing day and a few of the locals would gather in the pub to watch and bet on the horses. Abby and his wife Rose always put titbits on the bar, not your usual nuts and crisps - it would be cheeses, Conger eel, tripe or sweetbreads - not all the customers would sample them. Alf Hulme would ring the bets through for the customers to the betting shop and on Wednesday or Thursday Pat Newbrook would bring any winnings.

One Sunday afternoon Abby asked the lads in the bar if they would knock a hole through the bar wall to where the dartboard was in a private lounge. Unknown to the lads the Brewery Representative had said 'no' to the idea. The hole was knocked through with the help of Gilly (Gilbert Roberts), Sam (Brian Roberts), Nigel Hanmer and Benny (Keith Whitfield). A month later when the Brewery Rep. returned he was not pleased, and Abby told him, 'if you don't like it you can rebuild it yourself'. Abby used the space in this lounge for a pool table and put the old dartboard up on the wall. There was much more space for the customers. Abby and Rose Bywater left the Crown in 1983.

In 1985 Dave Lant wanted the Brewery to replace the fence and get rid of a 'disgusting eyesore'.

In 1987 Rose Hindmarsh and Ernie Harrop were one of a number of managers that the Brewery put in but none of them lasted very long.

Competition for trade inevitably meant it was not viable for two pubs in such close proximity to survive. The village hall could hold functions, meetings and parties etc. and also a licence could be obtained for the event and this meant less trade for the pubs. In 1997 Bob Greenaway, the licensee of the Red Lion bought the Crown from the brewery, after the pub had been closed for six months. The Crown's licence lapsed and it became a residential property.

Left to right from top: Eric and Esme Leave the Crown, David Oliver and his wife take over, Abby and Rose Bywater during their time at the Crown, Dave and Christine Lant take over the Crown, Replacement fence is needed, Rose and Ernie.

The Red Lion

The Lion buildings are not as old as the Crown or the Golden Lion. The Red Lion was built as a coaching inn on the Shrewsbury to Chester Road. The Earl Brownlow was the owner of the property and in 1860 Thomas Townsend moved from the Golden Lion, across the road, to take up the licence at the Red Lion. The attraction of the move was to have more stabling and a bigger yard and barn at the rear. The church bought the Golden Lion and it became the Vicarage. The requirements by law were that the waggoners and coaches must make stops at regular intervals of time to make a change of horses. The main A528, as we now call it, was a very busy route with trade between Shrewsbury, Chester and Liverpool. The inn made full use of its barns, sometimes using one to store extra beer over and above the normal cellarage ready for weddings and fairs when much more drink was needed. Farmlands, barns and a pigsty were a part of the contract when becoming licensee of the Red Lion. In 1891 the name was changed to The Brownlow Arms Inn but by 1893 it had reverted back to being the Red Lion.

In later years, but still members of the Townsend family, the Dickin name was above the door. Now the outbuildings were used as a slaughterhouse and a butchers shop.

During the time the Dickins were at the Red Lion they were responsible for the change of both the external and internal appearance. They altered the upper floor giving an extra dimension of space and raising the attic floor level. The dormer windows were a result of this construction.

Apart from passing trade, local events mainly centred on the use of the Red Lion. The steeplechase meant the winnings were collected at the Red Lion. The Oddfellows parade fun fair was set up in the yard and a marquee was erected for the meal afterwards. The Hunt frequented the Lion for dinners and parties.

In the years 1913–1950 Cecil Evans and Walter Tomlinson worked as slaughterers for the Dickins. Walter contracted anthrax in a scratch on his arm when he handled an infected animal from Marsh's farm at Crosemere Manor. This is a serious and highly infectious condition. He was tended by Dr Rogers from Ellesmere who scraped the wound with a spoon. His ministrations were successful and Walter continued to work for the Dickins for over forty years.

Following the Dickins as licensees were Rodney Baker, James Cooke, 'Tank' Mouland, Steve Bonnet, Jack Saunders, Mr Little, Les Humphreys, Sid Orme-Smith, Sid Buckle and Ken Coley.

During the time Steve Bonnet was licencee, he sent out a special Christmas Card to his friends

During 1982 Graham and Margaret Smith became licensee's at the Red Lion and as there was no paper shop in the village, their duties included selling Sunday Newspapers over the bar.

WISHING YOU A
MERRY CHRISTMAS
AND A
HAPPY NEW YEAR

from

SQUADRON LEADER & MRS. S. F. BONNET

THE RED LION INN,
COCKSHUTT,
NR. ELLESMERE.

Above: Christmas Card sent by Steve Bonnet

Right: Graham and Margaret Smith at the Lion

The Red Lion was bought by Bob Greenaway (below) in 1986.

During Bob's time in charge at the Lion it was very much a drinking-man's pub with darts and dominoes being very popular. The pool room was frequented by the younger members of the village. The Red Lion car park/yard has been changed over the last few years.

The Christmas draw was transferred from the Crown to the Red Lion and Peter Brown continued to run them. They were very successful for a number of years.

One large barn at the top of the yard, has been taken down and three Holiday cottages have been built. The barn still left in the yard is in a state of disrepair. This is a Listed building.

When Bob sold the pub in 1999 to John Veglio a big change took place. The pool room wall was knocked down to open up the inside and get rid of the narrow dark passage. The name was changed to the Terra Nuova (left) and advertised as probably Shropshire's finest real food restaurant. The outside was painted and looked a lot more inviting.

Once again in September 2003 the name was changed to 'The Leaking Tap' (left) when an ex-plumber, Nick Law and his partner Jenny bought the building only.

It is now a very well established restaurant and pub. The outside has been repainted white and it's looking bright and well cared for.

The Golden Lion

The Golden Lion was an inn in 1775 it was made of brick with a slate roof and stone window frames and lovely old oak beams inside. It was owned in its early days by a member of the Joyce family and let to victuallers. It stated on the licence, that one condition should be that John Joyce had a room for his workshop in the inn.

A John Yates of Ford was the innkeeper in 1785 for the sum of £40 a year. The inn was taken over by the Townsend family in 1808 – Thomas and his young wife Ann. In the same year there was a clerical error by the licensing justices when the Golden Lion was referred to as the White Lion. This may well suggest that the inn was a black and white building in the architectural style of the period and the heavy oak beams would corroborate this. The Townsend family remained at the Golden Lion until 1860 when this coaching inn was bought by the church as the Vicarage. The Townsends moved across the road. There was land alongside and at the back and they farmed as well as looked after the inn. This land now became part of the Vicarage.

The listed liquors on one inventory were brandy, rum, arrack (a Chinese concoction of cocoa, rice and sugar), uisce beatha (an Irish distilled equivalent of whisky), Geneva (gin) and Aqua Vitae (an Italian version of brandy).

In those days a woman could only stay the night at a coaching inn if she was wearing a hat, not a shawl over her head, and neither could she stay at a lower class place such as a beerhouse.

The Lloyd Arms

In 1856 the Lloyd Arms was part of the square or market place. The road from Loppington came past Crosemere Hall and met the main road to form a crossroads with Park Lane. This square was used for lots of village activities and is mentioned many times in the book.

In 1861 the Lloyd Arms was an inn and was also used as a magistrates' court, which held petty sessions at the court room on the second Thursday in every month, except during April and November when they were held on the first Thursday in those months.

The presiding magistrates were: – Sir John Kynaston, Bart.; CK Mainwaring Esq; Richard G. Jebb Esq and William Sparling Esq

An example of a prosecution before the magistrates TJ Prouis Esq and Capt. H.D Champman was as follows:

Wm. Austin of Cockshutt, a labourer, was before the bench for 'Drunkenness'. He was fined eight shillings with seven shillings costs or, in default of payment, seven days imprisonment.

The Innkeeper in 1841 was Jeffery Chesters aged 60 and his wife Elizabeth aged 20 and Ann, Jeffery's 15 year old daughter. The Chesters family were still in the inn in 1856 and no more has been found about the inn.

When it did close down as an inn, it was converted into three houses. Most of the timbers within the building came from old ships and can still be seen today. Later the building was altered again into two larger houses, known as The Ducking House and 21 Shrewsbury Road.

Petton Arms

Not much is known about the Petton Arms because most of these 'Brewers and Victuallers' could just open as a Public house, and were not recorded and did not have a licence to be a Beer House.

In 1861 a John Jones and his family ran the Petton Arms, Stanwardine Road, Cockshutt.

Chapel Cottages seem to be the likely location for this pub . Of course the old Methodist Chapel was also in one of the Chapel Cottages certainly as early as 1842 and until the new chapel was built in 1889.

The Green Gate

Clockwise from left: Green Gate; Storage sheds (today); and below; Cross Keys

In 1861 the Green Gate (left) was another example of a minor one-room drinking house. Its location was down in Crosemere near Crosemere Hall, where the potato sheds are today. (left)

The semi-detached cottages were owned by the Hulme family of the Hall. Not a great deal is known about the Green Gate, but on the Beerhouse Keepers register of 1861 lists George Chesters and family as the innkeeper.

The Cross Keys

The location of the Cross Keys (bottom left) was on the Ellesmere side of the village, on Shrewsbury Road, where Kenwick Close is today. Nothing was found in the archives about it as a beerhouse but it is mentioned in the horse racing in Cockshutt in 1852 when the Handicap Stewards were to be found in the Cross Keys. The Cross Keys was part of a terrace of sandstone cottages that were pulled down in the 1980s.

Kenwick Hotel

No information was found regarding the Kenwick Hotel. I wonder if it was up Park Lane near to Kenwick Park, as the rest of the village was well served by drinking houses. But with it being called Hotel was it more upmarket?

Our researcher of the pubs is still very busy trying to find out more information about these long lost buildings which were an important part of our village heritage.

No history of the parish of Cockshutt would be complete without mentioning Pongo (Les Jones), Alf Hulme, Stumpy (Stanley Hulme, Kenwick Lodge) and Joe Brookfield.

During our research and talking to the people of the village we were told many stories about their exploits. As requested by one of the families we are not putting any of the stories in the book, but you who remember these characterers will agree the village would have been a much duller place without them.

CHAPTER 11
VILLAGE HALL • PARISH HALL • MILLENNIUM HALL

*Call it what you will, we have a building to be proud of but it
certainly took a long time to build!*

Cockshutt Millennium Hall

The history of Millennium Hall has its origins in a decision by village elders in 1927, when they started a drive to collect funds for the construction of a village hall. In the 1930s they persuaded Lord Brownlow to donate a plot of land specifically for this purpose. During the depression of the 1930s and the Second World War they continued to raise funds and by 1946 they had £700, which, considering the difficulties of the time was a considerable amount of money. At that time it would have been about two years wages for the average farm worker.

Lord Brownlow had given the land on the condition that it was up and running by October 1939. Of course it wasn't, and as it was wartime nothing happened. The bank book was handed to Captain Robinson RN. He was churchwarden and vice chairman of the school managers – very, very conservative and trustworthy but utterly opposed to a village hall because all social functions were held in the school and brought in money. When it came time for the village to decide what memorial they wanted for the victims of the Second World War the money was used to install the organ in the church. This decision divided the village as some wanted the hall. Efforts continued over the next few years, until in 1965 a decision was made to purchase an ex-army hut rather than wait for a brick building.

Mr Hassall, Headmaster of the school, and the Reverend Peppercorn were very involved in fundraising and before the Second World War they used to hold 'Beanos' when the whole

village joined in. The school at Petton and vicarage lawn Cockshutt were used as venues and lots of dressing up was involved.

Ern and Nancy Roberts were up to their necks in fund raising, also Phil Morris from Petton and lots of others. Mr and Mrs Cox were very involved and Tim Cox was chairman of the Village Hall Committee when it opened in 1967.

Above, Village Hall Committee at the opening in 1967: Back Left - Ern Roberts, John Husbands, Frank Holliday, Bob Sutton, Bob Dommett, Arthur Clarke, Tom Roberts, Mac Griffiths, Bill Ralphs. 2nd Row – Phil Morris, Mrs Rodenhurst, Nancy Roberts, Nellie Sutton, Ivy Nicholas, Nellie Smith. Sitting at the table – Lady Dyer, Tim Cox, Ted Hassall, Mrs Hassall, Rev. Lansdale, Rev. C Skirrit (Ellesmere).

COCKSHUTT BEANO

THURSDAY, JULY 23rd, 1936

To be opened at 3 p.m. by

THE MAYOR OF SHREWSBURY - Alderman Charles Beddard

ATTRACTIONS INCLUDE THE FOLLOWING

CONCERTS in the Schools by Mr. and Mrs. T. J. Parry and Party, Petton Hall, at 3-30, 5-30, and 8 p.m. Admission 6d.

STALLS of Needlework, Produce, Sweets, Toys, etc.   "Daily Mail" Treasure Hunt

GRAND BALLOON RACE

Various Side Shows by Cockshutt Oddfellows, Directed by Mr. J. Birch

Everything stops for Mrs. J. Dickin's TEAS at 3 p.m. on the delightful Vicarage Lawn

A GRAND PROGRAMME OF SPORTS at 6.30 p.m. Organised by Mr. W. Worthington on Mr. Pratt's field (by kind permission) including Final of six-a-side Football Competition

At 7-30 p.m. Mr. Frank Batho will sell by **AUCTION** in the "Red Lion Yard"
A veritable Mixem's Mart. Live Stock and Dead Stock (any breed)
Furniture (young and old)   Eggs (hatched or unhatched)
Pots and Pans (empty or full)   Cheeses (graded or ungraded)
In fact, we sell all we can get, and get all we can on our sales

Mr. and Mrs. E. W. Parker's **DANCE** at 8 p.m. on the Vicarage Lawn will end a perfect day. Music for Dancing and during afternoon by WEM RADIO Co.   Admission 1/-

Electric light at last, illuminations for Dance kindly supplied by Wilfred Thomasson, Electrical Engineer, 65, Mardol, Shrewsbury (Next to Messrs. Jay's Ltd.)

Leave your worries at home, come and enjoy yourselves and enable us to achieve our object—

THE COCKSHUTT PARISH HALL

The Site is ready we now have £250

A grand Competition of Word Making for all children under 14 years of age. Entrance Fee 1d. Two Prizes of 2/6 will be given for first two solutions opened which correspond with sealed solution. Make 8 words out of the following :

    (1) **SPLIADY**   (2) **UDECORP**   (3) **EECCLRIT**   (4) **RREOCN**
    (5) **AEESLD**   (6) **ALNSI**   .   (7) **UDNORG**   (8) **CAIFTRF**

Send your entry together with your name, age, and address and 1d. stamp in sealed envelope to reach Mr. Hassall, School House, Cockshutt not later than July 20th, 1936. Mark your envelope "Beano Competition" in top left hand corner. Winners will be announced at 6 p.m. at the Beano.

Above, Ted Hassall performs the opening ceremony of the village hall

Looking to the future, the village hall committee asked Lord Wimbourne if they could rent the adjacent three-acre field for use as a sports field. He agreed to this at a very modest annual rent and that continues to this day. A concrete foundation was laid and the hall erected by the late Bill Humphries and village volunteers. The treasurer at the time was Mr R E Dommett who is still a village resident and celebrated his 90th birthday as I write this in the summer of 2003.

Above, Old Village Hall with Extension added later. Right, Karen and Keith Whitfield all dressed up at the 1965 Fete.

The old hall was a success from the start and fulfilled an obvious need in the village social life, being used for dances, bingo, whist, playgroup and a weekly doctor's surgery.

Fund raising continued and the annual fete was always well supported.

1977 brought the Silver Jubilee Festivities and the village really went to town!

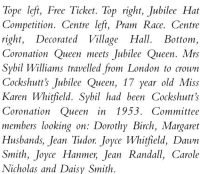

Tope left, Free Ticket. Top right, Jubilee Hat Competition. Centre left, Pram Race. Centre right, Decorated Village Hall. Bottom, Coronation Queen meets Jubilee Queen. Mrs Sybil Williams travelled from London to crown Cockshutt's Jubilee Queen, 17 year old Miss Karen Whitfield. Sybil had been Cockshutt's Coronation Queen in 1953. Committee members looking on: Dorothy Birch, Margaret Husbands, Jean Tudor. Joyce Whitfield, Dawn Smith, Joyce Hanmer, Jean Randall, Carole Nicholas and Daisy Smith.

Donkey derby at Cockshutt

A donkey derby was held in aid of Cockshutt Church and Village Hall funds on the village hall playing fields.
1—*The races get under way.*
2—*Sharon Duncan, Heather Woodcock, Jayne Roberts.*
3—*Mrs Margaret Johnson, Mrs Jean James, Mrs Isabel Sankey.*
4—*Mrs Winifred Davies, Mrs Dorothy North, Mrs Hilda Manford, Mrs Rene Jones.*

In 1992 the Village Hall celebrated its 25th Anniversary Above left, Some of the committee George Whitfield, Joyce Hanmer, Syd Davies, Pam Hanmer, Edna Evans and Ev Clarke and Right, Nellie Sutton cuts the cake.

The Play Area in 1992

After a couple of decades, voices were raised seeking to expand or improve the facilities to meet the area's growing needs. The Hall is reported to have had more bookings than the Albert Hall. However, it was not until the mid 90s when Lottery grants started to become available that this proved feasible.

In the summer of 1995 the Village Hall Committee chaired by Syd Davis, took the decision to apply for a lottery grant to build the new village hall. George Reeves was asked to undertake the task of securing the lottery funding and other grants. After reviewing the options he decided on the Millennium Commission with the hope of completing the new building by the Millennium.

At the same time Adrian Farmer was asked to produce a design for the new hall. Adrian produced a first-class design incorporating all the features that the Committee and the village had asked for. These included rooms for scouts and guides, playgroup, changing rooms for home and away sports teams and referees, complete with showers. Also included were a Doctor's office, the main hall and stage for concerts and an ancillary room for smaller functions. The main hall even included a sprung hardwood dance floor. Initial costings were approximately £250,000 and George Reeves started the application process to the Millennium Commission in August 1995. At the same time he sent out letters to many charities and Government bodies seeking other grants in the knowledge that lotteries would only fund 50% of the cost.

In the meantime the Village Hall Committee consisting of: Syd Davis Chairman, C.E.; 'Pat' Burns, Treasurer; Jean James, Secretary; George Reeves ,Project Manager; John Dickin, Ron and Joyce Whitfield, George Whitfield, Adrian Farmer, Chris Ashton, Alan Biggs, Alan Davies, Sheila Davis, Sharon Dean, Terry and Jenny Goodall, Edna Evans, Dave and Paula Griffiths, Caroline Griffiths, Debbie Haywood, Steve Milns, Ev Clark and Pam Hanmer were busy raising funds in a variety of ways. These ranged from raffles, pig roasts and concerts - some of which became annual events.

In December 1995 we were advised by the Millennium Commission that out of 1,460 applicants we and 300 others had gone forward to the next round. We were then asked to prepare a detailed appraisal review on feasibility and costs and prepare a presentation to the Millennium Commission team in May 1996. After this a further presentation and review was called for in June to provide more details. When this was done we were told that we were through to the next round with only 100 applicants.

During 1996 the committee was asked to demonstrate our ability to provide the £125,000 in matching funds. Grants were secured from The Rural Development Commission, North Shropshire District Council, Shropshire County Council, Shropshire Rural Arts Committee, Fullwoods Community Fund, BT, and Hawk Equipment. At the same time local fundraising had continued with all the committee and volunteers named above in a variety of ways.

During one raffle the group met to discuss progress and each member was asked how many books they had sold. The answers varied from member to member – 20, 50, until they got to Ev Clark who said "720 and I haven't finished yet"! It was a tremendous effort by an elderly lady who had difficulty getting around and eventually finished up in a wheelchair. She epitomized the spirit of that very hard-working group. Needless to say we convinced the commission that we could raise the funds.

In May 1996 we were visited by one of the head commissioners and his team who wished to discuss the building's design. During the meeting attended by Syd Davis, George Reeves and Terry Goodall, we were told that the building was not attractive enough. We were given four weeks to improve its external design, as the Commission was meeting to decide final grants within six weeks. We agreed the deadline and appointed Robert Netherwood, an Architect from Ellesmere, to redesign the front of the building, but to leave the basic design intact. He achieved this in three weeks and the new design was sent to London with a note stressing that there would be additional costs which had yet to be finalised.

During all this Steve Milns who is a Quantity Surveyor was doing a sterling job of settling the revising costs. These ultimately came to £325,000 and this information was passed to London, with the firm commitment that we would raise our 50% in matching funds. With only a few weeks left George Reeves was able to persuade the Rural Development Commission, Shropshire County Council and North Shropshire District Council to increase their grants to meet some of the deficit, with the assurance that we were confident in raising the rest locally.

In July 1996 we received a fax from Richard Rice of the Millennium Commission advising that we had provisionally been granted £162,500 subject to our meeting our obligations. However no announcement could be made until November as it was embargoed, but we should go ahead with raising the balance of funds. During this busy period we were finalising the balance of funding from other sources and defining the building costs more clearly. Steve Milns who is an excellent Quantity Surveyor produced the bill of quantities for us, working around the clock, and it generally confirmed the original estimates.

Throughout the previous two years the village had been running a weekly lottery and each member of our group had to collect money around the village. I think it would be fair to say that fund collection fatigue had set in. Despite this our Treasurer Pat Burns spent most

Saturday nights and Sundays as well as many other evenings sorting out the funds and any discrepancies; she did a first class job.

At this point with most of the funding lined up it appeared that we would be about £5,000 short. The Commission was assured that all the matching funds would be available and another campaign got underway by the Village Hall Committee to sell £100 named bricks to be fitted in the hall feature wall. The first to buy one were Mr and Mrs J M Sankey who have the top brick in the wall pattern as they got it started. We eventually raised £2,800 through this endeavour and the balance was raised through more hard work by the committee driven by Syd Davis.

In November we were formally advised by the commission that a grant of £162,500 had been made and the news was released. I gathered that we were only one of forty grants and that we were the first village hall to get a grant from the Millennium Commission and that there had been considerable nervousness about it as they usually funded larger projects.

As we were going to tender the Bill of Quantities was finalised by Steve Milns and the tenders were let in February '97. The lowest bid was by Onions Construction Ltd. and it fortunately fell within our cost parameters. It would be necessary to take down the old village hall which had been sold.

However, before we did this it was decided to hold a village concert. This was a great success and completely sold out, special mention has to be made of Bob Dommett who accompanied all the acts on the organ, Neil Gamble who looked after our electronics and made everything work. On the performance front Mark Smith did a great job of presenting his Scout Jamboree and Tom Jones led the Cockshutt Male Voice choir for a very successful finale to salute the old hall.

With the old hall taken down all that remained were the concrete foundations on which it was built. There is no doubt whoever put them in intended them to last. They were 2ft deep in places. Syd Davis hired a compressor and he and Ron Whitfield completed this in less than a week through driving rain. Only the supply of hot tea and cakes by Ron's wife Joyce saved the day.

On 29th April 1997 Onions Construction Ltd broke ground and laid new foundations for the new hall. On July 2nd 1997 Onions Construction Ltd announced they were bankrupt and a receiver was appointed. To say that the Millennium Commission was in a panic would be an understatement, the phone never stopped ringing. George Reeves made a trip to London to meet with their legal chief Jerry Michel and their solicitors. He gave them the assurance that the contract would be quickly renegotiated and that it would be

finished on time and to budget and they finally accepted these assurances.

The contract was given to Frank Galliers Ltd. at no additional cost and the work was completed on time in December 1997. It ran some £5,000 over budget largely due to last minute changes in specification to improve the building. Since then it has served the community well. turning a small profit each year thus establishing a fund for future repairs and alterations.

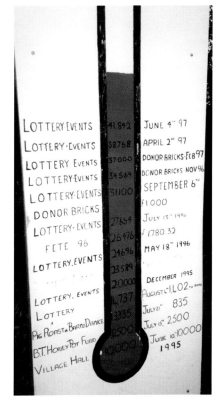

Top left, Building going ahead.
Top right, Fund raising at a glance: The village always knew how much money had been raised.
Centre left, The new building was opened in December 1997 by Dr Edwin Sawacha of the Millennium Commission.
Bottom left, Inside and right, Outside the Hall

Above, Cockshutt Millennium Hall Fund Raising Committee and Management Committee: Left to Right- Linda Biggs, Caroline Griffiths, Joyce Whitfield, Edna Evans, Jenny Goodall, Pam Hanmer, Jean James, Alan Biggs, Sheila Davies, Ron Whitfield, Pat Burns, Dave Griffiths, Debbie Hayward, Ev Clarke, George Reeves, John Dickin, Joyce Hanmer, Terry Goodall, Syd Davies, Paula Griffiths, George Whitfield.

The Ladies being presented with flowers are: Left to right Mrs Boughey, Mrs Betty Mulroy (Village Hall Adviser), Miss Sawacha, Mrs ?, Mrs Joan Reeves, Mrs Sheila Davies, Mrs Pat Burns (Treasurer)

The Committee has changed somewhat since then. Neil Gamble served as Chairman for a couple of years. Syd Davis is now back as chairman after a sabbatical. Pat Burns is still Treasurer and they all continue to do an excellent job of managing the hall. The one outstanding fact in all this must be acknowledged, that a small group of people with the aid of a small village raised over £40,000 in cash over a two-year period to ensure the building of the Millennium Hall. It was, and is, a major achievement and the building is a tribute to their dedication.

Fund Raising continues throughout each year and includes the Annual Fete.

Top four pictures. This 1998 Fete included a Parade through the Village what a specactular sight it was. Of course we are not allowed to parade through the village these days without paying a large amount of money for the road to be closed.

Bottom two pictures. The Play Area today. Thank you to the Play Area Committee for all their hard work over many years. Cockshutt is the only Play Area not managed by their Parish Council so the Village Hall takes on the responsibility of looking after this amenity.

CHAPTER 12
THE COCKSHUTT PARISH COUNCIL

The Development Boundary as it is in 2003.

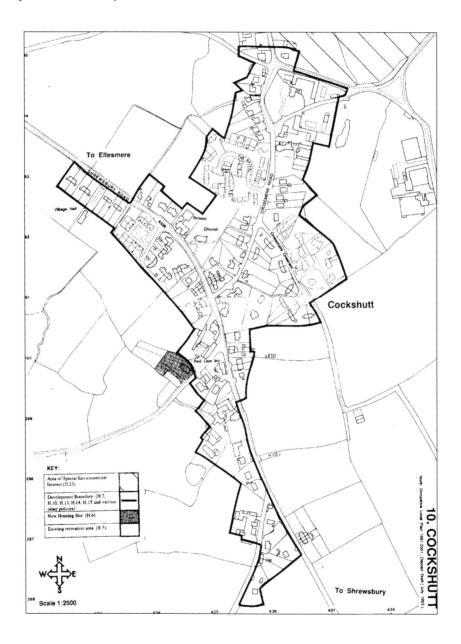

The Development Boundary as it was in 2003. From Local Plan 1991 – 2001,
permission granted by North Shropshire District Council

In 1894 the Local Government Act came into force. The Parish Council in those days was called a Parish Meeting and all electors were entitled to attend. They had the power to elect councillors and oversee the spending.

John Green, Headmaster of Cockshutt School, was the first Parish Clerk. The Parish Council was within the Ellesmere Rural District Council until 1973 when Local Government was reorganised.

The Parish Council does not have any powers but in the early days time was spent on discussing what to request from Ellesmere Rural District Council, Salop County Council, the Oswestry Postmaster and North Wales Power Company.

The Council Minutes from 1894 to 1931 are held in the Archives in Shrewsbury and the rest of the Minutes are with the Parish Clerk at the time of writing, but will soon be placed in the County Archives. The rest of this Chapter is concerned with the notes taken from 1931 to 2003 and, after reading through these Minutes, it appears that the majority of Parish Councils' efforts are spent requesting help from the 'powers that be' namely the District Council, Highways Department, Shropshire County Council and MANWEB, with matters that need their attention. It was also obvious that nothing was done very quickly. For example it took thirty years to get the sewerage scheme for the village up and running. The Clerk, from time to time, had to write to villagers to request that they trim their hedges, when there had been a complaint. The only item which the Parish Council is financially responsible for is street lighting. Local organisations also receive financial support from the Council's precept where they consider the request worthwhile.

1931

John Moore, Headmaster of Cockshutt School, became Parish Clerk.

1931, The Parish Council

Tom J Marsh	Farmer	Crosemere
John Brookfield	Postmaster	Cockshutt
Tom Sutton	Wheelwright	Cockshutt
John Peel	Sexton	Cockshutt
William Wilkinson	Farmer	Crosemere
George Tatton	Wheelwright	Cockshutt
Thomas Emberton	Farmer	Ferneyhough
Edmund Parker	Farmer	English Frankton
Thomas Dickin	Farmer	Cockshutt

Tom J Marsh was elected Chairman, and John Peel Vice Chairman.

In these early days when footpaths and footbridges were well used the Parish Clerk sent many, many letters to Salop County Council asking for them to be repaired. There is evidence of very poor drainage outside the school and in front of Primrose Terrace that needed addressing urgently.

1934

The vicar, Reverend Walter Peppercorn, was co-opted onto the Council.

North Wales Power Company were asked if there was any hope of electricity coming to the village, as many households were waiting to be connected. In 1937 Cockshutt was still waiting for electricity to be brought to the village.

1935

A special meeting was called to consider Lord Brownlow's application for the transfer of the licence from the Red Lion, Cockshutt, to the Boathouse Restaurant, Ellesmere. The Parish Council were very much against this transfer as it would cause great inconvenience to the parish, and remove from their midst an important centre of social and business activity. The four council houses on Shrewsbury Road were built; it was perhaps in 1919 that council houses had been requested for the village.

The Parish Council became the owners of the proposed site for the Village Hall.

1938

John Moore resigned as Parish Clerk, Mr R Gwilliam of Brook House appointed in his place.

1939

When war was declared the council houses in English Frankton were being built. To mark this historic event, the third and fourth houses from the village have got the corbling standing on end instead of flat, as on the other houses. Council houses were also started in Kenwick Park but took much longer because the first builder went out of business.

The village had at last been connected to the electricity grid but it was 1960 before it reached English Frankton and Kenwick Park. Of course there was no piped water in the village until 1953/1954 but much later in the outlying hamlets.

1941

Edmund Parker was elected Trustee of Ellesmere Dispensary Charity. He held this position until 1999.

1943

The Government's Ministry of Works needed to requisition iron railings and gates for the war effort. The following were considered by the Parish Council:

1. Dr Rogers' cottage had an iron gate.

2. School had railings on top of the wall along the roadside (left), but as they were for the safety of the children. Council objected to them being taken away.

3. Church yard tomb rails and as these served no useful purpose the Council could see no reason why they should not be removed.

4. The Vicarage railings and gate.

5. The Primitive Methodists Chapel railings

Only the railings around tombs at the back of Church were taken.

1944

The Alley walk leading from Crosemere Road to Crosemere Crescent is where George Gyles made a bowling alley on wasteland that belonged to the Lord of the Manor for which he was fined two shillings in May 1607. In 1944 Alley walk was unusable because it was so overgrown, mainly from the Vicarage hedge. Alley walk crops up almost annually when the District Council are asked for gravel for the locals to spread. Surfacing and hedge trimming are a continuous concern along Alley walk.

This year was when the Sewerage Scheme was suggested for the village. The scheme was completed in 1976 some thirty years later.

Street lighting was talked about as soon as electricity came to the village but the Parish Council was financially responsible for the cost of installation and upkeep of the street lighting. It was suggested that only streets that benefit from the lights were to be charged extra on the rates. A public meeting was arranged. The Council had to arrange a loan spread over ten years in order to light up Shrewsbury Road, Crosemere Crescent and Crosemere Road. Again it took a long time to for the project to be in place; in fact it was 1968 when Cockshutt was finally lit up!

1950

Crosemere Crescent was completed by 1952 in time for the Coronation of Queen Elizabeth 11

1953/1954

Piped water was installed in the village.

1955

Mr Dommett resigned as a Councillor to take up the post of Clerk.

1961

(Left) Some of the shop garden was taken to improve the junction of Crosemere Road and Shrewsbury Road. Below, Cockshutt was awarded a certificate of merit in the Best kept village competition.

1963

The Petton and Cockshutt Flower Show Committee set the ball rolling once again to get a Village Hall built. Another sub-committee was formed and by 1967 the hall was opened some forty years after the inaugural meeting in 1927.

1964

Mrs Rene Jones (the Garage) was given permission to enclose the official water pump in her garden, but access had to be available through a gate.

1966

An underground reservoir was built up the bank towards Kenwick Park as a holding tank. This was done to improve the water supply to the village.

1967

Old Village Hall was opened (above)

1970, Council members

Pat Blundred	Teacher	Cockshutt
Randle Carr	Farmer	Crosemere
John Hodnet	Farmer	Petton

Stanley Hulme	Farmer	Kenwick
John Kynaston	Farmer	Cockshutt
Edmund Parker	Farmer	English Frankton
Tom Povall	Farmer	English Frankton
Ernest Roberts	Milking Machine Engineer	Crosemere
W E Tomlinson	Farmer	Petton

There was still no sewerage scheme in place. The hold-up at this time was a suitable site for a pumping station.

Alley walk was once again on the agenda, and the Council asked for a crash barrier to be fitted at the Crosemere Road end. Once again they had to wait.

The council houses at English Frankton were modernised and running water piped to each property 16 years after the village had running water.

The sewerage scheme seemed to be progressing and the sewage from Cockshutt was to be pumped through pipes in the ground to Baschurch. Owners of septic tanks could opt out of the scheme if their tanks passed the inspection. There was to be no charge for connection.

Left, Pumping Station and below, Telephone Exchange and Extension.

1971

Cockshutt was declared a Class A village and was scheduled for development in the county plan. As there was still no sewerage scheme in operation, development was not going to happen at this time.

The telephone service in the village was causing problems, you did not get the number you dialled.

1972

Bungalows had been built down Crosemere Road and Crosemere Lane and more street lighting was needed.

1973

Local Government reorganisation and North Shropshire District Council was born with a new centre in Wem.

1974

The population of the village was 443 and more council houses and bungalows were needed as there was a long list of people waiting for accommodation in Cockshutt.

This was a bad year for the Village Hall and no accounts were available, no Chairman, no Treasurer, so an extraordinary general meeting was to be held in May, hoping that more people would attend.

The Parish Council had been Trustees of the Village Hall Fund since 1952 and an annual report was to be given to them – this is still true today.

1975

Money was allocated for four bungalows by the school(bottom right). They would replace Primrose Terrace.

The first lady was co-opted onto the Council in March, but Mrs Elsey, the vicar's wife, only stayed until the end of the year as the Elseys moved away.

The Village Hall was back on track and all posts were filled, but more help was needed - exactly the same as today.

At last plans for about eighteen dwellings on the site opposite the school were in the building programme of the District Council.

Above, Church Green in the building programme

1976

This was the year that two ladies joined the Parish Council, Mrs Carole Gimbert and Miss Carole Nicholas who is still a member today.

The trees in Shrewsbury Road between Wimborne Cottages and the Dobbin were checked for safety. It was many years later when they were felled.

1977

Mr Dommett resigned as Parish Clerk after serving more than twenty years. Reverend Tye was appointed as the new Clerk.

The houses in Kenwick Park were to be modernised and at last Church Green was to be started.

The Village Hall organised Jubilee celebrations for the village.

The Doctor's surgery, which was held in Stone Villa on Friday Mornings, may prove no longer feasible and it was suggested a side room in the Village Hall as a possible new venue.

1978

Up until now Cockshutt and Petton had their own Parish Councils. In June the Cockshutt–cum–Petton Parish had its first meeting. There were twelve members in all, three of whom must be from Petton. John Hodnet was elected Chairman, Tony Fowler Vice Chairman and Rene Jones, Pat Blundred, Carole Nicholas, Ernest Roberts, Derek Griffiths, Frank Tomlinson, Stanley Hulme, Frank Dickin, Edmund Parker and W.B. Homan-Russell made up the Council.

1980

A social car scheme had been suggested but more drivers would be needed. It was increasingly necessary for passenger contributions by 1981 although the scheme was being well used.

1981

Philip Holbourn was appointed Parish Clerk after the resignation of Reverend Tye.

1982

The building of bungalows in Crosemere Crescent was agreed although concern was expressed about the narrow junction with Crosemere Road.

The Council also considered planning for nine bungalows at the side of Church Green. The District Council intended to sell this land to a Housing Association.

1983

The Parish Council was reduced in size from twelve to eight and only one needed to be from Petton.

Mrs Gregory, the Postmistress in Crosemere Crescent, had resigned and a new suitable person and location needed to be found. The transfer of the Post Office to School House was approved and once again the Post Office was back where it was in 1882, although it had been at other locations – in Shrewsbury Road, Brookfields at No. 21 and Gladys Stokes' at No. 33 and then to Crosemere Crescent. It had now gone full circle.

The Old Post Office and Telephone Exchange 21, Shrewsbury Road

1984

Jean Radley was appointed Parish Clerk on the resignation of Philip Holbourn who had been in the post for three years.

1985

It was suggested by the Parish Council that a contingency fund be set up for the eventual replacement of the Village Hall.

The planned extension to the Hall for a Doctor's surgery still had not been completed so the Doctor was using a very small room at the Hall.

Two children were knocked off their bikes and a petition was signed by 119 people objecting to the speed of traffic through the village. Over the years some measures and signs for 30 mph. have been erected but we are still very concerned about the speed of traffic through the village.

City Meats threatened to close if they were not allowed to expand.

The picture (right) shows Knocking down the Cross Keys and adjoining houses to build Kenwick Close. The site had been sold to a Housing Association. Building work beginning is shown below.

1986

Dairy Crest in Ellesmere did close its doors.

1987

The Opening Ceremony of Kenwick Close was performed by the Duke of Westminster.

Shropshire Rural Housing Association Ltd. were the owners at this time.

Another building project was underway on Crosemere Road. Permission was given for 15 but 26 dwellings were agreed and now 30 were being requested; eventually permission was given for 28. The Briars was being built.

The Clerk wrote to the District Council suggesting the need for a cricket pitch, bowling green and tennis courts in the village.

1997

Parklands, off Park Lane, were being built (left) and affordable housing and social housing schemes involving a partnership with Housing Associations had been agreed.

A Rural Housing Survey showed that Cockshutt was quite well stocked, with Kenwick Close, Parklands and other various council properties.

Planning permission was granted for a Café facility at the local shop. As Alan Biggs recited at one village concert 'It was the only Café in Shropshire that closed at lunch time!

Meetings were held in the school while the Millennium Hall was being built.

1998

The Parish Council held its first meeting in the new Hall in January. Jean Radley resigned as Clerk, after 14 years in the post. Helen Eatough was appointed in her place.

A bit of history was made when The Crown was to be converted from a public house to a dwelling leaving the village with just one public house.

1999

A planning application for five dwellings at Crosemere Farm was approved.

J A Veglio proposed internal alterations to the ground floor at the Red Lion, repositioning of the bar, removal of two internal doorways and removal of a wall to the poolroom.

2000

The Millennium Project at school to provide a Mug for each pupil was paid for by the Parish Council, (opposite top).

Children from Cockshutt Primary School receive their Millennium Mugs from Cockshutt Parish Council representatives Eddie Jones and Joan Dickin. Children (from the front) are Emma Jones, Simon Postans, Felicity Cooksey, William Groombridge, Thomas Carr, Donna Millward and Daniel Wallace.

The Shropshire Star Millennium Oak Tree, given to the village, was planted out of sight by the Play area to avoid it being vandalized; unfortunately it has been damaged but is still alive although a slightly different shape!

Great concern about a possible erection of a 15-metre high telecommunications mast, with three antennae, two microwave dishes and an equipment cabin at English Frankton. Objections to the mast were sent to the District Council by the Clerk.

Manor Farm development had increased to six houses and the proposed demolition of Manor Farmhouse. There were no objections. A new code of conduct was introduced for Town and Parish Councillors to make them more accountable to the electorate.

It was in May 2000 that the Local Plan review proposed the building of twenty dwellings on the north site which the Parish Council approved. At a special North Shropshire District Council Meeting in Wem the preferred site was changed to the south site.

2001

In January the Council was informed about the GM oilseed rape being planted in Bagley as part of the farm trials.

Many villagers expressed concern about the effect of the GM Farm Trials on the local environment and the Organic Nursery on Shrewbury Road displayed a sign (above), 'Say NO to GM Crops'.

'Pick up' and 'drop off' parking outside school was causing problems, particularly for the school bus.

Re-opening of footpaths after the Foot and Mouth outbreak took place on 25th June.

The Highways Maintenance Plan was to include Cockshutt for traffic-calming measures in 2001/2002 budget.

After years of asking for Kenwick Close to be adopted, at last the District Council took over responsibility for the road and footpath.

The District Council also promised the outside of the houses in Crosemere Crescent would be painted, but plans for central heating were deferred.

2002

A very lukewarm response for the Queen's Jubilee from the village so no plans were made for a village effort.

There were ongoing problems with the sewage pumping station when both pumps failed. The station had to be emptied into tankers and driven away. (Right, New Extra pumping station was built).

The Parish Bus Grant Scheme was to be managed by five Parishes and Cockshutt Parish Council expressed extreme scepticism about the project. Eventually they did join the scheme when no money was expected to be paid. This bus was to provide a service for both Cockshutt and Petton.

2003

People in Cockshutt must be sending more mail as the present Post Box is not big enough! At the moment an alternative site has not been found; one suggestion was across the road, which was rejected by the Parish Council.

After going to appeal, the Red Lion Cottages have been changed from Holiday cottages to residential.

Water pressure has been a problem in certain parts of the village from time to time.

Stanwardine Hall and farm were without water for four days. Not a good thing when you have over 100 cows to milk and other animals to care for.

The Ellesmere Charities who had supported needy causes for a very long time were abandoned and the funds redirected within the area.

The Local Plan Public Enquiry was held on December 2nd 2003.

The Cockshutt Parish Council at this time:

Clerk	Helen Eatough
Chairman	John Hodnet
Vice Chairman	Terry Goodall;

John Dickin, Brian Hotham, Eddie Jones, Rosemary Milns, Carole Nicholas and Steve Hodnet.

Over the years many village organisations have been financially supported by the Parish Council including Cockshutt Church organ, clock and churchyard upkeep; Petton churchyard; Playgroup; Play area; Village Hall and School.

CHAPTER 13

WAR

Throughout the centuries Cockshutt, although not actually documented as a place of fighting during the English Civil War 1642 – 1651 the village must have been affected by skirmishes and troops travelling through the region. From early times the Welsh and English border kept changing and both sides attacked each other to gain or regain land. Owen Glendower was a visitor to Ellesmere and occupied land around the region. During the Civil War of the Roundheads and Royalists, Cockshutt was in the middle.

Cromwell's Roundheads were encamped in Wem and the King's troops were around Stanwardine Hall, so the village must have been involved on one side or the other. It is documented that the Roundheads and Royalists did fight by Loppington Church and the porch was damaged.

When the Battle of Shrewsbury was fought in 1403 troops travelled from the north led by the Percy family from Northumberland to meet Henry IV and it is possible that they passed not far from the village. Henry 'Hotspur' Percy met his death at the Battle of Shrewsbury - another victory for the King's army.

The First World War – 'The Great War'

Farming was a deferred occupation so many men in the village did not go to war. The men had to have a Certificate of Exemption, below, otherwise they could be called up for service.

RECUITING OFFICE,
OSWESTRY.

Dear Sir,
I have to inform you that it has now been decided that all men marked on the Military Register as being in a Reserved Occupation are liable to be called up for service with the Colours immediately, unless in possession of a Certificate of Exemption granted either by the Local Tribunal or Recruiting Officer. Under these circumstances it will be necessary for you, within seven days from the receipt of this letter, to obtain a Certificate of Exemption from your Local Tribunal, or from the Recruiting Officer where you are registered. Failing this you will be called up to join the Army.

Recruiting Officer

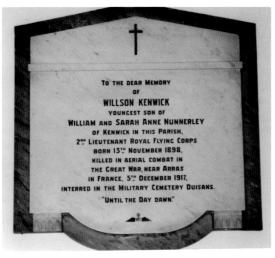

The War Memorial in the churchyard and three marble wall tablets in the church (right) commemorate the fallen. They are: Second Lieutenant Wilson Kenwick Nunnerley aged 19 from Kenwick Hall who died in aerial combat near Arras, France 5th December 1917. He was interred in the Military Cemetery Divisions.

Second Lieutenant Frank Harold Elwin of Cacar, India, died in action 12th March 1915 at Neuve Chapelle aged 19 years and was the son of a friend of the vicar of Cockshutt, the Reverend Peppercorn, who had the memorial erected.

The last marble tablet is in memory of Private William Stanley Marsh of the Coldstream Guards from Crosemere Farm. A letter written by Stanley to Bettie his sister in 1915 illustrates what our soldiers thought about having to go into action.

In Memory of

William Stanley Marsh

Private
16526
3rd Bn, Coldstream Guards
who died on
Wednesday, 10th October 1917. Age 21.

Additional Information:	Son of Thomas John and Emma Marsh, of Croesmere Farm, Ellesmere, Salop.

Commemorative Information

Memorial:	TYNE COT MEMORIAL, Zonnebeke, West-Vlaanderen, Belgium
Grave Reference/ Panel Number:	Panel 9 to 10
Location:	The Tyne Cot Memorial to the Missing forms the north-eastern boundary of Tyne Cot Cemetery, which is located 9 kilometres north east of Ieper town centre, on the Tynecotstraat, a road leading from the Zonnebeekseweg (N332).

Below, cards sent and received by Marsh family and below Stanley Marsh

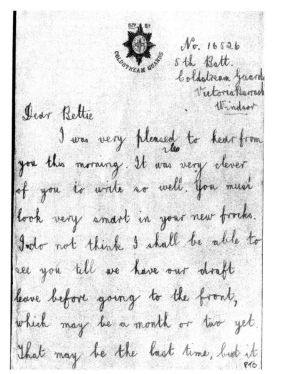

No. 16526
5th Batt.
Coldstream Guards
Victoria Barracks
Windsor

Dear Bettie

I was very pleased to hear from you this morning. It was very clever of you to write so well. You must look very smart in your new frocks. I do not think I shall be able to see you till we have our draft leave before going to the front, which may be a month or two yet. That may be the last time, but it

PTO

will be nice to come home altogether when the war is over, if I get through alright. We are having a good time here, not near as much to do as at Caterham. These barracks are fine places, billiard rooms, writing rooms, bath rooms with hot water, the worst of it being so dark outside because of the Zeppelins. Windsor is nearly as dark as Cockshutt. I have not heard from Sarah or May yet how are they getting on. We are going for a long route march tomorrow with full pack on. We have been out in the fields doing field work today. We had a nice march through Windsor for about 2 miles each way singing songs. Tell Mother that our letters must have crossed as I received her letter the post after I wrote, with the postal order. I think I will try and have my photo took in barracks with full pack, rifle and bayonet, it will show you how I look. I will write to Uncle Tom I may be able to get there some week end. A lot more are going to the front this week end

I shall be glad when our turn comes although no one wants to go back who has been. There are a lot who have been wounded here. The war looks no better yet, it looks like as if it is never going to end, everybody will soon be fighting I must close now as there is not much more news. How is Johny from the Lodge. Tell Mr. Moore I will write to him one of these days, remember me to Frances and all, hoping this will find you quite well. From your loving brother

Stanley

*Above and left :
Letter from Stanley Marsh to his sister Bettie*

*Above, E Marsh, Harry Marsh and above right opposite page,
John James Moore with his father "Gaffer" Moore*

THE GLORIOUS
MEMORY OF THE
MEN OF THIS
PARISH WHO LAID
DOWN THEIR LIVES
IN A
RICHTEOUS WAR.
1914 - 1918.

JOHN OWEN CLAWLEY
JAMES DONALD
FRANK HAROLD ELWIN
JOHN ARTHUR EVANS
GEORGE GIBSON
GEORGE HANMER
JOHN HANMER
ELLIS HUMPHREYS
WILLIAM STANLEY MARSH
WILLSON KENWICK NUNNERLEY
JOHN EDMUND ROGERS
ROBERT EVANS STONE
HENRY THOMAS
THOMAS EDWARD TOWNSEND
WILLIAM YOUNG

John James Moore and Thomas Moore, two sons of 'Gaffer' Moore the Headmaster of Cockshutt School, were away at the war but came home again.

Right is the War Memorial in Cockshutt Churchyard and bottom right a close-up showing the names on ther memorial.

Henry Husbands was injured several times in the trenches; his arm was bayoneted, became infected and was amputated during the Battle of the Somme. Henry returned to the village in 1916. He was given a hook as a replacement limb. He suffered long bouts of screaming and shouting in his sleep which would be so bad that his daughters were taken next door to try and get some sleep when the bouts continued. There was no such thing as counselling in those days. A hook would, with practice, be used with skill for some tasks but he was never able to milk again. Henry was an agricultural worker and there was no Welfare State. He managed layering of hedges, but at one stage when his fellow workers on the farm asked for a shilling pay rise – he did the same. They got it; he didn't. The answer was, 'I can't sell what you do'. This is a cold callous comment because to some extent the labourers were part of the productive food chain that has to create the money to earn a rise. Hedge layering was not putting food in anyone's belly. Today he would have been classed as disabled with a disability pension or a War Pension, or both.

The Second World War

The memorial in memory of the fallen of Cockshutt is the organ in church and a brass plaque bearing their names.

An Agreement made this *eleventh* day of *December*

one thousand nine hundred and Forty Seven BETWEEN THE

JOHN COMPTON ORGAN COMPANY, LIMITED, whose registered office is situate at

Chase Road, North Acton, N.W. 10., in the County of London (hereinafter called the

Company) of the one part and The ~~Parochial Church Council~~ *Cockshutt War Memorial Committee*

of Cockshutt Church,

Ellesmere, Salop.

(hereinafter called the Purchasers) of the other part.

WHEREBY IT IS AGREED AS FOLLOWS.---

Agreement for Organ, below, The Organ

Plaque on Organ showing Names of the men who did not return, the order for the Dedication Service.

ST. SIMON AND ST. JUDE'S CHURCH,

COCKSHUTT

———

ORDER OF SERVICE

for the

DEDICATION

by the

LORD BISHOP OF SHREWSBURY

(The Rt. Rev. Robert Leighton Hodson, M.A.)

of the

MEMORIAL ORGAN

to the

FALLEN MEN OF PETTON AND COCKSHUTT

1939—1945

Thursday, April 1st

at 7 p.m.

In 1942 there was a funeral at Cockshutt Church of Sergeant Eric Parker RAF from English Frankton. Eric was a Clapham policeman and he was one of the first London Metropolitan Force to volunteer for the RAF in 1940. He served as a wireless operator and gunner, and was badly wounded in a raid on Cologne; although the plane was brought back, he died from his wounds. He was a well known sportsman and a member of Wem Cricket Club. His coffin was covered with a Union Jack and had lain in church overnight. There was a very large congregation to thank God for his bravery and self sacrifice and he was interred in the cemetery. His name, along with the other six from Cockshutt, who did not return, is on the plaque on the side of the organ.

During the Second World War Cockshutt was part of the war effort in many ways. At Ferneyhough Farm, across the fields from Kenwick Lodge, there was a searchlight camp where enemy aircraft were spotted and the British planes based at Rednal would try to intercept them. The soldiers were under canvas and some outbuildings at Ferneyhough were used as well. Beacons were installed on the top gate, on Park lane, of Kenwick Lodge Farm, owned by James Hulme at the time and his son Stanley, known by everyone as 'Stumpy'. The beacon was claimed to be as high as the church steeple. The beacon was moved every three days or so to different villages in Shropshire. Only the British Army knew of the change, not the enemy.

Stanwardine Hall was another military camp. The yard was fitted with taps and troughs for the soldiers to drink and wash. They had tanks and large guns and one field is still known as The Gun field.

ARP (Air Raid Precautions) were in force, Edgar Roberts and his dad Tom from Petton had blue uniforms and a whistle. I will relate some of the stories we have been told about this dangerous time in our history. The spitfires were stationed at Rednal, and Sleap was used for the Flying Fortress. After the first landing of this very large plane the runway had to be strengthened as it went through the original surface. A very large tree by the church in Petton, and used as the landing mark for Sleap Airfield, was the tree that had to be cut down some time later as it was unsafe. Petton and Cockshutt were on the route for enemy planes going to and from Liverpool. One plane on its way back from an attack dropped an incendiary bomb on a hen house and pen by Nilgreen. They were trying to breach the canal which ran from Weston Lullingfields to Hordley at the time. The explosion was tremendous and the crater it left was enormous. The story goes that the hen house and hen pen were totally obliterated but two eggs were found later untouched in the field.

All houses had to have blackout and many families spent hours listening to and feeling the vibrations as the aircraft flew overhead. On the night of the Nilgreen bomb there was a gathering of a few people in Petton Farm and a couple wanted their cigarette lighters filled with fuel. Someone offered to go and fill the lighters from a vehicle that dripped petrol. While they were doing the job the bomb exploded at Nilgreen and everyone in the house thought that it was the vehicle that had gone up. What a relief when they went to look!

Another story is of a barrage balloon that had broken free from its moorings and was blown low over Petton and towards English Frankton. Spitfires from Rednal were alerted and sent to burst the balloon. The idea was to get underneath the balloon and shoot into the sky. Well one shot ricocheted off the road and caught 'Sticky Tom' in the hip. Many villagers had souvenirs of the balloon including Stanwardine Hall.

Another event happened near Weston Lullingfields church when a plane broke both its wings off as it hit two trees.

Entertainment during the war was the dances in Cockshutt and Ellesmere when the soldiers camped around the area were invited. The men organised long distance running events starting at The Crown towards Shrewsbury up Stanwardine Road past Stonehill to Stanwardine, turning left to Petton then down Lea Lane to the main Shrewsbury Road and back to The Crown. There was always a bookie to take your bets and Alf Hulme and Bob Burden were usually in the frame.

Interesting visitors from America had Bed and Breakfast at the Red Lion. These girls were known as the 'Doughnut Girls' and were from the Red Cross. They came in a converted London Green Line Bus equipped to make doughnuts. The flour and sugar were delivered to the Red Lion and with the help of Nancy Roberts they made the doughnuts while parked in the car park and then set off to sell them in the camps around the area. The girls were accompanied by a couple of soldiers who also drove the bus.

Home Guard

They would each have been given a certificate which read,

'In years when our country was in mortal danger name . . . gave gen-erously of his time and powers to make himself ready for defence by force of arms and with his life if need be.'

The Cockshutt platoon with their Captain; Mr G Glover (seated in the middle of second row) to his left is Lt. R Case and to his right Lt. E L Williams.

Left to right - Back row- Bob Sutton, Harry Thomas, George Tatton, Lawrie Sawbridge, Dick Chidlow, Unknown, Tom Latham, Bob Henshaw, Harry Pratt, Ben Sutton. Middle row- Jack Brich, Unknown, Unknown, Ted Hassall, Unknown, Unknown. Bottom row- Tom Gregory, Walter Worthington, Jim Chidlow, William Birch.

Cockshutt Royal Observer Corps

Left to right - Back row – Dick Chidlow, Harry Thomas, Bob Sutton, Jack Williams, George Tatton, Harry Brown, Lambert Jones, Joe Emberton, Harry Pratt. Middle row - Frank Edwards, John James Brich, Tom Gregory, Ted Hassall, L Sawbridge, Unknown. Bottom row – Walter Worthington, Bill Birch, Jim Chidlow, Ben Sutton, Bob Henshaw.

The ROC was set up in a field on the left going up Park Lane soon after leaving the village. It was set up to track enemy aircraft and transmit essential information to other authorities. They would have been equipped with a telephone for this purpose. The post was opened in July 1938 and closed in 1968. Firstly it was known as a Granite Post with a shed as shelter from the weather, equipped with red flares for warning aircraft of high ground – a Micklewaite indicator, which looked like a cross between a sundial disc and a sextant and stood on a tripod. This would read height/elevation and took bearings and distance. The observers became so skilled they could tell by the sound how many aircraft were approaching. It was of course a very visual observation and low cloud caused problems. This work of warning would link up with the soldiers further up the lane manning searchlights. The ROC played a vital role in the protection of our country. The post was very much improved over the years when an underground bunker was constructed on a low mound within a large square compound, SJ 432885.

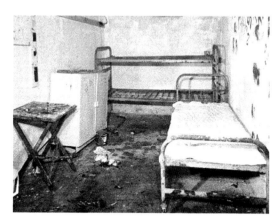

Top left: ROC Post above ground.

Top right: ROC Post below ground.

Centre left: Margaret Husbands, Jack Ridgeway, Dossie Birch and in front Gladys Williams visit Shawbury.

Centre right: The men from Shawbury and back row Gladys Williams, middle row Dossie Birch, in front Olive Chidlow and Margaret Husbands.

Bottom left: ROC Members Wedding - Left front to back Dossie Birch, Mr Money, Olive Chidlow, Bert Hanmer, Right front to back Gladys Williams, Albert Gregory, Margaret Husbands, Jack Ridgeway form a guard of honour at the wedding of John (Jack) and Glenys Griffiths.

COCKSHUTT Shropshire

ROYAL OBSERVER CORPS
~ An on-Line Survey of the U.K's R.O.C
& U.K.W.M.O Monitoring Posts.

**SUBTERRANEA
BRITANNICA**

Record added	2/5/2001
Post Name	**COCKSHUTT**
OS Grid Reference	SJ43232885
County	Shropshire
Date opened	April 1965
Date closed	October 1968
Location	On a low mound within a large square compound 20 yards south of an un-named minor road.
Description	OPEN All surface features remain intact with some green paint remaining. One louvre is still in place on the ventilation shaft. Slots have been cut in the top of the hatch for added ventilation and a framework for closing them welded on the top. The hatch is detached and open. Internally the cupboard remains in place with its top missing together with twin bunks and a single bed, a jerry can, card table, GPO wiring and one ventilation louvre.
Remaining Surface Structures	None
Date of Visit	21.7.2000
Future Actions	

Latest Inspection of ROC Post 2000

Rob – War Dog No. 471/322

Early in 1942 the War Office broadcast an appeal for suitable dogs for war work . Rob was offered and accepted by the War Dogs Training School at Northaw. On completion of his training as a guard and patrol dog, Rob and his handler were sent to an Infantry Regiment in North Africa and at the close of that campaign he was held at the Dog Holding Section near Constantine. He was then sent to the 2nd SAS training base at Sousse to act as a guard dog when stores were disappearing and it was there that Rob was first smuggled up in a plane by the men practising their parachute drops. Rob made his first jump without panic and so he was trained to drop silently and lie still until released from the parachute, then stealthily round up his patrol in daylight or darkness. Trained never to bark, the men were secure in the knowledge that Rob would keep ceaseless vigil guarding them. If he saw, heard or scented the enemy he would move silently to lick the faces of the sleeping men to wake them. Rob made over 20 parachute jumps in North Africa and Italy. On one highly dangerous mission Rob and his party were missing for six weeks, causing great anxiety. When they eventually reappeared Rob was given the entire credit for their safe return. For this and other operational jumps behind enemy lines, Rob was awarded the Dickin Medal (above) - the animal VC, and later the RSPCAs Red collar with its silver medallion 'For Valour'.

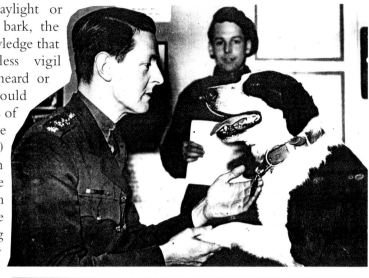

Rob was Britain's first parachute dog and at the end of the war he led the victory parade at Wembley Stadium for War Dog heroes. He was returned to his owners under escort in November 1945. No longer suitable as a cattle dog he was pensioned off until old age and infirmity overtook him and he was put painlessly to sleep in 1952. Rob was buried at Springfields, Kenwick Park and an engraved marble stone - the gift of the sculptor F A Cox stands in the garden - a tribute to a loyal and gallant dog.

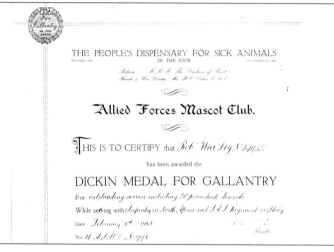

THE PEOPLE'S DISPENSARY FOR SICK ANIMALS
OF THE POOR

Patron   H.R.H. The Duchess of Kent
Founder & Hon Director Mrs M E Dickin O.B.E

Allied Forces Mascot Club.

THIS IS TO CERTIFY that *Rob War Dog N 471/322*

has been awarded the

DICKIN MEDAL FOR GALLANTRY

For *outstanding service including 20 parachute descents*

While serving with *Infantry in North Africa and S A S Regiment in Italy*

Date *February 8th 1945*

No. *11 A.F.M.C. N 498*

War Dog N 471/322 'Rob' took part in the landings in the North African campaign, with an Infantry Unit.

Since September 1943 he has served with a Special Air Force Regiment and took part in operations with that Unit in Italy, most of which were of an unpleasant nature.

He was used as patrol and guard over small parties who were lying up in enemy occupied territory.

There is no doubt that his presence with these parties saved many of them from being discovered and thereby captured or killed.

The Dog has made over 20 parachute descents.

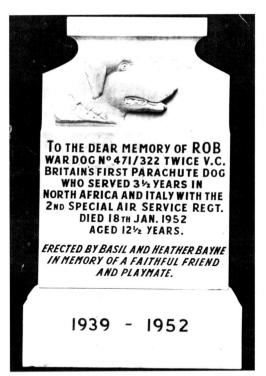

TO THE DEAR MEMORY OF **ROB**
WAR DOG N° 471/322 TWICE V.C.
BRITAIN'S FIRST PARACHUTE DOG
WHO SERVED 3½ YEARS IN
NORTH AFRICA AND ITALY WITH THE
2ND SPECIAL AIR SERVICE REGT.
DIED 18TH JAN. 1952
AGED 12½ YEARS.

*ERECTED BY BASIL AND HEATHER BAYNE
IN MEMORY OF A FAITHFUL FRIEND
AND PLAYMATE.*

1939 - 1952

Top left: A memorial to Rob the war dog

Top right: Poem about the Ex Servicemen's Dinner, author unknown

Bottom: An Ex-Servicemen's Club was thriving in the village and they held an annual dinner.

On VE day school was closed and all pupils were invited to a tea–party at school when they also had games and races.

To Dear Old Jack

The shades of night were falling fast,
As the Ex-servicemen's Committee passed
A resolution, brave and bold,
Their dinner on November 12th to hold.
Straightway they told the news to Jack
That an extension they should not lack.
"Oh yes, oh yes" did Jack reply
"I'll attend to the matter bye and bye".
"And Jack", said Worthington with a wink
"Don't forget the extension so that we can drink".
"Oh no, said Jack with answer pat
"Did you know me forget a thing like that".

Then came the night of November third
The day before the application was heard.
In the Lion the voice of some poor sinner
Said, "Walter, when's the Ex-Servicemen's Dinner?"
"November 12th" the Secretary replied with a grin,
"We shall all have a grand tuck-in".
"Jack" he shouts, "the Court's tommorer".
Poor Jack, he heard these words in horror
What to do was quite unknown
Till he got the Sergeant on 'phone.

For Jack's bad memory, well known here,
Had forgotten the extension for supping beer.
When Jack went to the Court on Monday morn
Looking sad and quite forlorn,
The Magistrates said, "Is that the lot"?
He cried "no, that damned extension I forgot".

CHAPTER 14

BRIDGEWATER ESTATE

Cockshutt was once part of the Bridgewater Estate, owned and looked after by Lord Brownlow and his family. During our research we came upon a beautiful illuminated book which was about to be thrown away by one of our villagers. Fortunately it was rescued by Dean Bywater and is now in the Archives in Shrewsbury.

Just a little history of the Brownlow family:

Henry Francis Cockayne-Cust – a direct descendant of Sir Brownlow-Cust (created Baron Brownlow in 1776) married and had several children, one being a daughter called Marion Isabella.

Major Cust, who had been Bridgewater Estate Agent for many years, died in 1884. His successor as Bridgewater Estate Agent was Brownlow Richard Christopher Tower. He married Marion Isabella Cust, and a Royal Warrant in 1921 granted Mrs Tower the title and precedence of the daughter of a baron. Thus Brownlow Richard Christopher and Marion Isabella became Mr and the Hon. Mrs Tower. They were great grandchildren of the 1st Lord Brownlow-Earl. (they were also second cousins to each other).

The illuminated book, dated 27th September 1892 (sample pages shown right), is beautifully leather bound and monogrammed, which records the birth of the said 'Brownlow Tower R.C. Esquire'. It was paid for by a lengthy list of noted people in the surrounding area and makes interesting reading. It begins;-

'We as neighbours and tenants on Earl Brownlow's Estate desire to offer to yourself and Mrs Tower our hearty congratulations on the birth of a son. We trust that it may please God that he should grow up a comfort, blessing to his parents and a joy to the whole neighbourhood'

Many people from Cockshutt and Crosemere area contributed to the beautifully leather bound book. Everyone who had contributed is listed in the book. The list includes: Reverend H.J. Wilcox, Vicar of Cockshutt; J. Moore, Headmaster of

Cockshutt School; George Burroughs, Crosemere; Mrs E. Prince, Crosemere; Nicholas Robinson, Frankton Grange; William Sheraton, Crosemere; Thomas Smith, Cockshutt; T. Townsend, Cockshutt; Andrew Wilkinson, Crosemere; Thomas Jones, Kenwick Park; William Jones, Kenwick Park; Mrs Marsh, Crosemere; William Nunnerley, Kenwick; William Marsh, Crosemere; E. Parker, English Frankton; John Hayward, Kenwick Park.

Brownlow Tower became Bridgewater Estate Manager when he grew up and was also a Governor of Cockshutt School at one time.

The Joyce Family

John Joyce (1) lived in Cockshutt. He carried on business as a chandler and also had a small-holding on which he kept cattle, sheep and pigs, as well as growing corn and barley. He married around 1600 and he and his wife Ann had two children John (2) and Dorothy.

When John (1) died in 1632 his son John continued to live in Cockshutt and in his will his father also gave him several pieces of land in Cockshutt and Kenwick. To his daughter Dorothy he gave the lease of land in English Frankton. Part of the house was used as a shop and as a result of an inventory on his death the following were part of the contents:

8 cattle, 3 nags, a mare, 44 sheep, 5 pigs and some poultry, candles, tallow and wick yarn; food-stuffs, such as treacle, sugar, currants, groats, prunes, also cloth, silk, thread and lace, oils, quick-silver, and tobacco, gunpowder, weights and scales. Total inventory came to £268.2s 6d.

A number of people owed him money with debts ranging from one shilling to £25 and when a farmhouse would cost about £40 to build some of the debts were substantial.

John requested to be buried in the grave in Ellesmere with his first wife who had died a few years before him. He had married for the second time and his goods and chattels were divided one-third to his son and two-thirds to his wife Susan. But his best feather bed, bedstead, bolster, coverlet and blankets he left to John and his second best bedstead and bedding to Susan.

In 1650 Francis Lloyd and John Joyce became joint landlords of a property in the village.

The Joyce family has a vague connection with the Gunpowder Plot in the Houses of Parliament of 1605. Sir Everard Digby was executed for his part in the plot and he had dis-covered the 'magic' powder when trying to find a solution for ships finding longitude when at sea. His son Kenelm Digby had a great grand daughter Lewey Conway who married William Joyce of The Lodge, Cockshutt in Wrexham Parish Church 1714.

Evidently the Joyce family had lived in the locality for centuries for there are entries on the Hearth Tax Roll of 1672, one was George Joyce living in Kenwick. Another George Joyce – perhaps his son, who was apprentice to Nathaniel Pyne a clock maker in London in 1684, founded what was to become the oldest independent clock-making firm in the world. Over the next three centuries the Joyce dynasty produced some 25 eminent clock and watchmak-ers, becoming one of the most highly respected names in the history of horology. The early small workshop was in the Golden Lion which Joyces owned and one condition of the let was that John Joyce had a room for a workshop and this was stated in the license. The little garret at the top of the stairs seems to have been where it all started.

John Joyce the fourth was married in a timber-built chapel in Cockshutt on 24th December 1685. John lived at The Lodge in Kenwick Park, probably the house of his grandfather. He was appointed supervisor in 1699 of Highways, which meant he was responsible for the roadways leading to the market towns. The road mending work itself was done by the unpaid labour of every householder, cottager and labourer for six days each year. John Joyce the fourth and his wife Elizabeth, who outlived her husband, had two sons and a daughter. It was in 1714 when John the fourth died.

A William Joyce was born in 1692 and it appears that he learned his skills as a clock maker from a relative John William Joyce in Wrexham and took over the business in Wrexham. John the fifth was born in 1687 and was married in 1727 to Tabitha Hodson from Montgomeryshire. On the death of John the fifth his brother William Joyce, a practising clock maker in Wrexham, inherited from his brother after his wife had returned to Montgomeryshire. William was named as executor of his Uncle Arthur Joyce, an innkeeper of Cockshutt. This is probably the reason for his return to his native Cockshutt where he was living when his son Arthur was born. The following year tragedy struck again, at the age of 23 William had become a widower for the second time and had also lost at least two of his children. He did marry again for the third time to Ann Jones of Ellesmere. William Joyce 1692 – 1771 spent most of his working life as a clock maker in Cockshutt and he made the sundial for Cockshutt church – the date 1774 was added later and it is supposed to mark a family grave. This happened three years before the present church was built and it is still in the churchyard, right.

In 1734 on the death of Edmund Bullock, William Joyce took over looking after the Ellesmere Parish Church clock and continued for twenty years until he passed the job over to his son John the sixth. It is this John and his sister Elizabeth who lie buried just outside the door of Cockshutt church (right). The inscription on the grave has been made on a brass dial originally intended for a long case clock and dated 1787 and his sister 1792.

At least five of his seven sons born at Cockshutt

became clock and watchmakers. John Joyce the seventh moved to Ruthin and Conway. Joyce founded a London branch of the business in Lombard Street where they made a wonderful jewelled watch for the Emperor of China. Robert went to Dublin and then to New York and James Joyce the third son removed the business from Cockshutt to Whitchurch where the firm gained international fame. This was before 1782 but the exact date is unknown.

The claim that Joyce of Whitchurch is the oldest firm of clockmakers in the world is often made without reference to the fact that it was originally established in Cockshutt. Another fact that is often wrongly assumed is that Cockshutt Church Clock was made by the Joyces. In fact it was made in Ellesmere by Bullock and Davies.

Cockshutt Murder

Randulph Maynwaring of the Dycheys? (The Ditches at Wem) in the 12th year of the King's reign – 1497 or 1521, made the following complaint. He said there is a chapel in Cockshutt (Cockisshod) where a priest administers a divine service daily. He is paid by the support of alms and charity for this dedication. These alms are given to the chapel each year on the Feast of Corpus Christi.

On the particular day of the Feast, Randulph Maynwaring sent his servant, Richard Manfield with a gift of money to the chapel. He was set upon by Humphrey Kynaston and his two sons - George and John - and an armed crowd of about one hundred strong. Richard Manfield was then attacked and murdered.

This accusation, George Kynaston said was untrue and designed to malign his character and create costs.

There was a long running strife between the Kynastons and Maynwaring families. It was of sufficient animosity that their respective attendance at Cockshutt (Cockisshod) chapel was arranged for attendance at different times to avoid confrontation. At the time of the murder, the Kynastons had attended on Trinity Sunday and the Maynwarings , on the Feast of Corpus Christi had attended on the following Thursday.

 Trinity Sunday passed peacefully but on the Feast of Corpus Christi three members of the Kynaston Family and approximately 120-140 ruffians and thieves lay in wait for Randulph Maynwaring. In the fracas that followed, Randulph Egg and Richard Manfield, two of his servants, were killed.

The three accused members of the Kynaston family appeared before the President (Lord Bishop of Exeter) of the Council of the Marches of Wales. In the evidence presented, it was said that Manfield, who came from Crosemere, had been threatened three to four days prior to his murder, when he was weeding his master's field. He only escaped by running into a nearby marsh. Kynastons party of horsemen could not follow.

The Kynastons and their mob succeeded in their pursuance of him three days later and murdered him. The Bishop on hearing both parties ordered the Kynastons to pay £100 fine and they were bound over to keep the peace and appear in court in twelve days' time. Their next appearance before the Manor Court in Ellesmere was before the Earl of Derby. They were found 'Not guilty' of the greater part of the offences and consequently pardoned.

(This article is a précis from a detailed account that appeared in the *Mere News* written by Christopher Jobson).

The following is an excerpt from the July *Chronicle* of 1888

Sudden Death at Cockshutt

An inquest held at the Red Lion in Cockshutt before Mr John Pay, Coroner, on the body of Elizabeth Ashley, wife of Thomas Ashley. His wife was forty-six years old and enjoyed the best of health. Thomas Ashley left for work at just after 6.00 am. At 8.00 am he was called home because his wife was ill. She was dead before he arrived home. Dr Roe was sent for.

She had been discovered in the closet by Emma Husbands who in turn had sent for John Husbands to give assistance. They carried the deceased into the house but she never recovered consciousness.

William Henry Evans, the medical practitioner from Ellesmere, said he could not give an opinion as to the cause of death and therefore a postmortem was required. The verdict was that death was due to heart disease.

There are two unusual features that are unique to the village of cockshutt and must be mentioned before the book moves onto Petton.

The railway signal stands in the garden of Canley, Crosemere Road

The steam engine known as Lady Heketh belongs to the Milns family of Crosemere, the steam engine can be heard, felt and seen on high days and holidyas going through the village usually on its way to a steam rally somewhere with one of the family at the wheel.

CHAPTER 15

A HISTORY OF PETTON AND ITS PEOPLE

Early Petton

The hamlet of Petton and the surrounding area shows very early traces of habitation. A stone adze/axe was found two feet down in peaty soil by Mr Tatton near Petton Farm. It was ground and probably polished, together with some unworked flints and were given by his wife to Shrewsbury Museum. Other finds include two large flakes of grey flint. Two spindle whorls and a bronze javelin head, were discovered in the moat in 1925. There are two mounds between the road and the church, one was thought to have been a tumulus or burial mound but is now taken to be a motte. From here the earliest settlers lived with the strategic advantage of seeing all the surrounding area. This was probably a wooden structure. There are lots of possible explanations regarding Petton's early development but is best defined as a migrated settlement starting from the area around the present church.

The other mound is the old Ice House for the Hall this may be late 18th early 19th century. There was a red brick structure under the earth mound forming an egg shaped cavity now filled in. Mr Philip Morris, teacher from Petton Hall School, had been down it and described it as 'laddered, deep, round and tiled throughout with white tiles.' The entrance arch tunnel is visible but blocked off. On old maps there is another ice house marked further down Church bank field towards Petton Hall.

The earliest documented evidence of Petton is in the Domesday Book, showing that in Saxon times it was held by Leuenot. Its Saxon value was 5s, which doubled in 1086. In 1066 it states that two villagers and two smallholders with one plough lived in 'Pectone', its Domesday Book name, which is derived from the Old English 'paec-tun' meaning settlement by the peak or hill. In Domesday times the manor was held by Robert Pincerna, with Radulph, who was possibly an ancestor of the Lord's Constantines. Next, the manor was held under the Lord of Montgomery by a family of De Petton, who all seem to be called Richard or Peter. People tended to adapt a name from the place where they lived. The Lords of the Manor appear in different juries, court cases involving land, witnessed deeds and one acted as coroner. Half a hide in Petton had been given by Hugh de Constantine to Shrewsbury Abbey. A hide is a unit of measure usually between 60 and 120 acres. In 1255 Richard de Petton II held half a hide in Petton by service of attending in wartime George Cantilupe, the Lord of Stanwardine with a bow and two un-feathered arrows for fifteen days at the cost of the said Lord. He held half a hide in Petton under the Abbot of Shropshire at a rent of 2s a year. This information was taken from the Shropshire Lay Subsidy Roll 1327, which also describes Richard de Petton IV in 1302 being patron of the Chapel of Petton.

The next Lord of the Manor who is documented was Sir Peter Newton. In 1503 he was Sheriff of Shropshire. Sir Peter Newton was a prominent person in the Council of the Marshes of Wales and in the Court of Henry VII, he was styled as Chancellor to Henry VII. Later he acquired the Council House in Shrewsbury; his will is dated 1524 and he styled himself as 'of Petton', he is buried at St Mary's Shrewsbury. It is thought that he had his Petton

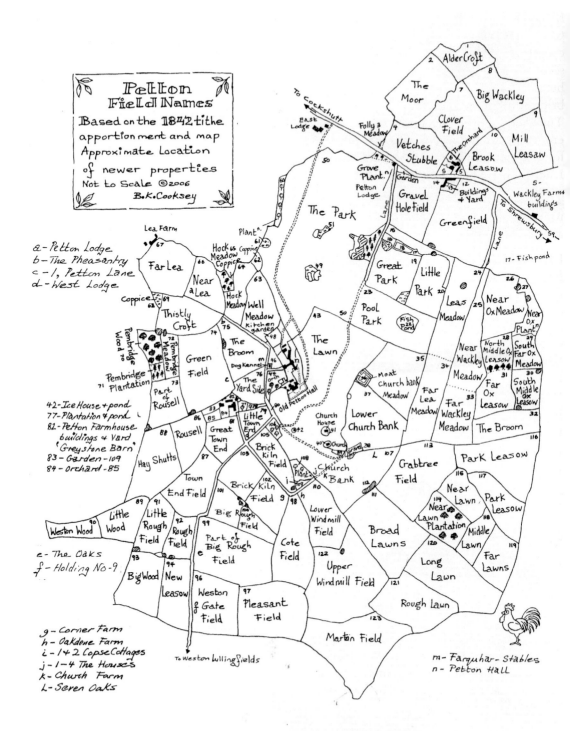

Petton
Field Names
Based on the 1842 tithe
apportionment and map
Approximate Location
of newer properties
Not to Scale ©2006
B.K.Cooksey

a - Petton Lodge
b - The Pheasantry
c - 1, Petton Lane
d - West Lodge

42 - Ice House + pond
77 - Plantation & pond
82 - Petton Farmhouse
     buildings & Yard
     'Greystone Barn'
83 - Garden - 109
84 - Orchard - 85

e - The Oaks
f - Holding No. 9

g - Corner Farm
h - Oakdene Farm
i - 1 + 2 Copse Cottages
j - 1 - 4 The Houses
k - Church Farm
L - Seven Oaks

m - Farquhar - Stables
n - Petton Hall

Manor house in the moated area, down the slope and out of the wind, east of the present Church. The moat is squared and is 'a good example of a medieval moated site with an associated fish pond.' (Shropshire CL Environmental Records). Unfortunately nothing can be seen of any buildings or occupation. It is said that the stone from this Manor house went to build Burlton Hall. There is a double arched bridge but it is made from Victorian hand made bricks. There are a number of large fish ponds that are built on the north and east of the moat. They were fed by streams and inter connected with the reservoir. Some are now dry and eroded by modern agriculture and ploughing. The fish ponds would have been an important food source when the Catholic Church had many feast days when only fish was allowed. Later they continued being a good source of fresh food.

The soil from the moat ditch was used to raise the land a little higher. The area is now surrounded and covered with trees and is a scheduled ancient monument. It is on private land and so is not open to the public and can only be viewed from public footpaths or the road.

Following Sir Peter Newton, the next people to acquire Petton was the Chambre family. The first Johanne de Chambre had settled in Denbighshire after the Norman invasion, then the family split, with Jenkin Chambre settling in Burlton. His son Richard was a wool merchant and he it was who bought Petton. His eldest son, Arthur, was Patron of Myddle church. He died in 1564 and was buried at Petton. The estate stayed in the Chambre family till 1650 when Arthur's great grandson Henry Chambre, went to Ireland. He sold it to a Roger Wilbraham whose name appears on the Hearth tax in 1662. The bell in the church has an inscription 'Long live Roger Wilbraham Esq. 1662'. He may have been one of the Wilbrahams of Delamere Cheshire, born in 1623, and one of the intended Knights of the Royal Oak or the bell may be for his father-in-law of the same name who was Sheriff of Cheshire.

Petton then passed back into the Chambre family via the second son of Jenkin Chambre of Burlton, Francis, son of John Chambre of Wolverley hall. There is a plaque on the north wall of the church written in Latin. The translation says that he had great faith and piety, hoped to go to heaven and that he was the first to suggest the restoration of the church and contributing half towards its rebuilding and decoration. He had married in 1714 and died 13th March 1734, aged 53. The estate then passed to his son John who had no surviving male heir to inherit, so the estate went to his widow and daughters, Hannah, Rebecca and Mary. Hannah and her husband Edward Maurice also known as Corbett, later bought out the sisters share in the estate, which she in turn sold on her divorce. Hannah was however buried at Petton in 1803. Rebecca never married and Mary married John Hill of Hawkstone. Their son became Lord Hill.

The family crest showed 'a greyhound's head erased argent, collared with a garter azure, edged and buckled or another a camel's(?)head quarterly argent and or, eared gules, and charged with a fesse between three annulets, one above and two below, of the last', Visitation of Shropshire 1623.

The Sparlings of Petton

John Sparling bought the Petton estate from Hannah Corbett (Maurice) in 1786 or 1790. John Sparling was born in 1731 and married Elizabeth Greenhow, daughter and heiress of John Greenhow. She died in 1816 at the age of seventy-five. Mr John Sparling was a wealthy shipping merchant, living in St Domingo Hall, Lancashire. He was an influential man being High Sheriff of Lancashire preferring to live in his house in Everton. Mr Sparling was described as being of the old school of Liverpool merchants 'he was dressed with precision and care, generally wearing a gold-laced waistcoat, as was the fashion in his day, and a three-cornered or cocked hat. He was one of those wealthy and upright traders of Britain of the eighteenth century whose attire and conduct were on a par so far as plainness, precision, regularity and substantial worth were concerned'. (Shropshire Mag. June 1957, E.V. Bayne).

They had twins Elizabeth and William, born 20th September 1777. William was involved in a trial for murder and one of the last duels to be fought in Britain. In November 1802 William was engaged to Ann Renshaw, daughter of Samuel Renshaw of St James Street Liverpool. They planned to live in Petton. On returning from a trip William found an anonymous letter 'implying that if certain circumstances were true it would have afforded an objection to his marriage'. Mr Renshaw was shown the letter and the matter was to be sorted, but Williams's mother and friends became involved and objected to the marriage. This resulted in much letter writing and Mr Renshaw accusing Mrs Sparling of writing the letter. Ann's uncle Mr Grayson became involved culminating in William demanding an immediate retraction and apology or Mr Grayson to name a time and place for a duel. So on Sunday February 24th 1804, in a hollow dingle outside Liverpool at just after 7 o'clock in the morning the duel took place. Mr Grayson's shot missed William, but his entered Mr Grayson's thigh by his hip bone. He died a week later of his wounds. William and his second Captain Colquitt where charged with murder and tried on April 4th 1804. The jury took just 20 minutes to return a verdict of 'not guilty'.

Elizabeth, William's twin married a West Indian planter called Mr Matthew Abedego of Bulekleys on the island of St Christopher, with her fortune they bought and built 'The Lyth' near Ellesmere, they had no children. John and Elizabeth's other daughter Ann married John Hopper of Whitton Castle, Durham.

The family was said to have had links or even made their money from slavery. The evidence from a will is that Mr Sparlings youngest brother James had a son called John who was said to have run away to sea and became the captain of a ship called 'Joseph', upon which he died on a voyage to Barbados. He left an unsigned will from which this extract is taken.

'I, Captain John Sparling, master of the good ship Joseph, now on her way [with the blessing of God] bound to Barbadoes, and afterwards to other of the West Indian Islands to dispose of a cargo of slaves, amounting to the number of 271, the privilege and commission of which (if sol) are as follows, say four in every hundred and four on the neat sales, and two per cent. On the gross sales which is my property. And if it should please Almighty God, to call me from this earthly and wicked world. I, the said John Sparling, the younger , aforesaid, do give and bequeath unto my dearly loved mother. Jane Sparling. All monies and other benefits arising from the above-mentioned voyage, together with £433 19s. 3d. now in the hands of

William Dean the younger.' (Pages from *The Life of John Sparling*). So he is not to be confused with the other John Sparling of Petton.

William Sparling's youngest son John wrote about his father and family in his diaries which his daughter was to edit and publish years later. His descriptions and character analysis are very personnel and carry much feeling as does all of his writing. He wrote of his father's character 'My father was a man of unquestionable abilities of a certain kind. Speculatively, he was a person of shrewd and accurate, if not of profound, judgment. He had great and rapid powers of calculation. His reading was prodigious and his memory tolerably retentive. His taste was fastidious, if not highly refined. Educated at Eton and Oxford subsequently placed in the 10th Hussars (at the time commanded by the Prince Regent, and considered, par excellence, the most patrician corps in the service), his mind was, betimes, highly cultivated and his manner polished. There was no mistaking that he was a gentleman. It is equally certain that he had ever the welfare of his family at heart. His children must always remember with thankfulness that for half-a-century he practiced the most vigorous self denial, and lived a life of almost penury, in order to leave them a comfortable provision at his death. Nevertheless, in practical matters he was almost a baby. At the moment of trial he was never equal to the occasion. In dealing with all the graver interests of life he failed signally. With all his varied stores of learning, he was never more than an intellectual voluptuary. Though capable of enlightening most of his acquaintances on most subjects, he never made his opinion to be sought, and he shrank from measuring himself with persons infinitely inferior in capacity to himself. It is characteristic of his unpractical mind that though he taught himself French and Spanish, to almost theoretical perfection, he was never heard to converse in either. In the management of his estate he blundered egregiously. He was unsuccessful even in the investing of his favourite money. Were I to be asked which was the most conspicuous infirmity of his mind I should without hesitation say it was indolence. It absorbed him. He would do anything to escape being plagued, and would live contentedly in a fool's paradise'.

He wrote similarly about his aunts and uncles but cut the pages out later maybe regretting what he wrote.

William Sparling went on to marry Emma Elizabeth only daughter of John Walmsley of Ince Hall, Lancashire. She was considered a great beauty and they were said to have been happy together from when they married, on 21st May 1805, to when William died in October 1870, aged 93. Emma died in 21st May 1876 aged 85.

Their grand daughter wrote this about her grandparents, 'To the last my grandfather and grandmother were lovers and he always treated her with an 'old world' courtesy that was delightful to see. My grandmother, who in her youth was a great beauty, and a toast at Bath when Bath was in its palmy days'.

They had eight children but not all survived childhood or they died in early adulthood. On 23rd January 1811 their two year old son John Charles died and tragically the next day their daughter Sophia, who had been born in Petton on 16th November 1810, died. Their daughter Frances was born 26th Feb 1812 and died April 1832 aged 20. A year later, on May 3rd 1833, Mary Elizabeth Sparling who was their eldest daughter died aged 27. Both 'departed this life in the bloom of youth' this is written on their memorial in the church.

Petton Park Salop
Friday May 8th 1868 —

Dear Sir

Old Jacks is farming about 140 acres of land under Captain first they are considered steady tidy & well to do sort of people & I should say you might venture to take him as a surety for the mun stated he has a son living under Wm Lovett of Fernhill & I believe he gives satisfaction but I really do not know what they are worth beyond what I have stated.

I remain yours truly
W. Sparling Junr

A Reference letter written by Mr Sparling 1868

Surviving into adulthood were twin boys William and Charles. They were born on the 14th March 1813. John Sparling was born on 19th July 1815. We also have Emma Anne Sparling who died 1880 aged 72 in London, but was buried in Petton.

William and Emma's son John started keeping a diary in January 1854, his earliest memories were of an illness 'and of the house at Petton being nearly rebuilt. I remember the kind face of my nurs , Mary Whitfield, who was ever ready to protect me from the slaps and snubs which her next-in-command, 'Lyddy' (old-Pot-Lid I called her), was no less ready to inflict. Lyddy had a worthy successor in Betty Renshaw, and certainly if I was spoiled, it was not by them. I have a very distinct recollection of my fifth birthday. It was the corona-tion of George the Forth. I was to have a bottle of brandy to regale the servants with in the evening. In the morning I walked with Mrs Whitfield to Burlton. In the afternoon the brandy was opened, and when I tasted that genuine British compound (duly diluted) I experienced the first disappointment which my memory retains!'

He wrote of a lonely childhood, his brothers away at school, his sisters older and Emma in the schoolroom. 'My father hated to be bored, and of course, saw little of me. My mother was so frequently suffering from neuralgia that my company would have painfully distracted her. And so for months I was left to the servants and to myself. It was no privilege to be sent for into the parlour. Oh, that library of a winter's night! That low, hot library, with the 'winding sheets' flickering murkily round the wicks of the two mould candles, and its silence broken only by the ticking of the clock and the rustling of the leaves of my father's book as he turned them over. To him the romping of a child was about as agreeable as the buzzing of a mosquito. How glad I was to escape into the kitchen'.

There was a significant occurrence at this early time, John was accused of stealing a candle-stick which he maintained all day that he had not. That night their first governess Miss Wood kept him up "preaching repentance until my eyelids drooped and my legs tottered under me and finally told me she would not let me go to bed that night unless I confessed my guilt. So I told her the lie she asked for, received absolution, and was allowed to rest. For years I was taunted with that theft. But from that night all moral influence over me was gone! I hope God has forgiven the poor woman, for she meant it well, but she spoiled my character on that dismal night for years. One good, however, it has done. It made me resolve, if ever I had a child, to treat it with confidence, and never break its spirit with a sense of injustice."

John Sparling went to school at Myddle Rectory with Mr Burd, his brothers to a Mr Corfield at Pitchford. He learnt of his new school when he was in the library being fitted for new clothes by Mr Parker the tailor from Cockshutt. As the tailor was leaving his mother said to him 'Mind you send the things tomorrow, for he goes to school on Monday.' 'Thus was the fatal intelligence broken to me!'. He spent ten years there, the first year went quiet well but then he was to receive terrible treatment from four new boys over a period of four years he wrote in his diary that 'I was daily and hourly beaten, mercilessly and wantonly beaten, for the sole and avowed reason that it was 'good fun' seeing me cry. It will hardly be credited that I was compelled often ten times a day to hold out my hands to be stung by wasps. Once they applied a wasp to my nose.' He goes on to describe many cruel incidences he had to endure, and then he seems to enjoy writing that all the bullies either died early or led a wretched life.

John Sparling wrote of Petton at Christmas in his diaries that it was kept 'after the fashion of olden times'. The hall was all cleaned and his mother would have the schoolchildren from Cockshutt and Burlton brought up for examination, as was her due as one of the main families in the area, as well as their patron and supporter. An ox was killed and distributed among the poor when each portion was labelled with a sprig of holly.

On St Thomas's Day old women came begging corn, then carol singers and morris dancers. On Christmas Day everyone went to church and a dinner was given for all the retainers. John remembers waiting as a young boy for the sound of the fiddle player outside the dining room window when they would start to play 'God save the King'. There was a dance in the servant's hall to which everyone came, a magic lantern show in the dining room, with the butler having a card party in the pantry and the old labourers a smoking party in the bake house. He writes that 'Thomas Birch sang 'John Barleycorn', old Teece sang 'Cheyney Metal,' and old Baker, the blacksmith, followed with 'I married a wife, and her name was Grace'. Neither my parents nor sisters took any part in these festivities. I think it must have been as early as Christmas 1827 that mother sent for me at ten o'clock from the servants' hall and told me I was getting too old for such companionship. I acquiesced readily enough, but I felt somewhat sorrowfully that childhood was over.'

(Extracts taken from pages of *The Life of John Sparling*).

William and Charles the twin's 21st birthday celebration in 1834 was on a major scale, lasting from March 14th to 26th. There were roasted ox and sheep, dances, tea drinking, bonfires, fireworks and lots of drinking carrying on over the two weeks. The motto for the event was 'success to the House of Petton. Peace and plenty Speed the Plough'. An account was given in the Shropshire magazine describing the events that started with a procession from Cockshutt to Petton Hall with a band of musician's adorned with ribbons and gilded laurels, on horseback tenants and neighbours riding in pairs, followed by forty pupils from Cockshutt School wearing hats with mottos. There followed a decorated wagon carrying the carcasses of an ox and four sheep with two mounted butchers. On arrival at the Hall the procession was received by the family and guests.

The important people in the procession were entertained in the dining room, the rest given bread and beef and 'good old stingo'. On returning to Cockshutt the beef and mutton were given to the poor with bread and ale. The three inns also gave free beer, a dinner at the 'Crown and Lion' and a dance for the ladies, the discharging of canon and the ringing of bells throughout the day. The day after this the women were given a tea, another dance and ran races for white stockings, prices of gown pieces and handkerchiefs were drawn in lots. The final festivities took place on 26th March, when tenants, tradesmen and other people from the area were entertained to a dinner and a ball. Finally two oak trees were planted on Church Bank to commemorate the occasion, *Shropshire Magazine* December 1953

Charles Sparling was a Captain in the 15th Hussars and died in 30th April 1876 at the age of 63. William died 27th March 1887. Neither married, so the estate passed to their youngest brother Reverend John Sparling M.A.

John went to Oriel College Oxford in early 1834. During the August while he was in Petton he contracted an illness which lasted several months and through which he lost the sight in one eye. In one account of his character, *Shropshire Magazine* July 1957, he is described as 'dashing, intelligent with a sparkling sense of humour'. Finding this extract from his autobiographical notes I think he must have been a very interesting man. He wrote of the curate at Cockshutt that he was 'a drinking, cockfighting speechifying, self-sufficient little scamp as ever there was. He was just five feet high; had fifty-two indifferent sermons and kept two concubines, adding a wife to them later in life', *Shropshire Magazine* July 1957.

The author of *Extinct Mansions of Shrewsbury* wrote of his visit, when he was shown the moat which had been cleared the previous year and described being shown round by Rev. John Sparling, describing him as 'a man of remarkable ability and shrewdness concealed by an assumed rustic manner'.

On a journey home after he had resumed his studies at Oxford on 23rd March 1836, he narrowly escaped an ambush near Wackley Brook, when a holly bush was placed in the road to make the horse shy. Because his horse was supposedly blind it didn't react. Unfortunately the next travellers from the opposite direction two gentlemen on their way from Wrexham Fair to Shrewsbury were not so lucky and the men waiting in ambush beat, robbed and left the men for dead. Fortunately they were found and eventually recovered. The thieves had been seen on a number of occasions that day and had been wandering around the country-side robbing affluent travellers. The five Irishmen responsible were eventually caught in

Manchester and charged with several crimes. However it was only at Petton that they could be identified, so they were sent for trial to Shrewsbury. The charge was brutal assault, amounting to attempted murder and robbery. They were found guilty, three were sentenced to death by hanging and the other two transported to Australia for life. On the day of execution there were supposed to be 10,000 people present.

Shortly after a walking tour across Northern Italy, France and then Germany, John met his future wife Catherine Sybilla de Trafford, the seventh daughter of Sir Thomas Joseph de Trafford. She was seated next to him at a society dinner apparently looking stunning in a crimson satin dress. They must have formed quite an impression on each other. Unfortunately she was engaged and had been for the last six years to an Irish protestant. Catherine was a Catholic and her father thought she had wasted her youth waiting for him. So on meeting John she broke off her engagement and quit the Catholic Church. The next day, when John found out from his sister Emma, he wrote offering himself to Catherine. After a whirlwind courtship of two months, they married on 19th September 1843 at Eccles Parish Church.

Their wedding announcement was the first in the very first edition of 'The News of the World' in 1843. They honeymooned for three years around Europe. While in Florence, on 21st November, 1845, Catherine gave birth to a son John William Rudolf. Unfortunately he died very suddenly on 13th August 1846 after a short illness while they were in Dresden. They returned to England, but were soon off again to Europe. While in Baden-Baden Germany on 5th June 1848, their only daughter Emma Florence was born.

John settled his family in Eccleston near Manchester, which was then a thriving town with a wool mill, two cotton mills, coal mine and large farming community. He had the best house there and a good income from his living.

William Sparling's daughter loved and admired her father very much, but like her father before her she also wrote a telling character study of her father. She wrote "In whatsoever company he found himself he was nine times out of ten, head and shoulders above it intellectually. But he was a shy man, and keenly alive to anything like a slight. He never forgot an injury nor a kindness; but, as he likewise never forgot to return good for evil, I can truthfully say that he lived and died a Christian gentleman. He would not nowadays have been considered a model clergyman. Virile and full of humour he had a scarcely veiled contempt for sanctimonious pretensions and for all manner of extremes. He reveals his character far better than I can delineate it, as the extracts from his manuscript will show. To me he never mentioned that he was writing a memorial of his life; but I think it would have pleased him could he have foreseen that some day I should edit it. It has been a labour of love, mingled with some sadness, for I know that the latter portion of his life story was written partly as a means of relieving his deep despondency after parting from the daughter whose future had been the sole object of his solicitude".

He inherited Petton Hall and its large estate in 1888 at the age of 72. He only lived there as master for a very short time before he died on 11th March 1890. His wife Sybella had died on 22nd May 1886. Their daughter Emma Florence inherited.

Petton Church

The church in Petton stands in a prominent position next to the old mound of the motte and the ice house. There has been a chapel on the site since about 1159 during the reign of Henry II (1159-1189) and the time of Bishop Durdent. The present church was rebuilt after a fire in 1727 probably by Francis Chambre and R Wilbraham. A badly worn plaque dedicated to Francis Chambre is on the wall by the pulpit. The owners of the Hall were always closely linked to the church and due to their support it has thrived; it was used as if it were their own chapel. The church is now in the Deanery of Ellesmere but was a chapelry of Baschurch in the Norman period. In 1086 it was in the Baschurch hundred, later the Pimhill hundred; these where a collection of places formed into an administrative district. The Patrons of Petton church were the Abbot of Shrewsbury from 1344 until 1616, then successive Kings, Queens and the Lord Chancellor. From 1960 -79 the patron was Mr R G Wall. When he died he left a substantial legacy for the church in Baschurch and a smaller one to Petton for capital expenses. This paid for re-roofing the church. After Mr Wall the patron was the Bishop of the Diocese and the Church Patronage Society acting jointly. The patronage finished when Rev Thorold took up his post in 1999.

The medieval church was probably only a small building with no tower. The present Georgian brick built church was a plain rectangular building in a smaller plot than now. The vestry was probably added later, as the bricks are a little wider. There are a collection of watercolours that show the church exterior as it was. One was painted by Rev Edward Williams c.1800, he was very prolific and painted many churches around Shropshire. His painting shows the tower or bellcote being not so pointed with a weathervane, square slatted windows and the doorway flanked by attached pilasters. The boundary wall was just a rough sawn picket fence with only some sandstone showing. The large yew tree at the front of the church can be seen as a very thin sapling and there are no monuments or headstones showing. The porch was built in sandstone and timber under a slate roof and the Church re-roofed by William Sparling Esq in 1st September 1870. There is a stone above the door of the church to this effect, although there appears to be a square raised area shown in an earlier watercolour. Limited edition prints were produced and sold in aid of church funds in 1996 by Barbara Cooksey. They show the roof with the old air vents before they were removed when the church was re-roofed. Other views of the church have also been used for notelets and Christmas cards for church fund raising. In 1896 Emma Florence Cunliffe as the 'Lady of the Manor 'started her course of 'beautification' of the church and changed the Georgian interior from being 'chaste and neat' (Bagshaw's Directory of Shropshire' 1851) interior to Victorian tastes. This she did with great energy using many salvaged or reclaimed materials, fixtures and fittings as her mother had done.

The church is filled with fine woodwork mostly dating from 1727 and earlier. The Jacobean pulpit dated 1625 and reredos (the ornamental screen behind the altar), were given to the church by her mother, Emma Elizabeth Sparling. These are very richly carved oak and were brought from Wrexham Church. Rev George Cunliffe was the Rector of both Wrexham and Petton; he was Mr Cunliffe's uncle. The Jacobean woodwork is mixed with late Gothic carving; a sacred monogram is carved at the back of the pulpit and the letters G & W at either side.

An Early interior photograph of Petton Church and below, The Pulpit decorated for the Flower Festival 1994

There are also 17th century carvings mixed onto the 'squires' pew. The nine boxed pews are a rarity now and are of differing sizes. The H-hinges and benches around the sides are probably c. 1727. They are panelled using pieces taken from the nearby Elizabethan Stanwardine Hall which the Sparlings and Cunliffes also owned. Mr William Sparling bought it when he sold property of his mother's. The ancient linen fold carved paneling which is now fronting the gallery was hidden under the seats and put in its present position in the 1896 refurbishment.

The pair of deeply carved pillars covered with oval, oblong and diamond shaped carving, with lion's heads at the top are just inside the main doors. They are supporting the gallery and were brought from the old Council House in Shrewsbury which used to be owned by Sir. Peter Newton, who used to live in Petton on the site of the moated area.

More wooden carvings include the font cover depicting the resurrection of 'Our Lord' and by the vestry door (which was originally in the Abbey church Shrewsbury) a very old Dutch piece coming from Bridgnorth. The small carving of St Martin sharing his cloak with a beggar came from Ellesmere in 1920.

There are Minton tiles in the Chancel and the Altar floor is of lovely Italian mosaic provided by Mrs Cunliffe, as well as the large carved wooden eagle, given in 1896. The altar table was given to the church in 1901 by Rev. Edward Reith. The electric light pendants and two storage batteries where installed by Mrs Cunliffe in 1913 as a memento of 14 years ministry by him; mains electricity was installed in 1951.

Memorials

There are many memorials to members of the Sparling and Cunliffe family around the church. Going round the church the oldest is to the Chambre family. It is marble and alabaster near the pulpit but the inscription has disappeared. Next to this is a metal monument to Rev. Walter Clement Tabor who was for twelve years the curate and fifteen years Rector at Petton 1837-1898.

On the left of the vestry door are monuments to Ellis Cunliffe and on the right a lovely angel in coloured stone and gold mosaic for Verbena Williams, Mrs Cunliffe's granddaughter (shown right).

On either side of the altar are white marble memorials to Elizabeth and John Sparling, Mrs Cunliffe's grandparents. In the corner are memorials to William, Charles and Emma Sparling and their sisters.

There is a large white marble memorial to Mrs Cunliffe's father, Rev.d John Sparling and mother Catherine Sybella, and further memorials to their son John William Rudolph, Caroline Muriel Valencia le Champion Mr and Mrs Cunliffe's 5th daughter, Vera Nina Williams, Ellis Sparling Cunliffe, Legendre Watkins Cunliffe , Major John Brooke Cunliffe and grandson Ellis Robert Cunliffe Stone.

On the north wall is a large alabaster monument in memory of Ellis Brooke Cunliffe who died in 4th March 1915. The central panel of Italian mosaic depicts an armoured King Arthur, a copy of a life size bronze figure, one of twenty eight surrounding the tomb of the Emperor Maximillian at Innsbruck. Beneath is the Cunliffe family motto 'Fideliter' (faithful), on either side his dates and information about his life.

Under the gallery there are certificates won by the church in the best churchyard competition and a memorial to George Tatton. He was church warden and organist, the son of Henry Tatton the head gardener for Petton Hall for many years. There is also a plaque to Mr Wall the last Patron of Petton church. One memorial at the very back, in white marble, is to 'Thomas Bretheton nearly 40 years faithful friend and servant of the Cunliffe family, 'Fear no more the heart of the sun, nor the furious winter rages, Thou, thy wordly task hast done home art gone & lain thy wages' (Cymbeline). He was the butler and must have been special to warrant such a memorial and also to have worked for Mrs Cunliffe for so long. He was married to Alice and they had three children born in Petton. He lived at West Lodge and died on 31st March 1924, aged 58. Mrs Husbands mentions him in her history of the area.

In 1917 in the font pew a simple wooden Roll of Honour was erected to those who died in the 1st World War. The central panel was originally an old oak pew door from Cockshutt church removed many years previously and given by Mr Henry Tatton. We know about those who died in the Cunliffe family in the war, others who died from Petton were Herbert Tatton, who was the youngest son of Henry Tatton. Herbert was a gardener according to the 1901 census. William Kirkham was a Corporal with the 1st Kings Liverpool Regiment, he died in Richebourg.

There are lots of small items in the church that at first glance do not hold much significance but are very interesting, like the wooden 'alms box' which is Jacobean and was found under the floor of the church at the time of Emma Florence's beautification in 1896. There is a small stone measure on a shelf at the back that was found in the moat when it was drained and cleared. It may have been thrown away during the reformation because of its use as a Holy Water Stoup, a romantic notion, but with the indents for pouring and handles it was probably for grinding and domestic use. There is a Prayer and Service Book chained to the rear pew behind the font dated 1745.

Windows

One of the more colourful additions to the church are the stained glass windows, they where uniquely designed for Petton with lots of very personal details and input from Emma Florence Cunliffe. All but one of the windows was made by Ward & Hughs of 67, Frith Street Soho Square, London, they were a well known and reputable firm of glass painters and contemporaries of William Morris. They made the East window for Lincoln cathedral and a window in the Guildhall in London.

The first window to be installed on the north side of the church in 1907 depicts the 'Angel of the Revelation.' It was placed in memory of Legendre Watkin Cunliffe their youngest son, by his parents, brothers and sisters. He died 24th October 1907 aged 27. Between the pulpit and vestry door is a small window, this was copied from Sir Joshua Reynolds' 'Heads of Angels' with the other half having a local touch, showing a familiar view across to Grinshill and Clive church. When commissioned in 1909 the window cost £44.15s. Parishioners of Petton contributed from Harvest, Easter and Christmas collections with the main donation from Mrs Cunliffe of £10.00. The local farmers like Mr and Mrs Parker and Mr Emberton gave around £2.2s while others like the butler Mr Bretherton and Head Gardener Mr Tatton gave 2s 6d, the deficit was defrayed by Mrs Cunliffe. Above the altar is a beautiful window dedicated to the glory of God and in memory of William, Charles and Emma Sparling, Mrs Cunliffe's uncles and aunt, it is framed by carved arched woodwork and is a copy of the Pre-Raphaelite's William Holman Hunt's painting, 'The Light of the World'.

The middle window on the north side is in 'loyal' memory of Queen Victoria and King Edward with medallion portraits of them at the bottom (shown right). It was designed and paid for by Mrs Cunliffe in 1911. It shows a beautiful woman, her face and manner very much in the Pre- Raphaelite School and it is full of symbolism. It is best described in Mrs Cunliffe's

own words, 'The white robed figure is symbolical of peace. The attitude suggests rest. The left arm bears a sheaf of olive branches. On the knees are some fruit of the Earth and surrounding the figure are near and distant sheaves of corn. All these symbols of peace denote the work of King Edward', The Peace Maker'. Behind the figure are red Tudor roses and an English oak. In the middle distance are the figures of a mother and two children. These symbolize the virtues of Queen Victoria The Good, the 'mother of her people'. In the further distance is shown an English homestead, typical of Queen Victoria's beautiful home life. In the far distance rises a church spire, expressive of both sovereigns being Defenders of the faith and beyond all roll 'The Seas of Empire'. All this was made clear to the congregation on June 25th, when a service in celebration of the coronation of King George V and Queen Mary was held in Petton church'.

The next window down placed in December 1911 (shown left) is of St Francis of Assisi showing him with a lamb that always followed him, the rabbit that he sheltered and delicately painted details like the insects and vegetation. The window was in memory of Mr and Mrs Cunliffe's son-in-law Robert D'Oyley Freeman Thomas of whom she was extremely fond; he was married to their third daughter and fifth child Florence Vanda. Again it is packed with details symbolizing stories associated with Saint Francis and personal details of Robert's own life and his love of animals. The distant landscape shows the bridge over Blenheim Lake which was the view from the house where he was born and died at the age of 45. In the background there is a broken column symbolizing a life cut short. Two falcons on a branch who were supposed to wake the saint to prayer and a verse from Coleridge 'He prayeth best who loveth best all things both Great and small, for the dear God who loveth us, He made and loveth all' completes the window.

The window behind the font (shown right) was probably the most poignant for Mrs Cunliffe because it was in memory of her grandson who died in the First World War. She wrote, 'The terrible year 1914 brought grief and desolation to countless English homes. Among the slain was Ellis Robert Cunliffe Stone, age 21. To Major and Mrs Stone it was the end of all their hopes. It was fitting that a memorial should find a place in Petton church, the subject chosen being, 'The Christian Soldier' clad in the whole armour of God.' The youthful figure (the face a likeness of the dead soldier) stands on a rampart with his back to Calais, in defence of which the allies were fighting in the middle distance the 15th century 'Hotel de Ville of Calais and the 12th century Church of Notre Dame de Calais '. In the far distance are shown the sea and English Battle ships. Above lowers a lurid and staring sky across which the Red Cross flag of St Andrew'. In the hollow of the boys left arm is the spear which carries the flag, and the arm also holds the 'Helmet of Salvation'. The right hand rest upon the 'Shield of Faith'. The breast is covered by the 'Brest plate of Righteousness the Body' girt about with Truth; the feet shod with Peace. Near the feet spring forget-me-nots'. There is a border of two spears and ribbon twisted with the initials ERCS, the Welsh dragon and English lion, rose and oak leaves."

There are lines by Sir Owen Seaman 'Tears for the dead, Who shall not come again Homeward to any shore on any tide. Tears for the Dead! But throu 'bitter rain, Shines like an April sun the smile of Pride' Also the words, 'Take unto you the whole Armour of God' on the arch of the window. It was dedicated on 21st March 1915. The window in memory of Emma Florence Cunliffe is on the far south side shows a mother figure in a blue cloak with her arm around a child. It was placed there by her surviving children. It was made by a different firm.

Ironwork and interior

Petton church's intricate iron work is another interesting feature. The chancel screen was erected in 1897 to commemorate the 67th year of Queen Victoria's reign. There are candle sconces mounted on the box pew sides and gallery and more hinged on the walls. There are four free standing candelabras; two were placed in the Chancel by Mrs Cunliffe in the Christmas of 1909. They are lit in the evenings for the Christmas carol service or on special occasions such as weddings when care has to be taken with hair and large hats.

In July 1924 Mrs Cunliffe was presented with a chair, from the people of Petton as a token of their love. She was obviously touched by this gesture and wrote, 'I hope that when I am no longer here to occupy that chair you will sometimes keep a corner of your hearts for me and now & then one pleasant memory'.

Generations of parishioners since and many visitors to the church have come to remember Mrs Cunliffe with gratitude. More than any other individual she has been responsible for making Petton church the unique and beautiful building that it is today.

A scheme of refurbishment took place in 1974 when a double gravestone was found under the floorboards in the rear pew on the south side of the church when a sunken floorboard was removed. It is thought it may have originally been placed against the interior wall of the church and removed when the paneling was installed, it may be the actual burial place. What was visible of the inscription reads ' . . . Here also lies the body of Thomas Lee who departed this life; Nov. 22nd 1762 aged 73 years'

Petton church was used as an alibi in the late seventeenth century in an attempted burglary and brutal murder at Eyton. Hugh Elks with a companion tried to rob one of his neighbours on Sunday morning when they thought everyone would be at church. He was recognized by a servant maid who had been making cheese; he slit the poor girl's throat. His accomplice fled to Baschuch church and Hugh ran home to Marton, then he ran to Petton church and slipped in just before the end of the service. Unfortunately he had locked his dog in the house at Eyton so when the crime was discovered by the family it led them home to his master's house. Hugh Elks was eventually found guilty and hanged at Shrewsbury.

Among the church archives there is part of a book detailing the people of Petton, the expenses of the church and two clothing clubs, 'Mrs Cottles Clothing Club' and 'Squire Sparlings Club'. Working from the census it is from the early 1870s. The monthly payments for both clubs were collected by John Birch who was the clerk for the church and monies were handed over to the clergyman at the end of every quarter. The members subscribed 6d a week that is six shillings 6d or £1.6s. a year. A donation of five shillings was added to each subscription. In Mrs Cottle's club there were six people, in the Squire's club there were twenty people and they each got a donation of seven shillings.

A savings bank also operated with Mr Sparling's butler receiving 2/6 a week from Henry Tatton and William Jones, carpenter who worked for the Squire for many years. This was then handed over to the clergyman on each quarter day to be put by him into Ellesmere Savings Bank, that was £1.12.6 in total.

Mr John Birch was a shoemaker and the clerk of the church in Petton his family lived in a cottage at 'Pick Hill near Petton on road side to Burlton but in Loppington Parish'. He was described as 'dyspeptic and invalidish' for his work as clerk he was paid £2.10.0 including the washing of the surplice, he also cut the grass in the church yard.

Next door to him lived Charles Bright, Mr Sparling's groom, his wife and two or three children, the son Charles 'out at service at Ellesmere'. According to Mrs Marjorie Jones book on 'Burlton', Sallie their daughter was a ladies maid at the Hall who on her retirement became a 'post lady' in Burlton in around 1920.

John Haycocks was the gamekeeper, his wife cleaned the church and lit the stove; she was paid £2.00 a year for this. They had four or five children, the two girls Mary and Sarah and the Birch's daughters Sarah and Jane sang in the church and at Christmas they were given half a crown each.

The book has an entry for 'The lodge in Petton Park but in Cockshutt Parish' this is where the Bailiff Mr Thomas lived with his wife and children. This may be what is now known as Lea Farm as that seemed to be where the estate manager/ bailiff lived before the building of 'The Grange 'for the Estate manager Mr Clarke by the Cunliffe's. The Thomas family went to Petton church and the one child is described as an 'asthmatic invalid too delicate to be sent to school & cannot read'.

Churchyard

On 25th June 1911 the wrought iron churchyard gate was installed in memory of King Edward VII, it has the letters E.R. and an Imperial Crown underneath two olive branches. It

was used as the main access to the church from the Hall. From an early photo you can see quite clearly the track that they called 'Dog Kennel Lane ' that ran across the field up to the church, the raised area can still be seen quite clearly when the grass is short, leading towards the back of Farquhar, the old stable block for Petton Hall. There is a mounting block and steps near the gate, originally put there for ladies riding side saddle to church.

There is an interesting memorial fixed to the outside wall of the church which reads 'In Memory of Edward Haywood whose death was caused by the wheels going over his head on 3rd September ---4'. The date has flaked off and he is not in the church burial records so cannot be verified, but a report about an accident was reprinted in the 'Shrewsbury Chronicle' 16th Sept 04 in it's 'Memory Corner'. It reads '200 years ago, Friday, September 14, 1884. Accident last week, as the waggoner on Mr Menloves, of Whackley, near Ellesmere, was walking backwards and whipping one of the horses in the harvesting field. His foot got tangled in some undergrowth which threw him down and the wheels passed over him and he was killed on the spot.' So it may be the same person as the dates and story are so similar.

A war memorial cross was bought by parochial subscription and erected over the steps of the Sparling vault. It has the names of those that died in the 1st World War.

There are a number of boxed graves on the East wall which are late 18th early 19th century. The inscriptions are quite worn but a lot are the early tenants of the Hall and the Menlove family. The graveyard was extended in 1933 at a total cost of £23.5.0. The base of the foundations of the original circular wall can still be seen.

Recent times

To mark the 250th year of Petton and 200th year of Cockshutt Church 4th – 6th June 1977 there was a 'Festival of Countrywork and Countryways'.

In 1979 the benefice was united in a new pastoral scheme as part of the United Benefice of Petton with Cockshutt, Weston Lullingfields and Hordley. In 1982 it was reorganised again, this time Petton with Cockshutt, Welshhampton and Lyneal cum Colemere.

The church was re-roofed using the original slates; this was possible because of the legacy left by Mr R G Wall. The old redundant metal air vents were removed at this time.

Petton has an active if small congregation and organises many fund raising events. One of the largest was a flower festival in September 1994; the theme was the hymn, 'We plough the fields and scatter the good seed on the ground'. Each boxed pew was decorated based on a verse from the hymn. The event lasted the whole weekend with a marquee erected on the lawn of Church House next to the church by kind invitation of Lady Newborough who lived there at the time. Teas and refreshment were served throughout the weekend which concluded with a Harvest Festival service on the Sunday evening conducted by Bishop David. It was one of his first official functions on becoming Bishop of Shrewsbury. The evening finished with a cold supper. The occasion attracted more visitors than expected and cakes had to be hastily baked due to the demand, it raised £2,000.

The Diocese did not have any records of the name of Petton church, so to mark the

Millennium the church was dedicated to St Raphael and St Isidore. The congregation chose their favourite Saint from a shortlist of four and two names were chosen St Isidore and St Raphael. A special ceremony of dedication was held on 14th May 2000 with Bishop Keith of Lichfield and a shared lunch followed in the Millennium Hall.

There are regular church services on the second and fourth Sundays in the month. Special services are held at Harvest Festival and on Easter Sunday after the service, decorated eggs are judged and are then rolled down the mounds outside church, the furthest winning a prize. It comes from an old custom based on the rolling away of the stone from Our Lord's tomb. An evening candle lit Carol service is held each year and new services have been introduced, like the old custom of Rogation when you are supposed to walk the parish bounds. A shortened version is done with a walk and readings around Petton. Mr Dommett the organist from Cockshutt Church comes to play on special occasions.

There are a number of trees in the church yard, the oldest are the four yew trees with a fifth one planted for the millennium taken from a tree that was a thousand years old. A copper beech was planted for the wedding of Prince Charles and Diana Princess of Wales. A crab apple tree was donated and planted by Mr and Mrs Sambridge and a cherry tree by Lady Newborough.

Mrs Cunliffe started her history of the church in 1906, she wrote 'It is desirable that future Squires of Petton will furnish information & future Rectors of Petton enter the same in this book thus carrying on the History of Petton Church keeping the same up to date'.

This they have done and the book has been a major source of information on the history of Petton and its church.

Cunliffe Family

Emma Florence Sparling inherited the old Petton Hall from her father John; she had married Captain Ellis Brooke Cunliffe when she was 19 on 17th July1867. He was born 6th July 1832, so was 16 years her senior and a Captain in the 6th Dragoon Guards. He was the eldest son of Ellis Watkin and Caroline Cunliffe of London and the grandson of Sir Foster Cunliffe first Baronet of Acton Park, Wrexham. He served in the Crimea war and Delhi in the Indian Mutiny and was present at the battle of Tchernaya. Captain Cunliffe left the running of the estate to his wife and was not as prominent as she in village affairs. He died in 1915 aged 82.

There are many written and anecdotal stories about Emma Florence Cunliffe, shown right, reproduced from *Shropshire Magazine*, who had a strong mind and character, was a devout Christian, mother and wife, modeling herself on the monarch whom she so admired and respected, Queen

The Colonel and Mrs Cunliffe

Victoria. She also ruled like a monarch on the estate, her word was law because usually people's livelihoods depended on her. In church she would sit at the very front directly looking at the pulpit and would start tapping her cane if she found the sermon too long or boring. The vicar on hearing would stop, even in mid sentence. The servant wearing an inappropriate blouse to church would be told never to wear it again or if you did not go to church she would want to know why. These stories were told to Mrs Pickering of 'The Grange' by her mother-in-law.

She expected respect when she rode in her yellow and black brougham with its pair of fine bays; the coachman and footman were dressed in the fashionable livery with cockades in their silk hats. The little girls had to curtsey and boys salute, if not the vicar and schoolmaster were informed and given a lecture about the 'duty towards their betters'.

In Marjorie Jones' book about Burlton she recounts the story about Squire Edward Goldisborough Chambre Vaughen who lived at Burlton Hall at the turn of the century. He was said to have been a very 'irascible old man' who had feuds with most of his neighbours and peers in the area. His disagreement with Mrs Cunliffe was well known and she relates it thus 'the Squire built a fence across the Pick Hill Lane to prevent Mrs Cunliffe's carriage from using it to reach Burlton and the main Shrewsbury to Ellesmere road. Mrs Cunliffe sent a man in the night to remove the fence and the Squire promptly had it erected again.' She overcame this problem by building herself a new road down to the main road which is still called the 'new' road by older inhabitants.

She bore much sorrow and disaster in her life with dignity. It is evident in the 'beautification' of the church that she was well read, cultured with an artistic and literary temperament. Although she was austere and domineering in her manner she could be very generous with a kind heart. When her favorite son Brooke returned from the Boer War she treated the children from Weston Lullingfield and Cockshutt School to a tea on trestle tables in rooms at the Farquhar House. There were rides on roundabouts and swing boats in the meadow between the Hall and the church and the children were all given a present.

In the latter part of her life when she had been widowed she did much writing; there was *Life of John Sparling*, an autobiography *Fifty Years of Sunshine, Storm and Rain* then a small volume called *Verses at Sunset* followed by *Seven Small Sermons,* these had all been privately published to be given as presents to family, friends and loyal servants.

The estate started to be dispersed by Emma Florence Cunliffe under instruction of her husband in 1920. She died on 13th May 1925 and was succeeded by her son Ellis, but he sadly died in June 1925. As he was unmarried it then passed to his brother William Noel their fourth and only surviving son. He had married Nellie Phyllis in 1910 and had a daughter called Gundred, they lived at Petton but moved to their other property in Suffolk when the Hall was sold in 1928.

Mr and Mrs Cunliffe had ten children, their eldest son was Ellis Sparling who was a Lieutenant Colnel in the 3rd Battalion of the King's Shropshire Light Infantry. He was also a Justice of the Peace in Shropshire from 1899, he never married and died at 17 Portland Place, Bath on 12th June 1925 aged 56, four weeks after his mother.

Their second son was John Brooke. He served as a Lieutenant in the Imperial Yeomanry (Northumberland Hussars) in the South African War receiving the Queens medal and two clasps. He was then a Major in the Northants Yeomanry from 1915- 1917 and died of sickness contracted in France on 20th April died 1917, aged 47 at the Princess Christian Hospital for Officers.

William Noel Cunliffe was born 25th December 1877, he married Nellie Phyllis Curd of London, eldest daughter of Sir John Aird, on 12th July 1910. He was to finally inherit the estate.

Their youngest son Legendre Watkins was born in 1878 and died October 1906 aged twenty seven, supposedly after an operation. A window is dedicated to him in the church.

Their daughter Catherine Violet first marriage was to J PG Hodgson Roberts and second to Percival Ayton Onley Whitaker of Suffolk.

Emma Veronica was married in 1890 to Lt. Col Henry Jessop Stone, they had a son Henry Cunliffe, he died, aged eleven months in 1892 and was buried at Petton. Their other son Ellis Robert Cunliffe Stone died in 1914 during the First World War. His family dedicated a window to him on Passion Sunday March 1915, the Rev Stainer read out an appreciation of him and a moving account of how he died by Colonel Radcliffe, who commanded him in the Royal Welsh Fusiliers; 'I cannot adequately express my grief at losing young Stone who was one of the finest young officers I ever had under my command. He was absolutely fearless and dashing to a degree, He was killed in the trenches on October 25th after doing excellent work with his men throughout and his loss is most deeply felt by every officer & man in the regiment. The place where he lost his life was in a trench 700 or 800 yards east of a little farm Cordouniere opposite the villages of Vertouguet and Rouge Baues, from whence the enemy were attacking us in force, their main force being further back at Fromelles from whence they kept pushing forward fresh reinforcements acquired our trenches. The line held by the regiment in their trenches was about one-quarter of a mile long and was subjected to constant attacks day and night and was also heavily shelled with heavy guns and field guns. Young stone behaved with exceptional gallantry and handled his men with great skill in the fighting at La Ferte Sous Touarre on the Marne. I had every intention of sending in a special report on young Stone on account of the excellent work he did on several occasions. His death was an irreparable loss to the regiment and I cannot wholly express my sympathy with Mrs Stone and all his relatives'. Mrs Stone also received a telegram at Petton Park from the King and Queen expressing their sympathy.

Florence Vanda was married at Petton Church in 1891 to R D'Oyly Freeman Thomas. It is to him the St Francis of Assisi window in Petton Church is dedicated. (See section on church windows).

Verbena Caroline married Masterman Stanley Williams of Kent in 1893 at Petton Church. They had a daughter Vera Nina in 1894, but she sadly died when she was twenty four. Verbena divorced and seemed to be living on her own means at Petton Park, she later married Lt Col Edwin James Fell.

In 1894 Caroline Muriel Valencia married Loftus de Launay Mollenus-le-Champion at Petton.

Mabel Virginia married on 18th February 1901 to Arthur Watson who unfortunately died of wounds in action 5th August 1917. They had a daughter named Diana who never married. Mr Robert Pickering met Miss Cunliffe Watson in 1968 when he and his father were required for inspection at her home 11, Chester Square, Belgravia. This was to see if they were suitable prospective buyers of 'Church House', it was the final Cunliffe property in Petton to be sold. He remembers her as a very small woman dressed in crinolines looking like Queen Victoria being attended by her two maids; they must have passed the inspection as they were allowed to buy it.

The Petton Estate

In 1891 George Bryson Clarke was estate agent to Petton Park and Henry Tatton head gardener. Around the time of the major building of the hall and other buildings, the 1891 census shows the family or any servants not in residence, but a lot of resident workman ranging from clerk of works to joiner, bricklayer and foreman joiner. Mrs Cunliffe was mainly credited for the responsibility for the building of the new Hall and was a major employer in the area. Once the new Hall had been built the Hall's staff increased, employing up to sixteen

The Cunliffe family crest

full time gardeners and live in staff of a butler, footman, under footman, cook, two ladies maids, two house maids and one kitchen maid. The Cunliffe family owned much land and property in the surrounding area as well as Cockshutt and Weston Lullingfields. Staff lived in tied property there or travelled in from the surrounding villages; from Burlton came boot boys, pantry boys, under gardeners and grooms.

Petton Hall

Petton Hall today stands not far from the old Hall which Mrs Cunliffe had pulled down to make way for her more imposing new house in around 1892. In Bagshaw's directory of Shropshire in 1851 the old hall was described as 'a handsome stuccoed mansion of considerable extent. It is approached by a lofty portico, supported by stone pillars and in the front of the mansion are beautiful pleasure gardens and shrubberies, which open into a park of considerable extent, having a fine undulating surface, richly wooded with noble timber and occasionally studded with thriving plantations. The kitchen gardens and vineries are extensive and highly productive at the time'. Another description was of a 'Georgian- type large building with pillars at the front.' From the earliest census of 1841 there lived at the Hall the Squire, William Sparling, his brother Captain Charles Sparling, Miss Sparling, Thomas Davies the gardener, Thomas Drury coachman, Richard Danneley groom and Henry Smith steward.

The new Hall was finished around 1892 and is the third Hall or Manor House to be built in the surrounding area. At the same time the access approach, the drive and gardens were rearranged and a major course of building took place. She wrote on 6th July 1896 'twas here the old house stood, but not a stone remains to mark the spot. I only know and care; remembering that here, alone in a dim room (where now the roses blow) An old man patiently for hours would sit close to the window, till the mist and gloom blotted the landscape.'

Nikolaus Pevsner described the present hall as 'Neo- Elizabethan'. It is built of red brick and cream sandstone with large bay windows and gables. The main house is now approached along a new road made to best show off the house. The East and West Lodge were built at the same time as the Hall. The front of the Hall has an imposing and practical portico. It is designed so that you would not get wet alighting from your carriage, the drive has a good sweep round. The kitchens, extensive cold rooms and all the practical rooms needed for running a large country house are to the left of the main hall in a single story building. The middle of the house has a square tower which commands great views over the surrounding countryside. The accommodation is extensive and very grand, displaying the family wealth which they were not averse to flaunting. In 1906 the *Shropshire Magazine* mentions the house being filled with many valuable pictures including ones by Sir Joshua Reynolds. The gardens were planted with many rare, exotic trees and shrubs with many still surviving today.

The Cunliffe's last remaining son William Noel finally sold the rest of the Petton Estate and Hall. It was sold on his behalf by John D. Wood & Co on Tuesday 26th June 1928, at the George Hotel, Shrewsbury. There was a comprehensive description in the sale details as follows: 'The remainder of the Petton Park Estate including the fine modern mansion known as 'Petton Hall', twenty-five bed and dressing rooms, five bathrooms, fine suite of reception rooms, ample offices, electric light and modern conveniences together with the beautiful old world gardens including tennis courts and a good deal of valuable timber in all about 16 ? acres. The whole suitable for residence, school, institution or demolition purposes.

Lot 1 at a low upset price of £4,500 The Magnificent mansion known as 'Petton Hall'.

A fine example of modern Tutor architecture, well-built of brick and stone, having charac-

THE BILLIARDS ROOM, PETTON HALL.

teristic stone mullioned and transomedwindows, stone quoins, ball finials and copings to the gables, in the slated roof, occupying a beautiful situation about 400 ft above sea level, facing South and East in the finely-timbered and undulating parklands, extending altogether to about 16 acres. It is approached by a well-metalled drive terminating in a wide graveled forecourt with centre grass plot.

Entrance is gained under a stone porte-cochere with iron-studded oak doors opening to the paved vestibule leading to the hall, which is entered through oak panelled doors with modern Tudor canopy fireplace. Cloak room with two lavatory basins and W.C. The Oak Gallery overlooking the main hall has an oak-ribbed ceiling and is panelled in oak to a height of 8ft. Connecting trough an archway is the staircase hall.

Front of Petton Hall 1928

The beautiful double drawing room, exclusive of wide bays with south and east aspects, panelled wainscotting and two fireplaces with carved mantelpieces and overmantels.

The dining room has a square bay and stone Tudor style arch to fireplace. Serving room is adjoining. Hot plate enclosed by oak panelled doors. The Library faces west and is a pleasant apartment, fitted with oak mantelpiece.

The Boudoir has Dutch tile surround to modern grate and adjoining is a bedroom fitted with lavatory basin and also oak mantle and overmantle. The Billiard Room has a mantel and over-mantel in oak and open fireplace. Note-The Reception Rooms have fine oak doors with oak architraves and oak boarded floors. The window fittings and furniture are of iron.

The office wing on the north side of the house comprises butler's pantry with sink, fitted cupboards and drawers, butler's bedroom, servants hall (now used as a brush room), house-keeper's room, lofty and light kitchen with tiled floor, glazed tiled walls and double Flavel range and a second range, scullery with double range, two sinks and cupboard, and an excellent range of four north larders with slate shelves. Game larder. Separate entrance to back yard and door to coal and coke house. W.C. boot hole, large soft water tanks under house. Luggage lift to first and second floors. In the Basement are arched cellars with two store, beer and wine cellars, fitted with brick and stone bins, with a beer shoot from back yard. Two W.C.s.

On the first floor approached by principal oak staircase is the fine wide gallery landing and ten principal bed and dressing rooms. Two bathrooms, two W.C.s. housemaid's cupboard, fitted sinks, store cupboard. Heated linen cupboard and off the black staircase is heated linen room. Radiators in corridors.

On the second floor are twelve nursery, secondary and servants' bedrooms and on another level are two large boxrooms, range of linen cupboards, and another principal bedroom, com-municating with bathroom, with heated towel rail and lavatory basin. Also two maids' bathrooms and pedestal W.C., heated towel rail. There are two back staircases, a spiral from the First Floor and another from the servants' floor to the domestic offices.

In addition there is the menservants' accommodation over the offices which comprises: Two bedrooms and bathroom, fitted radiator and four cubicles on the second floor, making a total of twenty-five bed and dressing rooms, four cubicles and fie bathrooms. Large tanks for storing water.

Conveniences. Electric light is generated by a 15 h.p. Crosseley engine with Newton dynamo and 54 cells. Heating – the principal rooms and corridors are warmed by radiators in convenient positions. Service by 'Ideal' boiler. Water is pumped by engine to two large tanks at the top of the house. Drainage is on modern principles and has a good fall to the east of the house. Telephone.

Some of the outbuildings adjoining the house could readily be converted into garages and rooms for menservants erected over.

The gardens and pleasure grounds were carefully laid out and tended by a knowledgeable and able gardener of the late owner. Adorning these gardens are beautiful specimens of Oak, Cedar, Beech, Wellingtonia, Acacia and numerous shrubs with an abundance of Rhododendrons. From the south side there is a charming peep over the beautifully proportioned clipped yews, enclosing the bowling green in the old manner with space for two

The old stable block showing the cobbled yard and the covered car washing area

tennis courts, to the finely-timbered parklands with a glimpse of the old church in the park'.

The Estate was sold in 11 lots with the Hall as lot one. Directly facing the Hall were the stables which also comprised the laundry, a cottage and yards. The description from 1928 sales catalogue is detailed, 'The buildings are conveniently arranged around a cobbled yard, which is entered under a wide arch with Clock tower over. They are well built of brick with slated roofs and comprise large garages taking 4-5 cars; one garage has a pit and there is also covered glazed washing place. A large room over the garage has been used for fencing and could be converted into a small flat. Range of 4 loose boxes with glazed brick and white-tiled sides, Musgrave's fittings, and with hat shoot from loft over. Also an exactly similar 4 stall stable and above is a large corn store and loft' large hay loft with two shoots. In this stable block is a laundry with brick-tiled floor and ironing stove, washing room with copper and fitted sink and a laundry cottage, comprising kitchen with copper and fitted sink and a bedroom over the archway. Tank room for water supply to stables of about 1,000 gallons. Drying ground. In this same building is another cottage containing five rooms and larder'.

The Park and Grounds

The 'Walled Garden' predates the present Hall, it is shown on early maps in an irregular shape. The walls show lots of alterations and an assortment of bricks from hand made to Victorian. The arched doorways were probably original and the front entrance the latest remodeling by Mrs Cunliffe. Ordinance survey maps of 1889 show it planted with just trees which support the present owner's view that there was no long term cultivation with organic matter. Old plans of 1900 show the greenhouses, paths and the buildings clearly marked with a sun dial in the middle.

The 'Kitchen Garden' and a portion of the 'magnificent pleasure grounds' extending to over 5 acres were sold together as lot two in the 1928 sale. They were said to be 'suitable for a splendid residence, suitable for conversion into a nursery or market garden'. The walled garden is nearly 1 acre and at the time of the sale was 'well stocked with all wall fruits and espalier trees, and adjoining is a Vinery, Fernery, Lean-to Peach and Conservatory with ample potting sheds and frames. Near by is a small orchard and adjoining on the south side are part of the Petton Pleasure grounds including a most attractive rock garden the whole shaded by magnificent and valuable timber.' (Details from sales catalogue).

Mr Philip Morris was a teacher at Petton Hall from 1950. He describes the walled garden in his 'Brief history of Petton' when he first came to the school as follows: 'I suppose the walled garden was almost as it had been, but totally overgrown- a wilderness. I was given the job of clearing it (I suppose that, as one of my specialist subjects is Rural Science, it was felt that I had the necessary qualifications for jungle warfare!) It was literally head-high in weeds, shrubs, etc. Suffice to say that four years later we had got it cleared and into good shape. There was a tile-edged path all round the garden (rope-edged tiles I remember) some 12 feet from the wall, and one right down the middle. On the wall were peach and apricot trees. It took me a long time to figure out how this was possible until, quiet by chance, we found that the garden wall must have been heated. It is hollow and we found evidence of smoke and soot between the outer and inner brick layers. We concluded that, somehow, hot air had been circulated round the wall from the boiler house. On each side of the path down the middle of the garden, some 12 feet again from it, were espalier and cordon apple and pear trees. At the far side of the garden([on the north wall) there was a big conservatory reaching to the top of that north wall (outline is still visible). We repaired this, and for quite a long time it was used as a classroom during the nice weather. Through the conservatory, and thus through the north wall, there were the tool-shed, the potting-shed and a big boiler house which supplied all the requirements of the conservatory, two greenhouses, and the vinery (all this was knocked down and the doorway sealed up when the orchard area went to Mr Pickering of The Grange). On the right of the conservatory, was a large greenhouse. Evidence of this is still remaining, and there was another large greenhouse almost where we have ours now. Halfway between the two greenhouses was the vinery. The vines were still there so we sorted them out and fed them with animal offal and had some quite good crops of nice, dark, grapes.' Across the central path there were metal arches 10 feet apart. It is unfortunate that the Hall and grounds were left empty for so long before being sold again and the walled garden became a jungle once more.

Extract from Mr Morris: 'As far as could be seen, the area which is now our playing field was formal gardens of various kinds bordering the driveway which ran from the existing drive, across the playing fields to what was then the main gate to the east of the goalpost furthest from 'Farquhar'. (The gate was still usable and the outline of the original main drive bordered by trees, was evident down to 'East Lodge', on the Ellesmere Road. There used to be many lovely mushrooms around this drive area and a carrier bag full was often picked on the way back). At this end of the playing field there were the remains of what had obviously been an Italian garden, running the length of the garden wall and about 20 ft from it on the playing-field side was a brick and stone structure about 3ft high and 8 ft wide in which was water. There were still a few water-lilies surviving so I suppose it had been an enormous fish pond.

The area which we still refer to as 'the bowling green' (left) was in fact a bowling green (lawn to the south side of the hall). It was surrounded by a privet hedge of considerable age, which was about 4ft thick and 4ft 6" tall and which had 4 entrances through it. As was to be expected, it was dead level and of good grass. We played bowls and other games on there for quite a long time. Eventually this hedge was taken out, but the bowling green made an excellent cricket wicket, the only snag being the boundary limitations.

To the right of the far end of the bowling green, just across the path that joins the main drive, was the dog's cemetery. In the centre of this there was a kind of obelisk mounted on a stone base and all around were the places where dogs had been buried and around each place there was a low privet hedge.'

There are some photographs from the 1928 sale catalogue showing the manicured lawns and the clipped 'bowling green'. The trees have matured and the snowdrops, daffodils and bluebells multiplied.

Petton Hall as a School

Mrs Cunliffe had started to sell off parts of the estate in 1920 on instruction from her husband, but the Hall was not sold till her death and the unfortunate death of her unmarried son Ellis very soon after her. The Cunliffe's only surviving son William Noel must have had to pay death duties, so it had to be sold. It was bought by Mr Parry and his wife Isabel who set up a private Kindergarten and Preparatory school for boys of well off parents whose children were delicate with special needs and could not go to the usual prep schools, or as described in Kelly's Directory for 'nervous and backward boys'. The school used the name 'The West of England School of Handicrafts' and had been originally founded in 1923 in Harlech. They used the Montessori and Foebel method of teaching with the curriculum as follows:

Mental	Religious Instruction, Reading, Writing, Arithmetic, General Intelligence, History, Geography, Nature study.
Manual	Gardening, Pig and Poultry rearing, Building, Carpentry, Leatherwork, Basketry, Rugmaking, Art Metal Work, Painting, Concrete Modelling, Raffia.
Physical	Drill, Tennis, Football, Cricket, Swimming, Singing, Pianoforte Playing, Elocution.

The boys had practical lessons in gardening and they used to pick blackcurrants and gooseberries at 'The Grange' and learnt brick laying, house building, carpentry and joinery when they built 1 and 2 Copse Cottages. The ratio of teachers or instructors was one staff member to seven pupils. The Matron was a fully qualified hospital nurse.

There was a Boy Scout and Cub troop, a billiard room and a cinema 'for talking pictures of educational and instructional value'. The school uniform for week days was green blazer with grey flannels and green and grey tie. Sundays was black coat and vest with black and pin striped trousers. (Details taken from an original prospectus of the school).

The main structure of the Hall was little changed when it was a school with grand fireplaces, wooden panelled rooms, wood- block and tiled floors. This is evident from the prospectus which detailed all the boys needs complete with photographs of principal rooms, accommodation and facilities.

The detached building to the side of Farquhar was the Hall's and later the schools workshops. A photograph from Mr Parry's school prospectus shows boys working at their workbenches, model making and wood working in their clean aprons.

The description in Mr Morris', 'Short history of Petton' is that 'The workshop area has changed considerably over the years primarily by the introduction of more modern equipment, but it must have been quite an extensive concern, able to cope with many of the Hall's needs, as was evidenced when I first came by the large number of big wheels and pulleys in and around the workshop (some of these still remain). We are still using the big circular saw. This is now driven by an electric motor, but used to be powered by a big petrol or diesel engine which also provided the power for all the other wheels, belts and pulleys. On the garden side of the workshop there was a long shed, roofed but without sides, in which there were supports and platforms on which tree trunks and planks were seasoned. This wood came from the immediate estate.'

'Farquhar' may have been a family name for the Parry's as their memorial in the church yard has

Above, single bedroom from school prospectus and below, boys working in the school workshop

Farquhar as a middle name and the name above the door of the stable block was added to a latter addition when they blocked off the archway to the courtyard. 'Farquhar House' held the extensive stabling and accommodation for horses, coaches and grooms for the house. When the school was run by the council as a boarding school it housed much of the accommodation, the bottom floor was the Housemaster's flat. There is evidence of the buildings former use. At the front there was a covered archway open through to the courtyard. It is now enclosed and used to be the housemasters lounge, the boys had a clubroom in the classroom next to this and behind this there used to be a gym later becoming a domestic science classroom. This was not a permanent structure and is now demolished. The flat above was for the seamstress, who Mr Morris remembers as a Miss Cole and Miss Tunnah. There were up to 52 senior boys who all lived in 'Farquhar'. Domestic staff and the children's help slept in what were the schools single dormitories on the top floor. Mr Edgar Roberts formerly of 'Petton Farm' said there were between 80 and 90 boys at the time when Mr Parry ran the school. Mr Parry's wife Isabel died in 1933 and the school was sold for a reputed £26,000 plus the same amount again for fixtures and fittings to Shropshire Education authority in 1947. The main Hall housed the youngest children on the top floor and on the bottom floor the middle age group. The "Headmaster's bungalow" was built at the back of the Hall; it was

Aerial photographs of the school taken around 1967

a flat roofed building. One of the longest serving head masters was Mr Speak, a few of the other headmasters were Mr Schofield, Mr Barnes, Duncan Boston and Mervyn Pugh. It was a residential, seven day special boarding school for boys. Girls were admitted as day pupils in 1976 and it became a five day residential co-educational school in 1977 with about thirty mixed day pupils. It was closed as a school in July 1990, when it stood empty for many years.

'Petton Hall' was finally sold in 1996 with planning permission for eleven individual units, for the purchasers to develop themselves. The main house was split into three with the kitchens, cold stores and gym forming three more houses, the old headmaster's house stayed as a bungalow in its own grounds. Farquhar was split into three houses and the school's old craft workshops were sold with the walled garden.

Lodges and Cottages

There were three lodges for the 'Petton Park Estate'; the oldest is 'Petton Lodge' a white painted house on the main Shrewsbury road. It has part of a curved sandstone wall that was a main entrance to the old Petton Hall, this passed between the fish ponds and across the park and lawn, the moat and then between the church and the hall to connect with 'Dog Kennel Lane' this can be seen on maps of 1842. This lodge seems to have housed the gardeners for the Hall, from the 1841 and 1851 census we have the gardener as Mr Davies who was from Lancashire, he was described by John Sparling as a 'character' and wrote of him that 'he was good at his trade, but full of professional conceit. He abounded in quaint sayings, and was extremely impudent, and a most barefaced thief. We always called him, even to his face, *Old Cabbage*. Withal, he was a kind of favourite with is. He died aged eighty-seven.'

In the 1861 census the gardener was Thomas Davies, his previous job on the estate was as cowman and bailiff. Again John Sparling wrote a not too flattering but affectionate account of the man in his diaries. 'He was emphatically what we called in Shropshire a 'gawby,' a chaw-bacon, a gowk, an irredeemable clod. He looked scarcely half sane, and one would have said, was born for the purpose of being victimized by keener hands. And yet this man, who had not a shilling when he came to live at Petton Lodge, is still alive, a prosperous farmer, has put both sons into large farms, and married his only daughter to a farmer.'

The next family to live there where Mr Henry Tatton and his wife Hannah. They came to Petton between 1868 and 1870, their first son Henry who was born in Lancashire was four at the time of the 1871 census, their second, William was born 1869 in Petton. Hannah died aged 34, on 20th April 1874; this may have been due to complications of childbirth as daughter Sarah Hannah was christened on 26th April 1874. Mr Tatton then married Sarah Tomkins of Ellesmere in July 1875, she died aged 71 on 1st September 1913 and finally in 1918 we have widower Henry Tatton marrying Mary Harriet Davies from Weston Lullingfields and their only son, Ernest Pax being born in 1919. He worked on the estate for many years and had eight children altogether. He played the Harmonium in the church and was paid £4.00 for this which was raised by subscriptions and collection. He was described by Peggy Husbands in her *History of Cockshutt* as 'a very small man with a beard which grew to his waist. He was very good at curing skins and stuffing birds. Many a pets coat has been made into a rug by this old gentleman for the owner to keep'. His youngest son Herbert was a gardener like his father and was living at home in 1901. He was killed in action on 21st October 1916 serving with the 3rd Shropshire Yeomanry. Henry Tatton died aged 85 on 2nd January 1930, his son George 1879-1951 was church warden for Petton for 20 years and organist for 30 and has a memorial inside the church placed there by his wife and daughter.

At the time of the 1928 sale of the estate 'West Lodge' was described in the sale catalogue as follows 'A capital modern cottage known as West Lodge Petton Park, situated in a quiet country road, built of brick and stone with slated roof, containing five bedrooms, two rooms downstairs with the usual offices and outbuildings.' The cottage was occupied by Mrs Austin on a service tenancy paying a nominal rent of 1 shilling per year but she should have a quarter's notice to leave.

Mr and Mrs Morris lived in quite a few places around Petton and for a number of years in 'West Lodge'. This extract taken from his *History of Petton* he remembered how it was when he first moved in: 'It was our first home after living in rooms and at my home and it seemed like a little palace. In fact, there was just one cold-water tap, no cooking facilities apart from an oil-stove and a very peculiar arrangement for lighting, together with a totally overgrown garden. Now I come to think of it there were two water taps, one from the mains and the other from a soft-water (rain) tank in one of the out sheds. These supplied one of those big, deep, rectangular, brown sinks that some of us may remember. The oil stove was a double burner – 'burner' being the operative word, as every so often it went on fire and did no good at all to whatever was being cooked. I remember, on one occasion taking a joint out of it and scrubbing it in the sink to get the soot off before trying again. The electricity supply had to be seen to be believed. It came on some wires suspended through the trees, from Farquhar. A high wind shorted it out on the branches and snow brought it to the ground. The most amazing thing was that our fuse-box was by the bathroom on the second floor at Farquhar. If a fuse blew, I had to travel up to Farquhar to replace it. Winter electricity was quite an exciting time. Our showpiece was the outside (and only) toilet across the yard. It was a bucket-job, of course, and had twin seats, the only one I've ever seen. Access to the buckets was gained from another shed adjoining. Winter, toilet-wise, was also an exciting time!'.

The house was only two bedrooms, but now has been extended by the current owners Mr and Mrs S. Hodnet bought the house from the council in 1984. The original entrance to the Hall was to the side of the house marked by a cattle grid and brick pillars. The Hall's entrance is now further down the road. 'East Lodge' was built in 1892 at the same time as the new Hall. It is now part of Cockshutt Parish, see Cockshutt history.

'Church House' or as it was called in 1928 'Church Cottage' has some of the best views in Petton, from its lofty position next to the church. It started out as a humble 'bothy' or worker cottage that has been added to and improved over the years. It is marked on maps of 1842, but may have been earlier as this was the area of some of the earliest settlement in Petton. In the 1841 census John Lewis and his wife Helen were living there with their family. They had their children christened at Petton church the earliest recorded was Sarah in 1799. Mr Lewis died aged 87 in 1847 and his wife ten years later so they had lived in Petton for most of their lives. In records Mr Lewis was responsible for the tithes on a garden which is now the site of 1 and 2 Copse Cottages.

The early gamekeepers seemed to have lived there as well as many farm workers from the estate. William Haycock was gamekeeper for many years around 1860, he and his wife Elizabeth lived there. They had a number of children born in Petton with his eldest also becoming a gamekeeper. Another occupant was Thomas Kirkham who was married to Sarah, he died aged 71 in 1915. He was employed on the estate for many years and in the 1901 census his occupation is electrical engineer; he was Sexton of the parish for 21 years.

The house had a long succession of tenants over the years before the being bought from the Cunliffe family by the Pickerings of 'The Grange'. Mr Robert Pickering and his wife Barbara lived there when they first married. The next owner was Lady Newborough who worked hard for the church and parish over many years; she landscaped the gardens and put in the ornamental gates looking on to the Park land. It was then sold to Mr and Mrs Johnson who moved there on their retirement from 'Top House Farm' near Cockshutt.

Ghosts

There are stories of a number of ghosts in Petton. There is supposed to be one in the walled garden, it is described as a whistling ghost, apparently you feel you are being observed and hear whistling and sounds that do not appear to come from anywhere. The sensible person will say it's the hollow walls or the strange acoustics of the four walls or is it an old gardener happily whistling at his work?

Other stories come from Farquhar when it was a boarding school when the boys would hear and see strange things they called the ghost 'Nellie'. The boys may have had over active imaginations or it may have been one of the many people to have lived there come to keep an eye on them. Other strange sightings and feelings have been felt and seen in the main hall but again it is an old house and creaky with age and modern central heating.

At 'Petton Hall Farm' quite recently, as a visitor drove into the yard, two strangely dressed figures were seen in old fashioned garb entering the house. The only people in the house at the time had been sitting watching television and had not moved, again an over active imagination, a trick of the light, or a paranormal sighting?

Farms, Farming and Houses

Petton has had a long association with farming which must have been successful to have had continuous occupation since neolithic times. It is higher than the surrounding area at just over 115 metres, the soil is sandy loam and clay and there is a small stone quarry. The area retains water and is very wet without the necessary drainage. Over the years there have been many wells sunk all over Petton to provide its own water supply. The Small Holdings had their own borehole and a well sunk

Working at Stanwardine Hall which at the time belonged to the Petton Estate. From left to right F Bennet - Jack Whitfield - D Chidlow - J Birch – T Kirkham

at the corner of Pick Hill lane located at the small brick building. The Hall had its own supply which during its time as a school was a borehole with an electric motor and pump outside the boiler house on the swimming pool side. With all its demands it never ran dry or diminished. There is a story related in 'History of Petton' by Phillip Morris that it is fed by an underground stream which runs from the Meres at Ellesmere to Marton Pool. 'Pump House Copse' did house a building as the name implies which supplied the Hall, but this was demolished many years ago. Remains of buff sandstone were found in the copse and show that it was quite grand and looks to have been built at the same time as the late Victorian Petton Hall.

A gentleman called Arthur Young travelled through England and Wales writing about farming practices around 1776. He visited Petton and his observations of agricultural practices are recorded in 'The Victoria History of Shropshire Vol. IV'. He met Edward Maurice who had reared Holderness cattle before 1776 and mentions one of the cows giving over $4\frac{1}{2}$ gallons of milk at one milking. He subsequently gave them up as being difficult to feed and tender, because their milk was not rich and their hinds too thin and so of no commercial value after slaughter. The Petton farmers in 1776 were buying the street and night soil of Shrewsbury at 5 shillings a cart load. They also used soot as a dressing for grass in the 1770s. In 1841 Petton had five houses and 39 inhabitants with a ratable value of £978.00. In 1871 it covered an area of 822 acres with a rateable value £900 and a population of 37 (Directories of Shropshire & Hereford 1879). In 1881 the population was 38 and the area was 829 acres it had a rateable value of £1,114. In 1885 the Petton Estate was 829 acres with a rateable value £1,186 with crops of cereals and roots (Kelly's directory of Shropshire 1885).

In the last century larger estates were lost when landowners and landed gentries levels of expenditure exceeded their income from the yield they could receive from their land. William Sparling (died 1870) was said to have 'saved all his life' and been very prudent. In 1874, 51% of Shropshire was owned by 52 peers and commoners owning over 3,000 acres each. Over the rest of England and Wales the percentage was 40%. In 1872-3 eight men owned over 10,000 acres there were a further 65 'squires' that owned between 1,000 – 3,000 acres each or 12% of Shropshire. (J.Bateman- Gt. Landowners of Gt. Brit. & Ireland 1883 & Ret. Of Owners of Land 1874- Victorian Histiry of Shropshire Vol.IV).

The early twentieth century saw farming and the distribution of land and the fortunes of the large estates change, especially immediately after the First World War, when there were large national land sales. Prior to this, sales in 1880s and 90s had been slow. From the Shrewsbury Chronicle sales catalogues, a rough estimate suggests that over 80,000 acres of land was for sale between 1918 and 1920s. This was an uneasy time for tenant farmers who had to consider buying their farms and being saddled with massive debt, moving or giving up. Landowners saw a buoyant real estate market after years of low values and tenants unwilling to pay market rents. It is at this time Mrs Cunliffe started to sell the outlying portions of the estate.

Petton Park Estate was extensive but in Petton itself when Mrs Cunliffe inherited there were only a few dwellings other than the old Hall itself. From early 19th century maps there were buildings on the site of the present Petton Hall Farm, Wackley Farm, Church House and a brickyard on the road to Weston Lullingfields.

Petton Farm

Petton Farm has been greatly extended over the years with the prosperity of the Petton estate and farm. The house is mainly brick with tiled or slated roof but parts of the house are timber framed. The back of the house is two storey but lower than the rest of the house and of a more humble appearance. There used to be eight bedrooms and downstairs plans show an ash pit, family earth closets, tool shed, blacksmiths shop, dairy and cold store at the back of the house and upstairs two bedrooms. These were demolished in the 1970s when they were deemed unsafe. The house seems to have been added onto as can be seen from the differing roof lines. The front has a 'Georgian' appearance with large windows and front door. To the side a two storey extension was added by Mr Charles Sadler tenant farmer during the time of the Cunliffes. This comprised of a French window with a porch which had wooden pillars supporting a balcony with turned banisters. What is now a window used to be a door leading from a bedroom which overlooked the old drive which swept in off the road that ended just past the barns (right). The barns are set out in a courtyard in sandstone, brick and wooden

slats under a slate roof. The saddle room in the barn nearest the house has a small fireplace. Recent historians have looked at the barns and say they may be 14th century.

Early tenants in the 1841 census were Mr Thomas Menlove and his wife Frances. We know Menloves were living in the area as early as 1789 from baptism records when John was born to a Thomas and Anne Menlove. In 1841 they had two daughters living with them and four sons. As a sign of the times they had two farm labourers as young as ten and one twelve year old with one female servant that lived in.

John Sparling wrote of Thomas Menlove as follows 'Thomas Menlove's impudence was boundless, but he was so whimsically absurd in his eccentricities that we never tired of being in his company. He was very quick at repartee, but he stammered in the strangest way. He was a great antagonist of Mr Vaughen of Burlton, with whom he had a lawsuit. He got £2,000 with his wife, but died in the debtor's prison; indeed, was suffocated there by an escape of gas.'

Although they moved out of the area, lots of the family was brought back for burial in Petton where there are a number of boxed graves of the Menlove family. Thomas died in April 1851 aged 66 after he had moved to Shrewsbury.

In the 1851 census the farm was tenanted by Edward Johnson. He was farming three hundred acres and employed a bailiff, five agricultural labourers and two servants. The next census shows Robert Hampson is farming two hundred and seventy acres with two labourers, two carters with a twelve year old carter's boy, cowman, housekeeper, dairy maid and house servant. His wife was called Elizabeth and they had three children born in Petton between

1853 and 1856. In the 1871 census the farm is being run by the fifteen year old son Edward and his seventeen year old sister Margaret as housekeeper.

Around the 1880s George and Elizabeth Key had moved from Dearnford Hall to farm at Petton Farm. During the time of Emma Florence Cunliffe the tenancy changed to Charles and Martha Sadler. In the 1891 they had five children ranging from twelve to one years of age. They employed three female staff, one being fourteen and two labourers and a living in housemaid, domestic cleaner, with a waggoner and a shepherd living at the farm. An interesting anecdote that has passed through the family is that on Mr Sadler on his wedding day, fell out of his carriage and it rolled over his leg, which then had to be amputated and is supposed to be buried in the paddock at the farm.

Mr Tom Roberts started working for Mr Charles Sadler after the First World War. He lived with his family in Bagley and would cycle over to work. Mr Sadler had a wooden leg so you could hear him coming across the yard. He found it difficult to drive although he managed it with a wooden block to put his heel in. Mr Roberts then took on the duties of chauffeuring him about in his lovely large car (below).

Mr Roberts' wife Dora would also help at the farm making the cheeses in the back dairy. The cheese would then be taken up through a trap door upstairs to dry out. The ready cheeses were put on a dray and taken down to Weston Wharf. The farm was large, over five hundred acres and employing a number of men. The women who came to help milk would walk across the fields from Weston twice a day carrying their stools, and wearing their aprons because they liked their own and did not like any one else using them. They had to milk a hundred cows by hand twice a day 362 days a year.

The council bought the Petton Estate but Mr Sadler did not want to move so he continued living at the farm with the new tenant Mr Tom Roberts his old employee. Mr Sadler lived in the downstairs sitting room that he had built. Martha Sadler had died in 1927 aged sixty nine and Charles Sadler died in 1939 aged eighty five. His gravestone is inscribed that he was of Petton Farm.

Mr and Mrs Roberts and their family had moved to live in Petton in 1929 from Bagley. They had six children, John, Ernest, Edgar, Irene, Verna and Ron. Edgar remembers them coming to Petton where they lived at the cottage in the stable block (Farquhar) at Petton Hall. They kept their cattle there in the stables. The front archway through to the courtyard had not been

blocked off and the Hall was empty at that time.

Mr Edgar Roberts remembers the Stable block as it used to be with a cobbled yard and the archway for the carriages and cars to pass through. There was a blue bricked area of the yard with a large glass covered area for washing the cars. The electricity for the Hall was produced in the

Engine House and he remembers the gleaming engine and the well polished rails round it and the other rooms for the coal to fuel the boiler.

Wackley Farm

The farm house is of red brick under a slate roof with boxed eaves. It is late 17th century which may also incorporate areas of an earlier building. It was extended and altered in the mid 18th century; it has a substantial range of sandstone barns across the busy road.

The earliest documented inhabitants were a family called Menlove in 1790s with Thomas and Abigail who died in 1818 and 1819 respectively. They were probably related to the Menloves at Petton Farm. The family farmed there till well into the next century. After them came John Menlove who was born in Petton and was married to Ann. They had quite a number of children, Parish records show that they had four boys and three girls born between 1827 and 1840. In the 1841 census they were farming one hundred acres and employed five agricultural workers. These were two fifteen year olds and two twelve year olds and four female servants, two of which were fifteen. They continued farming there for many years and there are many family burials in the church yard. In the 1861 census the farmers had changed to Thomas and Elizabeth Shingler, their daughters Elizabeth and Mary had been born in Myddle. The farm had increased to four hundred and twelve acres they employed six men and four boys. Living at the farm were the cowman, two waggoners two plough boys aged thrirteen and fourteen and a thirteen year old cow boy with two dairy maids and a house servant. Elizabeth died in 1865 aged 63 and Thomas aged 73 in 1870 the same year as William Sparling senior. Mary their daughter married John Bickerton Hiles. In the 1871 census the farm was two hundred and ninety acres employing four labourers, they also have a groom and a monthly nurse presumably waiting for the birth of their child born that year called John Shingler. Many women gave the children their family name as a second name as the daughters of Mrs Cunliffe of Petton Hall later did. In the census John Bickerton Hiles is down as a Yeoman farmer, they went on to have a daughter Beatrice Elizabeth, then three more girls until a boy called George was born in 1879. By the next census in 1881 the farm is being run by Margaret Cooke and her two sons Lewis and Charles. Living in were four labourers and two female servants. The situation changes in the next census with Lewis running the farm with his widowed sister as housekeeper, her daughter Mary and nephew John Cooke. A niece Margaret Adams was born at Wackley, her parents were Robert and Jemima Ann, he was a farmer and they moved to Burlton but had their five other children christened at Petton.

During the time of Mrs Cooke there was a tragedy at the farm. In 1902 Clara Lowndes had been employed to work on the farm for three years, unfortunately she then became pregnant. Mrs Cooke suspected she was pregnant but Clara denied this on numerous occasions and refused to see a doctor. On 24th March she rose at five and did the milking then while making breakfast she complained of pains so she was sent to bed. Mrs Cooke saw her later in the out house with blood on her clothing; when challenged she said it was from her mouth and pills she had been given and she denied giving birth, she was sent to bed again. Mrs Cooke went to the out building where she saw the feet and legs of a baby. When she accused

Clara of giving birth, she asked her employer not to say anything and no one would know. The police constables Bolderston and Rudge were called and they found the body of a female baby. When Dr Bathhurst from Ellesmere examined the body he found paper stuffed down the baby's throat, he deemed that the baby could not have done it herself and the post mortem confirmed death as from asphyxia due to the piece of paper. When Clara was sent to trial Mrs Cooke vouched for her hard work and good character and that she would employ her again. The defending counsel said the baby may not have lived and that Clara was not in a fit mental state to realise what she had been doing; with a very sympathetic judge he directed the jury to charge her with a concealment of birth. This she was found guilty of and sentenced to six months imprisonment. Mrs Cunliffe erected a tin shed in the farmyard for twelve cows as compensation for the building of the new road and loss of land.

Mr Charles Emberton was a tenant of the Cunliffes at 'Wackley Farm' or as it was called 'Bottem Wackley' from 1904 when he was sixteen, his father was the tenant at 'Top Wackley Farm''. Mr Charles Emberton and his wife Gwendoline bought the farm in 1926; they had two sons Charlie and Phillip. Cheese was made on the property till 1937; this was 'Choose Cheshire Cheese'. After the cheese was tested and found to be up to standard it was stamped in blue ink with three C's and their number 233, a solid brass stamp was used. Their cheese factors were 'Emberton Brothers of Crewe' who were cousins of the family. The Embertons took an active part in the Petton community as well as being church wardens; his son Charlie started the flying club at Sleap.

In December 1972 the farm was sold by Mr C Emberton and his sons. Mr Emberton wanted to see how much it made in his lifetime. When they sold the farm it was an arable and stock farm and an excellent shoot, it was 372 acres. They also sold two cottages down the road at the same time. More is written about them and how they bought the farm and cottages in the account of 'Cockshutt's History'. The present owners are Mr and Mrs Dakin who run a mixed farm with beef cattle, sheep and cereals. Mr Dakin's mother Connie is the grand daughter of Mr and Mrs Edmund Parker who were farming at 'The Grange' in Petton.

Wackley Farm

Left, the interior of Wackley Farm during the time of Mr and Mrs Emberton.
Right. Mr and Mrs Emberton outside Wackley Lodge with cups for Root Crops.

Petton Grange

Petton Grange (shown below on an early postcard) was built in 1893 as a fine brick late Victorian 'Gentleman's residence', it was built by the Cunliffe's with all the modern conveniences of the age.

The barns are large, two storey, brick built in a court yard with saddle rooms, coach house and every thing needed to run a large farm at the turn of the century. The first resident was Mr George Bryson William Clarke. He was the estate manager, his name is mentioned during the time of William Sparling in the 1881 census, he was 25 years old and living at the Old Hall. He married Jane and there were two boys Charles and Stanley then five girls born in Petton from 1889-94 Marian, Mercy, Muriel, Margery and Monica. He died aged 40 in April 1896; his wife was still living at the Grange in 1901 and living on her own means with a house maid and kitchen maid.

The next tenants were Mr Edmund Parker and his wife Marcia, they had eight children, George, John, Emma, William (father of Mrs Connie Dakin), Joseph, Eva, Lila and Bessie. Mr Parker died in 1912 and his wife in 1932. Their daughter Eva married the boy next door, Joseph Darlington; he was a prominent local farmer whose family farmed at Stanwardine

Farm. His father Richard came from Cheshire in 1890 and they had five children. Mr Joseph Darlington's daughter and her husband Mr and Mrs Higginson stayed at Stanwardine while he moved up the road to the 'The Grange' running the two together. He was very well known and from an article from 'The Borders County Advertizer' Feb.1926, we find that he was a very busy man working on numerous committees.

He was winning prizes with his 'Large Whites', the pigs he was breeding and for which he was world famous; he even went to Buenos Aires to judge them in 1922. He was breeding ewes (non pedigree Kerrys), pure bred Dairy Shorthorn cattle and his own Shire horses which he showed. At 'The Grange' he put twenty acres under wheat using the wheat straw for the pigs. He employed twelve men over the two farms and believed in labour saving devices. The water supply for 'The Grange' was forced up to the top of the house from the fields by an oil engine which also drove the chaffing and barn machinery. This also supplied the power for lighting the whole house and buildings. When he died he was buried at Weston Lullingfield.

'Petton Grange' was bought off the Cunliffe family in the 1930s during the depression by Mr and Mrs Darlington. The farm was then rented by their daughter Kathleen and her husband George Ernest Pickering, they had two children Pat and Robert. Mr George Pickering died

in 1978 and his wife Kathleen in 1987. Mr Robert Pickering is the fourth generation of the family to be farming at 'The Grange'. They have a very interesting snap shot into life on the farm in 1932 when Mr Pickering's parents were farming there, in the form of a set of accounts for that year. At the start of the year they had 48 cows, 1 bull, 8 heifers, 16 Yearlings, 4 horses, 30 poultry and their own 32 heifers. They bought in sheep, pigs and also reared chickens which were sold in Baschurch.

A staple industry for the farm and a major source of income was the cheese making. At 'The Grange' the vats and rooms still show

From left to right Owen Surveyor, Woodville, C E White, unknown, Davies Yearton, Jo Darlington of 'Petton Grange'

evidence of this and Mr and Mrs Darlington won prizes for their cheese. In 1932 the amount of cheese sold in each month varied from a good month like September producing forty seven cheeses to a slow month like December, when only two were sold and in some months none at all. Cheese prices also varied over the year from 6½d. to 9½d. per pound. The cheeses were sent to Liverpool to a firm called Lovell and Christmas and Walls. Everyone made cheese at the time as there was not the refrigeration to store the milk when there was surplus or a large local market for the fresh milk.

In 1932 the family owned a car and a telephone, one of the very few in the area. From a list of valuation of stock in April 1941 the farm had 70 cows milking and in calf, 21 in calf heifers, 26 yearling heifers, I bull, 4 working horses, 4 two year old colts and 2 ponies. Implements consisted of 1 binder, 2 grass cutters, 2 rollers, 1 corn drill, 2 sets of harrows, 4 carts, 2 electric motors, 2 ploughs and 1 lister engine.

In 1942 they employed five farm hands whose average wage was between £2.10s. and £1.13s.6d. The four women who milked the cows also made the cheese and helped in the house. As an employer he also took out insurance for 'men and girls' of £8.11s.2d. They paid a 'Tithe' to the church of £18.4s.7d. This was the old system of maintaining the church which all the local gentry and farmers paid. The agricultural workers slept above the stables and the female servants and dairy maids in the house. Mr Pryce Roberts was gardener and Herbert King was cowman, he used to be a regimental sergeant major and Mr Pickering said that you could hear him calling the cows in for miles. He also remembers the six large shire horses that Mr Andrew Manley looked after and that William Ralphs did the ploughing with three horses each side. The girls who worked at the farm were Marjorie Charlton, Isobel Armstrong, Maud Hanmer and Elsie Birch their wages ranged from £1.00 to 10 shillings a week.

During the first fortnight of the 1967 foot and mouth epidemic the farm had an out break, they had over two hundred cows which were all slaughtered by the R.A.F. all over the farm. It was eventually restocked but was suspected again but this time it was all clear. In 1974 the farm became purely arable under a government scheme. Mr Robert Pickering works the farm by himself and contracts out for the main harvesting; the crops are mainly wheat, oats, barley, beans and sugar beet.

Smallholdings

In 1908 the 'Small Holdings and Allotments Acts' came into being. The idea behind the Act was to get more people onto the land to work and distribute land into the hands of more people. At first land was leased, gifted or acquired through death duties, but this did not bring in enough so they then started to buy land. Shropshire's first 'Small Holding' were acquired in 1909. These were Albrighton and Barkers Green,

Shropshire County Council eventually owned or leased estates in forty nine areas, they were Albrighton, Alderton, All Stretton, Annscroft, Asterley, Barkers Green, Cantlop, Crickheath, Crowmoor, Cruckton, Cruckton Hall, Dairy House, Ditton Priors, Ellesmere, Emstrey, Frodesley, Harlescott, Haughmond, Henlle, Hincks, Lacon, Leebotwood, Lee Brockhurst, Long Lane, Lower Monkhall, Maesbury, Marton, Marton Grange, Newtown, Oxon, Petton, Pentre, Pothywaen, Rodington, Sherrifhales, Shropshire Gate, Shrawardine, Sibdon, Soulton, Stanwardine, Sweeney, Walford Manor, Walk Mills, Water's Upton, West Felton, Weston House, Weston Lullingfields, Whixall and Withington. Over the years the Council owned about 402 Small Holdings, but not all at the same time, with approximately 9,350 acres of land and 153 acres of woodland or there abouts.

Mr and Mrs Cunliffe were responsible for the first major building scheme with the new Hall, stable block, 'The Grange', 'Pheasantry' and lodges. The Council when they acquired the estate set about the next major building phase in 1933 with the building of seven new farms which were built by a firm from Church Stretton.

The Petton estate land was split up into six roughly equal size small holding and one starter holding. Shropshire had a number of different designs of small holdings, from two and three bedrooms, semi detached and some of the earlier houses were built of brick, as illustrated by some small holdings in neighbouring Weston Lulligfields. Petton's 'Small Holdings' were all roughly the same size, made of brick and pebble dash with a brick built court yard of barns that could house ten cows, stables and a loose box, some have a later addition of a room to house the new milk cooling tanks. The front door always faced off the road and the accommodation consisted of three bedrooms with originally a living room, small sitting room, small kitchen, pantry and dairy where the milk was kept cool. Outside there was a toilet and coal shed either to the side or back of the house. They were always painted white and the windows were made up of small panes of glass. The first land agent was Captain Pulford he lived at Montford Bridge, with other early agents being Mr Cooper from Clive and Mr Rees.

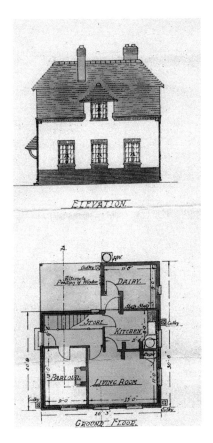

Original architects drawings of the Smallholdings and barns at Petton

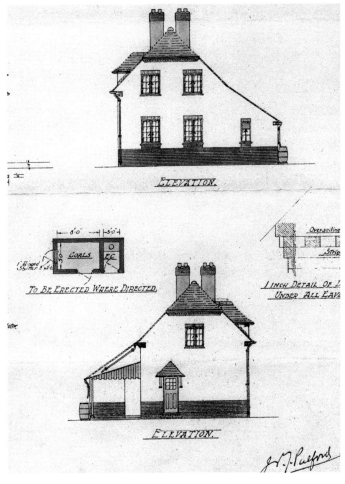

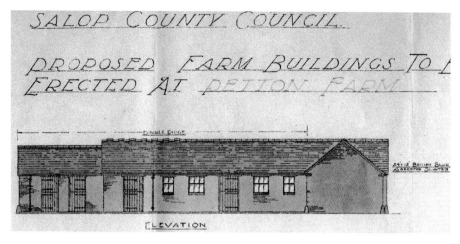

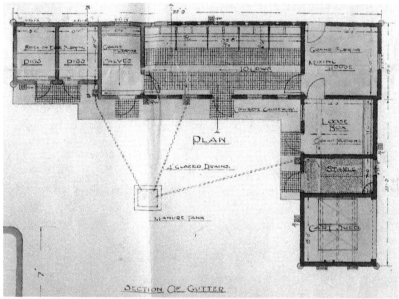

Original architects drawings of smallholding barns - Layout of barns showing which each section was originally used for,

Mr Edgar Roberts remembers them being very strict on the upkeep of the farms and anyone not following the rules was given a warning then asked to leave if they did not comply. The holdings were supposed to give enough work for a man and a boy. The usual procedure for getting a holding was by interview in front of a large committee as well as being over twenty five years old and married.

On the Petton estate the council took over 'Petton Farm' and 'The Pheasantry'. When 'Petton Farm' became a smallholding the first tenant was Mr Tom Roberts and his wife Dorothy, he had worked for many years for Mr Sadler. The rent in 1933 was £126.5s for the large farm house and the court yard of buildings with about 41.7acres. He farmed with his son Edgar, they had mainly dairy cattle with two horses. There was no demand for milk but they did supply Mr Parry at the school, taking it up to the school and putting it in jugs in the cool rooms. Milk was selling for 4½ d a gallon at the time.

The next tenants were Mr and Mrs Edwards who lived at 'Petton Farm' from 1968 to when they retired in 1993. They had been farming at Leebotwood on a smaller council holding. Mrs Colleen Edwards remembers the terrifying first interview before the committee wondering whether they would get their first farm in Leebotwood. When they wanted to move Council officials came out to inspect their small holding and see how they were managing that. Mr Edwards had broken ribs but still pretended every thing was fine because he thought they might think him unfit to farm. They passed the inspection and questioning and moved to Petton. Mrs Edwards remembers the old parts of the house which were uninhabitable and in a very poor state of repair so were knocked down. There was evidence of cheese making with the old vats and trap doors in the roof for hauling up the cheeses to store. They kept forty cows and seventy sows which they used for breeding. Mr Edwards also bred exotic birds. The farm was sold on Mr and Mrs Edwards retirement so they were the last council tenants.

Petton farm was sold in 1993 with 68 acres and a milk quota of 270,000 litres. It was bought by Mr and Mrs Powell who also bought the land and milk quota from 'The Oaks' smallholding which was sold about the same time, this consisted of 54½ acres and quota of 196,000 litres, they ran it as a dairy farm. They sold the farm house and 85 acres in 1996, and moved next door to convert the old sandstone barns which are now 'Greystone Barns'. These are set to the north of the house and used to be the pig sties and the old cart house (the large windowed area) It is from all the restoration of the old buildings that they developed their interest in salvaged and old materials. They bought 'Wackley Lodge' to which they moved to and now run their large reclamation yard from.

Holding number 332 'The Pheasantry' is marked on the 1901 map and as the name implies,

Aerial view of Petton Farm during the time of Mr and Mrs Edwards tenancy

the gamekeeper used to live there and it was another gatehouse or back entrance to the Hall. At the time of the 1928 sale the cottage was being rented to Mr Edgar Evans at a low rent of £10 a year and was described as a 'Picturesque and well built modern cottage of red brick construction, having black and white upper storey and slated roof, known as 'The Pheasantry' containing three bedrooms and two rooms with the usual offices downstairs, and standing in a good garden'. Mrs Husbands in her 'History of Cockshutt' called it 'Keeper's Lodge' and remembers Mr and Mrs William King living there. The first council tenant was Mr Andrew Manley and this was the smallest holding in Petton with 7.5 acres. Mr Manley also worked at the 'Grange', looking after the Shire horses. The tenancy then passed to his son George and his wife Winifred, he had come to Petton as a young boy. It is the only smallholding with the original family still living there.

Holding number 1- 330 – 1, Petton Lane had an original acreage of forty two acres and a rent of £117.14s. They used the barns from Petton farm the ones nearest the house which are now 'Greystone Barns'. The first tenants were Mr J Rhone then Mr Percy Birch helped by his nephew Percy Birch followed by Mr Sudlow. Mr and Mrs Sudlow are remembered as very hard working people, working from dawn to dusk all year round keeping an immaculate farm. Mr Sudlow never wore a coat but a sack across his shoulders to protect him from the rain and one round his waist too keep him warm. They retired to Cockshutt. The barn and land were then joined onto 'Petton Farm'. The house was used as accommodation for the school till it was sold to Mr and Mrs Ashdown who had been renting 'Stanwardine Farm' around 1986. Mr and Mrs Baumgartl are the present owners with their daughter Rosa. Mrs Linda Baumgartl has been involved with the researching, typing and work for this book.

Holding number 4 - 333, 'Corner Farm', originally 29 acres with a rent of £78. 6s. The first tenants were Mr and Mrs W.T. Sutton, they had come from working at Crosemere Hall. His father was the wheelwright in Cockshutt. They were very good friends of Mr and Mrs Roberts from Petton farm, helping at harvest times. On the death of her husband Mrs Sutton took over the farm, but it was too much even with Mr Edgar Roberts from Petton Farm helping so she moved, unfortunately she died the day the tenancy officially finished. Mr Bill

Taking a break, from left to right Jack Roberts, Tom Roberts, Mr and Mrs Sutton, Mr Jones

Tomley from 'Oakdene Farm' took over the tenancy and added most of the land from his neighbouring small holding next door, this he carried on till his death in 2004. It was sold at auction.

Holding number 5 - 334, 'Oakdene Farm', originally 41 acres with a rent of £109.4s. The original tenant was Mr . Jones, but he only stayed a few years. The next tenant was Mr H Tomley who was followed by his son (William) Bill who was born in 1940 in the house, as were most of the children of those first tenants. They farmed for many years mainly dairy with chickens and other animals. Bill was married to Chris and they had three boys. The house and a few acres were sold by the council and the remaining land was joined with 'Corner Farm'. The farm is still a registered smallholding with a mixture of poultry and pedigree angora goats; it now includes the land across the road known as 'The Copse'. The old single storey barns have been converted, one part into residential accommodation and the rest into holiday lets.

Above, early residents of Petton left to right Harold Dean, Tom Sutton, Walter Tomlinson, Herbert Tomley. Front, Tom Roberts. Below, Walter Tomlinson.

Holding number 6 - 335, 'Church Farm', 30 acres with a rent of £75.15s. This was the first new smallholding in Petton to be occupied and the first tenant was Mr Walter E. Tomlinson. It was recorded as an arable farm with seeds provided but became dairy, like the other farms.

He was the only tenant farmer who had been in the First World War. He was batman to Colonel Longsdale who was Chairman on the interview panel for the holdings. The Colonel vouched for him and told them Mr Tomlinson was having the farm so he did not have to go before the committee and be interviewed. Mr Tomlinsons wife was called Sarah they had two sons, but their first died at three days old. Their other son Frank was born in 1938. Unfortunately Mrs Tomlinson was house bound due to rheumatism, upon Mr Walter Tomlinson's retirement he moved to a bungalow they had built in Cockshutt.

Frank and his wife Anne took over the tenancy in 1962 and were milking cows until the late nineties, then raised beef cattle for which were rented additional fields in Petton. They had also kept pigs that used to roam freely over the fields in the winter eating acorns. The pigs worked their way round the oak trees and before Christmas they would be ready to go to market in Oswestry or Shrewsbury. The pigs would try and escape and get into neighbour's gardens.

Frank had a red David Brown tractor bought new for £400. His father told him it would 'see him out' which it did, selling at his closing farm sale for £1,800. Frank like the other children from the small holding went to Cockshutt School, he remembers walking to school for a time and also his father taking him in his

Morris 8 and then cycling.

Frank's father employed a man to help him through harvest to winter called George Thomas. As he had no other work to go to he asked to stay on and help as long as he could catch rabbits which he did. Farming was done with horses at first, when more were needed they were borrowed from a neighbouring farm, they helped each other out when needed at times like hay making.

Mr and Mrs Tomlinson remember that life was very different in Petton when they were first married. The neighbouring farms also had young families. Petton Hall School was a major employer in the area and the roads were very busy with traffic of cars, taxis and buses going to and from the school with teachers and pupils. The area was served by travelling shops coming each week: Perkins the grocers and Glovers coming from Weston Lullingfield; Green the grocer from Stanwardine; Billy Bedford the fishmonger from Wem who lived in Burlton and Rolfe and Green from Stanwardine green grocers. Mr and Mrs Tomlinson bought their farm but sold it in 2005 on their retirement when they moved to their bungalow in Cockshutt.

Holding number No.7 – 336 'Seven Oaks', 26 acres with rent of £62.5s. The first tenant was Mr James Griffiths and his wife Mary, the farm was to be an arable farm with seeds provided but soon became purely a dairy farm. They had come from working for a Mr Eric William at Nil Green and lived in Weston Lullingfields, they had three sons and a daughter.

Their son Tom lived with his wife Gladys at Petton. He was a joiner wheelwright and served time with Suttons of Cockshutt and at Tom Reeves in Burlton were he built carts and coffins. The trees used to be sawn down locally and brought to be converted in the saw mill at Burlton. They had four girls and two boys, unfortunately Tom died early of cancer at the age of fifty two in 1959.

The family thought they would have to leave the farm because Derrick, their oldest son did not fill any of the necessary criteria to take over the tenancy. He was not married, not twenty five and the council did not like the sons of tenants to go straight to the larger farm but preferred them to start on an allotment holding then move to a larger smallholding. Derrick went to Shirehall before the committee to try and persuade them to bend the. Rules, the committee was made up of lots of councillors and Derrick who had taken his future wife Audrey along, just to prove she existed, remembers it being very intimidating. They were

Left, Mr James Griffiths outside Seven Oaks barns.

Right, Mr Tom Griffiths

given the tenancy which they had never considered doing. Derrick married Audrey Pugh whose mother ran the 'Cross Keys' or as it is now called 'The Burlton Inn'. Audrey was one of seventeen children and was working there when they met.

The council only had the dairy converted to a bathroom in 1961, Audrey remembers this as she was expecting her son. They bought the farm but sold it on their retirement and moved to Ellesmere. It was bought by Mr and Mrs Edwards of 'The Rise' Weston Lullingfield who extended the house and still farm the land.

Holding number 8 - 337 – 'The Oaks', original acres 39 and rent was £104.11s. The first tenants were Mr John Lloyd and his wife Daisy; they had one daughter Ruby in Petton. There was an additional 6 acres at £15.00 and this pasture then reverted to the neighbouring farm with the next tenant Mr G. Bayliss. It was sold about the same time as Petton Farm around 1993. The barns are being converted to residential and holiday accommodation by the present owners Mr and Mrs Willock.

Holding number 9 - 338 - original acreage 25 and rent was 71.4s. The first tenant was Mr W Dean who came from Weston and then Mr W Pearce. The farm is still tenanted by Mr Mr Viner and producing milk.

The policy of the council was to sell off the houses when they became vacant and the land where possible, was amalgamated with other neighbouring holdings.

The Council then decided to sell any remaining small holding not bought by tenants to a private company or third party, but after the recent elections and changes in the council they have reversed the previous decision.

War years

As a farming community Petton played its part during the war. All spare land was put under cultivation, at least five or six acres each, so each farmer had to grow their own grain to feed the livestock. The farms were inspected by the War Agriculture Committee and if the inspectors deemed the farmer not to be doing enough they gave warnings because they had the power to confiscate the farms or evict the tenants. Mr Emberton of 'Wackley Farm' was responsible for the two threshing machines, each with two workers that went round the local farms at harvest time. A 'Minneapolis' tractor was given by the Americans and another called an 'Allis Chalmers U' was used with two threshing boxes. They would go all over the area from farm to farm. In Petton they would start at the bottom at 'Seven Oaks' and work their way up and round.

Mr Frank Tomlinson remembers as a very small boy lambing with his father and the German bombers going over head at night. He and Mr Edgar Roberts remember seeing the flashes and the skies lit up as they bombed Liverpool. Frank has vivid memories as a young boy watching the diving and acrobatics of the Spitfires over head as they went to Rednall and the bombers pulling the gliders behind them as they prepared for the Normandy landings, although he did not know it was for this purpose at the time. His father would take him on his handlebars to Sleap airfield where he would see all the bullet holes in the sides of the planes. The skies over Petton were busy and still are with gliders and light aircraft from Sleap and helicopters from Shawbury.

In the time of rationing any little extra food was welcome. Frank remembers the corn man Bill and his mate coming from Manchester on their regular deliveries once a month. He would take back 30 eggs and 10 – 12 rabbits caught on the farm. One day Frank's father Walter had some hares, the man asked what they were he said they were 'Shropshire rabbits' the man went away happy and always asked for more Shropshire rabbits.

'Church Farm' like all the other holdings was painted a uniform white colour, the house was on a line with the church and Petton Hall to Liverpool. The German bombers would head from the loop of the River Seven north then on moonlit nights with bombers needing land marks to guide them, this was deemed too obvious a landmark, so the War Ministry had the house painted green to camouflage it.

'The Grange' had seven officers billeted onto them after Dunkirk with the rest of the platoon going down to Stanwardine. The officers would inspect the bins and if there was too much waste their rations were cut. Mr Ernest Pickering was very worried about incendiary bombs dropping so Mr Manley was put on fire watch duty at night. Later in the war, prisoners of war started working on the farm; they came from Ifton camp and slept in the stable where there was a proper little house with a fireplace. There were Paulo and Guissepi from Italy and with the German prisoners Karl and Paul, one a Bavarian farmer the other in the German youth. Neither group would mix with the other and the Italians would rather sing opera than work. Robert Pickering spent lots of time with the German prisoners so much so that he spoke German more than English. Frank Tomlinson also remembers the prisoners with red and green patches on their uniforms working for the Embertons down at 'Wackley Farm' in the fields. He was very frightened of them and ran away when ever he saw them.

Mr Edgar Roberts remembers two land army girls in Petton, their names were Peggy Ayres and Lillian Elliot, they had come from Liverpool. They worked at 'The Grange' but slept at 'Petton Farm'. 'Petton Farm' was even fuller with a Mrs Penny and her son living there who were evacuees from Wallasey, they had their own entrance and self contained few rooms down stairs in the old scullery and dairy. Mr and Mrs Sutton at 'Corner Farm' also had two girl evacuees.

The Houses

1 and 2 Copse Cottages were built just before the Second World War by a builder called Bill Highley from Ellesmere. He was in charge but had the boys from Petton Hall School doing the labouring. The brickwork of the cottages has been described by a recent builder as being very 'interesting'. Were they learning a practical skill or just cheap labour? Their parents paid for them

to go to the school, so I doubt they were learning a trade they would carry on and use.

The houses were occupied by many members of staff and their families from Petton School. The houses had a connecting door when the matron lived in one half and the other house was used as an isolation area and sick bay. There were originally going to be two more houses built next door, the bricks had been delivered but were taken away to be used in the war effort at Sleap airfield.

The present owner of No. 1, Copse Cottage Mrs Helen Baldwin taught at 'Petton Hall School' in the last years before it closed. Mrs Mona Whitfield who lives at No 2 also used to work at the school, Mr Gordon Whitfield was born at Lea Cottage on the Petton parish boundary but in Cockshutt parish.

Around 1952 the council bought land from Mr E Pickering for two sets of semi-detached houses. One of the houses 'Fair View' was used for an agricultural worker from 'Petton Grange' called Harold Dean. He was their cowman and he and his wife Frances had previously lived at 'Church House', their grandson Gary and his family now lives in part of 'Petton Hall'. He said his grand mother loved their new home much better than Church House where they were living. Mr and Mrs Davies live at 'Wilmar' where they raised ten children. Mr Wilf Davies was caretaker at 'Petton Hall School' for many years and they are the only original occupiers left. All but one of the houses is now owner occupier.

BIBLIOGRAPHY & REFERENCES

Burlton Marjorie Jones

Census 1841–1851–1861–1871–1881–1891–1901

Shropshire County Council Smallholdings records, maps and documents

Domesday Book, Shropshire Phillimore Edition

The Victoria History of Shropshire Vol. I & Vol. II Agriculture Vol. IV

Petton Hall – A Brief History and a few Memories Mr Philip Morris (March 1981)

A brief history and guide of Petton and Church Mrs Mona Whitfield

History of Petton Church Mrs Emma Florence Cunliffe and others

English Architecture to 1900 Eric Mercer

Shropshire Murders George Glover

Extinct Moated Mansions of Shropshire

Buildings of England Niklaus Pevsner

Shropshire Place Names E W Bowcock

Kelly's Directory 1885-1891-1929 –1933 –1934

Directories of Shropshire & Herefordshire 1879

Bagshaw's Directory of Shropshire 1851

Mercer & Cracker's Directory of Shropshire 1877

History of Cockshutt 1910-1980 Margaret 'Peggy' Husbands

Shropshire Parish Collections Vol.

Antiquities of Shropshire Eyton

The Church Bells of Shropshire Walters

Churches of Shropshire Cranage

Stone Hill Donkeys-enquiries@donkeyline.co.uk

Ref. taken from a manuscript on *Ellesmere and the Welsh Princes* by Chris Jobson (it appeared in the *Mere News* Winter 2004, Issue 25)

Recollections of Cockshutt School by John Moore

The Key Story from a letter written by John Moore on June 20th 1971

The Toll House from a letter written by John Moore on June 20th 1971

Stone Villa an article that appeared in the *Chronicle*

Bear Baiting by Charlotte S Burne in *Shropshire Folklore*

Bear Baiting - A popular amusement not tolerated today by E V Baynes

Apple Tree Cottage, as described by the Estate Agents Aspden & Co

Rosemary Cottage - Sticky Tom story from www.stanwardine history.htm

Stanwardine in the wood – taken from the *Shropshire Gazetteer* by Michael Raven

Crosemere Hall, FPD Savills' a/c Estate Agents.

Shade Oak described by E V Bayne

Deeds of Wackley lent by Mr and Mrs Powell

The Sporting Parson by E V Bayne

Cockfighting was the popular sport of English people - E V Bayne; May 1958 – *Shropshire Magazine*

Mothers' Union, ref. extracts from the Minute Books of the Mothers' Union

WI - extracts from the Minute Books

Shropshire Star Article 1999; ref. report on Our Declining Villages

The Cockshutt Fire Engine; ref. to an article by E V Bayne on Milestones in History in a *North Shropshire Parish*

Glass Making - extracts from Encarta; also extracts from a letter dated 1970 with ref. to an 1827 Greenwood Map on glasshouses sent to E V Bayne, plus a letter by T C Hancox dated October 1970.

Browis Castle - an example of depopulation in the 19th Century by E V Bayne.

'Outcast' - extract from Shropshire Radio Show called *Monday's Place - searching the rich heritage of its locality*

Stockett – partially from *The History Gazetteer & Directory/Shropshire.*

Transport; The Railway in Ellesmere by Tony Hamlin/Katherine Jones.

The Wrexham and Ellesmere Railway by Stanley C Jenkins & John M Strange.

The Ellesmere and Llangollen canal by Edward Wilson.

Ellesmere Library; Documents concerning the parish of Ellesmere Rural incl. Cockshutt.

Map of Ellesmere canal from the above document.

A Cockshutt Murder; this is a précised article taken from a detailed account that appeared in the *Mere News*, 2003 issue 24, written by Chris Jobson.

Sudden death - an article from the *Shrewsbury Chronicle*, 20th July 1888.

Farming - Seasons of Change by Sadie Ward.

The English - A Social History 1066-1945 by Christopher Hibbert

Shropshire Historic Parks and Gardens by P Stamper.

Antiquities of Shropshire, Eyton.

Victorian History of Shropshire – Vol 2

Ellesmere Canal by E A Wilson.

History of Myddle, Gough

An English Rural Community Myddle under the Tudors and Stuarts by D G Hey

Bridgewater Millions, Faulk

The Shropshire Landscape, T Rowley.

Ellesmere, Shropshire 1889, J Peake

History of Shropshire, B Trinder

Tilley, The Secret History of a Secret Place by Alastair Reid

Gazateer of Shropshire, 1851, S Bagshaw

The Agricultural History Review Releasing of Bridgewater Estates, E Hopkins.

Some Old Shropshire Houses and their Owners, H E Forrester.

Material and Maps etc belonging to Bridgewater Estates - Shropshire Archives. and surrounding areas.

Shropshire Meres and Mosses, Nigel Jones

Dug Out Canoes from Shropshire, Lily F Chitty

Census 1841, 1851, 1861, 1871, 1881, 1891, 1901

Shropshire County Council Small holdings records, maps and documents

Shropshire Magazine Articles by E V Bayne (No. 78, June 1957, July 1957, Nov. 1958)

Shropshire 1906

Shropshire Magazine Dec. 1953

Shropshire County Council, Environment Record report on Petton Park Moat

Sales details, Petton Park Estate 1920

Shrewsbury Chronicle September 16th 1904, Memory Corner

Petton Church Records of Baptism, Marriage, Burial Tithes, Apportionment of Petton 1842 and map

Hearth Tax Roll 1672

Maps of Shropshire John Rocque 1752- Robert Baugh 1808- Ordnance Survey map – 1891

COVER PHOTOGRAPH INFORMATION

Front Cover

Top left: Petton Church

Top middle: Lawrie Sawbridge and helpers haymaking in the field where Crosemere Crescent is today

Top right: Cockshutt church

Bottom left: The Edge family from Quaikin, English Frankton, 1919
      Back: Amy Edge, Levi Edge, Nelly Edge
      Middle: Iris Edge, Marcia Edge, Willis Edge
      Front: Mrs Burroughs nursing Percy Edge

Bottom middle: Signpost and cattle at Church Farm

Bottom right: Three men digging 1926/27 just beforew Petton Estate was sold
      Standing: Jack Chetwood
      In trench: Charley Richards
      Sitting: Tom Roan

Back cover

Motor bike, Thomas Moore (outside the school)

Tractor, Andy and Roger Griffiths and Bingo the dog at Seven Oaks Farm, Petton

Main Road, Cockshutt around 1910, children across the road. No names for the children on the left-hand side fo the picture but Mrs Tatton is looking over the gate of Stone Villa – Rose Cottage (without thatch) and Primrose Terrace (Rag Row) can be seen before the school and church

Right-hand side of the group of children. Front from right: Elsie Birch with Tom Birch, May Austin, Popsie Humphreys, Hilda Matthews, Nellie Birch, Amy Birch and May Williams

Petton Hall

ACKNOWLEDGEMENTS

Many people kindly allowed their documents, photographs, family archives and memories to be used and gave invaluable help in the preparation of this book, they have helped to produce this book by offering their memories, photographs and pictures for which we are very grateful. To all listed below we thank you for all your help and advice in making this book possible.

Alan Jones

Alf Hulme from Radio Shropshire recording

Aif and Daisy Smith

Barbara Jones

Barry Hawkins

Beryl Ashley

Beryl Owen

Bill and Blodwen Smith

Bob and Amy Dommett

Bobtope left: Petton Church

enaway

Brian Brookfield

Carla Boulton, of www.naughtymutt.com

Carole Nicholas

Caroline Griffiths

Charlie Emberton

Charlie Thomas

Chris Jobson

Connie Dakin

Cyril Marsh

Dai Davies

Dave Pickett

David and Ann Hockenhull

David and Margaret Bridge

David Evans

Den Ridgeway

Derek Jones

Derek, L and Andrew Western

Derrick Pratt

Don and Carol Ashley

Dorothy Hambly

Dossie Birch

Ellesmere Angling Club

Ellesmere Countryside Unit

English Heritage

English Nature

Em and Nancy Roberts

Eva Grainger

Frank and Joyce Hanmer

Frank and Margaret Dickin

Frank Morris

George Reeves

Gill and Ian Webb

Graeme Kidd, LHI Advisor

Graham Humphries

Graham Wright of Shropshire Aero Club

Harold Davies

Helen Eatough

Herbert Hulme

Hugh Hannaford,

Community Archaeologist

Isabel Sherlock of Oddfellows, Wem

Ivy Ashley

Jackie Richards

Jayne Gray

Jean James

Jean and Tom Jones of Brick Kiln Farm

Jean Scrivens

Joan Tunes

John and Rose Sawbridge

John Griffiths

Johnny Husbands

Joyce Dickin

Joyce Durham

Kathleen Royle

Keith Egerton

Ken and Annette Kynaston

Ken Williams

Len Birch

Les Birch

Local Heritage Initiative

Lynda Hanmer

Mac and Marg Griffiths

Margaret Lycett and Betty Moseley

Margaret Watkins

Marilyn Yates

Mark Smith

Martin George

Mary Edwards

Mary Harrison

Mary McKenzie, Shropshire Archivist

Mary Parker

Mary Price

May Kynaston

Meryl and David Batho

Michael Hulme

Mike Faulkner

Mike Hawkins

Milly Wycherley

Mrs Birch of Stanwardine

Mrs Hanmer

Mrs Lansdale

Mrs Rodenhurst

Myrtle Holliday

National Archives

Nellie Benbow (Davies)

Nellie Sutton

North Shropshire Chronicle

North Shropshire District Council

Ordnance Survey

Oswestry Advertiser

Pam Hanmer

Pat and lona Blundred

Paula Griffiths

Penny Ward, Sites and Monument Records - Economy and Environment Sustainability Group

Phil Ralphs

Radio Shropshire

Randle Carr

Ray Jones

Ray and Pauline Povall

Raymond Jefferies

Raymond Richards

Research and Records Office

Rev. Cyril Elsey

Rev. John Tye

Rock IT Science, (Brian Dabinett)

Ron and Joyce Whitfield

Ron and Verna Roberts

Rose Jones

Roy Gregory

Royal Observer Corps

Rural Community Council

Sarah Faulkner, Farming and Wildlife Advisory Group

Shrewsbury Chronicle

Shropshire Archaeological Society

Shropshire Community Council

Shropshire Records and Research Library

Shropshire Star

Stan Horton

Stanley and Delphine Hulme

Stanley and Dorothea Hulme

Steven Taylor

Sue and Steve Hill

Sue Graham

Sue Page

Sue Turner

Syd and Sheila Davies

Terry and Jenny Goodall

The Countryside Agency

Tom Jones

Vera Roberts

Whitchurch Herald

Whilst every attempt has been made to identify and contact the copyright holders of material reproduced in this book the authors would be pleased to hear from any they have been unable to trace or have inadvertently failed to contact.